ESSAYS ON SOCIAL
ORGANIZATION AND VALUES

LONDON SCHOOL OF ECONOMICS
MONOGRAPHS ON SOCIAL ANTHROPOLOGY
No. 28

ESSAYS ON SOCIAL ORGANIZATION AND VALUES

BY

RAYMOND FIRTH

F.B.A.

THE ATHLONE PRESS
NEW YORK: HUMANITIES PRESS INC.

Published by
THE ATHLONE PRESS LTD
at 90-91 Great Russell Street, London WCI

U.S.A. and Canada
Humanities Press Inc.
New Jersey

First edition 1964
First paperback edition 1969
Reprinted 1981

© *Raymond Firth, 1964*

ISBN 0 485 19628 X

Printed and bound in Great Britain by
REDWOOD BURN LIMITED
Trowbridge & Esher

Preface

The essays in this volume were assembled in response to a request from my colleagues on the Editorial Board of this Monograph series. Except for Chapter IV, which has been substantially abridged, they have been reprinted almost exactly as originally published (details are given in the introductory notes to Parts I and II).

Though the essays vary considerably in date and in scope, each was written with some theoretical issue in mind. I have divided them broadly into two main sets to illustrate some of my views on social operations and on social ideas. But I make no attempt to present them as a complete theoretical system – and I would be sceptical of the validity of any such unitary holistic framework. I hope, however, that they may still provide useful sectors of an analytical approach to significant problems.

Most of the essays draw on my field material from Tikopia, a small Polynesian community in the Western Pacific. Chapters IV, V and VI embody some of the results of field research conducted in 1928–9 under the auspices of the Australian National Research Council, whose assistance I wish here to acknowledge as I have done in the earlier publications. Chapter VI also contains material obtained on my second field expedition to Tikopia in 1952, and Chapter VIII is based largely on data obtained during a brief exploratory visit to New Guinea in 1951. Both of these expeditions were made under the auspices of the Australian National University where, for a year, I was Acting-Director of the Research School of Pacific Studies. I am much indebted to the Australian National University for many facilities during this period. I had been a member of the Academic Advisory Committee of the University since its inception, and in part for this reason was invited to contribute to a symposium at the Sixth Commonwealth Universities Congress at Oxford in 1948 (see Chapter VII). The original drafts of Chapters VI and X were prepared in 1959 when I was a Fellow at the Center for Advanced Study in the Behavioral Sciences at Palo Alto. I was much helped by the facilities available to me at the Center, and by the scholarly atmosphere of discussion with my colleagues there.

For stimulating exchange of ideas during the years in which these essays were written I owe much to my colleagues and to my students in graduate seminars in London. I am particularly indebted to Dr. L. P. Mair for helpful comment on the introductory chapter, which has not been printed before. The preparation of several chapters of this book in their original form as articles, and of this collected version of them all, has been helped greatly by use of a part of personal grants-in-aid from the Behavioral Sciences Division of the Ford Foundation, to which I express my very grateful thanks. For much careful assistance in the preparation of these and other materials for publication I am grateful to Mrs. D. H. Alfandary.

For permission to publish these essays I am indebted to the President and Council of the Royal Anthropological Institute (for Chapters II, III, IV, IX, X and XI); to Professor Meyer Fortes as Editor, and the Clarendon Press (for Chapter V); to Professor A. P. Elkin, the Editor of *Oceania* (for Chapter VI); to the Officers of the Association of Commonwealth Universities (for Chapter VII); to the President and Council of the Royal Society of Arts (for Chapter VIII); and to the Rationalist Press Association (for Chapter XII).

London, 1962   R.F.

Contents

PART I
SOCIAL ORGANIZATION

Introductory Notes

My general aim in these essays has been to present samples of analysis of on-going social process, and to show the range and validity of an organizational approach to problems of social continuity and social change. Incidentally, some of the essays may show how far this approach has anticipated aspects of the study of the social implications of processes of decision-making, which is one of the modern trends in social anthropology.

Chapter I is the only new essay in this book, and is an attempt to see some recent developments in social anthropology in the light of developments in some other fields of social science. Chapter II was delivered as a Presidential Address before the Royal Anthropological Institute in 1954, and was followed the next year by the address which appears as Chapter III of this book. (They were published in the *Journal of the Royal Anthropological Institute*, vol. 84, pp. 1–20, 1954; and vol. 85, pp. 1–18, 1955.) The essays are closely related, and embody ideas with which I had been occupied for some years. The essence of my critique of social structure, for instance, was given in a paper read to the first meeting of the Association of Social Anthropologists, in 1946. It was not enthusiastically received at that time, when 'structuralism' was in its heyday, and I did not publish it, though part of the argument was presented in my *Elements of Social Organization* (Chapter I, 1951).

Chapter IV, on 'Marriage and the Classificatory System of Relationship', was originally published in more extensive form in the *Journal of the Royal Anthropological Institute*, vol. 60, pp. 235–268, 1930. Some genealogies also have been omitted here, and a few consequential alterations in wording made. Although this essay is now more than thirty years old, I have included the substance of it in this volume because it was my first exposition of a problem in what I have later come to call the organizational method of analysis. A brief reference to the history of the article will show how the problem arose and how theoretical formulations interact with the study of empirical situations. In Tikopia by the beginning of 1929 I had already obtained a working knowledge of the kinship system and its major structure. I also had managed to overcome the opposition of the chiefs to my study of the pagan religion and had finished an arduous participation in one seasonal cycle of the Work of the Gods. I was, therefore, then free to begin my sociological census, to make some assessment of my field material so far, and to think about collecting fresh data on a new variety of subjects. I turned again to some of the kinship sections in W. H. R. Rivers's *The History of Melanesian Society*. An entry in my diary in early February reads, 'Evening. Read Rivers's H.M.S. on anomalous marriages. He annoys me very much; all is hypothesis.' The next evening I spent sketching out a scheme for dealing with the Tikopia kinship system.

About this time I also began to collect material on changes of kinship terminology on marriage. I had previously regarded the kinship terms used by people for one another in a community as unalterable, fixed in a frame of usages so that each specific term-use was logically inferable from the general set of terms and relationships involved. I now found the logic unimpaired, but the relationships to be taken as assumptions more complex and more related to individual interests than I had previously perceived. I had realized some time earlier that some changes on marriage were implied, because as I had noted, since all the people of Tikopia are related, 'men *must* always marry their *kave* or *tamafine*, etc.' I did nothing more with this for about two months, but then took it up again as part of a general plan for presentation of my material. Then came an event which stimulated my interest – the only large-scale wedding which took place during my stay. The context of this actual marriage led to a great deal of discussion of genealogies and of the implication of marriage for kinship structure, especially terminology. Partly as a result of my reaction against Rivers's view, I began to examine these problems more closely. A comment on an incident in my notebook is 'Shows how kinship system not a rigid, inflexible mechanism, but one which is elastic, capable of being adapted to meet new situations'; and a note in my diary says, '"Anomalous relations" may be important as well as interesting.'

I currently began to work on the article, finishing the draft in Tikopia about two months later, though I still continued to collect further material which was incorporated in the final version. It was this experience, rooted in empirical observation, which as much as any other alerted me to the need for constant scrutiny of organizational elements in social situations.

Chapter V, 'Authority and Public Opinion in Tikopia', is reproduced from the volume on *Social Structure: Studies Presented to A. R. Radcliffe-Brown*, edited by Meyer Fortes (Oxford, 1949, pp. 168–88). The essay was offered as a general tribute to Radcliffe-Brown rather than as a specific token of allegiance to his system of ideas. Though never a pupil of his, as his junior colleague in Sydney in 1930–1 I learned much social anthropology from him. But I continually felt obliged to reject Radcliffe-Brown's more formalistic notions, in particular that of social systems in equilibrium – a rejection (see p. 143) hinted at in my introduction to the English edition of Lin Yueh-Hwa's book, *The Golden Wing*, two years before (Firth, 1947). This essay then was as much a study in political process as in political structure.

Since the orginal article was published my analysis of Tikopia political organization has been extended, not only by an examination of succession to chieftainship (Chapter VI, *infra*), but also by some more detail of the alleged practice of black magic by chiefs (Firth, 1954), and consideration of the status and role of executive officers (Firth, 1959, pp. 285–96). Problems of social control have also been examined (Firth, 1959, pp. 299–337) and an article on Tikopia suicide (Firth, 1961a) analyses the relation between personal intention and social pressures.

Chapter VI, 'Succession to Chieftainship in Tikopia', was published in *Oceania*, vol. 30, 1960, pp. 161–80. It involved some historical reconstruction, and in this respect has been supplemented by more detailed material, including stories of threats to the succession, in my analysis of Tikopia traditions (Firth, 1961b). It could be argued that such traditional material describes not the actual principles of succession but what the Tikopia thought they were, or thought they ought to have been, or wished it believed that they were. But two considerations are relevant here. The elaborate Tikopia genealogies and stories of the succession of their chiefs make on the whole not only a consistent and plausible account (which perhaps is what one might expect), but also one which accords with historical practice as far as I was able to check it (cf. Firth, 1959, p. 32; 1961b, p. 158). Moreover, during my absence of more than twenty years, four chiefs died. They had been succeeded by others along the lines indicated by the data I had gathered before. Again, even if this is not the presentation of an historical reality, but a projection of it on to a sociological plane, the theory of succession as outlined is of a flexible, sophisticated system. It makes due allowance for human frailty and variation in individual disposition and circumstance but displays an acute sense of political realities. In obtaining the stories and commentary from the Tikopia, I felt that I was receiving a contribution to my political understanding.

CHAPTER I

Comment on 'Dynamic Theory' in Social Anthropology[1]

(1962)

In 1954 I wrote: 'We are hardly yet on the threshold of any general theory of a dynamic kind which will enable us to handle comprehensively the range of material within our normal anthropological sphere' (p. 56, *infra*). In assembling these essays I have been led to consider contemporary anthropological theory again from this point of view.

Modern social anthropology is still sometimes said to be in need of, or in process of constructing, a 'dynamic' or 'more dynamic' social theory (e.g. C. Geertz, 1957, p. 34; Worsley, 1957, p. 266). Various anthropologists have described their own or other work, as 'dynamic' analysis (e.g. Belshaw, 1954, pp. 141 *et seq.*; Firth, 1939, p. xi; 1954, p. v. in Leach, 1954; 1959, p. 344; Powell, 1960, p. 143; Bailey, 1960, pp. 238 *et seq.*). But it is not always clear that they have meant the same by this expression.

What are the requirements and defining features of a 'dynamic' theory? What should it do which no other type of theory does?

I assume that the object of any anthropological theory is the statement of hypotheses which will be found to have an explanatory value in reference to problems of human social behaviour. Literally, from its Greek etymology (*dunamis* – power), dynamic theory should be of the kind which is concerned with the power mechanisms of social behaviour. But almost any kind of social theory is apt to be concerned with power mechanisms. To be meaningful, then, dynamic theory should be concerned with only certain types of power, or with the exercise of power in certain types of social conditions.

The types of social conditions to which analysis thought to have

---

[1] This essay is a revised version of a talk delivered at a Wenner-Gren Supper Conference in New York on 11 April 1962, and repeated in modified form at a staff-student colloquium in the Department of Anthropology, University of Chicago, on 16 April 1962. I am indebted to both audiences for helpful criticism and suggestions.

been appropriately termed 'dynamic' has been applied by anthropologists can be judged by examples. At least three types of conceptual approach seem to have been involved:

(a) The operation of forces in action within an unaltered social system. This is illustrated by Fortes's analysis (1945) of the 'dynamics' of Tale clanship and lineage. While pointing to an undercurrent of tension in every clan and lineage arising directly from their segmentary structure, and while recognizing occasional conflict in their relationships, Fortes saw lineage solidarity prevailing in the long run, based on the religious premises of the ancestor cult and the moral premises of kinship. In this study of the 'dynamics of clanship', Tale society is assumed to persist in the form there presented, with its major institutions unchanged. The power mechanisms operate, but not with disintegrative or disruptive effect on social forms.

(b) The operation of forces with immediate or partial disintegrative effect on the existing society, but in a developmental evolutionary manner, tending to the creation of social forms blending old and new elements. This viewpoint is represented, e.g., by some of Malinowski's emphases on the need for co-operation and the significance of the forces of consensus in the dynamics of culture change in modern Africa (1938, 1945). As Kaberry has said of Malinowski (1945, p. xiii), 'His approach is essentially dynamic in that he views the contact situation in terms of stresses and strains, of conflict and co-operation, and of compromise and passive resistance. . . .' This is not to be equated with an equilibrium analysis, as is sometimes thought. To me, it is pretty clear that what Malinowski was doing was not making an assumption but pleading a case. In essence, he was envisaging alternative outcomes of the African situation. Writing in the late 'thirties, he was pointing out to European opinion what he saw as the only solution for the continuance of European interests in Africa – a willingness to face unpalatable facts, and draw the necessary implications for action. The forces of radical change set in motion by new African aspirations, given the inequitable distribution of resources and incomes between them and Europeans, were certain to sweep away the Europeans unless the latter analysed the situation intelligently, saw where their common interest lay with the Africans, and made the inevitable compromises. Malinowski's *The Dynamics of Culture Change* was in this sense a political tract as well as a scientific analysis. Its dynamic was one of change, but of a facultative, conditional kind. This analysis is akin in assumption to e.g. W. W. Rostow's view that 'the outcome of conflict in a regularly growing society is likely to be governed by ultimate considerations of communal continuity' (1961, p. 151).

(c) The operation of forces tending to change the system by developmental movement of a revolutionary kind. The assumption here is that change is the resultant of the forces of opposition within a social system, and, moreover, that the opposition is of such radical nature that no permanent compromise is possible. The opposition may be suppressed, or it may lose impetus from other causes, but no lasting *modus vivendi* between the opposed forces is possible. Worsley's analysis of 'cargo cults' in Melanesia (1957) used this type of assumption.

We have here then what may be called both non-emergent and emergent dynamics – the one referring to a social system maintaining itself in essentially the same form, and the other referring to a social system in process of alteration, with issue in a different form. I think both conceptions of 'dynamic' are legitimate, but there is no doubt that in social anthropology it is the latter which has received most attention, and for which many anthropologists would wish to reserve the term.

From this point of view what should be the object of a dynamic theory?

It should be able to identify and measure or at least assess the general *magnitude* of *changes* in social form. It should indicate the *forces* responsible for such social change, i.e. demonstrate the relationship between the existing conditions and antecedent phenomena. It should also indicate the direction or *trend* of events, by relating antecedent and existing conditions to some further probabilities in the pattern of development. Ideally a fully worked-out 'dynamic' theory then should give some guide to prediction.[1] In this respect it may recognize a series of phases or stages in social change, with relative constancy of institutional form at each phase; or it may recognize a continuous process of change,

[1] Prediction may be only in the form of 'If such and such, then so and so' (cf. Firth, 1956, p. 209; Mair, 1957, pp. 14-15).

without marked stage identification. All this a 'dynamic' theory should do specifically for the societies under study. It should presumably also be capable of greater generalization – the results of analysis in a given society should be more widely applicable. There is also another objective held by some to be the prime aim of dynamic theory or a dynamic approach to social factors – it should be that theory or approach which is an instrument of social change. 'We study society not merely to understand it but to alter it' is the slogan.[1]

But the term 'dynamic' is overworked. Not only is it applied to a range of different approaches; it is also often prestigeful, and given a moral connotation – especially when it is identified theoretically with a scheme of developmental stages, and pragmatically with a socially useful instrument. Such 'dynamic' analysis is assigned a positive, approving character as against a 'static' analysis, regarded disapprovingly as a conservative, negativistic kind of approach. Theorists sometimes tend to be assigned definitively to one kind of approach as opposed to the other. They are regarded not as craftsmen who happen to be using one type of tool, but as doctrinaires who are committed to seeing the world around them in terms of their symbolic use of that tool. Now if the techniques of exploration of scientific thinking were sophisticated enough, perhaps relationships in personal temperament could be traced with enough refinement to identify such theoretical interests with other kinds of personal interests. Moreover, a concern with 'dynamic' elements of theory can be equated in a logical way with interest in on-going process, and therefore in past and future as different from, not identical with, present. But the identification of a conceptual approach necessarily with a personal view of how things actually are or of how they should be is in my view a fallacy, and not relevant to our present concern.

STATIC AND DYNAMIC

Yet the term 'dynamic' is convenient. A 'dynamic' social theory involves basically the idea of *movement* from one social condition to another. Such movement may be reversible or irreversible, gradual or rapid; it may occur in one major institution only or in several at the same time. It may be without noticeable disturbance of inter-personal relationships or it may be violent and dis-

[1] See e.g. Hader and Lindeman, 1933; cf. Wright Mills, 1959.

ruptive. But it is not social movement *per se* that is implied in the concept, but social movement resulting from the operation of social forces. The identification and analysis of these forces is as important a part of a dynamic social theory as is the charting and description of social movement. The more general relation between concepts of 'static' and of 'dynamic' is relevant here. In the older literature, following Herbert Spencer, 'social dynamics' and 'social statics' were regarded as opposed concepts. The situation is parallel in physics. Formerly kinetics or dynamics, the study of relations between the motions of bodies and the forces acting upon them, was contrasted with statics, the study of bodies in rest, in equilibrium. That contrast has now lost its importance. Statics tends to be treated as a part or particular set of cases in dynamics, since the state of rest of a body is only relative and forces continue to operate upon it. So also in social theory the old Spencerian frame no longer holds. Nowadays there would be no agreement to Spencer's propositions that 'equilibration must eventually become complete' and 'there is a gradual advance towards harmony between man's mental nature and the conditions of his existence' (Spencer, 1937, pp. 462–3). 'Static' conditions are particular cases of the operation of forces in society which, for the time being, result in social movement which has no major or structural consequences.[1] 'Static', then, implies a *relative* lack of movement, not a total lack of movement and not a *lack of force* operating. (A claim for a 'more dynamic' theory often ignores that such analyses of forces in movement have been made by 'static' procedures.)

But the argument for a 'more dynamic' theory tends to be based on two main premises: that 'static' theory has assumed conditions of rest or return to rest in spheres where there was ongoing social movement; and that sophisticated analysis would reveal more, or more significant, forces in operation than have been shown. In a modern critique of the theory of social anthropology, if labels be ignored, both these premises are probably justified. Certainly in reviewing my own work I recognize the force of the argument at some points. More generally, studies of

[1] I myself have used the concept of *social movement* in a specific sense to indicate social change within a continuing structural frame, and have distinguished it from *structural* changes of a major order (Firth, 1959, pp. 340, 352, etc.). Cf. Parsons and Smelser, 1956, pp. 247–8, who have distinguished between two main types of social dynamics according to whether changes are small in magnitude and short in duration, with return to an equilibrium state – changes *within* structure – or changes of a major character, *in* structure.

economic or of religious systems, or even of descent group structures, have often neglected the specific historical setting of the social forms they have described and so overlooked their contingent nature, their possibilities of change, their phase-character in a developing situation. Sometimes, with deliberate intent, they have concentrated on the traditional form of institutions in the society, ignoring the concepts and actions of some groups or members of the society which, at the very period of study, were making for a radical re-evaluation of those traditional forms and a modification of them.

But some of the critical argument seems to have been misdirected. Distinctions drawn between social structure and social organization, as by Radcliffe-Brown and by myself, have been represented (e.g. Worsley, 1961; cf. Worsley, 1957, p. 265) as equivalent to or as a revival of the 'statics-dynamics' 'model' of society. There is a sense, though a limited one, in which this is true. But such a 'model' is represented as being if not intellectually disreputable at least old-fashioned. Yet heuristic devices of this kind are legitimate enough and indeed necessary to some stages of inquiry, provided that they be taken as conceptual images to aid analysis, not representations of empirical situations.

In economics, which is far more advanced than social anthropology in the systematization of concepts in this field, the use of such models has long been customary. They are initially at least of a highly abstract order, with fairly rigorous assumptions of hypothetical conditions – a closed economy, a constant population, constant prices, workers who do not save, etc. Though there is some difference in the characterization by economists of the terms 'static' and 'dynamic', the essence of the concept of economic dynamics is the study of economic phenomena in relation to preceding and succeeding events, especially in respect of the process of change. A static analysis, taking a cross-section of the economy, eliminates the *passage* of time from the problem – though, as Baumol has emphasized (1959, pp. 3–36 *et seq.*), this does not necessarily eliminate the influence of time as such altogether. Anthropological usage, where it has been articulate, has tended to adopt a similar distinction,[1] in respect of allowance for variation and change over time. What is important to note is that the difference between static and dynamic in such contexts is

[1] e.g. F. G. Bailey, 1960, pp. 8–9, who states 'a static analysis is of necessity synchronic'.

not thought to lie in the character of situations but in the method of approach in studying them. Hence a static analysis may be followed by a dynamic analysis in the course of the same investigation.

There are, of course, complications in the economic treatment. Economists have distinguished firstly the *stationary state*, where no significant changes occur – nothing ever 'happens', i.e. no *structural* alteration takes place. No attention need be paid to past or future because the facts and analysis relating to the present will apply equally well at any other time. Study of the stationary state is a static analysis in the view of most economists, because the quantities involved need no time referent – in Hicks's terms, where we need not trouble about *dating*. But with slight shift of interpretation, dating, and even time passage, can be admitted into static analysis. Comparative statics is the study of a system in equilibrium *before* and *after* a change, which is, however, taken to be of the once-for-all variety. Again, Baumol has termed 'statics involving time', the study of a system in motion at *a specific point of time*. But the essential thing in all these uses of 'static' is that the analysis focuses on the particular conditions of the moment, and is not concerned with preceding and succeeding events, with the process of change in itself.

Following such usage, much anthropological study, especially in earlier years, has been either of stationary states, on the assumption that primitive societies were not changing and what was said about them at one period would apply equally well at another; or of statics at a point of time, regarding the social system as in motion but under examination for only a specific period, without reference to past or future. Fortes's analysis of the Tallensi, or my own first Tikopia book, come in this category for the most part – they can be classed as 'dynamics' only in the sense of movement within the system.

But it is important to note that in such contexts we speak of static and dynamic modes of analysis and not (except in a rather loose figurative sense) of static and dynamic societies or states of society.

Now consider the relation of static to structural analysis.

A static analysis and a structural analysis are not necessarily the same. They have an affinity in one respect; in neither does the factor of time *necessarily* enter as a significant variable. Both may admit time conceptually but as a relevant quantity it is neutral, a constant. The common definitions of social structure by anthropologists emphasize that it is concerned with the continuity and persistence, and the consistency of types, of social relationships – that is, the identification of a particular social structure depends on the selective types of relationship not having been altered by time. (If they have been so altered, then we are dealing to this extent with another structure.[1])

Logically, a concept of social structure which rests its definition on the notion of *continuity* of relationships (i.e. sameness, not-change), cannot equally embrace *discontinuity* (i.e. difference, change). Thus, the use of such a conventional concept of social structure *by itself* cannot account for structural change. Some additional elements must be introduced into the analysis, to allow for the *movement* from one type of continuity to another. This does not mean that studies which focus upon structural identifications cannot be concerned with problems of social change. It does mean, however, that some concepts of process must also be taken into the analysis, whether acknowledged or not. Nadel has seen this clearly when he states that without invariance as a condition we cannot talk intelligently about structure at all (1957, p. 133). A structural analysis may be conducted within a static frame by agreeing to regard as constant any effects due to the passage of

---

[1] Here I would draw attention to a point concerning the time dimension of social structure which I did not make clear in an earlier publication. In my *Elements of Social Organization* I wrote of the continuity expressed in social structure, of the firmness of expectations in its sets of relations. Yet I argued there must be room for variance which is found in the concept of social organization, the systematic ordering of social relations by acts of choice and decision. 'Time enters here' (1951, p. 40). This elliptical expression naturally attracted some criticism. Nadel, in the light of his exposition of social structure in terms of role theory, pointed out that social structure is an 'event-structure' in time, an abstraction from successive repetitive action. Processes such as recruitment of people into social roles and relationships, and conflict in social relationships, have a time dimension (Nadel, 1957, pp. 128 *et seq.*). Nadel was followed in this by Worsley (1961, p. 27). But such statements do not fully meet the point. Of course the concept of social structure must have its time frame – the very use of the term 'continuity' as a structural, defining characteristic implies extension over time. But what I was concerned to argue was that the concept of social structure as then generally used made no adequate allowance for time as a *significant variable*. My characterization of social organization was intended to make specific provision for the time factor as a necessary element in analysis. Assessment of social situation, choosing between alternatives, mobilizing personnel and other resources in implementing decisions – such processes require time for completion. When the situation is unstable, the passage of time allows for changes. The length of the time interval with its normal associate of activities, e.g. the agricultural cycle of a year, a human generation – may be a relevant factor in the situation. Time here is not a constant, a neutral element; the length of the elapsed period can be significant. Time 'enters' into the situation, and to some degree the result is a function of this.

time, that is, by ignoring events which do not conform to the pattern of consistency. But equally, a structural analysis may be conducted within a dynamic frame by taking account of such events and their implications, that is, by including in the study the effects of development over time.[1]

A static analysis is based on the assumption of the stability of the social system. If social movement is taken into account, it is regarded as being essentially repetitive or reversible or at least of such a type as not to disturb the basic character of the system. Such stability is only relative, being a function of the forces bearing upon the situation. But in a static analysis it is assumed that for the period of consideration any forces tending to destroy the situation are not powerful enough to take full effect. Therefore, for the period with which the analysis is concerned, time as a relevant factor may be ignored or treated as a constant. In the earlier history of social anthropology many structural analyses were of this static character. It was partly to argue that due allowance should be given to the effects of time as a variable that I drew attention to the need for supplementing the concept of social structure by a concept of social organization (see pp. 49–50, *infra*).

That a structural analysis need not necessarily be purely static may be illustrated by considering the structure of authority in patterns of chieftainship. As chiefs succeed one another, their authority in fact may vary considerably from that ostensibly given them by their formal endowment of power. Despite such personal variation, however, there is a continuity in the scheme by which their authority is exercised. An aggregate of such 'continuity features' may be recognized as an aspect of the social structure.[2] This recognition of continuity elements in the authority system – chief succeeds chief and no oligarchy or other form

[1] See e.g. Bailey, *loc. cit.* Cf. the usage of some economists, e.g. Dosser (1961, p. 574), who distinguishes between 'static-structure' and 'dynamic-structure' in income tax problems. The former refers to levies apportioned to *levels* of income and the latter to levies apportioned to *changes* in income. Note, however, that in the latter the principle of the tax structure still remains constant and allowance for changes over time is made by flexibility in the detail and application of the scheme. The term 'dynamic structure' has been used by other social scientists also, e.g. the Russian psychologist Luria in examining the psychology of conflict.

[2] Opinion may differ as to which elements are to be put into the 'structural' category. For example, Evans-Pritchard excluded the elementary family from Nuer social structure (1940, p. 262), though he regarded it as of no less importance than 'structural' groups, and elsewhere described the family as 'an economic unit and a simple local unit' (1951, pp. 108, 129). Cf. A. I. Richards, 1941, pp. 48–51.

of government intervenes – may assume either the empirical or the conceptual stability of the system. Empirically each chief may have been installed at the death of his predecessor almost automatically as a matter of unquestioned right and by full popular acceptance. But he may have succeeded his predecessor only by the exercise of political skill – say, by appealing to the people over the heads of other leaders who would have preferred an oligarchy; or by military action against them. In either event conceptually an anthropologist may concentrate on the analysis of the formal structure of the chief's authority, ignoring any challenges to it and the possibility of further development of such challenges to a point at which the system may be overthrown. Or he may assume that whatever be the nature of these challenges, they do not specifically weaken the system and may even contribute to strengthening its ideology. This could be regarded as a static analysis. Yet retrospectively viewed, chieftainship as an office and a form of government may often have been imperilled, and prospectively its chances of survival may be small. It has had continuity so far, but its relative stability has been slight. Conceptually it can be regarded as unstable in another way. Whether each chief succeeded unquestioned and as of right, or whether he had to struggle against opponents wishing not only to wrest power from him as a person but also to destroy his office, it may be held that as an institution chieftainship, by its nature, lacks the quality of a permanent, hence 'true' or 'correct', solution to the problem of power in a society. Further, it is conceivable, indeed plausible, that such instability of chieftainship is to be inferred most strongly in situations where – for various reasons such as demographic pressures or new technological opportunities – a radical change is taking place in the economic base and income structure of the society. From one point of view the only 'dynamic' theory in this respect would be one which recognizes the impermanence of chieftainship and focuses upon the forces tending to its overthrow. A structural analysis of the continuity elements involved, and of the forces bearing upon them and tending to modify them, could be pursued throughout.

The concept of social structure then is not simply equivalent to the acceptance of the notion of a static or stable society.[1] Nor is

[1] e.g. cf. Firth in regard to Tikopia by 1952 (1959, p. 343). 'In essence it may be said that the organizational changes so far were on the verge of taking structural effect.'

the notion of 'social organization' simply equivalent to that of the dynamics of society. What the concept of social organization does is to focus on those aspects of dynamics or process in which *choice* is exercised in a field of available alternatives, resources are mobilized and decisions are taken in the light of probable social costs and benefits. In my view, whether such terms be used or not, concepts such as 'static' and 'dynamic', 'structural' and 'organizational', are all needed in social theory. In particular, a dynamic analysis involves both structural and organizational components – as well as others concerning magnitude, growth, etc.

Generally speaking, a dynamic social theory represents an analysis of social systems in motion. It is a study of different *kinds* of social change – 'repetitive, structural, gradual, radical' (Worsley, 1957, p. 260). It also involves an investigation of the *forces responsible* for the social changes. Often prominent in the analysis is an emphasis upon the vital significance of power differences in social relationships, and the importance of the economic relations involved.

SOCIAL CONFLICT

But here there is room for a wide difference of interpretation. For some anthropologists one of the central characters, if not *the* defining character of a dynamic theory, has been a recognition of conflict between certain elements, principles or categories in social systems.[1]

As Coser has pointed out in an elaborate study (1956, pp. 15–31), there is a long history of sociological concern with social conflict. Social anthropologists too have examined conflict-phenomena of varying scale, including e.g. factionalism (Malinowski, 1938, 1945; Redfield, 1950, pp. 88–112; Leach, 1954, *passim*; Firth *et al.*, 1957; Murphy, 1957; Siegel and Beals, 1960; Fox, 1961).[2] Conflict has often been assumed, as by Robert Park, to be a basic form of human interaction. But there has been profound difference of view as to whether on the whole it is productive of socializing and unifying results in group life, as argued by Cooley or Simmel, or whether it is essentially dysfunctional, leading primarily to disintegration, as Parsons would seem to hold. These views have not always been exclusive. In social

---

[1] See e.g. Turner, 1957, p. xxii *et passim*; Bailey, 1960, pp. 238–41.
[2] For general review see Le Vine, 1961, pp. 3–15.

anthropology Radcliffe-Brown, Gluckman and others have favoured the theory that conflict in ritual forms, while temporarily disruptive, has ultimately cathartic functions of a symbolic order, tending to maintain the unity of a society. This self-sealing function, with its optimistic assumption, is not always easy to defend.[1] It is very difficult when applied to conflicts of an actual, not merely symbolic, order. Gluckman, for instance, holds that the South African social situation illustrates his central argument that conflicts in one set of relationships lead to the establishment of cohesion in a wider set of relationships (1955b, p. 164).[2] This seems to equate cohesion with realignment of interest. The point of view has been challenged, as for instance by Siegel and Beals. To what Le Vine has called the 'silver-lining' approach of Gluckman, they and others have opposed the view of social conflict as disruptive, maladjustive. To some extent differences of structural level (as Le Vine has pointed out) and differences of emphasis on internal or external pressures account for this divergence of interpretation. But I think the difference goes deeper. I may be wrong, but I see it as an expression of a contrast in viewpoint between the commonsense attitude that conflict is bad for social relations; and a more sophisticated attitude that it acts as a cathartic. Either may be true according to the conditions – and it is in the *specification of the conditions* that the real problem lies. Moreover, an interpretation of social dynamics in terms of conflict is apt to be one-sided if it ignores the problems of *consensus* – the forces which unite the members of each party to the conflict, as well as the forces which may operate at any point of reconcilement.[3] For a Marxist interpretation the study of *class-consciousness* must be an important theme – and this requires attention to shared conceptions, meanings, values and symbols as well as to structural and organizational considerations of behaviour.

Yet according to some views there can be *no* natural identity of interests, no 'normative consensus' between the various major

[1] Cf. Jarvie, 1961, on Nadel's teleological assumptions.

[2] Yet he points to the existence of 'irresoluble, unbalanced conflict' (p. 165) in the changing South African conditions, and presumably envisages no effective development of wider cohesion.

[3] e.g. J. A. Pitt-Rivers (1954, p. xiv) states that non-uniformity of values gives rise to strife and hence the necessity to reconcile conflicting social ties in the community. Modes of reconcilement give the structure of society many of its characteristics. His book traces the conflict of ties to divergent demands of the local community and of the central government – a problem in all centralized states.

parties in a social system. Such 'conflict-theory' does not necessarily use the concept of struggle between classes based on their
respective functions in production. But in anthropological theory
there is a growing emphasis on social opposition in interests and
in power related to differences in control of the resources at the
command of members of the society.

What forms of theoretical expression is this to take? Considering this emphasis upon the theoretical importance of conflict or
opposition – especially in relation to social change – one might
have expected in modern social anthropology more overt attention to Marxist theories of society, in which conflict between
social categories plays such a large part.

From the viewpoint of an anthropologist concerned with
social theory, perhaps Karl Marx's greatest service has been his
general contribution to the sharpening of sensitivity in sociological analysis, particularly by his insistence on historical specification, and by his emphasis on change. The Marxist view that a
description of a social situation is not an entity in itself but is to be
understood in terms of its particular historical setting – in modern
times, the positions, roles and statements of the actors in a scheme
of class interests and class ideology – has directed attention (even
if by counter-reaction) to significant social factors in interpretation. If the answers be not acceptable, the questions have been
very relevant.[1]

Several major features of the Marxist scheme which are well
known are, I think, still worth serious re-consideration. Marx
was pre-eminently concerned with the forces making for radical
change in society. He emphasized the significance of expansion
of productivity in giving rise to changes in economic and social
structure. More specifically, he emphasized the significance of the
association between control of the means of production and the
possession of political power. His interest in structures of domina-
tion was more firmly and systematically based in sociological
analysis than that of most of his predecessors. He pointed out how
the distinction between those who control economically and
those who operate technically the means of production can emerge

[1] See MacRae, 1961, p. 196: '. . . Marxism, imperfect as science, is diagnostically useful
and the grip it gives on the vital processes of society is genuine enough.' Cf. Korsch, 1938,
ch. ii; also Wright Mills: 'Classical Marxism has been central to the development of
modern sociology; Max Weber, like so many other sociologists, developed much of his
work in a dialogue with Karl Marx' (1959, p. 48). Cf. also Birnbaum, 1953.

in categories not merely of an economic order but also of a social and political order – constituting a system of classes. Between these classes, he argued, there must be basic incompatibility and conflict of interests. Moreover, Marx drew attention to the way in which systems of ideas about society – 'ideology' – are not to be regarded as objective, independent constructs, but in his view are related to class position and hence ultimately have a material economic referent.[1]

Why have social anthropologists responded in lukewarm fashion to the challenge of such ideas?[2] One general hindrance has obviously been Marx's overriding aim in using sociological argument as a political instrument – as illustrated by the exaggerations of the diatribe against (bourgeois) marriage and family in the *Communist Manifesto* (see Laski, 1948, pp. 147–9). Another more specific reason has been the obvious crudity of much of the earlier Soviet anthropological work, which followed in doctrinaire fashion the more arid theoretical schemes of Lewis H. Morgan and the Marx-Engels models related to them.[3] Anthropological lack of interest in Marxist political and economic constructs has been due also to the difficulty of relating them to the wide range of phenomena of the many technically underdeveloped communities mostly studied by anthropologists. Schematically, the over-generalization of the clan-type/pre-class/primitive 'com-

---

[1] This does not mean that in a Marxist view the ideology is directly based on economic conditions. As G. V. Plekhanov pointed out in his critique of the views of Espinas and of Eleutheropoulos on the relation of Greek philosophy to technology and economics, the evolution of ideologies is far from being a simple matter, involving other factors as well as conditions of production (1929, pp. 59–68).

[2] e.g. by contrast with the vast sociological literature on Karl Marx. Apart from writers in the U.S.S.R. and other Communist countries, few social anthropologists have explicitly considered Marxist theories. Worsley (1957, p. 266) stated that his analysis of millenarian movements was based on Marxist analysis, and David and Isabel Crook (1959) have adopted a Marxist-Mao viewpoint. Lévi-Strauss is obviously familiar with Marx's writing as part of his intellectual armoury. I myself have referred briefly to Marx's basic theory as it affects a primitive economic system (Firth, 1939, pp. 361–3). The historical materialism of Leslie A. White, though stated not to have been derived from Marx, would seem to have been influenced indirectly by Marxist views in combination with those of Morgan (see Harry Elmer Barnes, 1960, pp. xxvi, xxxv). Sahlins has also used some of Marx's views on capitalism to point up his analysis of the relation between economic condition and political power in society (1960, pp. 394–408). Some recent views in economic anthropology which would deny the validity of the concept of scarcity in the analysis of primitive economic systems may reflect an attitude of Soviet economists. Morris Opler's analysis (1962) of Plekhanov's *Unaddressed Letters* is in line with my argument for more appraisal of Marxist theories.

[3] See Plekhanov, 1929, pp. 36–53; Matorin, p. 6, and Kagarov, pp. 88–99, 1933; Korsch 1938, p. 50. Cf. recent work by Potekhin, Kroupianskaia and others which is much closer to the methods of Western ethnographic analysis.

munistic' society, for instance, presented too little differentiation, too little refinement in the analysis of social relationships to merit serious intellectual comparison.[1]

Again, lack of anthropological interest in Marxist theories of ideological constructs is perhaps due in part to our training in a comparative, relativistic view of what purport to be general formulations on social behaviour. It comes as no novelty in modern social anthropology to regard the analysis of a social situation and of the views expressed on it as adequate only when the economic and political positions of actors have been taken into the interpretation. The anthropologist's approach has been parallel to, rather than congruent with, a Marxist one, and the factors have been identified in other ways. Familiarity with difference between statement of ideal norm and the actuality of social behaviour has helped to deepen anthropological understanding of how people's interests dictate the form of their representations of society. Moreover, the operation of other strong theoretical influences – including the Durkheimian stress on social solidarity and the Weberian stress on the importance of the autonomous role of ideas in the historical process – may have tended to militate against any very deep preoccupation with Marxist theory as a professional concern.

Again, Marx's own substantial theories dealt with past phases of society – as Wright Mills points out, Marx's analysis does not refer either to the present Soviet type of society or to that of the 'underdeveloped' countries. Yet nowadays two conditions at least may tend to promote a growing anthropological interest in Marxist theses. One, the more specific, is an interest in theories of social evolution at a more sophisticated level than those presented in the nineteenth century. The other, the more general, is that modern social anthropologists have turned to the study of more complex economic and political conditions over a wide range of societies, often in rapid change. Of necessity, they must be more concerned with the effects of a progressive technology, of rapidly expanding productivity, of the creation of a wage-earning category of workers, of the problems of large-scale capital manipulation. They now require a more developed and more massive social theory to account for the phenomena which they observe,

---

[1] This position is likely to be corrected as the field research of Soviet ethnographers, and the breadth of their discussion with colleagues on an international basis, extends.

and they cannot pretend to supply that theory wholly from within their own resources. They are likely to seek elements of the theory in an eclectic way, and will be searching *inter alia* in historical sociology. A Marxist type of analysis (without the total Marxist system) offers a framework of theory which directs attention most keenly upon power structures, class formation and their economic pre-conditions. This is helped on the one hand by the greater flexibility of modern Marxist views, and on the other by the growing body of critical literature on Marxist theory.

An illustration of the kind of amalgam which is being created in this field is in the theory of institutions put forward by e.g. C. Wright Mills, H. Brotz, John Rex and others. Succinctly, Rex has argued, following Dahrendorf, that institutions may be looked upon not as an affair of participation in consciously shared common purposes, but as forms imposed and maintained by a ruling élite for their own purposes. There is then if not an overt struggle, at least a latent conflict of purposes, which would provide the dynamic for institutional change. This dynamic force may be provided partly by the ordinary men and women groping for new forms which will give more adequate expression to their needs, and partly by the efforts of intellectuals and prophets who serve as a creative minority to start new movements. No study of institutions which fails to take into account such incipient movements arising within the established forms can have anything much but ideological significance.[1]

Such a theoretical position stems from Troeltsch, Max Weber and Karl Mannheim, but the influence of Karl Marx may also be inferred.

As Dahrendorf has pointed out (1959, pp. 125–6), one of Marx's greatest contributions to social theory was his success in tracing conflicts that effect social change back to patterns of social structure. For Marx, social conflicts were not random occurrences which forbid explanation and hence prediction, but were the specific outgrowths of the structure of a society. While mistaken in his view that the only way in which social conflict could produce structural change was by revolutionary upheaval, Marx nevertheless in his use of a variant of the Hegelian dialectic did focus attention on the significance of looking for the seeds of change in the apparently stable forms under scrutiny.

[1] *Listener*, 30 Nov. 1961, p. 906. See also Brotz, 1961.

But is a dynamic social theory to be equated simply with conflict theory? Even if this equation be not an obvious oversimplification, certain distinctions must be drawn.

Conflict between individuals or between *specific groups* in a society – such as lineage segments, political parties, religious sects, etc. – may be generally studied in terms of overt or covert social actions by the parties concerned in an immediately observable field of operations. But conflict between *social categories* of persons may be a matter of inference rather than of observation. Here the view taken of the trend and ultimate character of historical process is significant. The particular dynamic scheme adopted by Karl Marx takes as a basic assumption a radical opposition of interests between certain socio-economic categories, of which ruler and ruled, feudal lord and peasant, master and slave, employer and employee, have been taken as conventional examples. But are these categories parallel and of the same order? In modern conditions it would probably be generally agreed that dictator or despot and his subjects, feudal lord and his servile peasantry, slave master and slave, do represent fundamentally opposed categories between which there can be only temporary accommodation. No one can nowadays claim more than a certain very limited set of rights over another person who is adult enough to take responsibility for his social existence. Rights over the actions of another person are legitimate, it is held, only when they are of very limited range, and refer to the alternative use of skills rather than to the disposal of personal life. But are employer and employee comparable categories to those just considered? The relation between employer and employee in a system of private enterprise in a capitalist economy is regarded by some as being a legitimate field for the exercise of reciprocal rights over skills, and not necessarily productive of basic antagonism. By others it is regarded as exploitation, an illegitimate, one-sided exercise of claims, and bound to produce conflict.

A second ground of distinction is in the meaning of the terms themselves. 'Employer and employee', 'master and slave', are fairly clear-cut in their explicit functional definition. 'Ruler and ruled' leave open a considerable area of interpretation. In societies where a limited monarchy is in operation it is a matter of some fine discernment, and perhaps of some argument, as to the extent to which the 'ruler' rules at the discretion of and along the lines dictated by the 'ruled'. In a political system with modern parliamentary government, and a written set of laws, if not a constitution, the margins for difference of interpretation are not very wide. The extent to which a Scandinavian or a British monarch 'rules' can easily be seen by reference to formal documents and to recent experience. But for many societies in which the social anthropologist has worked, no such clarity is obtainable. The degree to which a Polynesian or African chief is in the position of exploiting the economic powers of his people is a matter for considerable interpretation and difference of view. Similar differences can occur when the concepts of feudalism are lifted out of the Western context in which they were first used, and applied to the institutions of Oriental, African or Latin American society, where the relations between ownership and use of land, payment of rent and the performance of personal services, are often of a very different order than in European medieval society.[1]

Apart from questions on the nature of the categories between which basic conflict is assumed to lie, there is also a question about the existence of conflicts in analogous situations which in general fell outside Marx's own analysis. Marx stressed the difference between a capitalist economy and pre-capitalist conditions. The capitalist system presupposed a divorce between the workers and the unified owner of the property through which alone their labour can become effective. In pre-capitalist conditions, Marx argued, the workers are not so divorced, and the dispersed means of production are directed, held and used by the labourers themselves.[2] An implication sometimes drawn from this (not necessarily by Marx himself, cf. Korsch, 1938, p. 69) is that conditions in the pre-capitalist economy preclude basic conflict. Sahlins (1960, p. 409) quotes with approval Bücher's statement that in a household economy the relation of social dependence 'manifestly cannot come'. But here the weight of the argument turns upon what is to be regarded as 'basic' conflict. It is a matter of observation by many social anthropologists that in what may be allowed, for the sake of argument, to be a household economy, there are

[1] Cf. Potekhin, 1956; Schapera, 1928, pp. 175–6, 184; Chilver in Audrey I. Richards, 1960; Firth, 1959, p. 339; for some anthropological discussion of these points.

[2] Marx, 1930, pp. 844–6. Note the superficial resemblance in formal terms between Marx and L. H. Morgan's view (first expressed in 1868) that it is impossible to overestimate the influence of property upon the civilization of mankind. Morgan's strictures on private property are at the end of his *Ancient Society* (1877, p. 552).

often indeed deep-rooted conflicts between the controller of the
common household property and other members of the social
group whose share in the fruits of the property in their view is
less than equitable. Similar conflicts often exist between siblings,
especially where land resources are scarce and population is expanding. These conflicts rarely manifest themselves in an alteration of the structure of the whole system, it is true, but they may
be resolved only by splitting the system by migration of some of
the parties. Moreover, the threat of violence may sometimes be
not far below the surface (cf. Firth, 1959, pp. 93). It can be
argued, therefore, that conflicts between workers and the controllers of capital, which some Marxists seem to have regarded as
the product of specific developed economic conditions, can in
fact be seen to have their roots in economic systems which have
not reached the level of capitalist separation of ownership of the
means of productivity from the worker.

But what about cases where social actions of opposition between
family head and family members, or between siblings, do not
seem sufficiently crystallized to be described as conflict? To describe their relations as outwardly harmonious seems a reasonable
use of words, but may veil underlying antagonism of interests.
Here comes in a distinction sometimes drawn between *conflict* and
contradiction.[1] Since both terms indicate incompatibility, and both
have figurative as well as literal meaning, such a distinction can
easily be forced too far. But it can be argued that conflict is observable empirically in behavioural opposition between persons or
groups, whereas contradiction may be an inference referring
either to a logical opposition, or to an ideological opposition
between the parties.[2] In this sense conflict, which may be based on
misconception or temporary lack of adjustment by the parties,
may be resolved, whereas contradiction cannot be resolved so
long as the relevant conditions remain the same. (Conflict which
is not based on misconception but on underlying contradiction
can be resolved only temporarily while the basic opposed principles still remain.) But elements of incompatibility are built into
social life in many ways which are basic for social action. To

[1] See Bailey, 1960, pp. 238–9. Cf. MacRae, 1961, p. 183.

[2] By *logical opposition* here is meant incompatibility arising from general thought
structure and word use, and by *ideological opposition* an incompatibility arising from the
particular structure of a system of thinking about the nature of society, which is correlated
with a particular structural position of the thinker in the society.

Marx the basic incompatibility in economic terms was between the progressive capabilities of the material productive forces and the relatively fixed form of the social relations through which production took place in capitalist society. In social terms the basic incompatibility was thus in the power relationship between classes, founded on their different functions in the productive system. Against this one may argue, as has Dahrendorf, that not only the power relationship between economic classes but also any power structure bears within it its own contradictions. Further, it may be maintained that any authority relationship exercised by one person over another offers a perpetual challenge to individuality and hence a radical incompatibility in social existence.

It may be argued against this on Marxist lines that incompatibility or basic contradiction in dyadic relations between persons is not necessarily significant at the social level. Such categories of relations must be incorporated into class terms, with recognition of common interests between members of the class, before they can become fully effective as social forces. This point of view seems to have been undervalued in social anthropology. On the other hand, there is still the basic problem of how the common interests between the members of the class are recognized, defined and acted upon. Forces of consensus and co-operation as well as of conflict come then to be involved in the analysis.[1]

SOCIAL DEVELOPMENT

In historical perspective problems of growth and development would seem to be at least as significant as those of conflict. Indeed, when economists speak of dynamic theory they usually have in mind not the analysis of conflict but the analysis of economic growth. In any kind of society, even the most simple, conflict of one kind or another occurs. In this sense, then, if the stress in dynamic theory be only on conflict, then a 'dynamic' analysis may be made of a 'static' traditional society. Anthropologists may with profit take a leaf from the economists' book and focus on those aspects of social dynamics associated with elaboration of resources and development of social relationships. Conflict may

---

[1] e.g. as by Worsley, 1957, p. 237, who has to explain how the separate units of highly segmented societies unite under a prophet for common political action. Cf. Birnbaum's examination of Marx's position (1953, pp. 130–2).

occur in the allocation of these resources or in the restructuring of the relationships. But conflict may be regarded as a secondary not a primary object of study.

From the great range of theoretical treatment in the field of social development, an anthropologist should perhaps select Kroeber's monumental *Configurations of Culture Growth*. But as Kluckhohn and others have pointed out, this work, with its stress on the roles of clusters of exceptional individuals, falls far short of a sociological theory. It is my conviction that the theories which are most likely to be of use to social anthropologists searching for 'dynamic' interpretations of the phenomena they study are to be found for the most part outside the anthropological sphere. Sociologists, economists, economic historians, political scientists, for example, are accustomed not only to deal with material from complex societies, but to view it in a strictly historical perspective. Moreover, while we may reject the Marxist holistic theory, it is clear that there is little social development which is not underpinned by some economic growth. Economic analysis then must form some part of a dynamic theory of society.

I have mentioned earlier that for ordinary economic purposes the distinction between static and dynamic concepts is that of a mode of approach to the data rather than a characterization of the data themselves. At the same time, there is a tendency among economists and other social scientists to distinguish those systems in which economic growth is at a minimum or of a very low order, from those where significant growth is being achieved.

By economic growth essentially is meant increase of output per head. Such increase almost inevitably implies some re-ordering of human relationships, both for the production and the distribution of the results. Those societies in which no substantial increase of output per head is being achieved have been described as 'traditional', a term which in some cases is equated with 'static' and in others not (cf. Rostow, 1961, p. 4; Wilson, 1962, pp. 15–16). Characterization of a traditional society may be epitomized by Rostow's criteria – a high proportion of resources devoted to agriculture, an associated hierarchical social structure with relatively small scope for vertical mobility, prominence of family and wider kinship connexions, political power of mainly a regionalized type, generally in the hands of the controllers of land. In passing, such statements about 'traditional' societies sometimes offer points for critical comment by an anthropologist. Rostow's statement that family and 'clan' connexions play a large role in social organization, or Wilson's statement that in static societies values, techniques, skills, etc., are transmitted 'from father to son', invite anthropological qualifications. But the major interest for the anthropologist of theories of economic growth and social development is twofold. On the one hand, as with the work of W. Arthur Lewis (1955) or of Rostow, the social anthropologist can give content to the economist's or economic historian's statements about institutions, values and attitudes. On the other hand, these theories provide a directional frame within which the anthropologist may attempt to set his own findings. As general problems of significance in this field, we are concerned with the social concomitants of economic change – attitudes towards increase of productivity and the use of newly acquired wealth, problems arising in its distribution, tendencies to the formation of new class structures. We are concerned for example in how far the emergence of a middle class or, as John Gillin (1960, pp. 24–25) has termed it, a middle stratum or middle segment of society, is a pre-requisite to a period of economic take-off.

The present-day interest in dynamic theory for social anthropology is partly a response to increasing perception of deficiencies in earlier theoretical approaches. But it is partly a response to changed conditions in our field of observation itself, and it has been influenced by modern intellectual movements of a more general kind. Of this we must take advantage. In social anthropology we are not equipped to construct by ourselves what Baumol in economics has referred to as 'the magnificent dynamics of general theory'. There is now in economics and in history a climate of opinion which is favourable to co-operation with social anthropology, especially as regards problems of social change. Our general propositions for study and reformulation can be improved by such association – and we ourselves have a contribution to make.

To sum up, 'dynamic' analysis, then, if it is to be a representative study of the range of social phenomena, must have many components. It must allow for some degree of autonomy and flexibility in the operation of social factors and not assume unitary sequence in social affairs. It must take account of elements of status interest as well as of power interest in relationships between social groups or categories. It must deal with consensus as well as conflict. It must grasp the significance of economic factors, but not treat mass phenomena as being simply reactions of an economic order.

The anthropological contribution to dynamic theory lies in major part in the analysis of structures of interests and of power, of meanings and of values, not only at their ostensible 'realistic' level, but also as they express symbolically ideas of group identity and activity.

On the issue of 'dynamic' as a committal to change – an 'engagement', to use our analysis for alteration of the state of society – this is a personal issue which we will answer largely according to our inclination and training. What we cannot forget is that whatever position we adopt adds its implications for the structure and development of our own discipline in the surrounding world of social theory.

CHAPTER II
Social Organization and Social Change
(1954)

In responding to the invitation to give this address, I have been led to some retrospective thoughts. It is just thirty years since, as a postgraduate student from New Zealand, I attended my first meeting at this Institute. At that time the science – or sub-science – of social anthropology in Britain had not yet received any very clear definition. Rivers's book on the Todas and Malinowski's on the family among the Australian aborigines had long provided models – the one of field ethnography and the other of theoretical analysis of primitive institutions. But Radcliffe-Brown's work on the Andaman Islands, and Malinowski's study of the Kula were still so novel as not to have had great effect. The brilliance of Rivers, which had taken an unrealistic and somewhat perverse turn before his death in 1922, had left a powerful influence, and Elliot Smith and Perry were significant figures. Now, during these thirty years social anthropology has become firmly established as a scientific discipline, as a branch of instruction and research under intellectual control. In 1924 the only place in Britain where social anthropology was seriously taught was in Malinowski's seminar, and the students were only a handful. Now there are in Britain (leaving out the Commonwealth countries) at least seven centres where social anthropology is taught; students have multiplied and the membership of the Association of Social Anthropologists alone, though it is only eight years old, comprises over eighty people professionally engaged in teaching or research in the subject. (By 1962, eight years later, the number of members had more than doubled.)

All this is familiar to many of you. Familiar also are the problems of this rapid growth – problems of which the Institute itself has been well aware. One problem is to find occupation for the highly trained people thus produced. Another is to find research and maintenance funds to keep up that level of training, both in theoretical analysis and in field inquiry, which has brought British social anthropology a reputation second to none. These problems were no less acute thirty years ago – if anything, in choosing anthropology as a career, we had to leap into an even thicker darkness than did our successors. But fewer people were affected. Moreover, today, there is some light on the horizon. The normal flow of occupational openings is increased through the much greater range of academic posts. The creation of research institutes (and university departments) overseas, closer to the ordinary fields of the anthropologist, the interest in anthropology shown by the great general foundations, and the special support given by the uniquely devoted Wenner-Gren Foundation, have opened up new avenues of theoretical work. Apart from all this, but partly because of the results that have accrued, there is now the beginning of a realization in the public mind that a trained social anthropologist may have something to offer to the society in which he lives. Thirty years ago, applied anthropology meant doing ethnography for the government or being a missionary. Nowadays a much wider range of activities is open.

Overseas there are calls to study the social implications of rural community development projects, assimilation of immigrants, labour relations in new industries, effects of urbanization, operation of new legal measures, growth of new religious systems. The challenge and opportunities in such work are already drawing into it local anthropologists from the countries concerned. This is a most welcome development. It helps to increase greatly the mass of data gained and to broaden the personnel base of our science. It may also help to stimulate local interest and bring home the true nature of anthropology much more than alien scientists alone can do. Moreover, it opens up interesting methodological issues by increasing our sensitivity to local conditions and offering checks on the interpretation of field data – though of course it also raises the problem of objectivity in another guise. In modern Western society, too, the anthropologist is finding increasing interest and skill in the study of kinship and other associated systems, the position of ethnic minorities, the informal structures of industrial employment, the complex and subtle accompaniments of medical and welfare work and psychological rehabilitation. Such studies (in which this Institute has recently begun to take an increasing interest) are beginning to look as if they can be reasonably handled in theoretical and field terms by social anthropologists. They clearly have important practical implications. The next decade may well see a much closer approach of anthropological science and public interest than ever before, in seeking to define the fields where both sides can best make their contribution; in sorting out the roles and needs of theoretical and of applied analysis; and in promoting the experiment necessary to get reasonable answers on such issues.

In this kind of dynamic contemporary study the social anthropologist has certain assets. His comparative approach helps him to keep perspective; he is not put off by the seemingly familiar. His framework of theory, benefiting from constant reference to small-scale societies as 'going concerns', helps him to look at people's actions in context, as part of a system of actions into which other people also enter. His intensive methods of field study, using observation as much as questions, help him to keep close to the social reality, and check where he tends to depart from it.

But this impending role of contributor in the interpretation of modern civilization imposes new burdens on the anthropologist. The first is that of greater awareness of the theory and methods of his colleagues in other social disciplines. Sociologist, economist, psychologist, social administrator, are kept away from the social anthropologist nowadays more often by the practical preoccupations of their job than by radical difference of theoretical outlook. If they start with different points of view, their work on similar problems often may lead them to parallel conclusions. And even where their outlook is very alien, they may have a sophistication in approach to the data, and a knowledge of the local conditions and complex national structures of the social system, with which a social anthropologist at the outset may be totally unfamiliar, and on which he should be eager to draw.

The second burden is that of greater social responsibility. With any growing absorption into the study of what are regarded by most people as important fields of living – factory, hospital or welfare clinic, housing estate – the social anthropologist must pay closer attention to the way in which he proceeds to study his problem. Gone will be the happy days of ethnographic osmosis, when he could sit down and allow the fluid material from the primitive life around him to percolate his intellectual (and emotional) tissues! No longer will the material in itself be of no

outside interest, dealing with the customs of a remote and re-
condite group of which only experts will know the name. In
particular, the issues of quantification of his data will have to be
more squarely faced, and some of his generalizations will need
more substance.

Another burden may well be some sacrifice of ease of movement through the society. In the alien primitive communities that
have been the classic field of the anthropologist, he has usually
had remarkable social freedom. In studies in his own society he
may well find that he has a tendency to become status-bound.
This tendency will vary with his own personality and origins.
But to take an extreme example. An anthropologist could find it
relatively easy to make a first-hand study of the workings of a
Court system in almost any Asian or African state; but participant
observation might present some difficulty in Buckingham Palace.

With a change in emphasis in the fields or themes of modern
social anthropology, there may have to come then a closer
recognition of our limitations. With all this, social anthropology
may be becoming less romantic. I would deplore the passing of
some of the aesthetic experiences that primitive dance and drama,
acquaintance with technology, and even participation in funeral
ceremonies may give. These may have little scientific value in the
development of more acute perceptions for the observation of
behaviour. But they undoubtedly help to give incentive for field
work in difficult and sometimes dangerous circumstances. But
study of the contemporary problems of our own culture may
offer comparable excitements, in giving that feeling of contact
with – even committal to – dynamic issues of basic importance
in the large-scale affairs of the society in which we live.

There is something else that the change in the climate of public
opinion may allow in time. That is, the recognition of social
anthropology as a cultural subject. In academic training it may
come, say, to be on a par with history. In my view, social anthropology is not a subject that should be taught to young people in
schools. Unlike, for example, geography, it almost necessarily
involves consideration of questions of comparative human values
which demand some maturity for proper understanding. But at
the university level it could be a subject of general character; it
could clearly be part of a degree in which specialization lies elsewhere. Moreover, it should be acceptable in its own right as one

of the proper general bases for a non-anthropological career. If a training in classics, in history, or in philosophy is acceptable as a qualification for entry into, say, business or the Civil Service, then a training in another comparative study of human behaviour should stand on the same footing. To do all this with justice social anthropology must demonstrate that it has generalizations of interest about human and not merely primitive conduct; it must build up its comparative pretensions with solid material from the more developed, the more sophisticated societies. For this, it will have to have a closer alliance with sociology, giving as well as taking breadth and precision.[1]

Social anthropology will also have to continue to refine its theoretical framework, which has been responsible already for many important results. I am speaking today primarily about British anthropology, but I must pay a tribute here to the stimulus of our American colleagues, with whom, happily, contact has become increasingly close over the last decade. And while it may seem invidious to mention the names of our own colleagues, one cannot avoid referring once again to the fundamental importance of the complementary work of Malinowski and Radcliffe-Brown. Malinowski's great contribution, it so happens, was never formally recognized in full by this Institute – he was never either its President or its Huxley Lecturer – though he was awarded the Rivers Medal for his field research. But his spirit of broad humanistic inquiry, of intellectual honesty in exploration of a problem, still receives ample expression, and his theories still appear in various guise. Radcliffe-Brown, happily still writing and lecturing, has become a very Solon of his science.[2] Like Solon, he has been a lawmaker, and a wise one. Like him too, he has framed constitutions – though of academic departments, not of political states. And before passing on, I cannot omit mention of the work of Evans-Pritchard, with whom in temperament and in argument I am sometimes at variance, but to whom British social anthropology owes a great deal during the last twenty years for playing a leading part in developing the use of clear abstract formulations, and promoting high standards of scholarship.

I want now to speak about a few key ideas which have had a

[1] Probably the gap between professional and non-professional training in social anthropology will need to be widened also.
[2] Radcliffe-Brown died on 24 October 1955.

great deal of refinement during the last thirty years. This has not always led to clarification in the sense of agreed definitions. But it has meant an exploration of meanings – of alternative propositions – that has stimulated inquiry and generalization. These ideas relate to the framework of social action. Social action can be looked at in a number of different ways. One way is to examine it for its structure – to look for those major patterns of relationship in it which form a systematic arrangement and which as such serve to regulate further action along the same lines. These structural elements may be formal, given explicit recognition; or they may be informal, acted upon implicitly though not part of the overtly admitted patterning. In a large factory or business firm, for instance, there is a formal structure of directors, managers of various grades and functions, supervisors, foremen, and other people with various kinds of responsibilities and status. There is also an informal structure, at all grades. Distinctions of job or social condition may give a basis for recognized patterns of action, give status and social as well as technical role, and fit each newcomer into a regular scheme which may not be officially recognized at all. Knowledge of such informal structure, which can be gained only by empirical study on the spot, may be of profound importance for an understanding of how the formal structure works. Another way to look at social action is in terms of its organization. The structure provides a framework for action. But circumstances provide always new combinations of factors. Fresh choices open, fresh decisions have to be made, and the results affect the social action of other people in a ripple movement which may go far before it is spent. Usually this takes place within the structural framework, but it may carry action right outside it. If such departure from the structure tends to be permanent, we have one form of social change.

I want to consider these ideas further, because they are central to many modern discussions in social anthropology, and there is much difference of view about them. The first point I wish to make is that in discussions of social action the notions of structure and of organization are primarily matters of emphasis. They represent different ways of looking at the same body of material; they are complementary, not opposed concepts. Briefly, and crudely, they may be said to stand respectively for consideration of *form*, and of *process* in social life. But neither is precise, either as a theoretical concept or as a definition of an aspect of social reality.

Let me illustrate this from a preliminary consideration of the notion of social structure. This seems at first sight a clear enough idea. We think in the case of an African or Oceanic society, of its structure in terms of kinship groups such as clans or lineages; major kinship relations such as that between mother's brother and sister's son; status relations such as that of a chief to his people; ritual relations such as that of a priest to the congregation of worshippers at a shrine. In the classic address entitled 'On Social Structure', delivered before this Institute, Radcliffe-Brown (1940) defined his subject in terms of a complex *network* of social relations – 'actually existing relations'. Now no one has thought that he meant he was dealing with either a meshed fabric held together by knots, or an arrangement with intersecting lines and interstices recalling such a fabric. We can take it for granted that like a modern painter, when he wrote *network* he was expressing what he felt by describing metaphorically what he saw. The image is a vivid and useful one. We can figuratively speak of the relations between persons in a social context as links, and visualize them as lines, and it has probably helped many of us greatly in social analysis to think of social relations in this way. Barnes (1954) recently has found this metaphor convenient to describe the personal sets of relationships which characterize the particular structure of a Norwegian fishing community. But we must be aware of the vagueness of the concept of 'social relations'.

Jeremy Bentham (Ogden ed., 1931, pp. 68–9) protested against 'this obscure notion of *relations*', saying that this and other such abstract terms did not excite any idea in his mind at all. We can hardly do without this term now (especially since Max Weber's clarification of it), but there is no harm in reminding ourselves of its empirical content in the actions of people, and of the problems of meaning to which it gives rise. But Bentham has a further pertinent remark – about the danger of metaphors being used at first for illustration or ornament and afterwards made the basis of an argument. A network, a reticulation, is a very specific kind of structure, and a static one. Even if we imagine the net knots or nodules as more in the nature of nerve-ganglions from which fibres radiate, receiving and distributing nerve-impulses, the whole concept tends to give social structure a fixed form and a finite extent which are not borne out by analysis. Confusion arises between the metaphorical and concrete meanings of the term – or rather between the various degrees of generality and abstraction that can be given to it. This comes out in other views: Evans-Pritchard's concept of social structure as the consistent, constant groups in a society; Talcott Parsons's concept of social structure as a system of expectations; Leach's, of social structure as a set of ideal rules; Lévi-Strauss's, of social structures as models. And there are others. What do we now say if our critics tell us that our concept of social structure, the key-term of our analysis, is itself amorphous, lacking in form?

I think the first thing we say is that there is structure at all social levels. And the next is that each of these views does offer an important facet of the problem of definition. But we must not disguise from ourselves that this problem still exists, that there still remain several areas of uncertainty in its application.

The first concerns its scope. A 'social structure' in Radcliffe-Brown's sense can be conceived but never fully described. He includes as part of it not only persistent social groups, but also *all* social relations of person to person, and differentiation of 'individuals'[1] and classes by their social role. This all-inclusive definition merges the permanent and the temporary or ephemeral. (When I knock into someone on the street and apologize, we have a social relation. But is this to be reckoned as part of the social structure?) In addition, the study of social values is part of the study of social structure; the spread, unification and division of languages are 'phenomena of social structure'; and the study of how new forms of structure come into existence and the processes by which social structures change is a 'related aspect'. Little wonder then that 'many writers of ethnographical descriptions do not attempt to give us any systematic account of *the* social structure' (Radcliffe-Brown, 1940, p. 5 – my italics). There is indeed no such isolable entity. As Kroeber (1948, p. 325) has said, '. . . everything that is not wholly amorphous has a structure'. To give a systematic account of it in its entirety is impossible. '*The* social structure', viewed as something within the grasp of the ethnographer's account, is a myth. Social structure is a conceptual, not an operational or descriptive tool. As Radcliffe-Brown himself says in one comment – the 'structural point of view' is

[1] Despite his warning about confusion with 'persons' (Radcliffe-Brown, 1940, p. 5).

the important thing. If we want to compare structural systems, then, it is only in a selective, sectional way that this can be done. This is shown by Eggan (1949, p. 121), who observes cautiously that 'a limited number of structural principles' have been isolated by Radcliffe-Brown's method of structural or socio-logical analysis.

Another area of uncertainty in the understanding of social structure is the difference of stress between social ideal and social practice. Radcliffe-Brown was in no doubt on what he wanted considered – the practice. He distinguished between the structural form – the abstraction of general from particular behaviour made by the field-worker in his description – and the structure as concrete reality observed as the basis for description – the 'actually existing, concrete reality', as he termed it for double measure of emphasis. But it is what people actually do in forming and main-taining social relations that he stresses as basic data. The ideal comes into the picture in the consideration of rules of behaviour, the formulations of patterns and, presumably, also in the study of social values or interests as determinants of social behaviour. With this can be contrasted the notion of a social structure as a set of ideal patterns, of rules which may never receive their expression in other than verbal action. This conception of social structure as the set of relations which are regarded as proper to the maintenance of society, with its analogue of structure as a set of expectations, is important. It clarifies Radcliffe-Brown's usage and points up the methodological problems involved in relating ideal to empirical reality. But if the set of ideal rules is considered alone, or as the primary clue to the social structure, it can be mis-leading. The ideal may be no guide to reality.[1] It may be treated only as a substitute for it – just as in some ethical systems the possession of an ideal is regarded as absolving one from the neces-sity of any practical orientation towards it. Moreover, concentra-tion on this may lack perspective. How surprised the authors of *A Survey of the Social Structure of England and Wales* (Carr-Saunders and Caradog Jones, 1927) would have been if told that their subject should have been not actual units of marital associa-tion but ideal rules of marriage; not conditions of housing but the kind of homes it was thought proper for the people to have;

[1] Leach (1954, pp. 9, 15), who has used the 'ideal' definition, has dealt with this point in its structural context.

not actual distribution of the national income, but what people reckoned their incomes ought to be. Ideal relations are important in any conceptualization of a social structure, but they cannot by themselves be held to constitute *the* social structure (cf. Firth, 1951, pp. 29–31, and 3rd ed., pp. 29, 251).

A third area of uncertainty in the use of the concept of social structure is in the degree of abstraction that it entails. Abstraction is a necessary process in structural analysis, or in recognition of a structure. Radcliffe-Brown tried to distinguish between the actual structure, which is directly, empirically observed, and the 'form of the structure', which the field-worker describes by abstracting the general from the particular. As Fortes and others have argued, this distinction is invalid, if it is based just on the entry of abstraction at the second stage. But as I see it, Radcliffe-Brown was concerned with two things: on the one hand, he wanted to preserve the integrity of the analysis to ensure that the anthropologist is dealing with real entities, not fictions. On the other hand, he wanted to ensure comparability. Now it is true that while one can observe behaviour, one infers social relations. In that sense social structures cannot be directly observed. But Radcliffe-Brown was not so much denying that one uses abstraction at the primary level of structural study as pointing out the need of a different level of abstraction in order to get material for comparison.

Associated with this argument about abstraction in structural analysis are two other questions. One is the notion of social structures as models. This is a most promising line of inquiry, and already Bateson (1936, 1949), Leach (1945, 1954), and Lévi-Strauss (1949, 1953) have begun to develop it to good purpose. But among anthropologists in general there seems to be little clear idea of what a model is or should be. It is useful in thinking about models in social anthropology to take a leaf out of the economist's book, since, in economics, analysis by models is a customary device. For economists, a model is not just a personal way of looking at phenomena. It is a deliberate construct, simplified from, or departing from, real life situations, for heuristic purposes. It has been described as 'a closed symbolic representation of the interaction of certain economic phenomena' (Stone and Jackson, 1946, p. 555). Its use is still imprecise, in that there are economic models of different degrees of rigour, and different types, varying in the way in which they use mathematical or other symbols. Formula, diagram and model grade into one another. But, essentially, economic models follow the same general lines of construction. A problem is selected, a notation given to the various entities recognized in it, and propositions are put forward involving assumptions about the relations of the entities in specified conditions. Then, while certain elements in the model are held constant, others are allowed to vary, and the results of such variations are set out in further propositions. There are many economic models of this general kind, dealing with such matters as the relation between national income and savings; between national income, exchange rates, and balance of trade; employment policy; marginal costs; the income-generating effect known as the multiplier, etc. To be worth while, such a model must have logical consistency; it must have validity in standing up to test; and it must have utility ('power' as it has been called) in giving clarification to data and some basis for prediction.[1]

There are certain problems in the construction of these economic models – of logic, of time, and of reality – which may be mentioned for their bearing on our own problems. To secure that the set of relations posed is logically watertight, or to show that the logic is in some respects incomplete or off the track, is part of the ordinary process of economic argument. It is a stage which has hardly yet been reached in the construction and scrutiny of anthropological models.

The problem of correspondence of the model with reality is one which economists have on the whole now met fairly and squarely. They now see that the concepts and relations chosen for the construction of the model are not given by nature, but are largely the invention of the investigator. They are governed primarily by the way in which he thinks it 'profitable to represent experience'. They recognize that observations can be represented in many ways, and that the problem is to find the ways that are neatest, most efficient, most simple to represent the most important elements of the highly complex variable systems of the behaviour of human beings. (That such ways are also the most

[1] The literature on economic models is very full. Of special concern for the methodological interests of an anthropologist are perhaps the following: Stone and Jackson (1946); Baumol (1948); Phillips (1950); Joan Robinson (1952). A clear example of the use of an economic model is seen in Turvey (1948). In an allied field, a useful review of the work of Von Neumann and Morgenstern (1947) is given by Stone (1948).

satisfying aesthetically is one of the bonuses that the scientist allows himself.) Yet it must be noted that the aim is after all to represent experience, to 'save the phenomena', not just to construct a personal intellectual toy. Now this problem of the relation of the model to reality is one that the anthropologist will have to keep firmly before him. The reasons are twofold. The first is that the reputation of the anthropologist has been built up on his control of empirical material, on his first-hand knowledge and interpretation of the behaviour of people in actual named societies at particular periods of time; on his ability to make significant comparative generalizations which make sense in action, not just in theory. If he does not at each step try to relate his model to social reality, then he will lose one of his chief titles to status in the social sciences. The second reason is that the notion of model-making has become tangled up with that of the personal element in observation – the observer-effect. By this latter is meant that the observer's experience is viewed always through his personal lens. If one wishes to use Cassirer's (1953, pp. 57, 69–114) terms, there is no content which is not construed according to some form which is supplied by the human understanding at the start of apprehension. The primary experience is itself form-constituted. The scientist cannot immediately grasp or communicate reality; he can only mediate it. In knowledge, truth itself is whatever is in accordance with the form of understanding. But let us grant that the form-giving functions and symbolizing activity of consciousness mean that we can never get the 'crude facts' of Andamanese or Trobriand social life – the 'actually existing, concrete reality' of Radcliffe-Brown's (1940, p. 4) words.

Yet this does not justify intellectual retreat, or intoxication at the discovery of one's intellectual freedom. There is a tendency for frames of reference to be confused here. When one constructs an anthropological model of an aspect of social structure, one deliberately simplifies, or ignores, the material of observation. But one does so for specific purposes, and the only anthropological use of such a model is that it should in the end be related as closely as possible to what is understood of the behaviour of people in a specific society. This does not mean that all representations of social structures must be models. Still less does it mean that one is entitled to use any abstraction or distortion or personal construct and claim that it is as equally defensible as any other. Just as the model must fulfil certain requirements of relation to reality if it is to be of use, so the perception of system in social behaviour, and the description of ethnographic facts must be subject to test. Basically, this test is that of communication. When I describe a *kava* rite of the Tikopia and explain the meaning of the formulae uttered and the libations poured, I am doing so in terms of a system that I myself have perceived in Tikopia religious behaviour. But the validity of that system can be tested by the degree to which it is intelligible, to which it serves to describe and explain to others, both the Tikopia and those in contact with them, further items of behaviour within the field. At the ethnographic level, I think that my experience has proved this to be so, by prediction to a colleague and by our ability to partake with Tikopia people of the experience in a mutually intelligible way. In the philosophical frame of reference these may be matters of debate and difficulty. In the anthropological frame of reference, there is no need to assume an infinite regression of reality. What the field-worker describes must not be confused with what the armchair thinker invents. Both have their value. But they are different.

A problem which has caused more difficulty in economics is that of allowance for changes over time. For the most part, a model is assumed to operate over a period of given time dimension, which is the same and coincident for every element in the model. This is a non-historical dimension. The specific character of the time-period is irrelevant to the changes that are deemed to occur. In the construction of a dynamic theory, which is far from complete as yet in economics, various devices have been used, such as assumption about acceleration in rates of output, or lag in the development of different factors. For the most part, these imply the idea of steady change. And, as Joan Robinson (1952, p. 53) has pointed out, a theory conceived in terms of oscillations round a trend of steady growth may be inadequate to explain the structure of an economy from which this steadiness is absent. Part of the work of construction of a dynamic theory would seem to lie as well then in the laborious business of building up from economic reality a series of types and variants of such kind that changes over time – including erratic changes – can be studied with an approach to actuality. A difficulty here, of course, is the old one of comparability – of drawing out from the unique historical events the underlying regularities of social change. It is not for an anthropologist to advise economists here. But the relevance of the economic work for us is twofold. On the one hand it points to the importance of the construction of anthropological models, which, by their simplicity, the logical refinements possible in them, and the ability to study variation in them, give tentative answers to problems, provoke inquiry into empirical relations, and stimulate insight in ways not hitherto thought of. On the other hand, it indicates that an understanding of the dynamics of a social system needs in addition a constant study of observed social behaviour. The more abstraction is developed as a tool of logical analysis, the more the need for the corrective of data from the empirical situation. In addition, the experience of the economist suggests that a limitation may be speedily found to the use of models by an anthropologist through the difficulty of assigning magnitudes to many of the entities he wishes to incorporate into his treatment.

All of this bears on the notions of social organization and social change. If social structures *are* models, then we can call social organization the 'reality'. But even if they are not merely models, then as the set of primary forms of the society, they need supplementing by studies of process. The notion of social organization is of course not a new one. But one can distinguish at least three senses of the term. The first is general, even vague. In conventional descriptions or outlines of the earlier years of this century, the term has been used as equivalent to social groups and institutions – 'the social side', as C. G. Seligman used to call it. This is the undefined sense found in *Notes and Queries on Anthropology* (Royal Anthropological Institute, 1951), and giving the titles of W. H. R. Rivers's *Kinship and Social Organization* published in 1914, of his posthumous book in 1924, and that of Lowie's book of 1948. Even in Radcliffe-Brown's basic study of 1930, *The Social Organization of Australian Tribes*, the term 'organization' is not distinguished from 'structure', and both notions are used indiscriminately. This usage still persists in much anthropological writing.

The second usage relates to co-ordination or orientation of activities. Many years ago, Herbert Spencer (1885, pp. 473, 507) gave the term 'organization' the meaning of 'such a construction of the whole that its parts can carry on mutually-dependent activities'.[1] Max Weber (1947, pp. 138, 204) regarded organiza-

[1] In speaking of Old World priesthoods, Spencer (1885, p. 548) distinguished the structure, with subjection of rank to rank, from the 'sustaining organization'.

tion as a system of continuous purposive activity of a specified kind, and linked it closely with the notion of corporate groups, and with administration in the more technical sense. In the economic field, the term signified for him the ways in which the various types of services are continuously combined with one another and with non-human means of production. Malinowski (1944, pp. 39, 44, 52) used the term, in a somewhat similar though less technical sense, for the way in which a group of people equip themselves materially and adopt rules of status and rules of performance for carrying out their activities and satisfying certain needs.

The third usage attempts more precise definition, and offers systematic analysis along more specific lines. This is the concept put forward by G. G. Brown and J. H. Barnett (1942), who – rightly, I think – see value in distinguishing between social organization and social structure. They would treat *social organization* as the system of obligation-relations existing among individuals and groups in a society, and *social structure* as the placement and position of the individuals and groups in that system of obligation-relations. In these obligation-relations, elements of ideal behaviour, anticipated behaviour, and actual behaviour all enter. In particular, weight is laid on those relations of obligation entailed in public role behaviour. In line to some extent with this view is the recent standpoint of Radcliffe-Brown (1952), who now has made a distinction. He terms social structure an arrangement of persons in institutionally controlled or defined relations, and social organization an arrangement of activities. Alternatively, a structural system is concerned with a system of social positions, an organization with a system of roles.

My own view approaches that of Max Weber and Malinowski. It is difficult to follow Brown and Barnett in holding that the criterion of organization should be obligation, and especially in thinking as they do that the most accessible index of social organization is *anticipations*. Undoubtedly these are important elements in social organization. But when Brown and Barnett rely on anticipations because they represent 'uniformities of relationship existing in suspension within the cultural framework – in the minds of members of a society', this is too amorphous. And Radcliffe-Brown's conception of social organization as role-system seems to imply an invariant linkage between position and what one does in it, which would reduce the notion of organization to another aspect of structure. The notion of role, indeed, very useful though it is in defining the limits of a person's activity, can imply that a person does only what is assigned for him to do by his social position. It can thus imply a too mechanical view of social action. It does not make allowance for action to meet contingency, for adaptation to the highly variant circumstances and problems of social life. Organization is concerned with roles, but not with these alone; it also involves that more spontaneous, decisive activity which does not follow simply from role-playing.

I do not think that a neat single-sentence definition of the concept of social organization can be given any more than that such definitions have been successfully produced for social structure. But to begin with, one may think of social organization in terms of ordered action. It refers to concrete social activity. This activity is not random; it is ordered, arranged in interrelated sequences. Such ordering implies not simply chance patterns, but reference to socially defined ends. By such co-ordinated, orientated activity, a society is kept in being – its members kept in relation with one another. One may describe social organization, then, as the working arrangements of society. It is the processes of ordering of action and of relations in reference to given social ends, in terms of adjustments resulting from the exercise of choices by members of the society. This is not the same as describing social organization as the working *rules* of the society, which implies a conformity, an imperative, in the ordering of the activities of the members of the society which may be only partly true. People often do what rules lay down, but these rules alone are an incomplete account of their organized activities. Again, this ordering of social action may coincide with and support the structural features of the society, the major principles on which its form depends. But it may vary from the structural principles, and even bear against them in some particulars. Ultimately, the social structure may have to give way through a concatenation of organizational acts.

It will be clear that these concepts of social structure and social organization, though complementary, are not parallel. In speaking in this way of social organization, one is describing not so much an entity as a point of view. There can be no department of social life called social organization. Nor can it be subsumed, even with distortion, under the head of a few principles of group and status alignment, as social structure often is. The two concepts cross-cut each other, as it were, so that organizational results may become part of the structural scheme, and structural principles must be worked out in organizational ways and decisions. The relation between form and process may be difficult to elucidate; it may be easier for us to make generalizations about form than process. But this does not absolve us from the necessity of studying process.

At various times in the history of social anthropology attention has in fact been called to such necessity. In 1937 Sol Tax discussed what he called 'kinship accommodations' as an aid to the understanding of 'the science of social organization'. He was concerned to redress what he conceived to be an imbalance in Radcliffe-Brown's kinship theory by stressing the way in which elements of social organization are the result of a complex of social (or psychological) forces or principles, acting in particular social situations. Since culture is a continuum, some problems of accommodation can be solved once and for all. But in various kinds of situations tensions still exist and have to be solved again and again, no matter how much the solution is aided by precedent. Hence, in his view, the problem of kinship systems is reduced to a problem of choices that individuals must make if they are to live together. Modern descent group theory is coming to take this much more into consideration (see Fortes, 1953, p. 34; and cf. Firth, 1929, p. 100; 1936, pp. 582–3; 1951, pp. 56–7). Where descent is primarily a political matter – of reckoning one's membership of a kinship unit primarily by reference to one's residence, then it ceases to be automatic. Structural units are created and maintained through organization in which the exercise of individual choice is of basic importance.

This brings us to another point – the place of individuals in social organization. The working arrangements by which a society is kept in being, the ways in which relations between groups are made operative and become effective, rest upon individual choice and decision. Here is our great problem as anthropologists – to translate the acts of individuals into the regularities of social process. How do we do it? For brief exemplification, let us distinguish, as some sociologists have done, between manifest social structure and latent social structure. Manifest structure refers to the overtly recognizable patterns – of descent groups,

residential units, basic kinship ties, religious associations, formal
rank. Latent structure refers to those patterns which may be
equally fundamental to the character of the society, but are not
perceptible to observation until this is highly systematized.
Occupational distribution, relation between descent groups and
residential units, relative control of land by different social units,
incidence of marriage between various social categories, may all
need such special study.

Both manifest and latent social structure are kept in being by
individual actions, in the last resort. Even membership of a unilineal descent group involves continual *recognition* by individuals
of their categorization and that of others in those terms, and active
response to the duties and obligations involved. The interrelation
of these responses, the way in which one affects another, is an
aspect of the social organization. For the set of descent groups to
be treated as standard items in a description of the social structure,
the anthropologist must be sure that such recognitions and responses do in fact occur; he must also be aware of any situations
in which they may not occur, and the effects of this non-
occurrence. In other words, his analysis must include consideration
of *conformity and deviance*, and this means organizational data in
terms of individual action. Again, he must take account of what
may be termed *critical decisions*. In societies where segmentation
is a recognized process of group formation and a means to status
acquisition, the decision of individuals to constitute themselves as
a new lineage with a separate name and territory, of a headman
to migrate to a new location, are organizationally important
because they create fresh units for the interplay of social relationships and alter the scale of operations for each residual unit. The
decision of a ritual leader to remove the taboo on resources,
reserved from funerary respect, has organizational implications
by affecting amounts and division of labour, and the rate and scale
of exchanges. Such decisions are not the affair of leaders alone;
they involve action of acquiescence, possibly prolonged debate,
by followers. To understand them and their effects requires then
the study of *consensus* by the anthropologist (see, e.g., Chapter V).

In the formulation of rules of latent structure, by examination
of organizational detail, the only way may be by quantitative
means. In Tikopia, in 1929 and in 1952, I took sociological
censuses which gave, *inter alia*, the details of marriage arrange-

ments by clan and locality. There are in Tikopia no rules of preferred marriage and as far as one can see from superficial observation in such a small area the results are likely to be random. And yet the figures show certain marked preferences for marriages between specific clan members – for example, over one-half of Taumako unions are with Kafika, and over two-fifths of Kafika with Taumako, whereas only one-quarter of Taumako marriages are with Tafua and vice versa. As for Tafua, one-third of the marriages of its women and more than that of its men are intra-clan as against one-fifth and one-sixth intra-clan marriages of Kafika and Taumako respectively. Granted the facts, they can be explained to a considerable degree by traditional loyalties and antagonisms, and by various other ties. But the facts could not be inferred from any system of rules stated by the Tikopia. More-over, in terms of social change the interesting thing is that, despite the exposure of Tikopia society to external influence over the last quarter of the century, there had been practically no change in the marriage patterns. Similarly, as regards the residential aspect, nearly half of all marriages of men are to 'the girl next door' (in the same village) or in the next village. Marriages to a girl on the other side of the island are only one-seventh of all unions. Again, over a generation there has been practically no change in the average incidence, though some interesting local differences are shown. Analogous studies by other workers, for example Barnes (1949) and Schapera (1950), illustrate the use of such methods.

There is of course an area of uncertainty in the methodology of the study of social organization; the question of how far this involves the study of motivation in particular, and of psychology in general. What do we do about this? We can follow the econo-mists, and say that the *fact* of decision is the important thing, and that we are concerned only with the social implications of that fact. This is often what we do, and it is often enough. But some understanding of the reasons for action is frequently thought to be a necessary or advisable part of the analysis. These reasons are apt to be generalized. For example, such forms as 'a man's relation to his father's sister can be correctly described by saying that he regards her as a sort of female father'; or 'economic interests may pull a man to settle with his mother's kin' are common. But if they are to have any empirical validity they must be derived from observation of individual behaviour at some stage. Of recent years psychology has become rather a scare-word for social anthropologists in this country, and we have tended to practise a ritual avoidance of it. But I think we have created unnecessary difficulty for ourselves. It seems to be held that psychology is the study of individuals, rather than of thoughts, feelings, emotions. Hence, while imposing a ban on psychology, many of us have allowed to pass unquestioned statements about the thoughts, feelings, and emotions of men in the mass, or in generalized form. The introduction to *African Political Systems* (Fortes and Evans-Pritchard eds., 1940) – a book which has had, very rightly, a powerful influence in British social anthropology – stresses how Africans could not carry on their collective life if they could not think and feel about the interests which actuate them, their institutions and their group structure; how they feel their unity and see their common interests in symbols, in the form of myths, ritual, sacred places and persons; how it is their attachment to these symbols more than anything else which gives their society cohesion and persistence; how the values expressed in these symbols are common to the whole society. The whole treatment is shot through with statements of such a psychological kind. Moreover, statements about social solidarity, social integration, and the like, seem often to involve concealed assumptions about the ends of human action which are psychological at bottom. I do not think such statements should be avoided. But I think they need validation by evidence of speech and action.[1] But while we record as raw material what an individual says and does, our major concern is not his internal disposition. We are concerned primarily with the effect of his behaviour ·on the collectivity. There are no rigid borders among the social sciences, there are only spheres of relative interest. And our interest as anthropologists leads us into the sphere of the organization of social behaviour rather than into that of the organization of personal behaviour, though we cannot exclude the latter from our consideration. It is for such reasons that questions of whether the exercise of choice and decision is voluntary or involuntary, conscious or unconscious, are of relatively little concern to us. It is to the act of decision and its social consequences that we look primarily for our material.

Studies in social organization demand attention to three criteria: the magnitude of the situation (as in men and materials);

[1] Cf. my conception of *sentiment* in kinship study (Firth, 1936, pp. 170, 576).

the alternatives open for choice and decision; and the time dimension. The relevance of magnitude can be seen in a simple example. Radcliffe-Brown (1940) has pointed out that in a kinship system of the Aranda type (union of a man with his MMBDD or MFSisDD) it is often hard for a man to find a woman of the proper relationship to become his wife. The result is alternative marriage and consequential adjustment of the kinship ties. Clearly, the degree of adjustment that is needed will depend on how large the group is as a whole, and the relative size of its component units. In a group of normal random sex and age distribution, it might well require at least forty people in all for any one man to have a reasonable chance of finding a wife in the appropriate category. We know, thanks to Radcliffe-Brown and his successors, how the varieties of Australian kinship system work in theory, and the type of adjustments needed to meet deficiency. But for most of the tribes we still lack much of the quantitative information needed to see just how the system has worked out in practice for groups of varying size.

The importance of having alternatives for action is illustrated by the example of the relation of mother's brother to sister's son. In structural analysis this is often discussed in terms of *the* mother's brother and *the* sister's son alone, as if each existed in generalized form only. But if there is more than one of either, or if the mother has no brother, what happens? The conventional answer is that it is the type relation that is important. Arrangements are easily made in cases of plurality; some classificatory kinsman steps into the breach if there is no true mother's brother . . . and so on. This is adequate for structural analysis. But a real problem of organization remains. Lack of numerical equivalence between mother's brothers and sister's sons may necessitate considerable adjustments. A classificatory kinsman filling the role of mother's brother may have sisters and sister's children of his own with first claim on him. There may be conflict of obligation, and a problem of resources to be faced. Even if true and classificatory mother's brother be merged in a single vernacular term and category, there will still be a need to establish priorities. In some cases there may be defection, not fulfilment of obligation.

Examine the possibilities closer. The type situation is that of one mother's brother, one sister's son. Alternatives are: one mother's brother and several sister's (or sisters') sons; several mother's brothers with one sister's son jointly, or several sister's (or sisters') sons; no mother's brother (either because she never had one, or because he died – with the possibility of having left heirs to his obligations). Here, in addition to the structural type situation, are four major organizational possibilities from the point of view of a sister's son: having to share unitary avuncular resources with his peers; having undivided rights to multiple avuncular resources; having a share in such resources; having to rely on a substitute. This leaves out of account possible complications, as through any rights of sister's daughters as well. Considering the importance of the mother's brother relationship in many societies, as regards expenditure of goods and time, exercise of authority and support, transmission of magic and knowledge, some of these alternatives are likely to be relevant. Among the possibilities of resolution are: an undifferentiated collectivity; an effort at a one-to-one relation; a definite rule that, say, the eldest person represents the others in his category; a permissive relation whereby personal preference can be the guide. The kind of basis of resolution which is adopted in any society may well be related to the content of the relationship – varying according to whether the relation connotes only social support or involves economic or political transfers of cattle, land, or titles. It is a fair guess that whatever practices obtain will be related to the status interests and striving of individuals, and will affect the stability of the relationship as a whole.

How does the problem appear in anthropological literature? Not very fully. In the authoritative essay of Radcliffe-Brown (1924), the problem does not appear at all; the mother's brother holds the field. But this is reasonable, since he was concerned with establishing the type relationship. Only in a footnote is it implied that if the mother s brother is dead his sons fill the same role. In a later essay (Radcliffe-Brown, 1950) he follows the same line, though plurality is recognized as possible in the conception of a mother's brother.

In reviewing material from twenty-five African and Oceanic societies chosen haphazardly from well-known sources,[1] I have found diverse appreciations of the problem. For many, such as Ashanti, Ifaluk, Majuro, Tallensi, Trobriands, the rules of the

[1] It would be cumbersome to give detailed references in the text. The main works of interest are cited in the list of references at the end.

mother's brother-sister's son relationship are set out in type form: the mother's brother is singled out by a special term, is treated with respect, the sister's son inherits from him, etc. For other societies, some more specific orientation of the relationship is indicated, or some conditioning of the rule. Among the Mesakin (Nuba), a mother of children will receive annual gifts of grain from one of her brothers, as food for her offspring. In Dobu, a man never divides his magic among his sisters' sons, but gives it to one, usually the eldest. Among the Nuer, Nyakyusa, and Lovedu, a special tie of sister with cattle-linked brother gives a special tie between that man and a sister's son (usually eldest son). But in these cases further implications of variation in the mother's brother ratio, including lack of a true mother's brother, have not been exposed. For the Busama, Tikopia, Tswana, Yakö, and Yao we have more information. Among the Tswana, the high development of sibling linkage gives a linked maternal uncle a very special role in all matters affecting his particular sister's children. Provision is made both for substitutes in the case of absence, and for a successor in the case of death. For the Yakö, the principles of assumption of obligation are neatly set out. The role of mother's brother is assumed by the senior among a set of brothers when the marriage of a sister's daughter is in question. Where there is no true brother, a senior matrikinsman in the senior collateral line should act. And whereas avuncular obligations are fairly closely adhered to in ritual contexts, in situations requiring personal initiative and responsibility, rights and duties may be assumed by a younger brother or other matrikinsman with greater prestige. Thus marriage payments nowadays are often handed over by a senior to a more wealthy junior who is ready to accept the contingent responsibility of repayment. The Yao provide an interesting contrast. Since a man's status in a Yao community depends on the number of persons he is deemed to control, there is a strong tendency for brothers to compete for the right to care for their sisters. The eldest normally takes precedence. There are provisions for filling any gap or failure of obligation, to the extent even of a paternal half-brother or analogous kinsman taking the place of the uterine brother. Among Tikopia and Busama, there are similar provisions for gap-filling, and the element of selectivity is demonstrated. Thus, with the Busama, a person may stay with his father if his mother's brother has died young or neglected his obligations – in defiance of the custom which lays down that he should go to live with his mother's brother. Apart from this option, a person may prefer to live with a classificatory mother's brother from whom he may expect some status as heir, rather than with a true mother's brother, who may have chosen an heir elsewhere.

From data of this kind, which I have given here in outline only, we may still construct some organizational principles. We can divide the obligations and ties of the mother's brother-sister's son relationship into three categories – of generic, of specific, and of intermediate or optional implication. Of generic implication, for instance, are: use of the kin term; freedoms and restraints in behaviour; advice in time of trouble; social contacts by visiting and attendance at rituals. Here is no need for individual differentiation. All mother's brothers – or sister's sons – can behave alike; the problem of selection does not arise. Of specific implication are, for instance: inheritance of the personal name of the deceased; succession to headship of a kin group; widow inheritance. Normally, by social convention, there can be only one person carrying on the name, succeeding to a single office, marrying a widow, of a mother's brother. Hence there must be choice among sister's sons. Primogeniture commonly offers the social rule. But there may be some room for manœuvre, as Busama shows. Of an intermediate kind, for instance, are: inheritance of land rights; inheritance of magic by teaching; transfer or exchange of property, as with cattle on marriage. These do not necessarily imply that a single individual must be donor or recipient. But such resources are not unlimited, hence giving to one person lessens the shares of others. Here open up opportunities for favouritism, for tension, for conflict – let alone the possibilities of structural strain through claims or ties of mother's brothers to their own sons. Hence various mechanisms of organization are in vogue to lessen the difficulty and maintain specificity. Primogeniture is the simplest in some ways – invoking this structural principle offers a basis with a moral and social weight of its own. A one-to-one allocation also offers advantages, but suffers from the possibility that numbers will be uneven, as Schapera (1950, p. 142 n.) has noted for the Tswana linkage system. Individual choice according to wealth, prestige, capacity, or even personal preference gives flexibility. The situation cannot be determined *a priori*, but must be examined in the particular contexts of every society.

The significance of the time factor in social anthropology has been epitomized by Fortes (1949b). Yet it cannot be said that our handling of the time dimension of our material is satisfactory. This is due partly to lack of opportunity, partly to obscurities in our methodology. Among the results, some fairly obvious difficulties in our presentation of data have been noted. There is often an air of timelessness in ethnographic accounts – it is still apt to be 'the essential Kaffir' (in Dudley Kidd's phrase) or his equivalent, that is described. There is also a tendency to postulate a time scale from consideration of merely contemporary process. While giving 'structural time' a social dimension, the logic of this debatable notion has not been carried through, and the processes of lineage segmentation and genealogical adaptation are apt to be spoken of as occurring empirically in a certain manner when they have not been actually observed. And while ethnological reconstructions of the grosser sort are avoided nowadays, there is still some reconstitution of the 'original' society in pre-European days on a basis which is only partly that of historical documentation. Moreover, many statements of the structural interdependence of elements of a social system rest on short-period study of what may be only a temporary, casual association; they have not been tested in terms of their observed covariation over time.

Yet, granted this cavalier treatment of the time factor in some respects, social anthropologists can claim much solid advance in the study of social change, to which it is basic. Some, like Robert Redfield or Monica Hunter, have ingeniously translated space into time, by contrasting rural and urban environments, or kraal with farm. Others, like Keesing or Barbeau (and I would add myself here), have shown the way in which historical documents can be used in an anthropological context. Some again, like Redfield in Chan Kom, Kluckhohn and his collaborators among the Navaho, Eggan and others among the Pueblo, Schapera among the Kgatla, Margaret Mead in Manus, myself in Tikopia, have been able to use a sequence of long-spaced visits to a field for the specific study of social changes. Still others, like Oscar Lewis in Tepoztlán or H. Powell in the Trobriands, have been able to follow out the classic earlier studies of others with the same object of time-scale analysis. Most of this work has obvious methodological limitations. It is apt to be dual synchronic rather than truly diachronic, comparative at separate periods and ignorant of intervening events which might modify the interpretation of trends. There is the problem of how far changes that have occurred allow one to say that the same or similar social entities are being compared. And, as Li An-Che (1937) has shown in one example, the personal factor in interpretation may have greater weight than is sometimes reckoned. But despite this, such analyses do seem to have reasonable validity. Checks applied by later analysts by no means bear out all the conclusions of the earlier ones, but the main results are usually confirmed.[1] Moreover, the general patterns of change that have been revealed for these primitive and peasant societies studied by the anthropologist are conformable. They show many similar features which can be explained not merely in terms of a common universe of scientific discourse but of reactions to a common set of social forces of very general human significance.

Studies of social change by British social anthropologists lack the crispness of achievement such as Fortes (1953) has reported and enhanced in his study of unilineal descent groups. But significant advances have certainly been made. I may here cite from only a few fields. An early contribution which did much to crystallize thinking on these problems was the symposium headed by Malinowski (Mair ed., 1938). It would be valuable to have its analogue twenty years later, since we are now very conscious of differences in approach – exemplified by replacement of the term 'culture contact' by 'social change'. Among the various theoretical statements which have aided clarification of such issues are those by Gluckman (1940), G. and M. Wilson (1945), Nadel (1951), and Leach (1954). On family structure and marriage institutions, the formative work of Richards (1940a) and Schapera (1940) has been followed by many analyses, of which that by Phillips, Mair and Harries (1953) may be mentioned as a recent example which shows through collaborative work how far the influence of anthropological thinking on these matters has penetrated. Associated to some extent with such work on family structures are the various studies in change of pattern in large-scale corporate kinship units, of which an interesting example is given by Gough (1952). Many of such studies indicate the incompatibility of such units with many aspects of modern industrial, professional, urban

[1] To take an example from analysis of social change among the Maori. My own conclusions (1929) and those of F. M. Keesing (1928), worked out independently at the same time, agree in all essentials. A later review of my analysis, by Sir Apirana Ngata (1931, 1940), makes some criticisms, but accepts the major framework.

life, and their tendency to disintegrate or to retain or assume social and political functions in lieu of economic functions. In the economic field, there are the studies in the changing application of labour and the social implications of this, by Godfrey Wilson (1941–2), Margaret Read (1942), Schapera (1947), Hogbin (1951), Audrey Richards (1954), and members of the Rhodes-Livingstone Institute and the East African Social Research Institute. In the field of changing law and social controls, Schapera (1938), Freedman (1950), Nadel (1953), Epstein (1953, 1954), and Gluckman (1955a), have made significant contributions. In the field of religion, studies of Melanesian and of African Christianity by Hogbin (1947) and by Sundkler (1948), and of 'Cargo' and analogous movements by F. E. Williams (1928) and more recent writers, including Ronald M. Berndt (1952) and Peter Lawrence (1954), have presented us with a range of novel material.

With all this, we are hardly yet on the threshold of any general theory of a dynamic kind which will enable us to handle comprehensively the range of material within our normal anthropological sphere. We cannot ignore that the 'social change' of the anthropologist is only a facet of the great process of human history. It is a dimension of our subject-matter rather than a division of it. We need not share the view of Evans-Pritchard (1950b) that social anthropology should be described as historiography, not science, because it cannot produce laws of social behaviour – this is largely a verbal issue where it is not a matter of personal conviction. But social anthropology is close to history in another way. The time-place co-ordinates of the ethnographical material mean that for his empirical generalizations the anthropologist is using essentially the same kind of data as the historian does. The primary appearance of the latter in documentary or other solid form involves different techniques of handling it. But in generalizing about processes of social change the anthropologist does not stand alone among the social scientists. This implies both warning and support. We cannot ignore the long record of analyses of social change made by others. Aristotle distinguished between revolts against the person and revolts against the office long before Gluckman (1954) perceived the importance of this theme in Bantu Africa. On the other hand, our sociological responsibility is limited. We can leave to Sorokin and Toynbee those massive general interpretations which are so fascinating yet seem at times so curiously unreal. With a sigh, we may even find Kroeber's (1944) brilliant *Configurations of Culture Growth* stimulating but too rich to absorb completely. We find *The Analysis of Social Change* of Godfrey and Monica Wilson (1945) a valiant effort, more to our taste, though too compressed and elliptical to be always serviceable, and too African for direct comparability in all areas. The social anthropologist needs general concepts, but he needs them first as hypotheses. He is far as yet from a set of major concrete generalizations which can fill in the general framework of his study of social change in any comprehensive solid way.

In seeking his hypotheses, it is well for the anthropologist to continue to apply himself more systematically to his neighbours in the social sciences, especially the sociologists. From Durkheim and Max Weber to Talcott Parsons, Robert Merton, and Kingsley Davis – not disdaining also the less polemical aspects of Karl Marx and Friedrich Engels – we have much to learn still about the interpretation of our material in its more dynamic aspects. As Nadel (1951, 1953), for instance, has shown, there is great gain in breadth and sophistication of treatment to be had from such deliberate catholicity of approach. The social anthropologist has come under criticism at times either for looking at social change only in terms of breakdown, and disintegration; or for ignoring certain fundamental determinants in the situation, such as economic or political dependence (see, e.g., Balandier, 1952; Hield, 1954). There is something in this charge, and with such analyses have been linked that adherence of anthropology to equilibrium theory which has been challenged by Leach and others. But there is a great deal of modern anthropological work which looks for oppositions or 'contradiction' in the social structure, seeks explanations for change in shifts or pressures of power, and on the other hand, studies emergent social elements in terms of the manner in which they are contributing to the construction of new, more highly differentiated social entities. In all such work there is a distinction drawn, explicitly or implicitly, between *structural change*, in which basic elements of the society alter, and *detail change*, in which social action, while not merely repetitive, does not alter the basic social forms. It is becoming increasingly clearer that in order to understand both change in structure and change in detail we must look to a closer study of the setting and results of individual choice and decision, as they affect activity and social relations. In other words, we must look to analysis of social organization to help in the understanding of social change. In this, too, we must be prepared to quantify much more of the data.

CHAPTER III

Some Principles of Social Organization
(1955)

Last year, when I had the honour to address you for the first time, I took as my subject 'Social Organization and Social Change'. Since then it has been suggested to me that it will be useful to explore further some of the ideas involved in the notion of social organization, and to show how they may be applied.

The air of enchantment which for the last two decades has surrounded the 'structuralist' point of view has now begun to be dispelled. Now that this is so, the basic value of the concept of social structure as an heuristic tool rather than a substantial social entity has come to be more clearly recognized. All British social anthropologists are structuralists in their use of the analytical principles developed by this method. But the rigidity and limitations of a simple structuralism alone have come to be more widely perceived. This has been stimulated by closer examination of the concept of social structure itself. It has also been necessitated by the complexities of the ethnographic material to which structural analysis has been applied. A case in point here is the increasing understanding of the nature and formation of descent groups. The earlier emphasis upon the identification of lineages of simple form has given way to recognition of the wide variety of unilineal and non-unilineal descent arrangements allowing choice in the membership of perpetuating corporate kin groups. Variation in residence and in land-using are seen to be closely related to descent group affiliation, with no rigid structural principle of transmission as the sole determinant. (Perception of this trend recently induced G. P. Murdock to address an American gathering of anthropologists on the subject of the more 'dynamic' concept of social structure which he sees emerging.) It is in such more flexible connexions that I have suggested that a specific use of the term *social organization* is appropriate. The term itself is not important, but I think that we gain in clarity by making a distinction from social structure – which must of course still remain as a basic concept.

THE CONCEPT OF SOCIAL ORGANIZATION

As a general term in use by economists, sociologists and administrators, *organization* has long had dynamic implications.[1] In a narrow context, organization implies a systematic ordering of positions and duties which defines a chain of command and makes possible the administrative integration of specialized functions towards a recognized limited goal. In a broader context it implies diversity of the ends and activities of individuals in society, a pattern for their co-ordination in some particular sphere, and specific integration of them there by processes of choice and decision into a coherent system, to yield some envisaged result. It can be phrased again as that continuous set of operations in a field of social action which conduces to the control and combination of elements of action into a system by choice and limitation of their relations to any given ends.

There is structure at all levels; so also with organization. At the level of individual personality there is an organization of the person's bodily movements, the co-ordination of his muscular activity in walking and talking. He can affect this by drugs or by alcohol, or by emotional excitement as when in love, or in welcoming or bidding farewell to a dear relative. Such organization is not part of our inquiry – unless such effect is part of a regular socialized procedure, such as responding to an obligation to get drunk at a wedding party, or a funeral. At another level the individual is responsible for his mental co-ordination. He must plan his daily work, the relation between home cares and job requirements; he must keep his head about his expenditure and bank balance; he should not have a 'nervous breakdown' or a psychosomatic illness as a relief from his troubles of organization. This also is not our concern. We are concerned with these things only when the activity of organization concerns group as well as individual and is consequential for others in a system, or when regularity of decision is perceptible among many individuals, allowing observation of sequence and pattern. In speaking of *social* organization our aim is to extract the regularities from the social implications of the process of decision-making and allied processes. Ideally, generalizations should be produced indicating

[1] See Chapter II, also e.g. Marshall (1922, pp. 240–1); Cooley (1909, pp. vii, 21–2, 54); Homans (1950, pp. 106, 238–9); the very interesting analysis by Selznick (1948) and the useful little monograph by Greer (1955)

what solutions tend to be arrived at in specific situations in conformity with specific principles. We are a long way from achieving this aim. But this is the general position of social anthropology in which as yet classification and analysis are far ahead of explanation and prediction.

It is perhaps hardly necessary to point out that in speaking of social organization we are not dealing with any isolable, concrete social entity. Our analysis refers to a field of social action which is identified in terms of pattern-sequence. But in applying such notions as social organization we are not identifying separable things in the system so much as isolating separate elements as themes for study. In other words we are selecting for emphasis certain aspects of social behaviour, attaching significance to certain qualities recognizable in social relations.

In the concept of social structure, the qualities recognized are primarily those of persistence, continuity, form, and pervasiveness through the social field. But the continuity is essentially one of repetition. There is an expectation of sameness or an obligation to sameness, depending upon how the concept is phrased. A structural principle is one which provides a fixed line of social behaviour and represents the order which it manifests. The concept of social organization has a complementary emphasis. It recognizes adaptation of behaviour in respect of given ends, control of means in varying circumstances, which are set by changes in the external environment or by the necessity to resolve conflict between structural principles. If structure implies order, organization implies a working towards order – though not necessarily the same order. There is an arrangement of activity in reference to the possible reciprocal movements of the factors involved in the situation. An organizational principle also provides a standard of reference for behaviour, but of its nature is more flexible, to be operated in relation to other principles.

Organization is to be regarded as a primary aspect of cooperation, a co-ordination of individual behaviour for economic and social purposes. In any social group, organization involves the assignment of functions to different people, a process known as allocation; and the relation of these functions one to another and to group ends, a process known as integration.

From different angles, then, social organization is to be regarded as (a) adjustment of behaviour of *individuals* consequent on the selection they make from among alternative courses of action in reference to their social goals; (b) selection of *roles* and consequent adjustments in terms of responsibility and co-ordination; (c) arrangement of elements of *action* into a system by limitation of their social relations in reference to given ends as conceived by the actors. These are all modes of perception of phenomena for analytical treatment, and isolation of problems for working.

Social structure and social organization are both heuristic concepts. Both are essential to the handling of social material by an anthropologist. In terms of abstract approach to social phenomena, the conceptualization of the social framework (structure) must come first. But to form a knowledge of the social system there is still a whole sphere of activity of which the *quality* is not perceived by structural analysis alone. Take the efficiency of a productive undertaking. This is not responsive simply to the structural relations between members of the enterprise. In the conditions of operation alternatives are open. Choices must be made. Decisions have to be taken among these alternatives. In terms of a structural key, it is apt to be thought that one line of action only is the most probable or even possible in the circumstances – that the alternatives are not real but only apparent. The effectiveness of the undertaking 'reflects' the structure of personnel. In theory the chain of command and the other major types of social relation between the workers are such that their behaviour must conform to standard. Even where this does not happen the notion of *informal* structure is invoked – that is, further 'structural' (i.e. persistent, expected) relations are identified between the participants, but they are understood, not overt in formal rules. It is one of the discoveries of modern industrial analysis that such informal structures are often the most effective in regulating working behaviour.[1] In the 'primitive' field the informal structure and the formal structure may merge easily, if only because of the lack of any means such as charts or other written records by reference to which the formal structure can be maintained and established.

But beyond this, fields of choice which are still less rigid are open. Our task is to expose these, to delimit the range of alternatives; to observe the relative frequency of choice for one rather than for another; to explain as far as possible the social factors accounting

---

[1] As Selznick (1948, p. 25) has observed, the formal administrative design can never adequately or fully reflect the concrete organization to which it refers.

for such choices; to examine the implications of choice for social behaviour. It is sometimes thought that this means trying to explain social action in terms of individual action – to put the hands of the clock back in social theory to a pre-Durkheimian stage. This is not so. But it does emphasize that social action is *expressed* through individual action, and that this expression allows of alternative procedures.

EXAMPLE FROM THE ROLE OF MEDIATOR

An example which illustrates how such individual action forms a part of social organization is the process of use of a mediator. The use of an intermediary when one wishes to make a request or an arrangement or to transmit an order is a well-known process whereby one attempts to achieve one's ends while not assuming the full burden of responsibility and loss of status if one is un-successful. Anthropologists who have worked in oriental societies will recognize how widespread is the custom of the use of such an intermediary and how important his social functions may be. In some societies these functions may even be structuralized – be given a specific name or be regarded as a prime job of a person fulfilling a specific role. He may operate at the interpersonal level. In Samoa and to some extent in Tikopia, practically every young man has a *soa*, a bond friend with whom he co-operates in many social affairs and whom he uses in particular as his ambassador in love or in proposing marriage. But he may operate at the inter-group level. The *mangi-ugud* of the Kalinga, and analogous functionaries of the Ifugao and other Philippine mountain tribes act as go-betweens in arranging settlements between kinship groups involved in dispute, as through cases of homicide or wounding. In both cases the mediator is a kind of complement to the more formal structural group framework of the society. His operations may even help to maintain it. In Samoa and Tikopia he may be a kinsman but this is not relevant; he serves as an ally outside the immediate descent group, someone whose functions cut across those of the kinship structure and provide additional integrative ties. Among the Kalinga and Ifugao, who have no clearly demarcated descent groups, the mediator may well be a kinsman too. But here it is relevant. He should preferably be related to both sides in the dispute, or else to neither. Here again it is his function as an external element to the immediate units concerned that is very important. In fields of social action of this kind there are problems of conduct to be solved, and the solutions have ultimately to be found at the organizational, not the structural level. Bond friend or mediator must initially be chosen from a range of possible candidates; he must consent to the role required. In performing his functions he must continually examine issues, persuade, suggest, compromise – in other words he must *make* choices and endeavour to clarify issues and *suggest* choices. The upshot, a resolution of the problem, is the result of a process of organization.

In many social situations, an intermediary may be not actual but putative – he may be provided not by an external person but by an extrapolation, or extrajection of a part of the actor's personality. This putative agent is assigned the responsibility of decision and frequently has an authority unlikely to be exercised by the person himself. An obvious example of this is the use made by many primitive and other peoples of the organizing function of pronouncements made by spirit mediums in a dissociated state. I would indeed suggest that externalization of responsibility is an important function of spirit possession.

SIBLING UNITY AS STRUCTURAL ABSTRACTION AND AS ORGANIZATIONAL REALITY

I have been talking so far in somewhat abstract terms – abstraction, as we have been told, is a necessary process in anthropological thinking. But I suspect that all anthropologists have a touch of James Boswell. Boswell in his own way was a superb field worker. But in his discourse given before the Literary Society at Utrecht a couple of hundred years ago, he said, 'I never find myself prouder of my existence than when I walk with my head swathed in the solemn cloud of abstraction.' The relevant question is, of course, how far can such abstraction take us in understanding the workings of a social system.

From this point of view let us take a principle commonly used to explain phenomena in kinship behaviour – the principle of the solidarity and unity of the sibling group. This has been termed a sociological principle of a pure order, of a high degree of structural quality (Fortes, 1955, p. 20).

The principle is usually stated as if it were quite clear, needing no further inquiry. Yet when it is said, e.g. that the structural principle of the unity of the sibling group *explains* the levirate and sororate, what is implied?

There are at least four possibilities in this notion of sibling unity. The first, recognized by Radcliffe-Brown under the term 'solidarity', is that the internal relations of siblings among themselves are those of co-operation, amity, and easy substitution in relationships. The levirate and sororate could then result from the wish of one sibling to take the place of the other *vis-à-vis* spouse and children, and fulfil the appropriate social relationships. But this is not what is meant, as a rule, by explanation in sibling unity terms.

The second possibility is that siblings themselves are united in their external relations – that whatever be their obvious personal quarrels and rifts, they stand side by side against the social world outside. Levirate and sororate then are processes of gap-filling, not because the new spouses wish to make a personal replacement from a feeling of emotional identification with the dead, but because their interests or their family pride demand it. By the external world they may not be regarded as united, but they may wish to appear so. But this explanation also is not the one apparently implied.

The third possibility is the reverse of this. In the society at large, siblings may be regarded as united for social purposes, and treated as such. Their unity may be treated as a 'given' factor, as a primary feature of family and kinship in that particular type of society. On this view, which is the one generally put forward as explanation, levirate and sororate are an outcome, expression or 'reflection' of sibling unity because the jural position is empirically assumed; the marital behaviour automatically follows. To the extent that the unity of siblings is a jural assumption, I would prefer to speak of *unification* of the group.

For there is also a fourth possibility. The unity of the sibling group may be recognized not as a jural fact but as a moral ideal. It may be openly admitted that brothers ought to be but are not solidary among themselves, and that they are not 'united' in treatment by others. Even if there is not a basic *instability* of sibling relations – which would accord with much that we have learnt in both anthropology and psychology – there may well be such differences of age that the general social position of the siblings cannot be at all easily equated. So the jural assumption of sibling unity may not be a fact, but a fiction. A custom such as levirate or sororate may indeed be one means of keeping up or trying to keep up the fiction that siblings are united, or should be united, and ought to be treated as such. In other words, the relation of the levirate and sororate to the principle of the unity of the sibling group could be reversed; it could be not the outcome or evidence of this unity, but part of the process of attempting to maintain it.

It may be argued that all that is involved here is demonstration of the consistency between the two sets of facts, of their reciprocal interaction; that no causal relation is implied. But then what becomes of the 'explanation'? We must be careful that we do not offer a double-headed penny – presenting the levirate (or sororate) as both evidence for and outcome of sibling unity. It is preferable to look on the occurrence of levirate and sororate as resultants of a variety of social forces, of which sibling unity is only one – and that one needing to be viewed in a sophisticated way, with alternative meanings.

For the principle of unity of the sibling group to have full use as interpretation the structural principle must be supported by organizational analysis – concerned with allocation of responsibility, with definition of aims, with competing as well as with congruent interests, and with the effects of multiple structural principles in action together.

I have noted that the principle of the *unity* of the sibling group, as distinct from its *solidarity*, is said to refer only to the attitude towards siblings exhibited by the world at large. Yet it cannot be overlooked that lack of internal unity by siblings within their own group may lead to changes in external recognition and action. Sibling quarrels may necessitate remedial measures by other members of the society at large. They may involve processes of law or quasi-law. Again, they may involve segmentation. It may be precisely a breach in the unity of the sibling group *internally* which has a sociological effect by giving basis for the *external* changes which result in the formation of new groups by segmentation.

It is convenient to speak of identification, equivalence, solidarity, unity of the sibling group, when referring to those aspects of kinship which have been called *jural* – a useful but vague term to cover a mixture of law and morality in many types of obligation. But the notions of jural relation, jural status, jural aspect, have tended at times to be regarded as equivalent to that of obligation in general, and even apparently to be equated with the sphere of the strictly sociological (Fortes, 1955, pp. 20–21). It might be said that wherever the notion of obligation is perceived in a kinship relation this of itself makes the relation a sociological one – because the notion of obligation contains some element of appeal to an authority outside the will of the immediate person concerned. But the sphere of the sociological contains much more than obligations, and jural relations; in any case many internal relations of a sibling group are characterized by obligation. Moreover, there is still the question *how far* the principle of sibling unity explains norms of kinship behaviour. If it is more than a restatement of the basic fact of a classificatory kinship terminology, then what does it explain? The fact that siblings are treated as a single unit, or as equivalent in some social situations. But what does it not explain? It does not explain why they are not so treated in other situations. It does not explain differential allocation of functions and resources on the basis of sex difference. It does not explain the facts of kinship *grading* – of the distinctions made in behaviour towards different kinds of people called siblings, on the basis of their nearness or remoteness of genealogical relationship. It does not explain a range of variant relations towards siblings in the field of marital behaviour – e.g. fraternal polyandry or sororal polygyny. It does not normally explain also why the phenomena of joint succession do not occur in all societies with strong sibling unity. Siblings as a rule do not all succeed to the office of their parents; normally only one sibling succeeds. At the time of succession the principle of sibling unity is not complete – siblings are not regarded or stated as identical by the external world. Hence this 'structural principle of great importance' must be given a very hesitating validity when it is actually applied. A relationship to a particular person becomes a relation to his sibling group as a social unit in *some* similarity of behaviour; behaviour to a father's brother is *in some respects* similar to that towards the father; in *certain* circumstances a relative may take the place of another, as in *some* African societies the place of a father, etc., *may* be taken by his brother (Radcliffe-Brown, 1950, p. 26). In all this the facts of variation and choice are basic, and consideration of their implications for inter-personal relationships is part of a sociological analysis.

SUCCESSION AS AN ORGANIZATIONAL PROBLEM

I want now to consider this general question of social organization further, in the political field, in regard to a problem of succession. Structural changes depend upon organizational decisions and actions, and to understand structure it is necessary also to understand organization.

By 'political' I mean those elements of the social system of primary concern for social order. This is sometimes described as a concern with Law and War. This might seem like a concern only with dispute relations. But the political is concerned also with the position and operation of the community as an entity *vis-à-vis* the external social world. Moreover in the sense of an overall control of the community there is also implied an administrative organization with concern for the organization of resources, including personnel, as a whole.

From such a standpoint a series of questions can follow: how are the elements of this system arranged – in the form of an assembly or council, a chief and officers, etc.? How far do the elements of a political system as concerned with social order correspond to other features of the social system, for instance features of kinship and ritual? What kind of authority is involved in this system and how does it operate? What is its definition in terms of power potentials and actual exercise? What is the public concept of this authority? (There can be for example a concept of its exercise as a *right* as by a Divine King; or as a *privilege* delegated from a kin group or a community of the people; or as a *seizure* of power.) How far is this authority unified – there may be no single head, but by what arrangement then are the elements of authority brought together? Or are they not so brought together? If the authority is delegated explicitly or tacitly what is employed in the notion of *delegation* or *representation*? For instance if there is a notion of *effective decision* by a single individual or body of individuals, how far is the opinion intended to be subsumed by the representative, or exercised independently in the light of circumstances? Following from this, what kinds of notions of social responsibility are held and operated? Consideration of all this means organizational as well as structural analysis.

The assumption of responsibility is one of the crucial elements in organization.[1] By social responsibility is meant obligation to

---

[1] See e.g. the classical analysis by P. Fauconnet (1928).

envisage a situation in terms of the interest of others, of the widest group concerned, and to take decisions which shall be conformable to those interests. It also involves a readiness to be held accountable for the implications of those decisions, at least in so far as they are foreseen (Firth, 1951, p. 3). Conversely, the individual is representative of others, of a group. This means *delegation*. But the exercise of a sense of responsibility is not homogeneous. It is a matter of degree; it tends to vary in relation to the distribution of authority in a given situation, and the nature of the group or relationship concerned. Important questions for an anthropologist to consider are: What are the fields of responsibility, i.e. in what types of social action is it exercised and expected? What is its jurisdiction or range in terms of personnel and groups? What conflicts of responsibility occur through a person occupying different roles in a society? (As we know, even in a lineage-guided society, the jurisdiction of responsibility may be wider than the lineage.)

I want now to examine the operation of the concept of responsibility as an organizational principle by reference to a body of material dealing with succession to chieftainship.

Succession to office is a basic social process necessitated in the last resort by the waxing and waning of human physical and mental powers. Hence succession is a social requirement dependent ultimately on the situation and nature of the human organism. Every society, even the most primitive, has some measures for succession, and some more or less clearly formulated principles as a guide to those measures in individual cases. In ordinary anthropological terms the most general type of principle of succession is that of the structural order described, for example, by such terms as 'patrilineal' or 'matrilineal'. It is within such general frames of reference that succession is decided. But a patrilineal or matrilineal principle of succession is not automatic. It gives genealogical persistence, but it does not account for the actual succession of individual to individual in genealogical relation. Granted, say, that patrilineality in a particular society is invariable, selection is required from among patrilineal kin and secondary principles are needed as guide. Some societies adopt election from a general body of male kin. Others allow emergence by contest. Others have the principle of fraternal succession in birth order, others the principle of male primogeniture, or ultimogeniture.

Some of these principles are strong and rarely set aside, yet usually they are not invariable in the way in which the patrilineal principle is. Exercise of authority requires, for example, some recognition of responsibility, hence there is a tendency in most societies for a witless, irresponsible, or lunatic person not to be chosen as chief, although his genealogical claims qualify him. Moreover, in some societies, physical fitness in itself is a desideratum and in others it is regarded as an indication of spiritual favour, hence the physically unfit person may be passed over in the succession. Thirdly, recognition that the exercise of office may demand qualities of judgement and administrative capacity as well as those of fitness and responsibility, may mean that a predisposition in favour of, say, primogeniture may be ignored in favour of a person better endowed in these other respects. In other words succession itself is an organizational matter involving choice and decision. And the results of that decision in social terms may radically affect the integration and harmonious activity of the society. As Hilda Kuper (1947, pp. 88, 104) has shown for the Swazi, the results may have great structural importance; rules for choice of an heir to a chief are designed as much to counteract tendencies to fission owing to personal rivalries as to meet the specific administrative requirements of the community.

But despite much excellent work on succession to chieftainship in Africa and elsewhere, there are still many questions to be studied. From the Polynesian ethnographic area let me take Tikopia.

A CRISIS IN TIKOPIA

In Tikopia in 1929 there were four chiefs, one for each of the clans – Kafika, Tafua, Taumako, and Fangarere in that order of ritual precedence. All but the Ariki Tafua were pagan and practised elaborate religious rites, both individually and in concert in the 'Work of the Gods'. The Ariki Tafua, who had been converted to Christianity some few years before, had abandoned the 'Work of the Gods' and his private *kava* rites, though he still threw food offerings and performed other rituals to his traditional gods and ancestors (Firth, 1936, pp. 5, 8; 1939, pp. 177–8, 182; 1940, pp. 167–8, 327).

In 1952, when I revisited Tikopia, conditions were 'normal' in the three senior clans. In Kafika the former chief still ruled, although now a very old man. In Tafua there had been two changes, the eldest son having succeeded, and then only about two years before, his son in turn (his only male child). In Taumako the eldest son had succeeded his father. In both Tafua and Taumako succession had been by ordinary election. As regards religion, the chiefs of Kafika and Taumako were pagan, while the chief of Tafua, like his father and grandfather, was a Christian. In the fourth clan, Fangarere, there was a surprising difference. The old chief I knew had died, having been converted to Christianity, and in his place were *two* chiefs, one Christian and one pagan.

Each case of succession involved a range of organizational acts, and that in Fangarere in particular necessitated complex social adjustments. But I must examine the situation briefly here, and will discuss only the chieftainship of Kafika, as a case of potential succession illustrating organizational principles.

A Tikopia chief is regarded by his clanspeople in general, and by the members of his own lineage in particular, as having a great responsibility towards them. He so regards himself, too. This area of responsibility extends also over the community as a whole – for all the chiefs generally, and for the premier chief specifically. But the relation has several facets. A chief's responsibility in the field of pagan religious ideas embraces the role of intermediary between his people and the gods. The gods treat him in the Tikopia metaphor as their 'seating-mat'. This applies particularly to the chief of Kafika clan. If he is diseased, then (as tradition states happened on one occasion) he should abdicate from his office. If he is very old and feeble, then there is a possibility that he may not be so favoured by the gods as a vehicle for their transmission of welfare. In 1952 the Ariki Kafika, though in the region of eighty years old, and though he had recently had several severe illnesses, was for most of the time hale and hearty. However, in the private opinion of the people he had reigned for too long. Senior men of serious counsel told me how in Kafika family the old chief, toothless, pounded his betel in a mortar; his eldest son and heir, toothless also, pounded his betel – and now, they said, the eldest grandson in turn was beginning to lose his teeth! It was time for the old chief to die and hand on the succession to a younger man. I was told this first by the Ariki Tafua, who sententiously explained to me how his own father Pa Rangifuri, who had succeeded as chief about 1940, had devoted himself to death by starvation. He fell ill (from what was apparently influenza) in 1951. Plenty of food was offered to him, but he would not eat. Why? He looked at his son, who had become a man, and thought it was time he succeeded. Despite his son's urgings to take nourishment, he decided to die. Such was the story. The Ariki Tafua then compared this favourably with the conduct of the Ariki Kafika, and said it was not good. 'My idea is that Pa Fenuatara (the heir apparent) will die before the Ariki, and that the grandson will succeed', he said to me. He continued, 'It is good for a chief to go early, and to let a young man succeed.' Now this view could be regarded as not representative. The Ariki Tafua, succeeding as a young man, may have been rationalizing his own position, and using this as a point of contrast against his fellow chief. Or as a Christian he may have been taking an opportunity to denigrate a pagan. This is quite likely. But he was in fact also expressing a general view. Men of other clans, pagan and Christian, said much the same thing in confidential talk. It was not good for the Ariki Kafika to live so long. It was a sign that the spirit deities were rejecting him. 'The deities have begun not to like the chief; they have gone away from him. They have just left him to go on living.' Here emerges the notion, not uncommon in Tikopia discussion about death, that death is a boon granted by the gods to a man, since it means cessation of pain, and the pleasure of being taken to live in their abode. In 1952 the situation was complicated by the fact that though people of Kafika clan, with the usual Tikopia foresight, had long since accumulated supplies of perennial yams and other crops against the day of the old chief's death, they had been forced by the food shortage after the hurricane to consume them all. So if he did die suddenly they would be in an embarrassing position. (I did not, for obvious reasons, try to ascertain the ideas of the Ariki Kafika himself on all this.)

Then came a crisis. The chief's eldest grandson fell gravely ill. A message was sent to my friend Pa Fenuatara that his son was dying. When he hurried to the bedside he found his son in convulsive movement, with a severe pain in his lower ribs, on the right side (possibly a pleurisy). The Ariki Taumako and the Ariki Fangarere were laying hands on him to try to effect a cure. Then, as is common on such occasions, the principal spirit medium of the clan became possessed – in this case by the spirit of the long-dead father of the Ariki Kafika. The spirit discussed the illness and said that it was due to the fault of the Kafika lineage. Pa Fenuatara asked how could this be. He had not abandoned any rites nor shown disrespect to the spirits. The spirit answered, 'Because of your father! You have pulled him up to health.' (Each time the old man had been ill, Pa Fenuatara had done his best to assist his recovery.) In other words the illness of the grandson was a sign of the anger of the gods at the fact that the old chief still went on living. He would not yield up his life that they might have a younger and more active 'seating-mat'. The spirit said further that Pa Fenuatara should deny his father food and drink to accelerate his death.

This put Pa Fenuatara in a terrible dilemma. The occasion was one of great dramatic intensity, with the assembled kinsfolk mourning round his sick son. To be faced by such a spirit demand at this time was a strong emotional strain. He met it effectively. He answered in this way. He said, 'How can I deny my father food and drink? This is too much. Why should I turn the guilt upon myself? If you press me, then I will take my son (the sick man) and put him on a canoe and together he and I will voyage out to sea.' By this he meant in effect that he was prepared to commit suicide rather than be unfilial and sacrifice his father. This was a severe blow to the assembled crowd. It would have meant that they would have lost their most precious leaders. The spirit medium was undoubtedly expressing in dissociated form what may be regarded as general public opinion. It was an example of the externalization of responsibility. But the firm answer of Pa Fenuatara turned the dilemma back upon the medium. His reaction was characteristic; still in a state of possession he embraced Pa Fenuatara's knees, pressed his nose to them in apology and muttered the conventional formula of abasement, 'I eat ten times your excrement.' This restored the situation to what may be termed normality. Nothing more was said in public about the old chief.

A couple of days later the sick man recovered and things were as before. But after a week or so I referred to this matter in a talk with Pa Fenuatara and he described to me what had happened. Then after a pause he said in effect, 'The spirit was right.' He went on to explain to me how the premier god of Kafika clan, who is also in pagan belief the principal god for the island community as a whole, always wants a relatively young man as his chief. 'The expression is "The Ariki Kafika breaks (i.e. dies) while young – to go to the God." But if the Ariki Kafika grows old enough only to crawl with the aid of his hands, the deity becomes angry; he doesn't like the chief, because he has grown old. The God wishes his seating-mat to "break" while young and go to him – such is the custom of Kafika.' Pa Fenuatara had clearly shared the public view. But filial loyalty, ambition, and religious rationalization in conflict had had their result in public in a victory for filial loyalty. It was a victory also of another kind. Though it did not deny a basic religious premiss relating physical health to ritual fitness and in turn to welfare, it did assert what may be termed the rule of law and the primacy of family sentiment.[1]

This example illustrates the complex operations of the principle of responsibility. It shows an *exercise* of responsibility by chiefs for the people and the community; an *imputation* of responsibility by the people to the chief; an *externalization* of responsibility by the public through a spirit medium; a *delegation* or transfer of responsibility to the chief's heir; and an *acceptance* of it by him. The example also shows the principle of moderation or expediency, or what Nadel, I believe, has referred to as the 'principle of accommodation'. In a conflict between structural principles, either both manifest or one manifest and the other latent, it may not be easy to predict the resolution. But there is frequently a modification of the strict implications of a structural principle in favour of some measure of viable action. A person concerned will assume a lesser status or a different role than the structure would imply. This was illustrated in the behaviour of the spirit medium. Having enunciated a proper course of behaviour with all the authority given by a voice from the other world – and in fact expressing subconsciously a public attitude – he moderated his behaviour and status to meet the challenge of filial loyalty. In this he was, of course, behaving in fact as a member of the clan and of the society. Understanding of the entry of the notion of viable action

[1] I heard in June 1955 that the Ariki Kafika was still alive and active – 'that incredible old man is still going strong'. My informant, the Assistant District Commissioner, Eastern Solomons, to whom I am indebted for this note, added, 'I cannot help feeling that it must be a little wearing for Pa Fenuatara, who does all the work without the honour.' (Pa Fenuatara was in fact given great respect by the other chiefs and by the people in general. Although not a chief, he was accorded near chiefly status, and sat with the chiefs by invitation and almost of right, on public occasions. But he still, of course, lacked the final honours of the chiefly office.) Unhappily, it seems that both the Ariki Kafika and Pa Fenuatara died in an epidemic in August 1955.

involves reference to ends, to values. The principle of avoidance of extremes is very generally operative in Tikopia social action. There is an implied contrast here between the value of the *extreme* in conduct and the value of the *mean*. The value of the extreme lies in its lack of accommodation. Since its aims are pursued rigorously without compromise, action derives its strength from the simplicity of its rallying point. (Many charismatic leaders, both political and religious, have been characterized by this adherence to the extreme.) The value of the mean lies in the possibility of securing the adherence of many to whom the extreme is aesthetically or emotionally, as well as economically, repugnant. Whichever course will be pursued depends on ultimate ends. Now the conduct of the spirit medium, if he had insisted that Pa Fenuatara should deny sustenance to his father, would have shocked and alienated, to a certainty, a large number of the people. Moreover, he himself had to recognize a responsibility to the community not to let heirs to the chieftainship perish. Hence the principle of accommodation involved with the principle of responsibility provided a solution to the clash of structural issues. One may point out, too, that this resolution was at first impeded, but in the long run facilitated, by Pa Fenuatara's firm statement – a social counter. This had almost certainly an element of status involvement – he was not prepared to be pushed around in his actions, even by the spirit of his dead grandfather. Yet, when all was over, he showed that he too shared in the recognition of the principle of responsibility of chief to people expressed in symbolic terms. The solution was only interim – the situation could well arise again. But at least the immediate social tension was relieved by such organizational processes.

COMPARATIVE MYSTICAL AND ADMINISTRATIVE ISSUES

It is interesting to follow this situation out a little further in organizational terms, and for this purpose to compare it with the situation among the Shilluk, who have a somewhat similar problem analysed in an illuminating way by Evans-Pritchard (1948).

Like the Tikopia, the Shilluk have given a symbolic value to the physical vigour of their political head – so much so that they have been reported to have ceremonially put to death their kings when they showed signs of old age or ill health. This is one of the most famous examples of the divine kingship. Evans-Pritchard has argued that such ritual destruction probably never occurred, that it was a fiction.[1] He holds that Shilluk kings generally met a violent death through rebellion by another prince as the representative of public discontent. His opinion is that the idea that a sick or old king *should* be killed probably means that tensions inherent in disaster become manifest in the attribution of the disaster to his failing powers. This is strikingly supported by the specific analogue from Tikopia. But the Tikopia do not kill their ageing king; they merely wish that he were dead. They may, in extreme cases, make a suggestion for his demise, but they are unwilling to take any public responsibility for this. To judge by tradition, in olden days to kill the Ariki Kafika was regarded as a horrific crime, but it was not unthought of. Yet it had nothing to do with his waning powers, but was part of the struggle for personal supremacy which went on among the Tikopia leaders and is so interpreted, quite frankly, by the Tikopia nowadays. In present Tikopia conditions such a challenge in the form of physical struggle is out of the question, and regarded as inconceivable. But public opinion still pursues the theme of mystical linkage between social and personal health of the chief. Like the Shilluk apparently, the Tikopia have some organizational means of action to draw attention to the situation, if not to resolve it. A spirit medium in a state of possession, by serving as a vehicle of communication of public disquiet, can make the problem overt. Again, though physical force is out of the question to end the life of an ageing Tikopia chief, starvation is conceivable or at least mentionable as a possible means. This solution doubtless is likely to fail – as in the case cited, through filial sentiment. But it would be both theoretically and practically possible. That it is not a fantastic idea is indicated by the common Tikopia notion that an incurably diseased or very old person does in fact often deny himself nourishment, in order to end more quickly a life which has become painful to him. The idea of death by starvation, whether by self-denial or by the adamancy of others, is not a strange one to Tikopia. It is feasible that a sick chief, hearing of the public commotion, might decide, through shame, to end his life by such means, if he were allowed. But direct physical action, by ritual killing or rebellion, is ruled out.

[1] Brandon (1955, p. 328), relying on earlier sources, still refers to the killing as an actual fact.

The same basic problem has very different solutions in these two societies. But the Shilluk and Tikopia problem is in a sense self-created. There is no *necessary* mystical association between health of groups of people or of their social order, and the physical health of their chief representative. It would have seemed quite simple for the Shilluk to have assumed that the effectiveness of Nyikang can go on through the king no matter what his physical state may be. Indeed, if Nyikang 'participates' in the king, he might be conceived to be able to operate irrespective of how fit his human physical body is. So also with the Tikopia and their idea of the supreme god using the chief as his seating-mat and intermediary. The Shilluk and the Tikopia have bound themselves with chains they themselves have forged.

One is forced to conclude then – and here I think one can add something to Evans-Pritchard's interpretation – that it is not just the mystical bond which is the basic idea at the bottom of removal of an ageing king. It may well be equally the requirements of social administration.

It is fashionable nowadays to argue that it is just as rational for people to believe that the health and fertility of the land depend on the virility of the king as to believe otherwise. The gap in this argument is that 'rational' is a category we employ in philosophic and scientific discussion, and by these standards there is no demonstrable connexion of any direct kind between fertility of vegetation and virility of a king. To say that the Shilluk and the Tikopia are making symbolic statements about their social order (cf. Leach, 1954, p. 14) is a preferable form of expression.

What is symbolized? That a society needs vigour in its representatives if it is to remain an effective entity, a going concern. Grant that the mystical bond is the symbol of the effective state of the society, that the people in each case phrase an administrative issue in mystical terms. But they could drop this mystical bond and the same problem would still arise. It does in fact arise in all societies; leadership must follow some structural lines. But all societies do not have structural mechanisms for ending the leadership of a specific person when he can no longer fulfil his duties adequately. Many do, using the device of status change. Retirement from office into private life is an accepted procedure in Western societies. The Japanese historically used the practice in a characteristically flexible way, by means of the institution of a

'Retired Emperor', to manipulate power behind the governmental scenes (Brinkley, 1915, pp. 271, 330, 341; Sadler, 1946, p. 84). In a restricted form, retirement from office has even been a custom among such people as the Nyakyusa (Wilson, 1951, pp. 279, 281–2). Some societies reduce the element of personal decision by the device of a limited period of service, or an age-bar, which automatically (or such is intended) eliminate the difficulties of personal choice. But societies which do not have structural mechanisms must rely entirely on organizational ones. These have varying efficiency. In traditional times, the rebellion measure of the Shilluk was probably effective; we would judge that it is virtually inoperative now.[1] The Tikopia had nothing so clear-cut. On the other hand, they have evolved a working practice whereby the acknowledged heir to the chief acts in effect for him in all political affairs. But ˙this is not finally satisfactory; he lacks that ultimate authority which office alone gives.

In Tikopia, and among the Shilluk, there are certain ritual functions which it is ideologically essential for a political head to carry out effectively. But in fact the Tikopia chief and, I think, the Shilluk king hardly seem to need any particular bodily vigour for these performances, and certainly no sexual prowess to perform the sacrifices for rain and other rituals attached to the office. But in the administrative field some physical and mental competence is necessary. Here the need for *decision* is primary. If the society is to maintain its major political structure, the functions of counsel, arbitration, control, must be exercised by its leader. As a source of appeal he must be in full command of his faculties. If the ritual leader cannot exercise these political functions, then either they must be separated and assigned to more than one person, or another person must be chosen to supersede the ineffective one.

In structural terms, rebellion is the Shilluk mechanism for retaining the symbolism of the kingship unimpaired. ('Structural' because the kingship is a permanent office.) In organizational terms, this symbolism may represent the requirements of an underlying administrative efficiency. ('Organizational' because such efficiency is a variable condition needing care.) At one level it is

---

[1] Is it just feasible that the notion of ceremonially killing the Shilluk king may not have been entirely a fiction? Could this possibility have been held in reserve in case he was not removed by the normal process of rebellion as his powers began to wane?

care for the ritual purity and efficacy of the office that moves a prince to revolt and moves people to support him. At another level a prince revolts because of the status increase he acquires if he becomes king. People support him for loyalty and reward. But at another level they act because fundamentally they require a more efficient leader and decision-taker in their public affairs. Study at all these levels is important.

I think the significance of this administrative component could be supported from other African societies. Oberg's (1940, p. 157) material from Ankole shows the Bahima Mugabe in the position of a divine king killed when his physical powers began to wane. This was partly a reflex of belief in his magical powers being correlated with his physical condition. But it was also linked with his capacity to perform economic and political functions. There is a heavy emphasis in the Banyankole traditional system, for instance, on royal efficiency in war, and also on royal accumulation and distribution of cattle. It is true that the Dinka rainmakers, who seem to have had many administrative functions and much civil authority, are alleged to have been strangled for ritual reasons. But one probably becomes speedily exasperated with rainmakers anyway, in any society, and Dinka may well have felt that sooner or later they deserved strangling! More seriously, it would be interesting to have details as to whether there had been also a parallel decline in their administrative capacity. An illuminating case is given from the Nyakyusa (Wilson, *ibid.*), where an old chief is believed usually to die soon after the 'coming out' of his sons – which means his partial supersession. The 'breath' of the people is believed to kill him because men love his sons rather than himself; they prefer the younger generation. But on asking about one old chief who did not die for about fifteen years after his sons 'came out', the anthropologist was told that he was exceptional. 'The people loved him very much because he helped them with the government.' In other words, he was a good administrator and public servant, and the ritual requirement did not take its toll.

I am not arguing that all these peoples, any more than the Tikopia, do not believe in the mystical bond between land and chief, or that they do not act, up to a point, according to their beliefs. But I do argue that their mysticism in this respect does not fly in the face of common sense. From an organizational point of view the symbolic quality in their belief expresses and leads them to adopt good rational administrative practice.

The Tikopia case I have cited was a succession crisis. Analysis of other cases, of actual succession, would have shown different social situations, but analogous pressures.

POSTULATES IN SOCIAL ORGANIZATION

What I am showing here is how from situations of alternatives there have been solutions by a decision in reference to certain guiding themes or attitudes which may be termed principles or postulates of social organization. The principles of responsibility, accommodation, and status involvement have all been indicated as relevant. To some extent they operate in conjunction with one another, even, it may be, in opposition to one another. Social action is to be regarded in organizational terms as the resultant of the operation of such principles. Other principles might be examined in a similar way.

One of these is the principle of economy of effort. An illustration of the operation of this from quite another area but still within the field of succession is the practice which Audrey Richards (1940b, p. 101) records for the Bemba chieftainship. Through the custom of transmitting one large territorial chieftainship after another within the immediate family of the paramount chief a tradition has grown up that, for example, the holder of the Mwamba title should always succeed to the title of Citimukulu, whatever the kinship priorities involved. This claim was put forward in the succession dispute of 1925, and according to Richards was commonly supported by government officials, who naturally prefer a fixed system of succession to the discussion of rival candidates' rights that seems to have been the older procedure. In the succession of chiefs a fixed rule such as primogeniture or automatic moving-up from one grade to another is more economical of social effort since it tends to avoid the expenditure of time and energy in election and to obviate the disruptive effects of disputes. To government officials concerned with the smooth running of the administrative machine the promotion of such an economical practice has obvious appeal.

The principle of economy of effort is concerned with the disposal or allocation of resources and rests on the perception of their limited character. This principle, as has often been pointed out, operates far beyond the sphere of resources conventionally re-cognized by the economist as wealth, where price enters (e.g. Firth, 1951, p. 130; Stillman, 1955, p. 82). It has been expressed in many forms. (For example, as the general principle of least action it has been given as an explanation in classical terms of the dynamic system of nature.) Further examples of its operation can be seen in the acceptance of persons as right-holders. It frequently happens in societies of large scale that people claim to be members of social groups and thereby claim personal rights in social affairs. For example, take the case of an Australian aborigine who, moving from one tribal territory to another, identifies himself in sectional and kin terms and is received on the same footing as persons in the local society. Here no effort is normally made to check upon such claims; it is more economical of effort to accept them at face value and fit the claimant into the scheme of social action accordingly. On the other hand, advantage can be taken of this principle by people to elevate themselves in a graded series of rights. This happened when the migration of labourers from South India to Fiji took place in the latter part of the nineteenth century. Some men were able to take advantage of the fact that their background was unknown, to claim and operate in the new environment a social status in caste terms to which they had not been entitled in the old. Operation of the principle of economy of effort in such fields of social action rests upon two assumptions: a confidence that for the most part the initial statements are true; and a confidence that an ultimate check would be possible if the issue were of sufficient importance. Then a sacrifice of effort would be made.

This brings up the point that the economy of effort tends to be relative to the issue concerned. One may develop this by reference to social organization in ritual.

Social operations in ritual are governed by certain basic criteria, some of which may be stated in terms of first principles under the general head of economy of effort. The first of these is the criterion of social relativity. The implications of an action are propor-tionate to the situation in which it occurs. The same kind of action in different circumstances involves the actor in very different reactions. For instance, a Tikopia woman plaits a floor mat and lays it on the floor of a house. In one case this is a simple act of furnishing, providing a carpet. In another it is an act of ritual and political significance, as when it is part of a more general activity of recarpeting a sacred temple. For interpreting the act an appreciation of situation is important. Linked with this is the concept of a critical act. Any person in Tikopia may provide the coconut fronds for the mat and perhaps may even do the plaiting; it is the formal laying of the mat that is the important thing. This indicates a relation between the social group and god or dead ancestor. Again, there is the criterion of marginality of effort. This is not only applicable in the use of measurable resources of a material kind; it occurs also in actions. *Precision* in operations; *intensity* of taboos; *continuity* of activity are all subject to marginality. After a time the utility of what is done for the system in operation diminishes. This finally comes to a point at which the action can be changed or omitted, without a practical diminution thought to occur in the ritual efficacy of the operation as a whole. For example, there may be a rule that all the members of a descent group should assemble for a rite. In practice some may not, but it is not conceived that the ritual is affected. On the other hand, the more who refrain, the higher rises the marginal worth of those who attend. Or again, there may be a rule that loud noise is taboo during a certain stage of the ritual. Yet children may be allowed more licence than is given to adults; their actions are regarded as being marginal to the ritual scheme. Further, there is the criterion of climax and release of tension. Many ritual operations build up to a climax and then tension is released.[1] The value of climax is clear as focusing attention, helping to provide motivation in work. But to maintain a tension for a long period at the same level is physiologically and psychologically impossible, therefore socially the cyclical rhythm allows of the interspersion of ritual by non-ritual acts – attention to personal needs, eating, etc.

I now turn to the more general question of the use of such principles. I have cited four principles or postulates in this discussion: responsibility; status involvement; accommodation; and economy of effort. In earlier work I mentioned the principle of co-ordination, the principle of basic compensation, and the principle of foresight (Firth, 1951, pp. 78, 91–7, 234–6). Other principles may easily be adduced. I am not arguing that these are

[1] A clear example of this is given in the communion ceremony known as 'Hot Food' in Tikopia (Firth, 1940, I, pp. 101–3; 1951, pp. 227–9).

brought forward for the first time – they have in fact been used by other social scientists in various ways – but that more systematic use of them in conjunction leads us to a better understanding of social action.

The question will be asked, how far can a system be made out of all this, and how far indeed is it necessary to create a system? My own view is that in this whole field of explanation of social action, once we leave the formalities of structural analysis we are yet a long way from being able to produce schemes of any high degree of systematization, which at the same time have explanatory value. We are much indebted in anthropology to the admirable system formulations of Talcott Parsons, Marion Levy, and others. But within such broad constructs there are many ways of describing relevant social processes. The concept of social organization and the identification of principles or postulates within it are modes of conventional description. They are not just personal constructs. The aim in identifying them is to retain correspondence with the phenomena observable in the external social world. The test of this is a parallelism of description and phenomena in behaviour, including the validation of concrete prediction at various levels.

What kind of principles of social organization are these? How far are they psychological postulates, and sociologically irrelevant? They rest of course on a psychological base, that is they correspond to mental activity, and are related to conceptions and motivations of people. But so also do the principles of social structure. The principles of sibling unity and lineage unity are based on *recognitions*. What gives them validity is that these recognitions are homogeneous, i.e. all members of the society concerned recognize the division into corporate kin-units of the type specified, and act upon this recognition in *some* of their basic daily behaviour. Any statement about lineage segments of the same order being 'equal and opposite' rests upon assumptions about the attitudes of people. The 'equality' is rarely, if ever, in terms of numbers of persons, and therefore involves translation of multiplicity into unity. The notion of segments as 'opposite' involves recognition of their operation at a highly abstract, even symbolic, level. In the concept of the 'unity' of the sibling group, siblings are regarded as equivalent or united only for some social purposes, in defined conditions, and not in others. A problem is to show what these conditions are, where they obtain and do not obtain, and the implications in both eventualities.

SPHERES OF OPERATION

The principles of social organization are not so 'automatic' or homogeneous as those of social structure. But they can help to explain, in a way in which the principles of social structure cannot, social operations in a wide range of spheres of fields of action. Let me mention merely four of these.

First, there is the sphere of *allocation of rights and duties among persons*, having regard to structural principles of the society concerned, and the fact that they have to be implemented among a varying number of persons. Arrangements for maintaining relations between mother's brother and sister's child with varying numbers of each category have been discussed, with examples, in Chapter II. I might have added there that Malinowski (1935, I, pp. 189–95) was one of the writers who anticipated this problem and discussed it in terms of his Trobriand material.

Secondly, there is the sphere of *range of social recognition* and the degrees of conformity which operate within it. A clear example here is the non-verbal field of the classificatory system of kinship. Terminologically persons are called siblings over a wide range of genealogical relationship and this mode of identification is followed logically in the terms used for their descendants. But in the more concrete aspects of rights and duties to kin – observance of taboos, performance of economic obligations, etc. – there is a sharply decreasing magnitude. This illustrates the principle of economy of effort. Although there is an ideal uniformity, in practice there is a diminishing effect since resources and energy do not allow of indefinite extension of practical aid.

Thirdly, there is the sphere of *resolution of conflict* between two or more structural principles. One example here is the clash between ties of lineage or clan membership and those of membership of a local group. Here the principles of economy of effort on the one hand and of status involvement on the other tend to operate to resolve the issue in favour of the ties with the local group to the detriment of the fulfilment of lineage member obligations. As Henry Maine (1875, p. 72) put it, 'from the moment when a tribal community settles down finally upon a definite space of land, the land begins to be the basis of society in place of the

Kinship'. Some of the conditions of such resolution can be stated in terms of economic controls. Another example is the conflict between the structural principle of lineage membership and that of membership of the elementary family. This is the type of situation analysed by Malinowski from his Trobriand material, and taken up in an interesting manner by Richards in regard to the Bemba (Malinowski, 1927a, pp. 8–16, 84–6; 1935, I, p. 37; Richards, 1940a). A further example, closely related and relevant in understanding social changes, is the conflict between joint family obligations and elementary family interests in the case of the Irava and Nayar (Aiyappan, 1945, pp. 71–7; Gough, 1952, pp. 81–2, 84, 85; Mayer, 1952, pp. 100 *et seq.*). Here in general one may state a conclusion that the higher the status involvement and the greater the control of disposable wealth, the more is the tendency for the larger kin units to maintain their cohesion. The wealthy, the gentry, keep their joint families, their 'big houses' longer than do people of lesser status and wealth (Aiyappan, 1944, p. 66; Fei, 1946, pp. 4–5). But significant also are the opportunities for consumption of wealth, and especially its degree of liquidity. The greater these, the more the tendency for the elementary family to become independent of the larger kin unit.

Finally there is the sphere of *social control*. Here we are not concerned so directly with the resolution of conflict between two or more structural principles, but with the implications of crises in the personal experience of individuals who have found their actions or wishes in conflict with a structural principle or with the actions or wishes of others. At various stages in the processes of expression and social control come in the principles of social organization. They appear in the individual's own actions, but they are manifested particularly in the mobilization of community action and the application of sanctions. Questions as to who takes the initiative in mobilizing public opinion; as to the degree to which a sanction shall be applied; as to the manner in which a final resolution of the conflict is attained – all these involve operation of some of the principles of social organization indicated earlier.

I have said that social organization, like social structure, can be recognized at all levels. In the widest sense the actions of any individual resulting from his choices and decisions and involving the actions of others can be regarded as social organization. At the other end of the scale, social organization can be seen in terms of those actions which tend to promote the integration of society. Hence we have the associated term of social disorganization where the referent commonly is to some major group in society or to society in its totality. It is tempting to argue that the term social organization should be restricted in its reference to integration of the total society. One difficulty in this is that of judging what kind of actions do in fact promote or are calculated to promote that integration – and what indeed are the tests of such integration. What seems preferable is to look upon social organization as having reference to definable social ends, without necessarily relating these to the ends of a total society. For example, one can define ends of lineage activity in terms of defence of lineage territory, maintenance of lineage status, etc., without arguing whether this does or does not maintain integration of the total society. In other words, one may treat social organization as a relative concept in terms of an agent or set of agents; a set of ends or purposes towards which action is directed or thought to be directed; a set of choices, from alternative courses of action; and a set of implications, effects or results of decisions.

The explanation given by the kinds of principles of social organization outlined earlier is admittedly a statement of postulates rather than of final generalizations.

And there are many questions still outstanding. How far are these postulates discrete, or how far do they simply imply one another? Do the different postulates vary in their weight from one society to another? If so, will this variation not be random, but ultimately fit into some classification of societies? Are some postulates more relevant for social change than others – for example, does economic expansion demand a contraction of social accommodation in a peasant society? How far does structural change demand not merely an alteration in the objects of choice, but in the procedures and principles of making choices? It should be noted also that the very terms in which social structures are described tend in themselves to point to the fields of choice which are open, and in that sense to lead towards the identification of certain principles of organization. Finally, let me make the point that once the social anthropologist goes beyond the formal description of static social systems he is bound to introduce postulates of similar kind to those I have discussed. But he may not recognize them as such. There is all the more need then for further analysis along such lines.

I think, moreover, that we can already go some way in regarding such postulates as having an explanatory value. Look at modern conditions in Africa or the Orient, at situations where members of large-scale corporate descent groups are faced by new economic and social opportunities in an expanding universe of social contacts. We can say with some confidence that the area of kinship responsibility will contract, that shifts of authority will occur in certain directions – from mother's brother to father, from hereditary elders to new income-getting élites. But we can only show *how* such things will happen and *why* they must be so when we study the situations more fully in terms of such organizational principles as I have outlined.

It is told of a medieval Abbot of St. Albans how he incurred that mockery of which mention is made in the Gospel, namely that he who is about to build should compute the expenses which are necessary to finish the building, lest, after he has laid the foundations, being unable to finish it, all begin to mock him. In trying to build up social anthropology as a scientific study we have laid some solid foundations. But we are likely to find that the effort to raise the building further will involve us in heavier intellectual expenditure than we had anticipated. Yet anthropology is not architecture, and no building of ours can ever be completed. All that each of us can hope to do is to contribute some materials and labour and a few suggestions towards the plan.

CHAPTER IV

Marriage and the Classificatory System of Relationship

(1930)

The observer set down among a people, and finding their culture regulated by the classificatory system of relationship, should naturally begin, after satisfying himself as to the general working of the system, to search for the limits of its application, for the point at which relationship becomes so distant as to be ignored, or at which other social factors tend to circumscribe its field of operation. The misleading simplicity, the almost mathematical regularity of this system of denoting kinship, while stimulating speculation as to its origins, has rather baffled attempts to probe deeply into the actual significance of the facts underlying the terms which stand as their symbols. It is only recently that it has come to be realized that the presence among the social institutions of a people of this system of relationship termed, not too happily, *classificatory*, does not imply the existence of classes of relatives with identity of kinship function corresponding to identity of terminology. Analysis of the duties and obligations of a man to various relatives whom he addresses by the same term has revealed a distinct gradation, those in respect of near relatives being the most onerous and important, but lessening, shading off in intensity as the relationship bond becomes weaker. Study of the differential attitudes and behaviour of a child as it awakes to the realization of the extensiveness of its kinship affiliations leads to the same conclusion. The closer the acquaintance of the observer, the more he realizes that the relations of a person with his near kin are usually much more intimate, his emotional attitude much more sympathetic, or at all events more clearly defined, his duties much fuller and more binding, than they are with his more distant kin, in spite of the fact that these latter are addressed by precisely the same kinship terms.

This fundamental problem will receive consideration in the present article, but from another angle, that of marriage. It will be shown that in a society organized on such a wide-spreading kinship basis, and not complicated by any arrangement of matrimonial classes or other exogamous groups, marriage necessitates a definite reorganization of the ties of relationship, of modes of speech and behaviour, a conversion of relative status. But this adjustment to new conditions, though it involves whole groups of people, is by no means automatic, is not merely a matter of simple reclassification; the old ties undergo a differentiating scrutiny, and individual circumstances are frankly taken into account in making the final settlement. The opportunity of change in status gives play to selective adjustment on the basis of personal preference and degree of social significance.

THE REGULATION OF MARRIAGE IN TIKOPIA

According to W. H. R. Rivers, the marriage system in Tikopia is regulated entirely by kinship. Like most generalizations of such vaguely formulated type, this is only a half-truth; indeed, it would be just as correct to say that in Tikopia kinship is regulated by marriage.

Analysis of the factors which do actually regulate marriage in this community shows that normally kinship plays a very small part. The case usually resolves itself into one of personal choice on the part of the two people immediately concerned, or, failing this, on the part of the man's relatives. The question of the kinship ties of the two parties is rarely brought up for consideration; in fact, this is done only when the limits set by custom and popular sentiment are in danger of being overstepped. The kinship principle enters, not as a determinant, but merely as a barrier against the union of close relatives. But even here, as will be seen later, its power, backed up by the weight of public opinion and ridicule, is sometimes insufficient to prevent the marriage of two people who greatly desire each other. Generally speaking, there are three main factors which come into consideration in shaping the minds of those interested in a marriage: personal attraction, competence in economic affairs, and compatibility of temperament. As is but natural, the last two have the greater weight in influencing the relatives of the person wishing to marry, while he or she, though by no means insensible to these considerations, is usually ruled more by the initial factor. Often the credentials are satisfactory on every point to all parties concerned, and the match proceeds. But human susceptibility and desire are capricious in their choice of objects, so that a difference of opinion is not infrequent between a person and his or her family. In Tikopia, as elsewhere, the critical sense of the relatives is given full rein, and the shortcomings of the desired partner are vigorously canvassed, a discussion which is none the less keen because it has of necessity to be conducted in private. Such critical analysis is usually directed against the woman by the man's family, and not the reverse, since, marriage being patrilocal, it is they who will find themselves in intimate association with her. Moreover, Tikopia custom places the initiative in undertaking marriage upon the man and his relatives, while the girl's people are kept in ignorance of the proposed *coup* until it is too late for them to take action in the matter. A man usually gives his relatives some hint of his wishes in order to secure their co-operation; a woman rarely does so lest she be beaten for her effrontery in wishing to desert her home.

A not uncommon objection made against a proposed bride is that she will 'turn her back on the household', a metaphorical description of a woman who does not fraternize with her husband's relatives, eats apart from them, gives them the 'cold shoulder' in fact; a very undesirable person to receive into a closely knit family group. Objections on the score of youth, of laziness, of a scolding tongue, may be brought by relatives as other reasons against her acceptance, and may cause the man to abandon his project and look for someone who is more agreeable to the taste of his family. On the other hand, he may demur to a proposal from the side of his parents or father's sister, on the score that the woman is physically disagreeable through deformity or disease, or again that he simply does not desire her. The issue depends on the relative strength of mind of the people concerned. An obedient son or daughter will yield to the wishes of parents and kin, and seek a spouse elsewhere. One who is resolute, spurred on by the image of desire, will carry the day.

On the rare occasions on which a girl makes known her choice to her parents, her action is usually dictated by a passion of overwhelming strength, which makes her reckless as to consequences. A threat of suicide, if thwarted, not infrequently accompanies such a declaration. If firmly opposed she may say, 'Of all the men that go about, I see only one; if you object I will swim out to sea.' This announcement is usually intended seriously and, as the natives say, parental affection concedes her desire. It is unpleasant for a Tikopia, as for any other father, to contemplate the certain prospect of his daughter being devoured by sharks.

A man, if pushed to extremes, may threaten to take a canoe and set himself adrift, but usually before the argument reaches this stage his relatives fall silent. Nevertheless, their abandonment of the discussion does not mean concession. Secretly and hurriedly they decide upon a wife for their son; then, forming a strong party of his brothers, cousins and others of his father's kin, they sally out to seize the woman of their choice. They find her in the path, or in the cultivations, and bear her off, struggling and shrieking, to their house. A rough-and-tumble with the girl's people ensues, but the party of rescue or vengeance seldom gets her back. The man himself in such a case does not take too kindly to the situation for the first few hours, but the die has been cast and he has perforce to accept.

If, on the other hand, the wishes of a man are agreeable to his relatives and coincide with the desires of the girl, with whom he has probably been sleeping for some time, then the pair of them go quietly to his house one evening. On discovery in the morning, the usual marriage ceremonies take their course. A woman of rank, however, generally makes some show of resistance, even when eager to go, in order to save her reputation from wagging tongues.

One interesting phenomenon in Tikopia is the number of men and women who never marry. With some, as for instance the younger brothers of a household, it is for acknowledged economic reasons; with others it is ostensibly the result of personal preference for the single state; while with some women, of course, it is merely due to the fact that no men have been desirous of taking them as brides.

While kinship does play a very important part in marriage ceremonies and subsequent social relations, it is of minor significance in the actual prior regulation, i.e. in determining what parties shall marry. Its influence is seen as a purely negative principle prohibiting by custom the union of near kin, and even here, as the evidence will show, it has been disregarded on many occasions with impunity, with the infliction of no social penalty but that of mild scorn and amusement.

We are faced, then, by this problem: what actually is the position, in terms of kinship, of people who are about to marry? Rivers was led to formulate his general statement that marriage is regulated purely by kinship by his empirical conclusion that, 'A man does not marry anyone whom he would call *kave*, whether the daughter of brother or sister of father or mother or a more distant relative through the classificatory system.'[1] *Kave* is the reciprocal term used primarily between brother and sister, with all the extensions usual to Polynesian kinship. Now it is plain that in making this generalization Rivers did not formulate clearly to himself the issues involved. For, as he correctly states, the classificatory system of relationship in Tikopia is of a far-reaching kind, i.e. its terms, especially the basic ones for father, mother, brother, sister, are used for persons who are very many degrees removed from the true family circle. It is often necessary to inquire back for many generations in order to trace the origin of such connexion. But it is easily seen that if the classificatory principle is so catholic in its scope, then man and wife may reasonably be expected to have been related to each other before marriage. This is the more probable since the community is not large, kinship is reckoned bilaterally, and the clan groups are not exogamous. Considering these facts of Tikopia social organization, I soon came to realize that there could be very few, if any, people who were absolutely unrelated; consequently, a person was bound to marry some sort of relative. This opinion I found confirmed when I began to direct my inquiries on to this precise point; the evidence led, in fact, to a complete reversal of Rivers's generalization. Not only may a man and a girl who call each other *kave* marry, but such marriages are the most frequent and are held to be the most 'correct' if the connexion is not a very close one. Natives express it thus: 'It is good to marry the sister set on one side, the sister from another place.' Such, in fact, is the position in the majority of unions. The reference to the 'sister set on one side' means, as the term suggests, a distant relative of the *kave* status; the 'sister from another place' primarily refers to a difference of locality, a girl from another village, but in fact amounts to the same thing, since, normally speaking, difference

[1] W. H. R. Rivers, 1914b, I, p. 309.

in residence can be correlated with divergence of relationship.[1]

One of the fundamental facts about marriage is its social reverberation; the union of two individuals involves the creation of a whole set of new ties between their respective groups, social and economic obligations of weighty and even burdensome kind, very stringent in the case of close relatives of the married pair, but decreasing in intensity with the distance of relationship. In Tikopia this centres round the *tautau pariki*, a term indicative of persons under constraint of relationship. They must observe certain formalities in addressing each other, and special politeness in all social contacts; they must keep certain rules of avoidance in bathing or meeting in the path, and observe a certain niceness of expression in conversation. Above all, they must refrain from any angry, indecent, or even chaffing talk in each other's presence, such being termed *taranga pariki* (bad speech), whence the title of their relationship is derived. Father and son are under this ban to a mild degree, as also, to a greater extent, are brothers-in-law. But the *tautau pariki* par excellence are a husband and his father-in-law, a wife and her mother-in-law, and cross-sexually. Once the marriage ceremonies are concluded, the specific economic obligations between them are few, but the social impressiveness of their relation is great. Only after the birth of several children, and the approach of the husband to middle age, which places him more or less on a footing of equality with his father-in-law, does the severity of the prohibitions surrounding their contact tend to relax. As the Tikopia say, the *tautau pariki* becomes mild. But it is never really light. The social importance and responsibilities of this relation between a person and his or her affinal relatives must be borne in mind, especially when considering the reorientation of relationship that takes place in the case of the more abnormal types of marriage.

The scope of this *tautau pariki* relation is much widened by the fact that, in addition to the husband, his brothers and near cousins also assume the same constraint of relationship towards his father-in-law. Moreover, the brothers of the latter are included in the

---

[1] This offers a comment on Rivers's well-known view that forms of social organization and terminology are a sure index to forms of marriage. If, as he maintains, their forms of marriage, past or present, are enshrined in and can be deduced from the kinship system in vogue among a people, it is curious that his general statement as to the fundamental principle of marriage in Tikopia should be the opposite of the truth. Again – to anticipate – he quite failed to grasp that, with such a classificatory system of relationship, a variety of so-called anomalous marriages is bound to occur.

same category and receive similar treatment. With women the corresponding situation obtains. In a family group of a number of brothers and cousins, several of whom are married, each one, whether married or not, pays respect to all the *tautau pariki*, the parents, real and classificatory, of the various wives.

This analysis of the kinship implications of Tikopia marriage may be prefaced by a brief outline of the terminology in use for denoting kin; the detailed treatment of the system, with its bond of sentiment, its manifold obligations and links with economic, social and political life, has been given elsewhere (Firth, 1936).

THE KINSHIP SYSTEM

By the time that a Tikopia child has reached the age of seven or eight years it is equipped with a full set of terms by which to describe its own and its parents' relatives. The mother and the father are *toku nana* and *toku mana* par excellence, despite the extensive application of these kinship terms. In the wider use of the terms, not only the sisters of the mother and her more distant female kin, but also the wives of the father's and mother's brothers receive the appellation of *nana*, while the father's brothers, the husbands of the father's sisters, the father's father's brothers' sons, and his more distant cousins in the male line are each referred to as *toku mana* (my father). Such of these people as are unmarried are distinguished as *nana taka* and *mana maroa*, according to their sex, and are called *nau taka* and *pa maroa*, respectively, the qualifying terms indicating that they have not yet entered the state of matrimony. In the case of all 'fathers' and 'mothers', whether married or not, it is prohibited (*tapu*) to speak their proper names. To all of these people the child is *taku tama*, or, if it is a girl, the more specific designation of *taku tamafine* (my daughter) is given.

Parents of the mother and father, or, in the wider issue, anyone who is *nana* or *mana* to the mother or father, is a *puna* of the child, the term being applied to a person of either sex, though in actual address a distinction is made between *putangata* (grandfather) and *pufine* (grandmother). To these people the child is their *makopuna*, a term used irrespective of sex, both for address and reference.

In the child's own family and generation it soon learns to distinguish *taina*, sibling of the same sex, from *kave*, sibling of the opposite sex. To a boy, his *taina* are his brothers and male cousins, to a girl her sisters and female cousins, while their respective *kave* represent relatives of the other sex. Distinction is made, where specific reference is needed, between *taina* (or *kave*) *maori*, true brothers and sisters – which term is often applied to first cousins as well – and *taina* (or *kave*) *fakatafatafa*, distant brothers and sisters, literally 'set to one side'. A synonym for the latter is *taina* (or *kave*) *kesekese*, 'different' brothers and sisters.

Further categories of relationship are formed for the child through the kin of the parents. As already noted, all the *taina* of its mother are *nana*, and the *taina* of its father are *mana*. But the *kave* of its mother are another matter. Headed by her *kave maori*, her true brothers, they are the child's *tuatina*, most important people, from whom the child, as their *iramutu*, receives great attention, by whom he is presented with food and valuables on ceremonial occasions, and when death claims him is buried with due rites. If his actual *tuatina* have preceded him to the world of spirits, then their sons, or their sons' sons, take on themselves the same name and functions. In these matters of social obligation it is the real mother's brothers, the *tuatina maori*, who are chiefly concerned and, through constant association from infancy, for them the child's sentiments are correspondingly deeper.

The father's *kave*, his sisters and female cousins, though not bound to the child by any such set of duties and obligations as are the *tuatina*, are nevertheless treated with even greater respect by him. They are his *masikitanga* (*masakitanga*) – they call him *tama*, as do his parents – and to their wishes and opinions he pays great heed. They, or more accurately his *masikitanga maori*, his father's own sisters, are regarded as a kind of female counterpart of his father, a point of view which receives actual expression in native opinion and relationship terminology. On the death of the father, if he has no brothers who survive him, but a sister remains as the representative of his house, his son will confide in her as in his father, and according to the mood or fancy of the moment will address her as '*masikitanga e!*' (aunt), or '*pa e!*' (father). To the native mind there is nothing ludicrous in this contrasexual attribution. I cite an actual statement: 'Great is the weight of the father's sister. The double of the father since the sister of the father (is) living, is the same thing; the father, the father's sister. The father is absent (the euphemism for "dead"), but the father's sister is living;

(one) will "Father" to her. There, that is (why) its origin is weighty concerning her, it makes her *tapu*. To "*pa*" to her is correct because she alone remains living singly in the house.'

The unique position occupied by *tuatina* and *masikitanga* has its effect also on the kinship terminology and the behaviour in respect of their children. Whereas the children of one's *nana* and *mana* (mother's sister or father's brother) can be treated rather cavalierly, and even cursed freely on occasion, behaviour of this kind must be avoided in the case of children of the father's sister and reciprocally of the mother's brother. The former (parallel cousins) are *taina fakalaui*, the latter (cross-cousins) are *taina fakapariki*. Infringement of this rule, and in particular any physical injury offered to one's *taina* (or *kave*) *fakapariki*, will bring down the vengeance of the *masikitanga*, who is credited with particularly powerful influence in the matter of invoking supernatural punishment.

It is not my purpose to bring out the essentially individual character of the relationship system from this angle, hence it will be sufficient to point out that such a ban is intense only in the case of the father's own sisters and mother's own brothers; as the relationship becomes more distant, though the terminology is retained, the obligations become light. This is specifically recognized by the Tikopia.

NORMAL MARRIAGE AND ITS RELATIONSHIP TIES

There still remain for consideration the various relationships involved in marriage, the full force of which is felt by a person only after maturity is reached. Chief of these ties is that of *tau ma* (brothers-in-law, sisters-in-law) and *tau mana fongoai, tau nana fongoai* (father- and son- or daughter-in-law, mother- and daughter- or son-in-law). Since the main theme to be considered here is that of the ramifications of the relationship system in connexion with marriage, it is well to give an actual example in illustration.

It has already been mentioned that the typical or ideal marriage in Tikopia is that with the *kave fakatafatafa*, the distant classificatory cousin. Genealogy I shows such a marriage, where the prior bond of kinship can be traced only through a remote ancestor.

Manga, now known as Pa Teva, of the clan Taumako, married

the daughter of Pa Tavi of the clan Kafika.[1] She was his *kave fakatafatafa*, and also his *kave i take ngangea*, being from another village. By this marriage a new set of relationships was contracted between the *paito* or family group of Taumako and that of Tavi. The primary ties to be considered are those of *tautau pariki*, already mentioned.

Pa Teva speaks of his wife's father as '*Toku mana fongoai*', and his wife's mother as '*Toku nana fongoai*', and in actual conversation with them he calls them '*Pa*' and '*Nau*', or '*Pa fongoai*' and '*Nau fongoai*', respectively. They in their turn may call him '*Pa*' as a sign of respect, or may speak of and to him as their *fongōna*. Both sides commonly use the polite dual *korua* (you two) in speaking to one another, and more formally, may reinforce it by the inclusion of other relatives in the kinship term. (It does not matter whether these latter are present or not at the time; there is no intention of addressing them.) A man addressing his daughter's husband does not call out simply '*Au*', 'Come in', as he would to another visitor, but gives him his title '*O Mai, fongōna!*', 'Come in, son-in-law!', using the plural form of the verb. In the early stages of married life, especially at the first visit of ceremony paid by the new husband to the wife's people, great play is made with his new appellation. 'Go and invite *fongōna* to come', is the formal invitation, marking the first use by the girl's father of his son-in-law's title. But its significance is deeper than this, for it also conveys the first public recognition of the latter's existence, and a tacit abandonment of any resentment at his daughter's flight or abduction. 'Come in, *fongōna*', he calls as he sees him in the doorway. 'Take down the food basket that *fongōna* may eat', and so on. If a small child crawls inadvertently in front of the son-in-law, the father hurriedly interjects to it, '*A mata o fongōna*', 'Mind *fongōna*' (the conventional apology, literally 'eyes of son-in-law').

Again, a man may address his son-in-law as '*tau ma e!*', 'brothers-in-law', politely including a reference to his own son, who may not be present at all. Conversely, a person who wishes to attract the attention of his father-in-law does not call out '*Kaia*', the Tikopia equivalent of 'Hey', but says respectfully '*Tau puna E!*'

---

[1] I have used the expression 'clan' as the most convenient to designate the major divisions in Tikopia society; the appropriateness of the expression is discussed in Firth, 1936, pp. 369 *et seq.* Termed *kainanga* by the natives, these divisions are four in number: Kafika, Tafua, Taumako and Fangarere. They are not formally exogamous, though marriage outside the clan is usual.

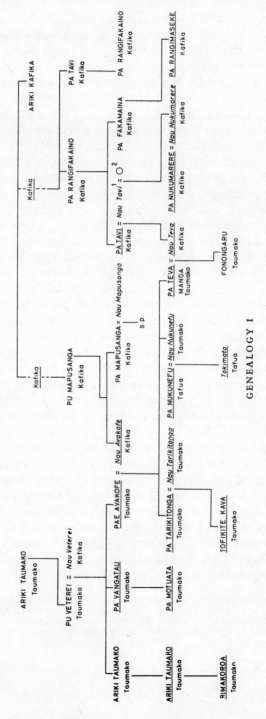

GENEALOGY I

(literally 'grandparent and grandchild'), coupling as it were his father-in-law with his own child. This convention of employing polite duals and coupled relationship terms to single individuals is to be regarded as a mode of showing respect by softening the forms of address. On very formal occasions a chief or other honoured person may be spoken to by the dual pronouns out of politeness, though no such relationship exists.

The same terms and rules apply to Pa Teva in his relations with Pa Fakamaina as with Pa Tavi and with Pa Rangifakaino, the father's brother's son of the latter. They are all his *mana fongoai*, his *tautau pariki*, before whom restraint must be observed, and he is their *fongōna*. In fact, all the men of this generation in the Tavi *paito* (family group) will be his *tautau pariki*, and their wives also. All the men of his own generation, as mentioned below, will become his *ma*, and the women, their sisters, his *taina*. The extension of terms carries still further, for not only Pa Teva, but also his brothers and sisters and even his more distant relatives are affected, and take on the corresponding relationships. Theoretically, this process is like the ripples formed by a stone when thrown into a pool; the circles keep on widening till they reach the bank, that is the limits of the community. But in actual fact some other marriage, like a second stone, always interferes, and it is this repercussion of opposed forces that forms the central field of our study.

To return to the genealogy. Pa Teva has now to speak of Pa Rangimaseke as his *ma* and to address him as '*Tāngāta*' (not to be confused with the well-known Oceanic word *tăngata*, man, plural form *tāngata*), being very careful, as in the case of his parents-in-law, never to mention his proper name, and if possible to avoid repeating his 'house name'. (On marriage, a Tikopia ceases to be called by his or her proper name, except occasionally by parents and brothers or sisters, but is addressed and referred to by the name of the house in which he or she lives, the terms *pa* or *nau* being prefixed to it according to sex.) It may be noted that Pa Rangimaseke is not the actual brother of Nau Teva, but her first cousin. Nevertheless, he is reckoned as her *kave maori*, and hence becomes a *ma maori*, a true brother-in-law. Generally speaking, all men who are *kave* (classificatory brothers) of the wife become *ma* of the husband. Similarly, all *kave* (classificatory sisters) of the husband become *ma* of the wife; they are addressed by her as 'fine'. The sisters, real or classificatory of the wife, her taina, are called taina by the husband as well, and they call him by the same term. Taina is primarily a term applied to a brother or sister when the speaker is of the same sex. The native explanation of its usage for the wife's sisters is that it conveys the idea of the unity of husband and wife. If a man's brother marries, then he calls the wife by the same term as he employs for his brother, and this is used reciprocally by her. 'You, your taina (brother) shall marry, go you and call out to his wife "my taina". Because she is married to the taina.'[1]

There seems to be no justification for correlating this usage with any idea of placing a barrier upon sexual relations between the people thus denominated brother and sister. There is no levirate in Tikopia, so that a man never has intercourse with his brother's wife, either before or after his death. It is quite common, however, for a man to marry his wife's sister, and for the three of them to live in a common ménage. The custom originates, so the Tikopia say, in the practice of the wife's unmarried sister coming to live in the household on the birth of the first child, in order to care for it and act as nurse. Thus situated, the man not uncommonly desires her, and marriage with or without previous intercourse is the result. Such a marriage is in no way regarded as reprehensible, and in olden days seems to have been fairly common.

Despite the disparity of sex, a man and his wife's sister, or a woman and her husband's brother, are called by the ordinary term of tau fanau, used in speaking of brothers and sisters of the same sex.

A slight linguistic digression is here necessary to make clear the usage of certain terms. As already noted, by kave is meant a brother or sister of the sex opposite to that of the person used as the referent. It is a reciprocal term. Now, a brother and sister together are spoken of as tau kave, the word tau implying the link or reciprocity between them. Thus in the genealogy, Pa Teva and Nau Nukunefu are tau kave, as are also Nau Teva and Pa Rangi-

---

[1] It is difficult to render quite adequately the native explanation here, because of the ambisexual use of the word taina. A parallel in English is where a man speaks of a woman as 'my cousin', since she has married his cousin. It may be noted that the application of the term taina, primarily used for brothers or sisters of the same sex to these affinals of the opposite sex, involves no real confusion, such as would be created by using the term kave, which at first sight seems the more natural because of its primarily heterosexual usage. The kave being the basis of the tuatina relationship, the whole structure of the kinship system would be thrown into a state of chaos. (For further discussion see Firth, 1958, pp. 4- 5.)

maseke. A qualification may be introduced, so that they may be *tau kave maori*, true brother and sister, or *tau kave fakatafatafa*, distant brother and sister, as were Pa Teva and Nau Teva before marriage. If there are three or more persons included in the relationship, then they are referred to in the plural as *nga tau kave*. Pa Teva, Nau Nukunefu and Pa Tarikitonga would be referred to together in this way; or to take a wider instance, any collection of children of mixed sexes of the former Ariki Taumako and his brothers Pa Avakofe and Pa Vangatau (see also Genealogy II). Sometimes, by a curious usage, the plural is singularized again, and the group is spoken of collectively as a single unit, *te nga tau kave* (the brothers and sisters). The same usage is applied throughout in Tikopia relationships. Thus *tau ma tangata* denotes a pair of brothers-in-law, *tau ma fafine* a pair of sisters-in-law, *nga tau fanau* several brothers or several sisters. (Note that the term *taina* is replaced by *fanau* in such a case.) Difference of generation is no bar to this terminology, which is very widely used in ordinary conversation. Thus a native, on being asked who are fishing in a certain canoe, will rarely give the names of the people concerned, but will reply: '*Nga tau fanau i Maneve*', meaning the brothers in that house, or '*Nga tau mana i Tafua*', meaning the chief of that clan and his sons. Or if someone inquires in the house: 'Who has gone to fill the water-bottles?' '*Tau masikitanga*' is the reply, meaning an aunt (man's sister) and her niece. The particular configuration of the household group makes it clear who are indicated; if this is not so, a further question soon settles the matter. The terms *tau* and *nga tau* thus imply persons of reciprocal relationship, the former a pair only, the latter several. I propose to refer to such expressions as 'coupled' and 'joint' relationship terms, respectively. As a rule the superior term of reference, that for the elder person, is used, as for instance, *tau puna*, grandparent and grandchild, instead of *tau makopuna*, in the reverse order. This is quite natural. Again, *tau tuatina*, mother's brother and nephew (or niece), is the term in general use; *tau iramutu*, nephew and uncle, is, I understand, a permissible expression, though I have never heard it employed.

This usage may seem curious, and even puzzling – at least it was so to me on the first occasion when I encountered it in conversation – the idea of two persons of different status and kinship designation being coupled merely under the single superior term of their relationship being rather novel. But when one becomes accustomed to its use, it is found to be not only simple to grasp, but also extremely convenient in ordinary conversation. It has the merit of brevity, and also the added advantage that in a society where personal names have often to be avoided, it offers an easy and unembarrassing means of reference and address.

It may be observed that the usages of the relationship system may be followed regardless of age. As a case in point, Pae Sao and the Ariki Kafika are *tau fanau*, through a distant connexion; their sons Katoarara and Pa Fenuatara are also *tau fanau*. Katoarara and Rakeivave, the son of Pa Fenuatara, are *tau mana*, though the two children are much of an age. Moreover, the former's sister, still a baby, is the *nana* (mother) of Rakeivave, although the latter is her senior by several years. Only rarely, when a young man is of the same kinship status or kinship grade as another greatly his senior, does any self-consciousness manifest itself. Thus Kavakiua, a man of twenty-five and unmarried, has as his *ma* (brother-in-law) one of the ancients of the district, white-haired and toothless, though still active. He confided to me with a laugh that he was shy (*fakama*) at calling this old man by the familiar title of equality, *tangata*, and so always addressed him by his 'house name', which is less intimate in tone.

MARRIAGE WITHIN THE PROHIBITED DEGREE

The union already considered, that of Pa Teva and Nau Teva, is of the normal type, that is with *kave* of distant relationship. Sometimes, however, the bounds of propriety are overstepped and a marriage takes place between two people who are *tau kave maori*, true brother and sister, in the native terminology. This may be termed an aberrant form of the typical marriage, people uniting with the same generation but within the narrower circle of the family group. Marriages of parallel cousins, cross-cousins, and even half-brother and sister, are thus recorded in my notes, and the genealogical bearings of some of them are given below.

Marriages of this type are not frequent, but on the other hand are not absolutely singular phenomena. If asked point-blank, 'Do *tau kave maori* ever marry?' a native will often reply categorically, 'No'. If pressed, however, and if he is on certain terms of intimacy with the questioner, he will qualify this statement with the remark that some people have done so, adding that it is a stupid or bad thing to do. Certain families have the reputation of being specially addicted to marriages of this kind, notorious among them being Sa Raropuka. People of other groups who marry within the proscribed degree are compared with them in disparagement.

In abstract discussion, once the subject has been broached, if mention of actual cases of people still living be avoided, Tikopia give very clear opinions on the inadvisability of such marriages. 'That is good, to marry the sister from another place, the sister set to one side, but marry the true sister, is bad; not good.' Or stating it another way: 'Is good to go and marry into another family group, but to return again is not good.' That is, to seek a bride in one's own family is bad; one should go out to another family. A particularly vivid expression was used by one man in discussion: 'The one flesh joined within itself; is not good, is bad. The idea from of old in Tikopia.' Here the reference to the 'one flesh' is to the near brother and sister, members of the one family group, whose union is regarded as evil.

No overwhelming social stigma attaches, however, to such a union once it has been consummated in marriage. Politeness naturally forbids allusion to it in the presence of the people concerned. 'We do not call out "*Tau kave*" (brother and sister) because it causes to quiver in shame', say the natives. But mention of it in other company usually provokes a smile, slightly contemptuous. Annoyance may cause a reference to the simile of eating *soi*, a certain bitter fruit. Indeed, it is the belief that such marriages are bound to be sterile, and definite instances are given in support of this generalization. This looks at first as though the Tikopia had formulated on empirical evidence some biological principle as to the evil effects of inbreeding. Their reasoning, however, is not at all of the scientific order, but belongs to the realm of religious belief. It is held that the parents of the guilty pair are angry at this foolish conduct on the part of their children. Though they may swallow their resentment in life, yet it becomes active after death. In the form of spirits they proceed to bewitch the married couple. Thus of one pair, son and daughter of a former Ariki Kafika by different wives, it was said: 'Died then their children; die because their sterility brother and sister true; their parents come and interfere with their children.' A more detailed explanation was given by one informant. 'The true brother and sister, their children are not good, are diseased and weakly. The true brother and sister shall marry, their children are kept alive only through their fathers while alive and dwelling. But die their fathers, ill befalls their children. That is, their fathers have come to bewitch the children of the married couple. Their fathers die, go to the *atua* (supernatural beings) go, go then to what the *atua* are doing, go and dance at it; go dance, dance, dance, call out the *atua*: "A! Come and dance! Thy notoriety in thy children who are living together." (That is the married pair who have united.) Thereupon shamed. Shamed; turn and strike their children.'

They may prevent conception or cause miscarriage, or smother the new-born child, or kill it by wasting sickness, but in any event they do their ghostly utmost to prevent the raising of any offspring. Like many other native generalizations, then, the one mentioned is scientific only in appearance, and rests on a basis of supernaturalism.

The attitude of Tikopia towards the marriage of close kin naturally varies somewhat according to personal situation. One who has married a distant relative is strong in his disapproval, while one whose marriage closely approaches the prohibited degree is apt to be more temperate in his opinions. Consequently, the ethnographer does not obtain a consistent series of opinions on this topic, but a graded set of views. But the emphasis is always on the negative, prohibitory side. It was of course impossible to discuss the position with the parties directly concerned in the more notorious cases of intermarriage, but opinions received from brothers of these people and from other persons who have married fairly close .kinswomen were all of a disapproving character. Public opinion, in general, is against such marriages. According to Pa Fenuatara, a man of considerable intelligence, the marriage of first cousins is barred, but the marriage of second cousins is not regarded with such severity, since they have 'gone aside'. It is said that their families have 'entered into one another', 'determined to dwell together' or 'intermarried'.[1]

Kavakiua, another good informant, discussing the marriage of cross-cousins, said, 'Some people married their cross-cousins; not

---

[1] I could find no hint of the idea suggested by G. Pitt-Rivers (1927, pp. 92, 134), that Polynesian chiefs deliberately practise intermarriage with close kin in order to perpetuate a fine physical strain. The Tikopia custom of chiefly families and commoners marrying each within their own class, which is quite different, is due to the desire to maintain exclusiveness of social and economic privilege, not to preserve any physical or mental qualities.

good, but their own mind' (i.e., it is their wish, and though it is not good, who is going to stop them?). We have here an expression of the toleration for other people's conduct which characterizes Tikopia society. There is much verbal criticism and back-biting, but little direct action taken. Of the marriage with near relatives in general, with members of the *kano a paito*, he re-marked: 'It is done; it is good, yet bad.' Such is the point of view generally elicited when the matter is discussed with more or less impartial Tikopia.

The marriage of closely connected relatives naturally involves a readjustment of kinship attitudes and of corresponding termi-nology. People who were former *tautau laui*, with whom it was proper to bathe, or to exchange chaff or even obscene jokes, have now become *tautau pariki*; their presence restricts freedom of speech and conduct, they must be addressed with considerable formality, and under no circumstances can one forget oneself and indulge in any *risqué* conversation.

The readjustment of relationships consequent on such a marriage is illustrated. The present Ariki Tafua took as his second wife the daughter of his mother's sister, a woman of the same clan. Before marriage he and her brother, Pa Korokoro, were *tau fanau maori*, true brothers, calling each other *taina* or using personal names; now they are *tau ma*, brothers-in-law, and call each other *tangata*. The old status is ignored, and they behave to one another in accordance with the rules of their new relation-ship. Such is the general custom; the former terms of address and reference are completely discarded, and both parties scrupulously adhere to the new state of things.

This difference is not felt so deeply when the persons thus drawn into the prohibited category were previously of no special social consequence to the new husband. But when they were called his own brothers, shared the intimacy of his family life, were co-partners with him in economic pursuits and co-sharers in the family wealth, when ordinarily they would come to his aid and help him to cope with the outlay of food and gifts for his wife's relatives, this sudden ranging of them in a separate group, with the imposition of a certain ban upon freedom of speech and intercourse, gives a severe jar to the equanimity of family life. This, perhaps, accounts to some extent for the dislike of such marriages in the mind of the average Tikopia.

It might be thought that there would be little objection to the marriage of close kin in Tikopia in the case of parallel cousins in the female line, the children of two sisters. Since patrilineal descent is the acknowledged system, such children are members of different *paito* (family groups). But the importance attached to the mother-line in kinship brings this marriage also under the public disapproval. The children are recognized as being close kin through their mothers, *tan kave fakalaui*. In one case which attracted considerable attention, a death occurred in the family of a man who had married his mother's sister's daughter. When I was first given news of this my informant, an old lady whom I knew well, added '*rau mara*' ('their sterility' or 'failure'); it was the natural result of the close kinship of husband and wife. Many times in the next few days I heard this opinion repeated by people who were discussing the event.

Even where such people come from different clans the attitude is the same. The fact of their mothers being sisters places them within the proscribed degree. With the offspring of brother and sister, of course, the same position holds.

The apparent indifference of Tikopia society as a whole to such unions, which in personal judgement they admit to be undesirable, is almost certainly due – apart from a general spirit of toleration – to the idea that the punishment may be safely left in the hands of the ancestral spirits; that it is, in fact, a case for interference from within the family.

On the same plane, in Tikopia eyes, is what appears to us to be a really incestuous marriage, that with the half-sister. Two cases at least have occurred to my knowledge, and in one of them I knew well the people concerned. They were, in fact, near neighbours of mine. The other, to which reference has been made already, was that of the son of the late Ariki Kafika by one wife to his daughter by another. When the subject of incestuous marriages with *tau kave maori* was brought forward, this was the stock example given by the natives in their endeavour to convince me that such a union was bad, and necessarily unproductive of children.

When I adduced the second case, where there was a numerous and handsome family of children, I was met by the statement that the earlier offspring had all died, and that it was only this, coupled with the simultaneous death of the parents of the married pair, that enabled them to rear the present family. The argument is not too logical, but obviously some reply had to be made.

THE ADJUSTMENT OF KINSHIP STATUS

One point has emerged in the discussion of these aberrant forms of marriage – that is, that the union involves not merely the assumption of new ties of relationship, but the discarding of former ones. There is no clinging to the old status, no attempt at blending the terminology. Of these changes, the principal is the substitution of brother-in-law for brother, real or classificatory, which is commonly the case in the more typical form of marriage also. As will have been gathered already, this change is, as a general rule, imposed not merely on the bridegroom, but also on all his *taina* in his *paito*. All the people in his own family group follow his lead and address the people whom the bride calls 'brother' as 'brother-in-law'. This is the natural outcome of the classificatory principle in the relationship system resulting from the prominence assumed by the new marriage tie.

The classificatory principle, however, is not operative in all cases – a fact which is of considerable importance to the general theory of kinship. Thus, to consider Genealogy II, Pa Tarikitonga and his wife before marriage were *tau kave fakapariki*, and he and Pa Maniva were *tau fanau fakapariki*. Now, as is natural, they have become *tau ma*. But contrary to the rule just given, Pa Rongonafa, own brother to Pa Tarikitonga, has not followed suit, but is still *tau fanau fakapariki* with Pa Maniva. The explanation goes to the root of the classificatory system of relationship – that is, it depends on the fact that *the kinship status and terminology is not an automatic conformity to a general principle of classification, but varies where necessary with the circumstances of the different individuals concerned.* The relation created by marriage between Pa Maniva and Pa Tarikitonga is sufficiently strong to override any previous kinship bonds, and takes precedence. But with Pa Maniva and the brothers of Pa Tarikitonga it is different. They have not married the former's sister, and the original cross-cousin tie of kin is thought to be too near to be abandoned. So they hold the old status and terminology, and let him take on the new alone. The same holds with regard to Pa Rongonafa. He married, successively, two daughters of a man, now dead, with whom he and his brothers were *tau fanau*. With Pa Niukaso, this man's son, he is

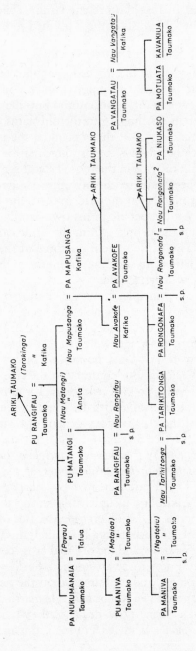

GENEALOGY II

now *tau ma*. But Kavakiua, his *taina maori* (his father's brother's son), has not followed suit, and still remains in the *tau mana* (father to son) relationship with Pa Niukaso, though to the latter's sister, Nau Rongonafa, he is a brother (*taina*), because she is his 'brother's' wife.

It must be emphasized that such differential adoption of relationship ties on these lines of conscious selection is not a mere inference on my part, but a statement of the Tikopia point of view as it is commonly expressed in concrete terms.

'With some people the true brother and sister unite; the man (who) marries like that has brothers-in-law himself alone.' To a man marrying thus his brothers say: 'You make your own brothers-in-law yourself alone, but our own brother group is made already.' The new husband then is the only one to contract the new ties of relationship; his brothers voluntarily keep to the old kinship situation. 'His *tautau pariki* (i.e. father-in-law, etc.) he only then makes, will leave he himself alone.' (That is, it will be left to him only to make the change.)

Such family discussion and individual choice in the assumption of new relationships is of frequent occurrence in Tikopia society.

In other words, the application of the classificatory system is not a blind following out of the one status by all members of the same class, but involves the principle of selection and differentiation with reference to individual cases. Where there is the likelihood of confusion, or the conflict of competing interests, each case is considered on its merits.

ANOMALOUS KIN-GRADE MARRIAGES AND THEIR EFFECTS

This is brought out most clearly by marriages of an apparently anomalous character – that is, those in which persons of different generations unite, as, for instance, mother and son, father and daughter, father's sister and nephew, mother's brother and niece, all such relatives being naturally of a classificatory kind. Such instances in Tikopia are by no means rare, and I select examples for illustration. Apart from the actual fact of the marriage of disparate generations, persons of different kinship grades – in itself a matter of interest – the feature worthy of consideration is the manner in which former relationship ties are adjusted to meet the altered conditions engendered by the marriage. In addition to providing data regarding the flexibility of the primitive kinship organization, this will also form a basis for certain more theoretical conclusions as to the nature of the classificatory system as a part of the social mechanism.

As a typical example, the marriage of Pa Taitai, illustrated in Genealogy III, may be considered. It was one of the first cases which came to my notice, and brought home to me the interest of the principle involved. Nau Taitai and Nau Paiu are two sisters, and are distant *kave* of the Ariki Kafika, from whose line their father's family sprang some generations ago. Other *kave* of the Ariki are Nau Raroakau and Nau Tafua, for similar reasons,

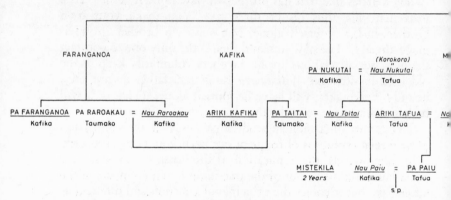

GENEALOGY III

and their respective sons, Pa Taitai and Pa Paiu, were formerly his *iramutu* and called him *tuatina*. On their marriage to the above-mentioned women, the question arose should they preserve the uncle-nephew status, or should they, having married his classificatory sisters, become his brothers-in-law. In the case of Pa Taitai, the latter was decided upon. After his marriage, when he met the Ariki, he tried to greet him as of old as '*Tuatina!*' 'Oh, no! We two are brothers-in-law', said the Ariki. And in spite of the protests of the younger man, they remain so. The Ariki finds the situation humorous. On his frequent visits to my house the small son of Pa Taitai, who lived near by, generally wandered up and stood in the doorway, gazing solemnly at him, after the manner of infants. 'Go away,' said the Ariki, 'go to *tangata*' – this with a chuckle, for calling his former nephew 'brother-in-law' is rather a joke. Pa Fenuatara, son of the Ariki, and the same age as Pa

Taitai, says of the latter: 'He comes and "brothers" me, but I object: I "Pa" him because he has married my father's sister.' Pa Taitai, thus overwhelmed, has submitted.

Pa Paiu, on the other hand, retains the former relationship. He insists on calling the Ariki *'tuatina'*, in spite of the latter's efforts to establish the new position. After the marriage, Pa Rangifuri, brother of Pa Paiu, said to the latter and the Ariki, 'You two are brothers-in-law.' 'Brothers-in-law, who? He and I are uncle and nephew', replied Pa Paiu, in his lazily determined style. And by his insistence he carried the point. When I questioned other people on this they said that the respect felt for the Ariki would make a young man shy at greeting him as 'brother-in-law', and that this was the reason for Pa Paiu's adherence to the old status.

Of Pa Taitai, the Ariki said: 'My nephew there has become my brother-in-law; not nephew, because he has married my sister. Will live his children, come then and make an uncle (mother's brother) of me.' This statement indicates how clearly and concisely a Tikopia is able to put a case of this kind.

In the family of Pa Taitai a further change has taken place. Before his marriage he and his wife were *tau masikitanga*; she was his classificatory father's sister. Moreover, she and his mother were classificatory sisters (*tau fanau*). Now, since a certain degree of constraint is observed between a wife and her mother-in-law these two have now become *tautau pariki*, with a corresponding gap of a generation between them, so that Nau Taitai now speaks of Nau Raroakau as her *nana fongoai*.

In this example, I have described at some length the precise mechanism by which the adjustment of relationships was settled. In the last resort, where there is ambiguity, and a choice must be made, the decisive factor is the opinion of the persons immediately concerned. Thus, I asked Pa Motuata one day in what relation he stood to the elder men of the *paito i Kafika*, into which I knew he had married. He said, in reply, that before marriage he was *tau tuatina* with them all. They were his mother's brothers, his mother coming from the allied *paito* of Tavi. But now, since he had married into the group, all the men of that generation had become his *tautau pariki*, his fathers-in-law. All, that is, except one man. On being asked the reason for this exception, he said that this man merely said he 'did not want to'. Hence he still retains the old status of *tuatina*, and is so addressed by Pa Motu-

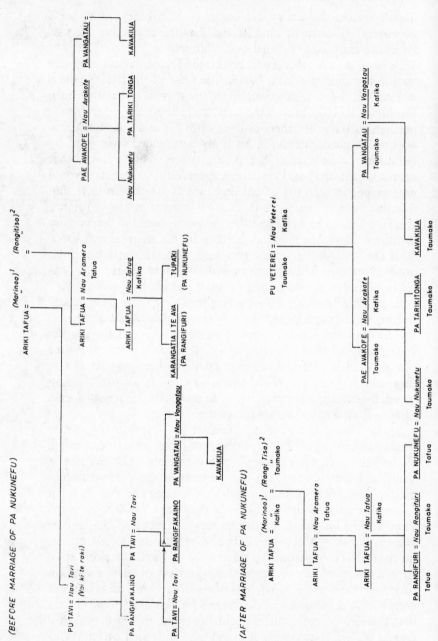

ata. This apparently casual attitude is due to the fact that the objector was not a close relative of the bride; for this reason the relation of *tautau pariki* would not be of great weight, and it made little or no difference whichever status obtained. It would have been very different if this man had happened to be the bride's own father.

In the usual analysis of a system of kinship terminology in ethnographic literature it is often impossible to tell from the observer's account whether this personal factor of differentiation plays any part or not in the social life. Considering the small size of many primitive communities, however, and the probable result of marriage leading to such interlacing of relationships, it is unlikely that such a characteristic is unique and confined only to Tikopia.

Other instances may now be given to indicate how frequent is this phenomenon of a 'glide' up or down in the scale of generations, an adjustment of the kinship terms to meet the inconsistencies of such marriages.

One of the cases which, at first sight, appears most involved is that represented in Genealogy IV. If we take, to begin with, one of the fundamental alliances which went to shape the present-day kinship status (for the Tikopia can usually trace back a relationship to its *tafito*, its origin), the *masikitanga* of the present Ariki Tafua, his father's half-sister by another mother, married into the *paito* of Tavi. Her son and the Ariki were then *tau fanau fakapariki*, and the children of the former regard the latter as their *mana*, their father. One of these, Nau Vangatau, in her turn has now got grown-up children, and these in their youth, as for instance, Kavakiua, called the Ariki their *puna* (grandparent). But Pa Vangatau, her husband, on the other hand, and his brother Pa (Pae) Avakofe, are *mana* of the Ariki, so that Kavakiua is both *tau puna* and *tau fanau* with the latter, grandchild through his mother, and brother through his father. The marriage of the children of the Ariki has both simplified and complicated matters. Pa Rangifuri, the eldest son, regards Pa Tavi as his *taina* (brother), and Nau Vangatau as his *kave* (sister), while Kavakiua on this side should be regarded as his *tama* (son). On the other hand, through the latter's father Pa Rangifuri is the *tama* of Kavakiua, and actually this was the relationship acknowledged socially. Such was the condition before marriage. But Nau Rangifuri, his wife, regards Pa Vangatau as her *tamana* (father), so that he becomes the *mana fongoai* (father-in-law) of Pa Rangifuri; while his son Kavakiua and Pa Rangifuri now become *tau ma* (brothers-in-law). This position was still further reinforced by the marriage of a younger son of the Ariki, Pa Nukunefu, to a daughter of Pa Avakofe. As Pa Vangatau is the latter's brother, he naturally becomes *tautau pariki* with Pa Nukunefu (i.e. his father-in-law), and also with the brother, Pa Rangifuri. And since Kavakiua is his son, and the *kave* of Nau Nukunefu, he (Kavakiua) has an additional reason for being *tau ma* with the sons of the Ariki. Moreover, Pa Rangifuri falls into line with his brother, and for him Pa Avakofe is *tautau pariki* also. But here is a point of interest. Pa Nukunefu is *tautau pariki* with both Pa Vangatau and Nau Vangatau, since his wife, Nau Nukunefu, is own brother's daughter to Pa Vangatau (see Genealogy I). But Pa Rangifuri, while he is *tautau pariki* with Pa Vangatau as befits the *tamana* of his wife, continues to call Nau Vangatau his *kave* (sister), as the *tamana* relationship between Pa Vangatau and Nau Rangifuri is fairly distant, and allows the prior bond in the case of the former's wife to be retained.

Furthermore, it has been mentioned that Kavakiua was *tau puna* with the Ariki Tafua through his mother, and *tau fanau* with him through his father; now the intermarriage of the two families introduces a third relationship, and he treats the Ariki as his *tautau pariki*, his father-in-law, since his *kave* (sister) has married the Ariki's son. Thus in terms of classificatory relationship he has passed from grandson, through brother to son-in-law. His *taina*, Pa Tarikitonga, the actual son of Pa Avakofe, was *tau fanau* with the Ariki formerly; they thus called one another 'brother' (*taina*). But he too, on the marriage of Nau Nukunefu, abandoned this status and now speaks of the Ariki as his father-in-law.

This apparent confusion of relationships seems less strange when one learns that the children of the Ariki Tafua, of Pa Avakofe and of Pa Vangatau are all more or less of an age, and that therefore the final reduction of their relationship in recent years, by inter-marriage, to that of brothers-in-law to one another, and sons-in-law to the other people's fathers, falls into line with the natural age-grading. It may be noted too, in passing, as a point of some theoretical interest, that the chief factor instrumental in resolving the confusion was that of a marriage between a man and his classificatory mother, *she being the same age as he*. Moreover, it was a match of mutual inclination, contracted in the face of the violent opposition of her relatives.

Natural choice, in fact, cuts across the tangles of kinship, and allows the thread to be joined up again at the most appropriate ends. The two principal marriages concerned, those of Pa Nuku-nefu and Pa Rangifuri, were in the one case with a classificatory mother, and in the other with a classificatory daughter (see Genealogy V), but in neither was it a question of a union involving any noticeable disparity of age. In the former case the woman

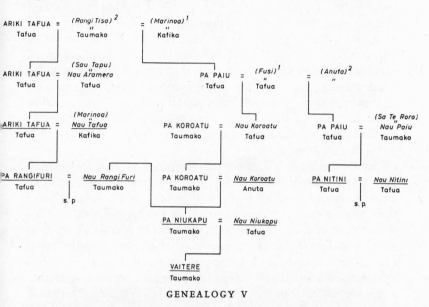

GENEALOGY V

is, if anything, slightly younger than her husband; in the latter she is apparently of the same age. In Tikopia such marriages, anomalous from the point of view of kinship status, are by no means infrequent, but neither do they represent any acquisition of young women by old men, nor the acceptance of elderly women by men who are their juniors. Approximate equality of age is one of the primary conditions of matrimony.

The immediate effects of the marriage of Pa Rangifuri with a woman who was his classificatory daughter are seen in Genealogy V. At an earlier date her real father and he were *taina* (brothers), but after the marriage their status necessarily changed to that of *tautau pariki*, the coupled term for father- and son-in-law. The association of these two families shows a further point of interest;

it was this, indeed, which first led me to realize the complexity of the apparently simple Tikopia relationship system. Vaitere, son of Pa Niukapu, is the *iramutu* (nephew) or *tama tapu* of the Ariki Tafua, his mother being the *kave maori*, own mother's brother's daughter, of the chief. It might be expected then that Pa Niukapu, having married the *kave maori* (true sister) of the Ariki, would be his *ma* (brother-in-law). This is not so, however. He is his son-in-law; they are *tautau pariki*. This puzzle is resolved by the fact that the *masikitanga* of Vaitere, the sister of Pa Niukapu, is married to Pa Rangifuri, the son of the Ariki. Hence, in the matter of relationship to the *paito* of Tafua, father and son in Niukapu are of equal status. Each traces his kinship through the nearest line, the father through his sister, the son through his mother. It is noteworthy, again, that though Pa Niukapu married a woman who, from one point of view, could be reckoned as being two generations above him, yet in the matter of age there is no perceptible difference between them.

The above example illustrates the difference between what may be termed *significant relationship* and *inferential relationship*. The latter is the relation between two persons which arises out of their relation to other persons, according to the rules of the kinship system in force. But in a society such as that of Tikopia, at all events, where the classificatory scheme is continually being crossed and recrossed by marriage affiliations, there may be several inferential relationships between the same two persons, according to the direction from which the relationship is traced. The result is not a blur of terms, obligations and privileges, but a definite selection, an insistence on one relationship to the exclusion of the others. And normally the relationship thus selected is the one of the greatest social importance either from the point of kinship sentiment, of ceremonial observance, or of economic obligations and privileges. It is the *socially significant relationship*.

In Tikopia society every person must have his or her *tuatina* (mother's brother) to whom he or she is *tama tapu* (literally 'sacred child'). On the *tuatina* devolves the duty of holding the child in his arms after birth and sending it gifts, of taking charge of it during the incision and other ceremonies of childhood, of making presents of food and bark-cloth on all the important occasions of its life, and finally of digging the grave after death. Hence for Vaitere, the obviously significant relationship which he cannot abandon is that to his mother's brothers; he therefore counts the Ariki as his *tuatina*. With Pa Niukapu there are two chief relationships to be considered. He has married the *kave maori* of the Ariki, and his own *kave maori* has married the son of the Ariki. He can then assume the relationship of brother-in-law either to the Ariki or to his son. But his wife is really only the first cousin of the Ariki, while it is his own sister who has married Pa Rangifuri. Moreover, the age and rank of the Ariki is such as to inspire respect. The situation is best met, therefore, by treating Pa Rangifuri as his brother-in-law on the one hand, and Pa Sautapu on the other, while the Ariki is elevated to the position of *tautau pariki* (father-in-law), a status consistent with his dignity and kinship to Pa Rangifuri.

Genealogy VI illustrates still more clearly the element of individual differentiation which exists in the classificatory system. Tokipare is the *mafine* of Uviaiteraki and also the *iramutu fakata-fatafa* of Pa Fenutapu, the latter through the Anutan connexion. She thus holds the same relative status with regard to both men, being a kinship grade below them. But the two men themselves belong to different kinship grades, Pa Fenutapu being the *mana* of Uviaiteraki. Now, Pa Fenutapu has married Tokipare, thus taking to wife the daughter of his son from one point of view, or his own niece from another, these terms being, of course, purely classificatory. This seems to present rather an involved problem for settlement, but the social system is equal to the occasion. Since Pa Fenutapu has married the 'daughter' of Uviaiteraki, the latter has become his father-in-law, but the original father-to-son status is not ignored. Each man, therefore, calls the other '*Pa*', which is the term of address for either relationship, and due respect is thus paid to both sides (*fetau pa katoa*). This is the usual Tikopia solution for marriages of this type which involve a complete reversal of former relations, to ignore which would carry a loss of respect.

One point must be emphasized in connexion with these so-called anomalous marriages; this, that the anomaly is really superficial. In all the cases given, and they are a fair sample, the husband and wife are approximately of the same age. Despite the difference in generation, or rather in kinship grade, there is little, if any, in years. Every marriage is essentially a normal one, contracted soon after maturity and offering no violence to any natural desire of

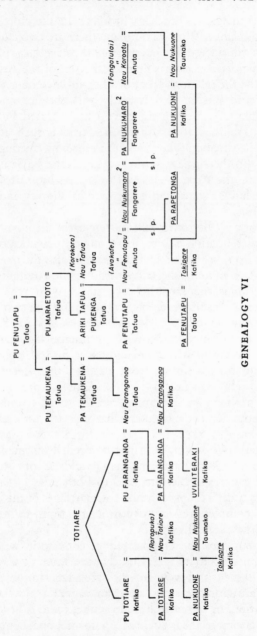

GENEALOGY VI

youth to mate with youth. The process just illustrated amounts to a correction by the ordinary avenue of marriage, of discrepancies between the kinship status of people when contrasted with their respective ages.

Of the few really anomalous marriages that I noted in Tikopia, one is where a man married one woman, and later took her brother's daughter also. In this case there is a real gap in generations. He is now an old man, grey-haired, and his first wife walks with the aid of a staff, while his second wife is still a comparatively young woman. But in this case there is a definite reason for his conduct. By his first wife he had no children and, after a long interval, being by this time middle-aged, he determined to take another wife. Naturally, in the circumstances, he desired a young woman; he returned to the *paito* of his first wife and took the woman whom he called his daughter, the child of his wife's brother. For this he was laughed at by people, but it is said that the woman was quite willing to live with him, and his action has been justified by the appearance of several children. A second case is of the same kind. A man, after some years of wedded life, had connexion with and later married a girl from another family who lived in his house. This union was contracted through his desire to have a male child, and with his first wife's approval. He, too, was successful in attaining his object.

Another instance is that of the marriage of a son of the Ariki Fangarere with a woman much his senior. She was, in fact, the girl just referred to above, having left her husband later and gone to live with her people. While there she was visited by the young man, and the pair were married. Here, again, it was entirely his own choice; he went to her, it is said, 'from his own desire'. There is a suspicion that his disability, a serious impediment in his speech, made such a match the most feasible for him; at all events, the pair live very happily together with their child.

The reflection is suggested, then, that really anomalous marriages, where there is a considerable discrepancy in age between the two parties, amounting perhaps to a generation, are to be accounted for on the principle that they are exceptional cases, and, moreover, are unions undertaken from purely personal inclination, or for some definite end, such as the production of children where previous attempts have been unfruitful.

GENERAL OBSERVATIONS UPON THE CLASSIFICATORY SYSTEM

Analysis of the Tikopia data here presented has shown that certain conclusions can be drawn which are of general interest to the theory of primitive kinship. The more important of them may be reformulated in conjunction as follows: In a community where the classificatory system of relationship is in force, and kinship is counted with almost equal strength through both the male and the female lines, it is clear that the more limited in numbers the population the more likelihood there is of the existence of a previous tie of kinship between people who marry. In the matter of this prior relationship it is immaterial whether the social organization is based upon exogamous clan groups or not. Marriage, then, involves a change of status not only for the husband and wife, but also for their relatives who have to make a readjustment of their kinship bonds to meet the altered situation.

This change is not automatic, a simple reclassification *in toto*. It takes place on the basis of individual circumstances and even personal selection, the most significant relationship, that one which has greatest social weight, being adopted from among the several possible or inferential relationships. Such a process is seen in its extreme form in what may be termed the 'parting' or 'splitting' of relationships, as in those cases quoted above where a husband holds the status of father-in-law, and his wife that of sister, to the same man, or where a father and his own son enter the same kinship grade, one being the son-in-law, the other the nephew of a third person. There is no attempt to combine or fuse the status or the terminology of kinship. The mode of such selection shows, incidentally, the existence of a very strong *individual* element in the classificatory system. The terms as used in ordinary life by the Tikopia connote for him not abstract undifferentiated groups of kinsfolk, but definite specific persons each linked to him by personal individual bonds.

This process of individuation, of selection and exclusion in adjustment, is necessary for the preservation of this particular type of kinship structure. It is, in fact, the compensatory principle which the classificatory system bears within itself for the purpose of its own functioning.

Under this form of social organization, where the classificatory system of relationship is in association with the bilateral recognition of kinship, and consequently marriage with a relative is the rule, the major proportion of such unions takes place between persons of the same kinship grade, as between those termed 'brother' and 'sister', that is, between cousins. Natural birth sequence, however, operating it may be over several generations, tends to cause a variation of kinship grade between persons of essentially the same age. Hence, a proportion of marriages tends to occur between people of different kinship grades, as between classificatory uncle and niece, nephew and aunt, father and daughter. To this extent such marriages are anomalous. It may be noted that they have not been inferred from any 'correspondences' in kinship terminology, but have actually been observed and recorded from native life. These marriages, however, are truly normal in character, their essential feature being that the union is contracted between people of approximately the same age, the same *tupuranga*, 'growth-stage', as the Tikopia say. Really anomalous marriages between people of widely different ages are rare and contracted for some special reason – as desire for children, or physical disability of one partner.

In general, then, the natural tendency of man to seek a mate in a woman of equivalent age, that is, soon after both have attained maturity, renders it inevitable that where such differences of kinship grade occur with no great disparity of age, marriage in many cases will eventuate, and the discrepancies in the kinship grading disappear. Age and status are thus once more reduced to a level of equality. Nature herself tends to correct in the sphere of marriage the balance of the social mechanism which was originally displaced by her own operations in the field of birth.

It seems to me probable that a careful study of the social organization of other Polynesian peoples, and perhaps of other culture types as well, will yield similar results to those obtained in the case of Tikopia.

To have given an adequate account of this subject of Tikopia kinship would have meant the inclusion of a vast mass of data showing the manner in which the system operates against the background of economic and religious affairs. But what the observer cannot help but perceive as he is actually studying the culture in all its bearings, is the essential practical utility of the classificatory system of counting relationship in its own cultural surroundings. Unlike the rigid travesty of it which is sometimes put forward by theorists for comment and criticism, it reveals itself as a convenient, flexible and commonsense piece of the social mechanism.

CHAPTER V

Authority and Public Opinion in Tikopia
(1949)

It is a commonplace in modern social anthropology that in any authority[1] system involving the pre-eminence of individuals, the power exercised by these individuals is not completely autocratic, whatever the local system of ideas about the nature of their control may be. In practice it is not that this control rests on the ultimate acquiescence of their people through virtue of some kind of initial covenant, as the earlier European political philosophers argued. The acquiescence may be due to no more than a dull apathy, an inability to see an alternative mode of government, or acceptance by them of some values regarded as absolute and not forming part of any contractual scheme. But in one way or another the people governed impose limitations and modifications on the actions of their leaders and rulers. In some societies formal institutions such as chiefs' councils or nominated elders help to provide checks to authority. In other societies these checks come through informal mechanisms such as a ruler's gossip with his retainers, the influence exercised upon him by his womenfolk, or some dramatic event which reveals to him the strength of popular feeling.

There has so far been little examination of the kinds of processes whereby such popular feeling becomes manifest and effective. This essay is therefore intended as a contribution to the analysis of public opinion as a force of social control. It is dedicated to Professor Radcliffe-Brown because, like all British and many other social anthropologists who have worked on problems in primitive law and allied fields, I am deeply sensible of the value of his clear and stimulating formulations – even though I have not always adopted either his terminology or his concepts.

---

[1] By authority is meant here the ability to exercise power through the application of sanctions.

DEFINITION OF THE PROBLEM

The term 'public opinion' is used here to indicate a view or a body of views on a matter of general concern expressed in some concerted form by a significant number of individuals in the community. From the point of view of empirical study and of social action it is the expression and not the mere holding of the views that is significant. The difference between overt and covert expression of views is relevant to most social situations, the former being usually much more effective as a force of social control. Action in regard to public opinion may be mobilized or unmobilized. The latter may range from exchange of views among small groups to simple crowd behaviour; the former implies elements of decision, leadership, and organization. It is situations of this last type especially that I shall discuss here, with particular reference to the sociology of Tikopia. Since the paper is an analysis of social process and not an exercise in definition, I refer to the material considered as phenomena of social control, not of law. I prefer here the term popularized by E. A. Ross, because, though I think one can usefully speak of law in Tikopia, there is no need to consider here the problem of the relation between social control and politically organized authority, which would be necessary if the term 'law' were to be employed.

The relevant principles of the Tikopia social organization may be briefly recapitulated. The major forces of social control are provided by the kinship organization – with which the religious organization is largely coincident – reinforcing authority to a considerable extent with ritual sanctions. The basic structural element in the kinship organization is provided by the segmentary kinship groups of ramifying type, which are now generally known in African ethnography as lineages,[1] but which I termed in a former publication *ramages*.[2] These are unilateral groups, and in Tikopia are patrilineal. There are more than twenty of them, aggregated by various processes of affiliation and assimilation into

[1] The term kinship system is sometimes used to indicate only ties derived from the bilateral family, and distinct from those of the lineage system, with ties from the unilateral descent group. I think this is inappropriate. A lineage system is part of a kinship system, i.e. of the system of recognition of social ties based on genealogical ties.

[2] See Firth, 1936, pp. 344–72. I now prefer to speak of those groups which are unilineal as *lineages* and to reserve the term *ramage* for descent groups of a non-unilineal kind. See Firth, 1957; 1959, pp. 213–14. Some writers, e.g. Sahlins, have adapted and elaborated my earlier usage by applying ramage to internally linked segmentary unilineal groups in Polynesia. To avoid confusion I have kept the original text here.

four primary kin groups which, though not exogamous, are most simply termed 'clans'. In each clan there is one ramage whose members are of senior rank and which furnishes the chief of the clan. The chief of each clan is supreme in authority as far as his own group is concerned, and autonomous. In public affairs for the island community as a whole, however, especially in religious affairs, the four chiefs are arranged in a hierarchy, each having specific ritual functions to perform. The order is as follows in terms of named offices: the Ariki Kafika; the Ariki Tafua; the Ariki Taumako; the Ariki Fangarere. The first is *primus inter pares*; he is the senior and takes precedence, but he is not a paramount chief; and the others defer to him rather than obey him. Any one of them is at liberty to refuse co-operation.

Our general problem, in more specific form, can be seen to have two aspects. The first is: within each clan, where a chief is ruler, what are the forces of social control and how does public opinion emerge *vis-à-vis* this dominant element of chieftainship, backed as it is by ritual sanctions? The second is: by what mechanisms of social control are relations among the four autonomous clan chiefs maintained in a way which allows of community action as a whole, and what role does public opinion play in this seemingly even more refractory type of situation?

Before adducing evidence to answer these questions, a few general points may be made. The first is that neither question is a hypothetical one. General community relations depending on the solution of difficulties among the clans exist in a number of ways in Tikopia, e.g. at dance festivals and in the ritual cycle known as the Work of the Gods, and public opinion can be effective both in intra-clan and inter-clan relations. The second point is that in such a society, where the institution of chieftainship is operative with great force and with important religious sanctions, for any mobilization of public opinion to be effective, its directing force, presumably in terms of the individual or individuals primarily responsible, must clearly be of great weight. *Ex hypothesi*, one might postulate that the principle relied upon in such case would be that of a ritual sanction different in kind from, though equal in magnitude to or greater than, that on which the power of the chiefs depends. In fact, this is not the case. The sanctions utilized are essentially non-sacerdotal, exoteric; the basis is a social, not a ritual one. The third point is that the social principle involved is overtly that of the appeal *ad misericordiam*; it is constraint by pleading; it takes the form of what may be termed a 'lead from weakness'. The final point to make at this juncture is that to a considerable degree it is the kinship system which provides the basic structure on which public opinion can operate most effectively. It is not the sole factor but the primary curb on the autocracy of the senior members of the community – that is, the chiefs – is provided by the recognition that juniority has claims which cannot be ignored. Kinship also enters in another way by providing lateral ties between the major participants in the situation.

Having outlined the main sociological aspects of the problem, I can now examine the ethnographic data bearing upon it.

STRUCTURE OF AUTHORITY

The first set of data concerns the structure of authority. In the ordinary everyday affairs of the Tikopia clan the ultimate decisive role is played by the chief. His word is effective, and is normally not questioned. Affairs between clans are decided by the chiefs in concert, with great display of courteous agreement. Seconding the efforts of the chief in each clan are his elders (*pure* or *matapure*), who are the heads of the various major ramages. They attain their position primarily by seniority of descent, but they must be confirmed in office by their clan chief, and in some twin ramages which continue to maintain a close relationship for generations after the point of branching the chief may select the joint elder alternately from one and then the other ramage. The role of the elder is, however, in essence a ritual one. His main task is to conduct the worship of the gods and ancestral spirits on behalf of the group he represents and to perform the appropriate rituals in connexion with sickness, sea voyaging, etc. This ritual function is symbolized by his investiture by the chief on election with a leaf necklet regarded as endowed with magical virtue. The elder exercises authority by right over all members of his ramage and obtains respect from the community at large. His position is analogous to, and in some degree is the outcome of, that of a father in the family. The Tikopia elder can, in fact, be regarded as fulfilling in part the role of a father-symbol to his ramage, just as the chief fills a similar role for his clan. But the elders may play a comparatively small part in general social control in the community. They are ranked in a ritual hierarchy in each clan according to the importance of the gods they serve, and only a few of the highest-ranking ones play much part in the maintenance of public order.

The role of sustainers of public order is played primarily by the men of rank known as *maru*. These, broadly speaking, are the brothers of a chief and his closer cousins in the male line. Ordinarily the chief's sons are not considered as *maru*; they become so on his death, when they act as supporters of the authority of the eldest of their number, who succeeds their father. The *maru* are essentially the executive officials of the chief; their function is to watch the land and to repress violence, to carry out the commands of the chief when sentence is passed on an offender and in general to keep the peace of the community. The influence and importance of the elders depend on the gods over whom they have control; that of the *maru* almost wholly on their personality backed by their rank. The *maru* has no gods to whom he addresses invocations; his position depends to some extent upon his birth, but a man without strength of character will exert no influence. The ideal *maru*, respected by the people, is a strong vigorous individual, secure in his high birth, unafraid of expressing his opinions or taking action, and well disposed towards the common folk. In the years before I arrived in Tikopia one *maru*, Pae Avakofe, became pre-eminent on this account. Father's brother to the chief of Taumako, and a man of strong personality, he had gained great influence by his firm assumption of authority in cases of dispute and his unwavering protection of strangers and the oppressed. When I was there he was still spoken of as *te maru sokotasi i fenua nei*, 'the one *maru* in this land', meaning by this not that he was the only one but that he exerted the supreme and final authority. In 1928 he was an old man and unable to take any active part in the administration of affairs, but he was still of premier importance in the community. His responsibilities had been delegated to his eldest son, Pa Tarikitonga. The latter told me that his father had said to him: 'Your brother, the eldest of the family, is dead, so it is for you to be the *maru* to the land. Do not trouble to remember formulae of the *kava* and other matters; leave those to the chiefs and the elders. Your work is one only: to look after this land. If a stranger comes, look after him; if a time comes when the chiefs and their people agree together in anger against him, you protect him that he may not be killed or sent off to sea. That and that only is your work: to look upon the land that it may be well.'

This speech emphasizes the one essential difference in function between the chiefs and the *maru*. They are close relatives, but the duty of the chief is to retain the esoteric knowledge of the community, embodied in the *kava* and other sacred formulae, and to exercise it for the public weal; that of the *maru* is to preserve peace in the purely social sphere. The injunctions of the old man illustrate also another extremely characteristic feature of the Tikopia social system. There is a marked sense of responsibility possessed by the leaders of the community – the chiefs and their assistant officials – for the maintenance of the social order and the well-being of the people, and for the exercise of hospitality towards strangers who have arrived on their shores. This is a traditional attitude handed down by each generation of men in authority to their successors; it represents the ideal and to a considerable degree also the reality of government in the island. It receives recognition in current sayings, and at critical times does indeed exert a definite influence on the course of events. Another aspect of this sense of responsibility is shown in the invocations of the chiefs and their elders to the presiding gods, who are addressed specifically not for the welfare of the reciter but for that of the group as a whole.

In speaking of the maintenance of peace the native expression is *fau te fenua*, to 'guard the land'. This is regarded as the predominant function of the *maru*. The ideal of order in the community is expressed in the words 'That the orphan child may sleep in the middle of the path'. This expression is figurative – no Tikopia, not even a child, would dream of behaving in such an uncouth manner as actually to lie down and sleep in the middle of a public way! It is intended to convey the sense of security felt when strong and benevolent authority is wielded in the land by men of rank – even one so defenceless as a parentless child is safe from oppression.

EXERCISE OF AUTHORITY

We may now consider the exercise of the functions of the chief and the *maru* in social control. No attempt can be made here to survey the whole field, but simply to indicate a series of type situations.

In ordinary quarrels of individuals about property or in family affairs the chief exercises no authority. The disputants settle the matter by themselves, or with the assistance of their kinsfolk, by wordy battle which sometimes, though rarely, ends in assault or the exchange of blows. The chief, in common with the rest of the community, displays a lively interest in the affair, and expresses his opinion freely as to the rights of the case; but it is not formally laid before him for judgement, nor is his opinion taken as a ruling by either side. Out of respect for him the quarrel will seldom take place in his immediate neighbourhood. However, if it should occur near his dwelling or that of a *maru* or other man of rank, the *maru* may intervene in the general interests of order. He usually admonishes both sides, bidding them cease their strife. In one case I knew a married woman committed adultery with her husband's brother. When her own brothers came to hear of it, they were greatly enraged, and after virulent reproaches one of them struck his sister a severe blow, and threatened violence to her paramour. The latter replied with spirit, and the noise of the resulting brawl reached the ears of the eldest son of the resident chief of the village, who was sitting in his house close by. Learning the reason for the disturbance he sent out a message in forceful language, which can be translated only in colloquial style as 'If I come out to you, there will be something doing!' Not wishing to brave his anger, the brawlers subsided. The most violent of them, indeed – one of the woman's brothers – withdrew to live for a few days in a village at some distance.

The wrath of a *maru* or of any man of a *paito ariki* – a 'chiefly house'[1] – is feared, since he may possibly strike the offender and the latter, especially if a commoner, is by custom expected not to retaliate.

Cases of dispute over land, due either to contested boundaries or to collateral inheritance, are common. Normally the people concerned settle their own differences. Sometimes, however, if a man of rank feels that public concord is being outraged too openly he will endeavour to reconcile the parties and suggest a form of amicable arrangement. This he does on his own initiative, not as a piece of set procedure. As a rule the chief does not act in the matter; he may in conversation state his opinion as to the

---

[1] i.e. a ramage from which the chief of the clan may be chosen, or the members of which are descended from a fairly recent chief.

relative merits of the claims advanced, but the settlement of the case does not immediately concern him. In certain circumstances, however, he may exercise his authority and give a pronouncement. In theory all the land of the clan is held at the disposal of the chief, and some portions of it were actually handed over by his ancestors to clan members in bygone generations. If land of this type is under dispute and the trouble appears to be serious, perhaps likely to lead to bloodshed, or if the chief becomes irritated at the news of the bickering, he sends a messenger with an ultimatum to the people concerned. This may embody a decision against one party, bidding them 'sit down' and yield to their opponents. More often it is to the effect that if they do not speedily resolve their differences he will resume the land himself and drive off both parties. This threat has usually the desired effect. Where land is so scarce the entire loss of a garden or orchard is a serious matter, apart from incurring the displeasure of the chief, so that some compromise is generally arranged.

Most of the disagreements so far described may be termed private disputes. They are essentially between individuals or small groups of individuals, such as families, and though the fact of dispute may invite the censure of the rest of the people, the action of either party is rarely in itself regarded as deleterious to the welfare of the community.

Theft is a phenomenon of a different type; it is regarded as reprehensible. *Te kaia, e pariki* – 'theft is bad' – is the conventional stricture. But, though stigmatized, theft in Tikopia is not punished by the community.[1] The essential reaction to theft is the idea of replacement by equivalent. The use of other people's property, especially food supplies, is much more free among Polynesians than among modern civilized folk. This is partly because of the ties of kinship extending throughout the entire community. Hence one man can distrain upon the property of another with comparative immunity. He should, however, first ask permission of the owner – which is normally not refused – and again he should, as soon as is convenient, give a *quid pro quo*. These are the points on which a Tikopia fastens when a question of theft arises. When articles have been stolen the people say, 'Theft is bad. It is good to come and ask permission (*fakataurongo*) of the man whose things they are', and again, 'It is good that the person who has

[1] Except when persistent, see later, p. 134.

taken these things shall come and lay down an equivalent of his own for what he has taken.' The question is treated on the basis of wants and satisfactions: it is argued that the person must have desired the articles, otherwise he would not have taken them away; let him therefore come and produce something in return. It will be noted that it is not suggested that the particular goods stolen be handed back to their former owner; it is deemed a satisfactory outcome to the situation if a proper equivalent is rendered. It is general restitution, not precise restoration, that is needed. Theft, then, though regarded as an outrage against personality, is primarily seen as a failure to present compensation. Hence it incurs reprobation, not punishment. This is in line with the ordinary canons of etiquette in connexion with the transfer of property.

In cases of theft the chief takes no official action, but leaves the person who has been robbed to prosecute his own inquiry and settle with the offender, if he locates him. When he is robbed himself, as happens occasionally, he acts as a private member of the community, not in his representative capacity.

The normal reaction of a person on finding that some of his property has been taken without leave is to *forua*. This means to shriek in a high-pitched, prolonged way, *Iefu! Iefu! Iefu!* At the same time he indulges in violent bodily action, such as beating the roof of his house with a stick, until his rage has exhausted itself. He also curses vigorously. This is not only a venting of his anger; it is also a formal protest against the theft, and serves to apprise other people of the village of his loss. If the thief is actually caught at work a vigorous tongue-lashing is administered to him. If he is seen at a distance a stone may be thrown in his vicinity to scare him. If he is later identified he will be asked for recompense, or the owner himself will reimburse his loss by seizing upon some goods of the culprit and appropriating them. But theft of durable property is rare; theft of food is more common, especially from the cultivations, and in this case the thief usually evades discovery.

In these matters the chief is in the same position as his clansfolk. His gardens and orchards are as subject to depredation as theirs, and his behaviour in response is of the same type. I have heard the Ariki Kafika, premier chief of the community, shriek and curse like any ordinary man – and with as little effect. Theft of coconut and areca-nut is the most common offence, and as a rule the perpetrators go undiscovered. Sometimes in exasperation the man who has been robbed will compose a song in ridicule of the thieves and introduce it at the next public dance display. There it is chanted as a chorus by all the performers, and the matter is thus brought to the notice of the people in general. When I was in Tikopia one of the chiefs, the Ariki Taumako, whose areca-palms had been raided time after time during the season despite all his precautions, took umbrage and composed a song of this type. In it he likened the thieves to paroquets who came and settled in the fronds of the palm and nipped off the nuts. In ironical style he asked them to come and dance with abandon after the completion of their nefarious task. The song of an aggrieved owner generally embodies some contemptuous reference of this kind, though he may confine himself simply to a plaint of his misfortune. The Tikopia idea is that the persons responsible, hearing the song thus chanted before all the people, feel ashamed of this publication of their misdeeds and of the derisive terms applied to them. They slink away from the dance ground, it is alleged, and are restrained from repeating the offence. Thus, while he gets no compensation in goods, the victim does get some emotional compensation – even though he has not discovered the persons who were to blame. The song is a kind of mobilization of the ridicule of the community, and a formal launching of it against the offender. More important, perhaps, though not explicitly recognized by the Tikopia, is the opportunity it affords of giving relief to the composer's feelings.

Apart from these ordinary measures the chief has one mode of reprisal in which he has exceptional advantages. This is the practice of black magic, *tautuku*. By its recital he is believed to be able to inflict illness on anyone who offends him, through the intermediacy of his gods. The power of a chief in this direction is feared, though not, apparently, to the extent of deterring persons from raiding his crops without authorization. But as a rule theft is not followed by an appeal to black magic. This is a secret measure of retaliation, and though its use may be regarded as justified, the consequences are not approved by the community. The *tautuku* is bad because, it is believed, it makes people ill, and they may die. Whatever the provocation then, the action of a person – commoner or chief – who employs or is believed to employ such a device is always condemned though not, of course, to his face. The *tautuku* is a traditional institution, regarded as a reality, utilized as a means of private retaliation, but regarded with disapprobation by the community in general. Its use in any specific instance is suspected but not normally disclosed.

FIAT AND EXECUTION

Offences against a chief's dignity or against a taboo he has set up are on a more serious plane than theft. The procedure in such a case illustrates how a chief crystallizes his attitudes into a specific declaration or fiat, and how this is acted upon. I give an example which I witnessed personally.

Most of the lands used for cultivating taro in Tikopia are aggregated in a number of areas known as *mara*. Each of these *mara* is subject to the authority of a chief, who names the day when it shall be broken up for cultivation. No member of the clan should begin to work there before the chief's permission has been secured. On one occasion the Ariki Taumako gave instructions that a *mara* on the Te Roro shore of the lake was to stand uncultivated for a season, to allow the grass and other vegetation to grow tall and provide a good mulch for the ensuing year. Contrary to his instructions his sister's husband (of the same clan) together with several other men of the clan, began one morning to break up the ground there. The chief had been bathing in the lake and from the farther shore perceived what was being done. He flew into a rage which was increased when he learned the identity of the transgressors, and shrieked out his anger till the lake side re-echoed and people came from their houses to investigate. On the return of the chief to his dwelling his sister crossed his path, and was cursed vigorously – 'Filthy household' – a term of abuse which is quite improper between members of the same family and shocking in public. What was to be done with the culprits? The chief summoned the leading elder in the Kafika clan, Pa Rarovi by name, who lived near, and ordered him to proceed at once round the lake shore to announce his indignation to the offenders. They were bidden to betake themselves immediately to the woods – a form of banishment. Pa Rarovi complied and sped along the path, uttering an occasional yell of *Iefu!* as he went, to proclaim that he was on a mission of wrath. Bursting out on the glade where the startled workers stood, he bade them fly to the woods, telling them that they had incurred the anger of the chief and that this was their punishment. Immediately they deserted the scene of their labour and, wailing, obeyed the command. The fiat meant that they could not re-enter the village of their chief, or inhabit their ordinary houses on pain of more serious bodily penalties. They must reside either in one of the scattered bush dwellings, which stand in the orchards as temporary shelter, or go and dwell for a time with relatives in another district. In this case, as generally happens, the culprits went over to the other side of the island. There they stayed till the anger of the chief had cooled; then having ascertained that he was prepared to receive them, they returned.

In order to regain the good graces of a chief once more and be reincorporated into the community the person concerned prepares food, then brings it to the house of the chief. Setting it down at the doorway, the offender begins to wail as he enters, then crawls along the floor mats to the feet of the chief and, bending down his head, salutes with his nose the chief's foot and knee. This denotes his abasement. At the same time he chants a formal dirge expressive of his sorrow for his lapse. The song chosen does not necessarily bear on the immediate situation, but is one of a type employed at funerals or other mourning occasions. When the dirge is completed the chief (who has hitherto taken no notice of the man) tells him to be quiet, lifts up his head and salutes him by pressing noses with him. This is the formal token of forgiveness, denoting that the offence has been expiated and that the man is received into favour again.

For graver offences the mode of procedure consists in 'banishment' of the culprit, likewise, but in a more permanent form by sending him out to sea in a canoe. This amounts to a sentence of death, since the remoteness of the island from other land renders it extremely unlikely that a man so launched on the face of the ocean will survive.

This punishment is seldom inflicted. It is said that in former times men who became known as persistent and incorrigible thieves were sometimes treated in this way, but no recent case had occurred when I was in Tikopia. The offences which are thus penalized are in general those which seriously infringe the dignity of the chief, either by bodily violence or by deep insult offered to his person or to that of a member of his immediate family. Thus to strike a chief's son in a quarrel, to engage in an intrigue with his daughter resulting in her pregnancy, to disregard the chief's welfare in a crisis, or to threaten his life, are all offences which are held to merit the extreme penalty. The duty of executing the punishment is delegated to the *maru*. After making his decision the chief summons the *maru*, mentions the name of the offender and says, 'Drag down his vessel to the sea.' The *maru* goes and with the help of other men hauls the canoe down to the water's edge. Then he visits the condemned man and announces to him his fate. Weeping, the victim goes and takes his seat in the canoe, and is set adrift. A paddle and sometimes a sail are given him which he may use if he wishes. A water-bottle or a few green coconuts are usually laid in the bottom by some sympathizer in case he should desire to attempt to reach another land. The sentence is thus theoretically one of exile, not death, though in practice there is little difference.

Sometimes, with hope of life still strong, the man endeavours by sailing or by paddling to preserve himself, with the faint prospect of eventually reaching another island. As a rule, however, the Tikopia say, he abandons himself to his fate, and either allows himself to drift on the ocean till he perishes of thirst, or is overwhelmed by the waves, or takes the initiative and slips overboard to meet his death in the maw of a hungry shark. To be eaten by these monsters of the deep is in fact regarded by the Tikopia as the normal conclusion to being set adrift in this manner.

In suicide the same procedure is followed. Voluntary self-destruction and the punishment of crime are intimately connected, since when a serious offence has been committed the guilty person often anticipates the sentence by setting off in a canoe on his own initiative. It is worthy of remark that in this case the vessel is often not his own. Women commit suicide or, in rare instances, suffer punishment by swimming out to sea. Unlike the men they do not go out to meet their fate in a canoe; such is not the custom. On this account their end is more speedy, though hardly more certain; sooner or later, the natives think, the shark gets his prey (Firth, 1961a).

So far we have dealt with the ordinary forms of punishment as following in logical sequence from the action of the chief. In this connexion the function of the *maru* is seen to be that of executive official; it is he who carries out the chief's orders and deals with the criminals in person.

THE RESTRAINT AND STIMULUS OF PUBLIC OPINION

This course of events, however, is not always followed in its theoretical or ideal plan, and here the interrelation of chief and people and *maru* is of distinct interest. The following illustration of procedure is from my own observation.

A brother of the Ariki Tafua had recently died. This chief, in accordance with a custom of mourning for a man of high rank, had set up a taboo sign and declared that no fish might be caught along a certain stretch of coast. This prohibition was observed by the majority of the people. But one afternoon as the chief went down to bathe, he saw on the reef a small party of men taking out a net in the forbidden area. This breach of his prohibition angered him intensely. He stood on the beach and yelled at them: *Iefu! Iefu!* in an expressive protest. Then, as they were startled and hastened inshore, he stalked up to his house to get his gun. By this time some members of his family, hearing the commotion, had run from their houses near by. As he seized the weapon they endeavoured to restrain him. In dealing with an angry chief every care and tact is used, since his power is absolute, and there is, for the time being at least, no appeal beyond him. His sons grasped the weapon and held it respectfully but firmly while they talked soothingly to him, adjuring him not to do damage to his people nor to cherish his anger. The old man sat silent, his whole form quivering with wrath, his eyes glaring, his face working. From time to time he ejaculated merely, 'May their fathers eat filth', and spat emphatically into the fireplace. At last, yielding to the continued exhortations of his sons, he allowed the gun to be drawn from his grasp and began nervously to pound up his betel mixture in his mortar. This took place inside his house. After sitting for a time he rose to his feet, seized an old sabre that hung on the wall – a relic of the early labour recruiting days in the Western Pacific – and made for the door. His youngest son, a man of 20, was sitting there. As his father crawled towards him on hands and knees – for Tikopia doorways are very low – he tried to block his exit. 'Get out of the way!' said the old man to him, threateningly, and pointed the sword at him. The son obeyed, slipping to one side, and the chief emerged. Standing up to his full height he began to stride purposefully down to the beach, brandishing the weapon over his head, his grey locks streaming out, an impressive,

even awe-inspiring figure. It was clearly his intention to proceed
to the next village where the offenders lived and punish them for
their transgression. At his side and behind him came his sons and
their wives, endeavouring to restrain him with placatory words,
but not interfering immediately with his progress. When he
reached the beach, however, one of the wives, a woman of rank
of another clan, slipped close and grasped his sword arm. A young
man also from another clan, and of *maru* status, ran in and clasped
him round the knees, making the *songi*, the salutation of respect to a
superior, by pressing his nose to them. Thus impeded the old man
stood still. Again he began to shout in fury, in a voice which
carried along the beach for nearly a mile. Mingled with the conventional *forua* were curses heaped on the heads of the offenders
and their progenitors. This exhibition lasted for several minutes
while more and more folk assembled from their houses and came
to soothe the chief by tactful words. At last the old man ceased to
rage. His frenzy had spent itself. Yielding up the sword he walked
back to the house, silent, but stiff and dignified, with his sons and
villagers in train. No further action was taken by him against the
offenders.

It is important to note that though this procedure is spontaneous
in certain respects it follows basically a well-defined course and
forms a recognized social reaction. The extravagant gestures, the
yelling and curses and grasping of weapons are the product of
real, not assumed emotion, but nevertheless they constitute an
expected norm of behaviour. So also the placation of the offended
chief proceeds on conventional lines, the outcome of which can
be fairly closely predicted. His own relatives acknowledge the
justice of his anger and reprobate the folly of the offenders,
while at the same time they counsel moderation and appeal to his
sympathy towards these people and themselves. They take no
active measures to restrain the chief; on such occasions it is
etiquette only for a person *of another clan* to bar his progress or
seize his weapon. Were one of his own family or clansfolk to
attempt to do so he might strike them for their temerity, but he
would not act thus to a person from a different clan. He shows this
respect especially to a married woman, since in Tikopia formulation 'a married woman is taboo'. The whole course of events, then,
including the protest of the chief and the efforts of the people to
pacify him, is a customary mechanism in which the behaviour of

all parties is based on real emotions, but expresses itself according to traditional rules. An offence of this type is thus liable to set in motion a whole chain of recognized procedures, of which each element is variable, but all in association conform to a more or less definite pattern. The chief has a customary form of action for expressing his displeasure; his people have one also for exerting restraint upon him. As for the culprits, the cause of the outbreak, they also have a recognized mode of expiating their offence: they remain in seclusion for some days and then bring to the chief a gift of food.

It will be observed that what we have been considering here is merely the social response to the breach of taboo. To use a terminology conveniently introduced by Professor Radcliffe-Brown in his studies of primitive law, it is the operation of a repressive sanction. It is not that of a ritual or religious sanction. It is in so far as the offenders have incurred the wrath of the chief and the action of the society that they have come within the scope of our study; they may also be visited with sickness or accident thought to be the result of supernatural agencies concerned with taboo, but this lies in another sphere.

A more dramatic case of the same general type indicates still more clearly the emollient and restraining influence of public opinion.

A son of the Ariki Tafua fell ill and the chief proclaimed a period of restriction, during which no festivities might take place. Such an edict was in conformity with public sentiment. When the crisis had passed some of the folk of Rofaea, a nearby village, instituted a dance one evening without troubling to ascertain the feeling of the chief. As the old chief sat in his house the rhythmic beat of the sounding-board was borne to his ears. Without a word to anyone he rose, seized his spear – which is also a chief's staff of office – and went along the path to the village. In order to avoid being seen he took the inland path through the bushes in the moonlight, and did not go along the beach, the main high road, lest he might be noticed. However, a youth caught sight of him before he disappeared, and guessing his errand ran on ahead to warn the dancers. 'Be off, you fools!' he shouted. 'The chief is coming.' Struck with fear they stopped the dance and fled in all directions to hide. When the chief arrived, furious at the breach of his edict, no one was left for him to confront but a few of the elders. Carried away with anger he stood up in front of the village and with yell after yell of the *forua* he roundly cursed the inhabitants of the village. Then he finished by giving the fatal order: 'Go to your land the sea.' This is the formal pronouncement of the sentence of exile and death. The people understood the command – to set themselves adrift in their canoes. In such a case as this the execution of the sentence is left to the people concerned; shame, injured pride, and the force of tradition cause them to carry out the obligation. By next morning the whole island had heard the news, that the villagers of Rofaea were going to *forau*, to voyage forth. It was said that even then they had begun to prepare barkcloth for their departure. Public opinion was decidedly against the Ariki Tafua. It was felt that his sentence was too harsh. It was admitted that his action in rebuking those people was justified, but it was said on all sides that the punishment was excessive. This point of view was held most firmly by the Ariki Kafika, to whose clan the unfortunate offenders belonged. He, however, could do nothing, since it is not etiquette for one chief to interfere in the decisions of another. During the ensuing days the projected departure of these folk was discussed on all sides as a definite event. The actual day was named to me. As time went on, however, I learned that this was in part a façade. Though the banishment was spoken of as about to be put into effect when the preparations were complete, yet it seemed to be tacitly understood by all parties that the affair would not be allowed to proceed to this conclusion. In such circumstances it is the custom for a man of rank of another clan, the eldest son of a chief, or a *maru*, to take the initiative. Without reference to the chief who imposed the sentence, he goes and bids the people settle down again and abandon their intention. After some demurring they obey this command. They then prepare food and take gifts of mats, sinnet cord, and a valuable bonito hook to the chief whom they have offended. Abasing themselves before him in the customary way, they lay down their presents and thus expiate their offence. This closes the incident. Such in fact actually occurred in the case cited.

It will be seen then that the *maru*, apart from their position as executive officials of the chief, have also a valuable place as abrogators of punishment and protectors against the chiefs' anger. It is their function, recognized by the chiefs themselves, thus to step in and mitigate a sentence. In so doing they help to guard the common people against the oppression of authority. But more subtly, they also sustain the power of the chief. A chief in the heat of his anger may utter sentiments which are uncalled for, and inflict an unjust penalty. To revoke this sentence later would cause his pride to suffer; it also might lower his dignity and authority in the eyes of the people at large. The usage, then, whereby the *maru* take it upon themselves to intervene and remit the sentence, thus allowing the offenders to go and make peace with their ruler, is of considerable value to the system of government of the community as a whole. This function of the *maru* is a feature of great interest in the social organization.

The principle of differential rank, based on difference of birth, is fundamental in Polynesian society. But with rank come power and privilege, and with these the possibilities of oppression. In obviating this consequence the Tikopia social system makes use of the ingenious procedure of complementary officials, whereby the *maru*, themselves of rank, act as a factor of adjustment between the men of higher rank, the chiefs, and their people. In so doing they represent the popular will and give expression to it.

In another direction also the *maru* serve to give expression to popular sentiment in contrast to the will of the chiefs. Sometimes an offence is committed and the chief for reasons of his own is unwilling to take action against the culprit. If public opinion is strongly against him, it may become mobilized through the agency of a *maru* and his relatives. These people, having observed that the proper penalty – banishment – will not be inflicted, determine to force the issue by a customary method of procedure. They assemble outside the house of the chief, then, on a given signal, they rush in and, catching him up in their arms, raise him from his seat into the air. While he is in this elevated position they pay him the utmost signs of respect. They press their noses to his knee and the sole of his foot. They use the most conciliatory and honorific forms of expression. At the same time they implore him to accede to their request and banish the criminal – to send him in his canoe out to sea to perish. The action of raising the chief in their arms is termed *sapai*, and is a mark of great respect. Their procedure is in fact a kind of compulsion by exaltation. For the chief to struggle would be undignified, so he is forced to remain on high until they release him. They on their side tacitly refuse to set him down until he has agreed to pronounce the sentence. In thus doing homage to the chief the *maru* and his relatives are putting him under an obligation. In recognition of this he is virtually forced to yield to their wishes. Theoretically it is possible for a chief to remain aloft in this manner, sitting still and making no reply to the men who thus abase themselves beneath him. But such conduct would be regarded as churlish on his part. However much he may inwardly resent their interference, he must show no sign. In practice, apparently, after a due pause to sustain his dignity, he always grants what they ask. His decision is probably affected by his realization of the strength of the public sentiment against the offender, which unless powerful, would not receive expression in this action of the *maru*.

The *maru*, then, can enforce punishment in cases where a chief is too mild, or mitigate it where the chief is too harsh. He helps, in fact, to complement the functions of the chief, to adapt his decisions to the sentiment of the community. The existence of a mechanism of this kind, whereby other members of the community, usually of another clan, force the chief's hand, indicates that actions such as killing or intrigue with a chief's daughter are definitely a matter for the exercise of judgement on the part of the community as a whole. The action taken against the culprit is then a punishment of a public kind, not merely private retaliation.

These examples which we have considered help to illustrate the principles of social control in Tikopia, and show the relation of the individual clan chief to the government of the whole society. Moreover, they indicate the difference between social theory and practice. In Tikopia theory, as formulated by the people themselves, the punishment of offences depends entirely on the will (or whim) of the chief; he and he alone is acknowledged by the people as the absolute power. In practice his decisions are subject to the general will of the community, or a large section of it, as interpreted by the action of some *maru* or other man of rank. If the offender is not deemed to have committed a severe offence, or if the circumstances are extenuating, then someone steps forward and saves him by forbidding him to obey the sentence. If popular opinion is against him then no one hinders him. And if he be sheltered from the consequences of his offence by the person who ought to punish him – the chief –

then public opinion takes action on the other side, and the chief is constrained through homage to pass the appropriate sentence.

The administration of social control, then, depends to some extent upon the reaction of personalities within the community. It is not merely automatic, as some writers on primitive politics have attempted to prove. The essence of the sentence of banishment passed on a Tikopia offender is that a *decision* has to be made. Moreover, the decision may have to be rescinded, which again involves personal choice on the part of the man taking the initiative. It is clear that the individual's conception of justice and expediency which prompts his action is dictated ultimately by the ideas derived from his group associations. Traditional precedent, sentiments of indignation and horror at the breach of custom, respect for the chief, sensitiveness to public opinion, sympathy for the offender and compassion for his children – all these factors combine to sway the individual in his interpretation and administration of the social controls. But, however close the social determinism of the individual's actions, there is a point of crystallization at which the anthropologist cannot predict the outcome exactly – the individual may decide one way or the other. Here the anthropologist has to give place to the psychologist and join the ranks of the historians, reduced to recording a sequence of events. Retrospective, not prospective, analysis then becomes his task, though he can still predict in terms of 'averages' of behaviour.

The Tikopia material given in this chapter demonstrates how, in an illiterate community with a kinship system of ramifying segmentary groups and a hierarchical class structure, social tension can be resolved and social control exercised. This is done by using as a counter-weight to the predominant representatives of authority – the chiefs – an amorphous set of officials drawn from the existing rank structure, and relying for their authority not on ritual powers but on social prestige and personality. Even public opinion, a control force of considerable effect, uses this feature of the organization. Nascent class conflict is recognized, but is damped down and checked by using members of the dominant class themselves as channels and leaders for expression of the common moral law. A cynic might admire the way in which a ruling class draws the teeth of opposition by making members of their own body 'protectors of the poor' from the exactions of their own kind, and accumulates a moral credit balance thereby. This would be an inverted way of seeing the situation. To all Tikopia, chiefs and people alike, the *maru* are governed by considerations of the common welfare. It is witness to the power of the common people that even the chiefs accept the convention that the *maru* represents the views of the people, and also accept his check on their pronouncements. This may be viewed in terms of a system of complementary forces. The principle is carried still farther in the use made of extra-clan pressures. A chief yields more easily to members of another clan than to his own. It is the fiction of the 'disinterested party', who in fact may be a very interested party in terms of the wider polity. The weakness of the whole mechanism as a regulating agency is that action depends on the personal decisions of the *maru*, and that his conceptions must to some extent be framed in terms of his class interests.

It would seem possible to translate these conclusions into wider terms. Each factor in an authority structure has its own assets, i.e. ability to exercise pressure and reap advantage – in material goods, in social goods (e.g. prestige) or in psychological goods (e.g. the satisfaction of seeing one's own opinion prevail). To separate out these factors and to examine the tension between them, to estimate the comparative advantages they possess and the comparative pressures they exercise or potentially have at command, is part of the business of the sociologist. To view them as systems in equilibrium seems to me to be an unwarranted assumption. In any society at any given time there *may* be such balance attained as to render the comparative pressures fairly even, and action by one factor or group of factors compensated for by that of others. On the other hand, there may not be such balance. To view this lack of balance as simply one stage in a disturbance of equilibrium or as a return to equilibrium seems meaningless, unless one has a vague belief in a sort of political entropy. One might affirm that there can be no equilibrium in any political system except a Spencerian anarchy, and that unless one believes that anarchy will be the result of social evolution, there can be no general trend to equilibrium. There is struggle, there are alliances; there is respect for the existing system and desire to change it; there is obedience to the moral law and attempt to get round it or to reinterpret it to sectional advantage. It is measurement of these forces in terms of a theory of comparative social advantage and relative social pressure that is necessary.

CHAPTER VI

Succession to Chieftainship in Tikopia
(1960)

The institution of chieftainship is basic to the Tikopia political system, and traditionally was one of the key features in Tikopia religious performance. It is of interest then to examine the principles and the process of succession whereby the chiefly roles were filled.

Succession in the social sense is a process of replacement, with public recognition, whereby titles, offices, authority, roles and other indicators of status are transferred from one person (incumbent) to another. Succession may be generational, after the socially active span of the incumbent has been completed by retirement or death, or periodic, after a definite interval. Succession to an office or title is very rarely open to every member of the community, without specific criteria demanded in the candidate; usually it is restricted and involves a sex limitation, qualities of maturity, membership of a given social group, etc. Part of the restriction may be in terms of a kin tie, making the succession hereditary.

In Tikopia succession to chieftainship is generational, restricted to males, and hereditary. It normally takes place only on the death of the incumbent; there is no rotation of office and no recognized provision for retirement (cf. pp. 69–75 above).

Succession to office and position of authority implies a need by the society for continuity of personnel. In any community it is desirable that the machinery for bringing a new official into being should operate as soon as possible in order that authority and social order shall continue unbroken and that essential services shall have their functionary. Where the official has the authority and the multiple functions of a chief it is particularly important that a replacement should be obtained as soon as possible. An interregnum affords opportunities of disorder in the body politic and may leave the group without its representative towards other groups and putatively (in traditional Tikopia) towards the gods. When a vacancy is caused by retirement, planning for succession is facilitated and the timing can be arranged. When the vacancy is caused by death, planning can only be imperfect and the necessity for succession may arise at any time. Succession at the death of a chief calls for some agreed principle of replacement by the society. The gap may arise at any moment, the emotional tension at the death of a man of rank is likely to be considerable, and it is functionally useful to have some mechanism which can be put into action to ensure that a replacement is obtained as soon as possible.

In some societies this issue has not been very clearly met. A period of confusion ensues on the death of a chief, and factional struggles of a violent order may take place until one person emerges as victor in the succession move. In some other societies it has been customary for the announcement of the death of a leader to be conjoined with the proclamation of his successor, presented in advance. '*Le Roi est mort; vive le Roi.*' In Tikopia the system was neither one of confused competition among candidates nor one of automatic succession. It was a somewhat curious system of election, in which the principal role was played by competing 'kingmakers' rather than by competing candidates.

In examining this system in detail, I want first to consider the type of qualities regarded as desirable in a chief by Tikopia society.

QUALITIES DESIRED IN A TIKOPIA CHIEF

If one asks the question, what has been demanded of a chief in Tikopia, what qualities should be possessed, one does not get a neatly rounded formulation of an ideal personality responding to a clearly demarcated set of obligations. The ideal of what a chief should be can only be extracted piecemeal from the judgements of people expressed upon his behaviour in concrete situations, and from isolated statements of principle often arising from these situations. The most explicit generalizations have come not from the people, but from the chiefs themselves and the members of their families, whose consciousness of the chiefly role has been most acute. From my experience in 1928–9 and 1952 it may be said very broadly that all Tikopia held that the chiefs were the guardians of the interests of their people, and that this demanded from a chief certain types of conduct, including abstention from direct injury to his people through selfish motives, and limitations upon his freedom of action where this freedom might be indirectly prejudicial to them. Traditionally this position was correlative with their function as priests, that is, as representatives and intermediaries with the Tikopia gods. The Tikopia chief could be, in theory, a dictator. In practice, his power and authority were subject to limitations imposed by the very character of that authority. The efficacy of the limitations upon him depended to a large extent on his conception of trusteeship.

This conception of responsibility and trusteeship received explicit expression in statements of the chiefs themselves about their own motivations, and in criticism of the actions of other chiefs in such terms. It was also given concrete manifestation in acts where a chief put himself to inconvenience or economic loss for the sake of his people.[1]

In many contexts it was implied that a Tikopia chief should be a mature man, capable of making responsible decisions. The Ariki Tafua described to me in 1952 how his father when very ill looked on his son who had become a man (*ku tangata*) and was ready then to abandon life, in the thought that it was time his son succeeded to the chieftainship. And I think it is significant that although at least one case is recorded of a chief having been elected as a minor there is no case of a chief having been elected *in absentia* – on a sea voyage abroad.

Of the other qualities that were demanded of a chief, one was physical health. If his body was not hale, then he could not serve efficiently as a representative of his people and a medium for his gods. This was exemplified by an Ariki Kafika, Pepe, about nine generations ago, according to tradition.[2] He was said to have been afflicted with severe yaws (framboesia), and therefore to have abdicated in favour of his younger brother, Tuisifo. In comment on this story, one of the senior men of rank in Kafika said, 'If a chief dwells and contracts yaws, then he is put on one side to the rear. He is taken to the rear since he has become bad. Even while the yaws is slight he goes to the rear, because it is an evil thing. When the yaws stands in (the body of) a chief, it is the doing of the gods. It is bad, therefore he is set to one side that another chief that is good may be taken.' The underlying reason for this setting

---

[1] See Firth, 1936; pp. 173, 360; 1939, p. 219; 1959, pp. 259–60.
[2] See Firth, 1936, Genealogy I, p. 347; 1961b, p. 126.

of a chief aside in Tikopia belief was not that the disease itself was physically contaminating or ritually destructive, but that it was a manifestation of the displeasure of the gods towards the chief. There was a suspicion that he had done something wrong. In any case, his power with the gods must have been ineffective, otherwise he would not be suffering. Yet such a general principle was not necessarily carried out in practice. The Ariki Fangarere in 1929, an elderly man, had been afflicted with a debilitating tropical ulcer in his foot for a number of years, but he still carried on his duties as chief, and I heard no suggestion that he ought to retire. He himself had not expressed any wish to abdicate. This may have been due to the fact that he was extremely active in economic and ritual affairs despite his lameness. Occasionally a concession was made to him as when, during the rites of the Work of the Gods, he came by canoe over the lake instead of walking round the shore with his co-chiefs. As I saw in 1952, such a concession could also be made to a chief on account of the weakness of old age. The affliction of the Ariki Fangarere was treated, then, rather as weakness than as fault. Yet that weakness of old age of the Ariki Kafika was regarded as deleterious to the welfare and prosperity of the land was borne out by opinions in 1952.[1]

In addition to physical purity, it was thought that a chief should have a certain moral purity. The ethical side of their religion was not strongly emphasized by the Tikopia, but it was asserted that sorcery should lie outside the province of a chief. In 1929 the Ariki Taumako said to me, 'A chief should continue to dwell beautifully only, to make the *kava*; it is made only for welfare, for food to be good.' The term translated as 'beautifully' could also be rendered as 'in proper style', that is, 'without evil intent'. The sanction given for this kind of behaviour was a reference to the traditional death of the great Tikopia culture hero, the premier deity of the whole community, who was said to have gone sinless to the realm of the gods without revenging himself on his slayer. It was said then that he objected to any 'cursing speech' (*taranga tautuku*), i.e. any formulae of sorcery, by chiefs who in so many rites and activities were said to have been following the model he created. The Ariki Taumako also told me that his father had said to him, 'We who make the *kava*, we follow the one god, the deity of Kafika.' His father instructed him that a

[1] See Chapter III, above.

chief who used sorcery lost his *manu*, the potency of his *kava*; a chief who practised sorcery had done wrong, his *manu* had thereby been directed into sorcery. His *kava* would be efficacious only on occasions of the prescriptive ritual itself. At other times the chief would call on the gods but they would not hear him; they no longer would desire him. Rain would no longer fall at his word, nor would the seas grow calm. As it was by the reputed control of such phenomena that the Tikopia chief was helped in maintaining the good opinion of his people, this belief might act as a deterrent against a chief's misuse of his relation to the gods. In 1929 Pa Fenuatara said, 'If a chief is angry, he scolds only with good speech; he curses by the father (i.e., "May your father eat filth"), but he does not use sorcery.' He added, however, 'It is true indeed, some chiefs are bad.' The Ariki Tafua was cited to me (in private) as one who had caused the deaths of several people and the illness of others by invoking his gods against them, and this was condemned as bad conduct by those who told me of it. Pa Fenuatara went so far as to admit that if his father, the Ariki Kafika, had used sorcery against a man, then, 'He would die indeed; he would not see the night; there would be no delay; he would die on the instant.' But, he said, 'The Ariki Kafika has sympathy for the land, that each stands there in his body of belief. If a man is sick anywhere and the news comes to the Ariki Kafika, he will recite the formula for the man to get well.'

The attitude of the Tikopia chiefs towards sorcery was not one of simple adherence to the traditional ethical code. Where adopted, it was partly in deference to a sense of responsibility and partly through fear of loss of power in ritual directions. Moreover, though given verbal allegiance, either it was disregarded on occasion or there was sufficient lack of faith by the ordinary people in its observance for them to make specific accusations of breach. But in effect such a code of abstinence from sorcery was promulgated among the chiefly families themselves, and that commoners also held it indicated that it was part of the general concept of the duty which the chief bore towards his people.[1]

But correlative with this attitude of responsibility and obligation towards the people of his clan and the community as a whole was the pride of a chief and his family in his position. In his daily life, each chief was continually subscribing to the thesis of his

[1] Cf. Firth, 1959, pp. 311-13.

supremacy and his unique role in his clan. He accepted gifts as a kind of tribute due; he gave largesse as a matter of right; he behaved in ways which in all other men would be described as arrogant; he was quick to criticize the actions of commoners which appeared to him to overstep the bounds of their status; he had outbursts of anger at anything seeming to offer him an affront. Going beyond his immediate personal interests, he spoke in approval of the actions of other chiefs in regard to their clansfolk, maintained their common interests, and on critical occasions was willing to lend his presence and authority in their support. A chief was apt to exemplify his status by special figurative expressions. The Ariki Kafika said to me in 1929, 'I who dwell here am the net-ripping *urua*, the man-eating shark' – comparing himself with the furious fish of the ocean. On another occasion he gave me a further set of metaphors. The Ariki Kafika is 'The mouth of the land, the confirmation of all things, that to which the land listens, the standing chief indeed.' In explaining to me a secret formula, he drew attention to a phrase which occurred in it, 'The deity of the land is one.' This, he said, was the chief who in his power stands over a commoner like a god. If a commoner of his clan disturbs the peace of the land, then the chief will hear him and will make him pay for it. In terms of the social framework, commoners were regarded by the families of chiefs as of minor importance. Pa Fenuatara said to me in 1929, 'The commoner who dwells, his ancestral tale is one, the chief; his deity is not heavy and did not go whither or whither.' This meant that the ordinary clansman had no history or traditional origins apart from those of his chief, which subsumed his. The gods to whom he appealed were of small influence ('light'). They performed no deeds of note which demonstrated their power, nor did they have adventures of that variety or interest which would have entitled them to a particular rank in a spiritual hierarchy.

A chief in relation to commoners, then, was expected to be someone superior, somewhat aloof, capable of fierceness when angered, but compassionate. In the family circle of the Ariki Tafua in 1929 I was given a set of honorific phrases for a chief concerned with his bounty towards his people. He was addressed thus: 'You are a chief who feeds voyaging sons, a chief of sympathetic appeal, a chief who feeds orphan children.' Now it is true that I heard some of these expressions from the lips of commoners and was given examples of songs in which they were used for formal thanksgiving and praise. But it is significant that it was in the family circles of the chiefs that I heard them quoted most.

This stereotype of the ideal of chiefly character and conduct was subscribed to by the commoners, though formulated mostly by the chiefs and their immediate kinsfolk. What was sociologically important about this code was that it put into a moral category conduct which was of practical service in maintaining the position of the chiefs. Up to a point it could be regarded as a realization of the need for putting a halo round autocracy and making the chief serve public interests if he was to exercise his privileges.

An index to the special position of a chief in Tikopia is the care that is taken over the marriage of the potential heir, a chief's eldest son. The history of the marital unions of the Ariki Taumako of 1952, before he became a chief, illustrates this.

As a young man he was first married to a woman of the lineage of Fetauta. The first wife had been the choice of Pa Tarikitonga, the father's brother's son of the young man's father. The choice was taken up by the agnatic kinsmen, but it had never been approved by the husband – he had never gone to her as his mistress. He had never given her betel materials or tobacco. But the woman was brought to him by his kinsfolk according to the traditional custom of *tukunga nofine*. They settled down together, but after a time the young man objected to her, saying she was no good. So she left him and after a while remarried, having as her husband a man of the district of Rofaea. Then the young man married Tauviitevasa, a girl from Akitunu lineage of Namo. He selected her himself, brought her back, the marriage feast was made, and they settled down. But then his present wife came over from Faea alone to him. He had gone to her as his mistress earlier, and it was said it was by the wish of her father, the Ariki Tafua (formerly Pa Rangifuri), that she went to marry him. Her father wished that his daughter should become the wife of the man who in time would be the chief – that she should be sheltered by Taumako. The young man obviously was willing to accept her as his wife and the marriage feast was made. Then the jealousy of the new wife drove out the earlier wife. This woman returned home and remarried, becoming Nau Te Aroaro. She had no child by the young man; she went home pregnant, but nothing was known of the results – possibly she procured an abortion, it was said.

The young man's father, the Ariki Taumako, then still alive, had been impressed by this second wife and was very angry when she was driven out. She was an instructed person who knew how to run the household affairs and in particular to provide food for members of the clan. The third wife, it was said, did not feed the people properly. 'Do you see how we do not go constantly to Motuata?' said my informant in 1952. (Motuata was the principal residence of the chief of Taumako.) 'The place of gathering of this clan from of old is Motuata, the place of assembly of the people. The reason why the brothers of the chief and other people of the clan do not go much to the Ariki Taumako is "because of the woman". One chief is good, another is so-so (na atamai e fefea). His brothers observe and behave accordingly. Each sits in his own house.'

When the first two wives remarried, in each case the men of Sa Taumako formed a party and went over to demonstrate against the marriage. It was held that a woman who had been the wife of a chief or of a potential chief should remain unmarried – even though he had thrown her off! When I protested, my informant made a face and said, 'I don't know, it is the custom of this land.'

The marriage feast of the girl from Fetauta was made in the house of Vangatau, that of the girl from Akitunu in the house of Te Aorere and that of the third wife, who remained as Nau Taumako, in Motuata, the chief's own house. In 1952 the chief's three marriages were not popular with some members of his clan. My informant said, 'We objected – the valuables disappeared, the sinnet cord and the paddles, because he married three times. The valuables and the food of the clan of Taumako and of us, the lineage of Taumako here, just went and went and went. Bowls and paddles were finished.'

Apart from the objection to the triple marriage, two points of importance are embodied in this whole statement. One is that the marital affairs of a chief or even of a potential chief are also the concern of the clan. They regard themselves as entitled to provide him with a wife and bound to protest if that wife leaves him, even although she may have been provoked into doing so. Secondly, the degree of attachment between clan and chief is to some extent dependent upon the hospitality which his wife will exercise. She is responsible for seeing to it that the clansfolk who visit the chief are well received and given food. By her conduct in this respect she can do much to make or mar the reputation of the chief and his relations with his clansfolk, even his close agnatic kin. The interest of the clan in providing the chief with a wife is therefore directly related to the quality of their own future relations with the chief. The Tikopia have no expression equivalent to the African one – 'The chief's wife is the wife of the tribe.' But in effect their behaviour bears much the same significance.

PRINCIPLES OF SUCCESSION

How were such general ideals recognized and put into effect when questions of succession arose? Aristotle laid down three qualifications required for those who have to fill the highest office. These are: loyalty to the established constitution; the greatest administrative capacity; and virtue and justice appropriate to the form of government. Since all these qualities do not necessarily meet in the same person, some selection is necessary. Aristotle advised us to make the choice in the light of the kind of functions the office has to exercise. In selecting a general, for instance, we should choose a man of skill in preference to a man of virtue without skill, since military skill is presumably rare. But we should choose virtue in a man required as a steward, since the administrative capacity required by this office (so he thought) is of a common kind.

In general, the Tikopia way of thinking can be related to Aristotle's conceptions. They have not appeared to feel the need of military skill in the organizational sense. Their leaders in such warfare as they had seem to have been aggressive individual fighters (*toa*) rather than generals. Loyalty to the constitution of Tikopia society might be assumed, since until recent years all Tikopia appear to have shared the same general values and attachment to their way of life, including the traditional social structure. As Westernization has come closer to the Tikopia, the greater interest of some men in modern ways has only just begun to raise the question of basic loyalty as a conscious issue. Administrative capacity the Tikopia have seemed in effect to have disregarded as a criterion for chieftainship – or rather to have assumed (with Aristotle) that all men possess it to a sufficient degree for the office. Moreover, a chief can have good advisers. Virtue they have regarded as an important, though not necessarily final, determinant in selection for office.

This may have been because the Tikopia realistically may have regarded it as simpler to secure virtuous conduct in a chief by demanding it after his election rather than by looking for it beforehand. In other words, with a somewhat cynical view of human frailty, they seem to have placed more reliance on the regulating effect of the social code upon an office-holder than upon any earlier inducement of virtue *per se*. They seem to have attached much more importance to a regular form of succession than to a search for the ideal qualities in the person who would succeed, though such qualities were not ignored. This type of abstract intellectualistic statement is not, of course, that of the Tikopia. It is my inference from the evidence which they produced.

Neither in 1929 nor in 1952 did an actual case of succession to chieftainship in Tikopia occur. But I was given a considerable amount of descriptive data about recent cases, and I had also for consideration the mass of genealogical material about the chiefly lineages of Tikopia. Though this cannot be taken as specifically historical case material, the types of succession there indicated conform to those of very recent occurrence and may be taken as illustrative of Tikopia theory, and probably, practice also.

Succession to chieftainship in Tikopia has been hereditary by descent in the male line. No woman has succeeded to chieftainship,[1] nor has any descendant in the female line. With the exception only of a founding ancestor, no one who was not an agnate in the chiefly lineage succeeded.

Material of succession to Tikopia chieftainship is obtainable from the genealogies of the four chiefly lineages, and comprised by 1952 a total of 49 cases of succession, 13 each in Kafika and Tafua, 15 in Taumako, and 8 in Fangarere. Succession has been of the following order:

Son succeeded in	27	cases
Son's son	3	,,
Brother	5	,,
Brother's son	7	,,
Other agnates	7	,,
	49	,,

[1] The title of *Ariki Fafine* (Female Chief) conferred sometimes upon the senior daughter in the chiefly house of Kafika was a token of ritual status with certain privileges and functions attached, but in no way comparable with the status and functions of the clan Ariki.

The principle of direct hereditary transmission of the office is clear from the material. There was also an emphasis on primogeniture.

In collecting the genealogical material I was told on various occasions that a particular man – usually one lost at sea – had been *te ariki fakasomo*, the 'growing chief', *te pupura*, the 'shoot' or 'seedling', or *te pupura nga atua*, the 'seedling of the gods'. The terms were used in every case only of the eldest son of a chief, and the analogies with growing plants illustrate how the Tikopia look upon the eldest son as the probable chiefly heir.[1] Special treatment might also be given to such an eldest son, as in taking gifts of food to him, 'since he is the coming chief'. Primogeniture was thus the normal Tikopia mode of succession.

In eleven cases of the 27 where sons succeeded, it was the eldest son in birth order; in four other cases an only son succeeded; and in the remainder it was the eldest surviving or the only surviving son, other potential heirs having died meanwhile (commonly lost at sea). No case is recorded where a younger son succeeded his father as chief when his elder brother was still alive. (Only one case is recorded, that referred to already in Kafika, where a younger brother succeeded his elder brother, the latter being alive but ill.) The pattern of filial succession was common to all clans. In Kafika and in Tafua son succeeded father in eight cases out of thirteen, in Taumako in seven cases out of fifteen, in Fangarere in four cases out of eight. In general, where a son did not succeed, the pattern seems to have been to select a brother or other agnate as close as possible to the dead chief. A problem, however, arose at the death of this man – whether he should be succeeded by his own son or whether the chieftainship should revert to the line of his predecessor. Here the Tikopia seem to have adopted the principle of reversion, but not automatically. It seemed to depend upon the relative availability of likely successors in the different lines, and it was here perhaps that the qualities regarded as desirable in a chief came most to the fore as criteria for selection. But succession in the case of brother's sons was for the most part a reversion to an elder line.

In the records of Kafika there appear to be three cases in which reversion to the senior branch did not occur after the succession had been so broken. The first of these was when the chief Pepe,

---

[1] Firth, 1939, p. 190, indicates the economic role of such a potential heir.

who abdicated by reason of disease, founded the house of Tavi. No attempt seems to have been made to seek later chiefs of Kafika from this house. The second case occurred two generations later. The chief, Tanakiforau, had succeeded his father; he was the second son, but his elder brother, Mourongo, *te pupura*, the 'chiefly seed', had died at sea. As Tanakiforau grew old, he was neglected by his sons. They used to go out and procure food, but they did not bring back to him the little delicacies which were due to an aged parent – forest fruits, land crabs, birds. They selfishly ate them in the woods themselves. Seeing this, one of his younger relatives, Vakauke, an adopted child in the house, used to bring him back such things to tickle his palate. This went on for a long time and one day the chief said to the lad, 'When I am gone, that which is hung round my neck shall be yours' – that is, the lad would be given the chiefly necklet of coconut frond which was worn by a chief on ritual occasions. Tanakiforau became ill and was about to die. All his kin assembled. Tereiteata, the Ariki Tafua, was summoned. When he arrived the chief of Kafika was to all appearances dead, but at intervals a long breath still assured the people that he lived. (As a matter of fact, said the Ariki Tafua who was telling me this tale in 1929, the chief really was dead, and it was only the god in his body waiting for the Ariki Tafua to come before leaving the corpse untenanted.) The Ariki Tafua came and asked, 'What did he say? Where is the speech he left?' All replied, 'He has said nothing.' Then he turned to the dying man, now motionless, and said, 'Speak to us, make known to whom the chiefly necklet shall be given.' The body made no sign of life. He addressed it again and again, but there was no response. Then he began to repeat the names of the dying man's sons, but there was no indication from the old chief whether he favoured one or not. The Ariki Tafua recited the names of all the sons and other close agnates and again repeated, 'Tell us who it is that shall have the chiefly necklet.' There was no response. At last he turned and said, 'It is this thieving thing that sits there?' – indicating Vakauke and using a term which is one of contempt. The apparently lifeless body rose, drew up its head in assent, and fell back motionless, now really dead. Thus the succession was confirmed and Vakauke became chief. He was the ancestor of the present line of chiefs who are thus the offshoot of a junior branch of the lineage of Kafika.

Such is the traditional tale, which has certain odd features, including the unusual specification of a successor by a dying chief. It might be interpreted as in part a moral story to influence sons to behave well to their fathers. But the Ariki Tafua told it to me with emphasis upon the political aspect to explain – and to some extent enjoy – the break in the direct Kafika line. I had in fact found it already impossible to ascertain precisely what was the ancestry of Vakauke; the story might have been a reconstruction originating in Kafika clan to bolster up the election of an outsider. Yet, if this were so, one would expect a more direct link in the succession to be given. In the story told by the Ariki Tafua, his own ancestor plays a most important part, and this entry of another chief in facilitating a decision as to the succession is in accordance with traditional rule. The use of the contemptuous term 'thieving thing' by the presiding chief indicates the un-expectedness of the choice. What is not explained is why the choice was left to the expiring chief. It is notable also that in this case the selection of a new chief was regarded as being in effect through a sign from the gods. Since a Tikopia chief traditionally had as primary function the job of serving as intermediary with the gods and at times even as their embodiment, it is interesting that normally no supernatural approval of the human selection seems to have been sought. What this tale suggests is an anomalous succession, probably because there were no obvious candidates available; it is probably significant that, although mention is made in the tale of the sons of Tanakiforau, I was not able to ascertain their names, which is unusual. As a speculation, one may advance the view that this was an instance of virtual ultimogeniture – that the old chief had no sons of proper calibre, that the senior line as a whole had no one outstanding, and that therefore the chieftain-ship devolved upon a very junior agnate actually living with and serving the chief. A member of the senior branch – a great-grandson of the Mourongo referred to above, was in fact chosen as chief of Kafika later. When, however, he died the title reverted to a brother of his predecessor and then to his predecessor's son, and not to any descendant of his own.

In Tafua, the direct line of succession was followed closely. The most marked divergence from it was in the case of the predecessor of the Arika Tafua, whom I knew in 1928-9. This man was an F.F.B.S.S. of his predecessor and the product of a third wife.

When he died, he was succeeded by the eldest son of his predecessor's first wife, and again the direct line resumed.

There was one case, told me by the Ariki Tafua in 1929, where a former chief of Tafua, Moritiaki, attempted to reserve the chiefly office for his younger son. By an Anuta wife he had Taupe. Though the boy was not his eldest, the chief wished him to have the *kasoa*, the chiefly necklet, because by reason of his mother's alien origin, he had no supporting body of kin in Tikopia. His half-brothers, on the other hand, had standing through their kin ties. But when the brothers heard of their father's proposal they were very angry, and all deserted Uta, where their father lived. Seeing this, Taupe was much ashamed at being the cause of so much disruption, and went to live alone in Namo. There he lived for a long time, catching fish, cooking and eating them, and sleeping, all alone. Finally he married there and became the progenitor of the lineage of Akitunu. At last his father summoned him to Uta. There he gave him a little basket of sacred adze blades (*toki tapu*) to carry and they went together to Maunga Faea. There the chief buried the blades in various spots, as 'blocks' (*pipi*) to secure the land for Taupe and his descendants in perpetuity, and ward off any possible encroachment by his brothers or their descendants. After their father's death the eldest of the brothers, Te Urumua, then became chief, but Taupe's economic future was assured.

In Taumako and Fangarere the line of the eldest son was left on one side in a few cases, presumably because there was no available candidate. But it seems that in nearly every case an attempt was made to return to the senior line as soon as possible. In Taumako, where a brother succeeded in three cases, on his death the succession went to a son of his elder brother in two cases and in the other the chieftainship reverted to an elder branch. Where a brother's son succeeded, on his death the succession reverted to the elder branch again. In Taumako, primogeniture with the right of the elder branch to succeed has been the dominant principle; save for the one case of refusal, youth or absence seems to have been the only bar.

Normally, a Tikopia chief is a married man at the time of his election. But this is not an invariable rule. Pakimoana of Taumako was elected while still a child (see later), and Tereiteata succeeded as a bachelor. He was lost at sea before he married and left no descendants, but in accordance with a Tikopia practice of respect to a chief he was given a title, Pu Tafua Lasi, equivalent to that of a married man and an ancestor.

The most outstanding exception to normal succession in Tikopia chieftainship was in the case of Fangarere in recent times. As I discovered in 1952, on the death of the Ariki Fangarere I had known earlier, *two* chiefs of the clan had been elected. This was a clear case of factional interests arising from difference of religion. The elder son of the late chief, personally not very desirable, and a Christian, had been made 'the Chief of the Gospel' at the instance of the Ariki Tafua. The younger son, personally much better fitted for the office, and a pagan, had been made 'the Chief of the Chiefs' by his pagan colleagues. He was the chief of higher status.[1]

Unlike the practice with some African peoples, Tikopia has no provision for a regency. The clan must have a chief as soon as possible after the death of its former leader, and he who leads the clan as chief must have full powers. In the traditional Tikopia society this absence of regency could be correlated with the necessity for the chief to perform ritual functions of direct relation with ancestors and with the understanding that he himself in turn would be incorporated into the ancestral line as an object of spiritual appeal. No one who had not been properly and fully inducted as chief could perform these roles. It might be understood generally that when a chief taken from a junior branch died the succession would probably revert to a descendant of the senior branch. But such a limitation could only be implicit in the Tikopia system. It was not structurally expressed as an explicit limitation; in other words, there were no purely regent's powers.

There is no recorded case of a Tikopia chieftainship ever having been seized by force, though reference is often made in tradition to attempts to seize power as such by violence, and origin tales (Firth, 1961b) speak of contests to gain office. In quasi-historical times certainly, it seems as though the combination of ritual and social sanctions for chieftainship was such that no legitimacy could be expected by such forcible seizure. (Of course such seizure may actually have happened, and been disguised under a story of normal succession, but this is unlikely since the interlocking kinship ties of the other clans would have probably revealed it.)

[1] See Firth, 1959, pp. 280-3.

MECHANISM OF ELECTION

It is curious that in the Tikopia system of succession despite the emphasis upon primogeniture there is no automatic rule by which a designated heir succeeds to a dead chief. No man, even the eldest son, could claim the chieftainship as his in advance. Instead, by a custom which is almost unique in Polynesia, a chief is chosen by what may be called a system of election. In this system the major active role is taken by leading men of clans other than that whose chief has died.[1]

The election takes place as soon as possible after the death of the reigning chief, usually in the midst of the uproar and wailing which begin the funeral ceremonies. The formal token of conferring office upon the new chief is the demonstration of seizing him and raising him into the air in the arms of his selectors. This public elevation is the notification to him of his election. It also serves as a sign to the people at large that the succession has been renewed. Apart from clothing the newly elected chief in a new bark waist-cloth, this is the only ceremonial act that is necessary to accomplish the election. There is no formal ritual induction by which he is introduced to the ancestors or in any other way consecrated to his new work. The choice of the funeral as the place of election has the advantage that it gives the widest publicity to the occasion, since at the obsequies of a chief a large number of people are present from all clans and from all parts of the island. The act of elevation (which may be performed on the person of the chief on other occasions also) is described by the term *sapai* and expresses in symbolic form the lofty status of the chief in regard to the mass of the people. By this act too those who select the chief acknowledge their own formal inferiority to him.[2]

[1] Lack of any heir designated during the lifetime of a chief is not uncommon in Polynesia (e.g., in succession to *matai* titles in Samoa). But the election of a leader of one group by leaders of *another* group seems uncommon. The closest analogy to the practice of Tikopia appears to be in Rarotonga where traditionally F. J. Moss (1894, p. 24) has reported, 'The *ariki* is supreme, but largely controlled by the *Mataiapos* (or nobles). The new *ariki* is named by the *arikis* of the other tribes from the *ariki* family of the deceased's tribe. But the confirmation depends on the *Mataiapos*, as the installation rests with them.' E. Beaglehole cites also from Moss, 'a bitter dispute among the five principal chiefs of Rarotonga over the right of one of them personally to appoint before her death an adopted son as her successor. The remaining chiefs refused to have what they called "a cockroach crawling on their mat"' (1957, p. 115). He also remarks upon the power of chiefs of *Mataiapo* status to elect and control to a large extent the supreme chief of the district in which the *Mataiapo* held land (*ibid.*, p. 169). The system of election is thus still not quite clear from the literature.

[2] Cf. Chapter V, above.

The point of especial note in this proceeding is that the choice and elevation of the chief are done by people whom he does not rule. Since no chief died while I was on Tikopia, I have no first-hand data, but descriptions given to me make the procedure clear. In 1929 the Ariki Kafika described to me how the then Ariki Taumako had been chosen. He said, 'The chief who was living there was taken by me; my chief whom I took. I went where people were crying (i.e. wailing for their chief who had just died). I called out, "Where is my chief?" The crowd pointed with their fingers.' Then the Ariki Kafika went up to the dead man's son, who was wailing for his father near the corpse, and gripped him tight despite his struggles to get free. Then came another man, also a member of the Kafika family, at the back of the Ariki to assist him. The Ariki said, 'Hold your chief and lift him into a man's lap.' He was held fast and raised from the floor while his kinsfolk strove to release him. Such, said the Ariki Kafika, is the general custom at the *sau ariki*, the taking of a chief. The party which has determined on a choice goes in a strong body of kins-folk (*paito soa*) to the house of mourning, and while some hold the man they have selected, the others engage in a rough and tumble with the members of his lineage. 'The body of kinsfolk of the man taken – to be a chief – object to his being taken. Great is the fighting at a chief-taking. When a chief is taken, it's terrific. Folk are struck and the kin of the new chief wail for their son who has been taken to rule.' It must be noted that although a chief making a selection indicates the man to be elevated, he does not himself raise the new chief in his arms. This would be derogatory to his own dignity. The job of elevation is done for him by one or more of his henchmen.

The struggle of the kin of the ruler-elect to dissuade those who would elevate the new chief seems paradoxical. Why should a man's kinsfolk object so strenuously? Why should they want a chief to be chosen elsewhere, as the Tikopia themselves say they do? For this attitude two reasons were given me by the Ariki Kafika. The first was that the body of kinsfolk lose some of the services of their man when he is elected, since he will not go and prepare food as consistently as formerly owing to his new status and obligations. There did not seem to me to be much practical weight in this objection because though a Tikopia chief takes little part in the actual preparation of food, and none at all in the oven work, he does occupy himself in cultivation of the soil, in fishing and in many other economic affairs. Moreover, there are other economic advantages which could compensate for immediate loss of services. The second reason, perhaps more plausible, was that the kin of the chief-elect are afraid lest they be called 'a family wishing to be chief' (*paito fia ariki*) – that is lest they be accused of ambition and greed. Yet both these reasons are probably nominal. The show of resistance seems to be largely a traditionalized move to 'save face'. This interpretation is borne out by the fact that I obtained no record at all of such resistance having been carried to the point of preventing the election altogether.

It is not only the kinsfolk of the chosen man who object. The man himself usually makes some show of avoiding election by struggle or by flight. I was told in 1929 how the then Ariki Kafika ran away when he thought that his election was near and hid on top of a shelf in a house, carefully arranging around himself a number of wooden bowls. But a man discovered him and announced his whereabouts to the crowd. Whereupon the reluctant ariki-elect got down and ran, but was intercepted by outstretched arms; he was caught and lifted up as chief. In this evasion there was quite conceivably an element of shyness at being thrust suddenly into the centre of public attention and at the threat of a radical change in his mode of life. But such conduct is also traditionally dictated as an expression of modesty and is adopted in order to avoid suspicion of a desire to grasp power. The Tikopia is peculiarly sensitive to the reproach of being 'a person wishing to exalt himself' (*tenea fia pasaki*); this simulated refusal of honour is thus in line with the behaviour of his kinsfolk.

Sensitiveness to such a public reproach provides an overt explanation of the anomalous custom of the election of a chief by members of another clan. But while it allows the chief's own followers to preserve a reputation for modesty and reticence, the custom has certain other functions, perhaps equally important, though they are not stressed by the Tikopia themselves. A reference to the persistent conditions of succession will reveal them. It is clear from what has been said already that there is no right of succession to the office of chief. However, certain probabilities are recognized informally in everyday life. Where a chief's eldest son is grown up, married, and has shown himself to be a person of mature judgement and ability, then normally it is assumed that he will be elected on his father's death. In 1929 it seemed almost certain that Pa Fenuatara would succeed the Ariki Kafika and Pa Rangifuri would succeed the Ariki Tafua. When the Ariki Tafua was very ill during my stay, I asked the Mission teacher who would be chief if the old man died. He replied, 'We do not know, but we think it will be Pa Rangifuri.' This prediction was fully borne out. In 1952 I learned that Pa Rangifuri had, in fact, succeeded his father, had died in his turn, and had been succeeded by his own sole remaining son. Similarly, in 1952 it was perfectly clear that all Tikopia expected and indeed desired Pa Fenuatara to succeed his father, the Ariki Kafika.[1] When there is no such obvious heir or when the chief's eldest son is still a child, the system of election by the outside group becomes more than formal. The decision then appears to lie in their hands – literally – as to which of several possible persons shall be chosen. In this case their decision removes from the people of the clan the necessity of making what might be a distinctly individious choice. Alternatively, it removes the possibility of internal disunion within the clan before arriving at a decision. Disagreement and lack of harmony, if there be any, are transferred outside the clan, where there is probably less tendency for permanent resentment to operate and more scope for salving wounded feelings.

The interest of the clan itself may come to expression in one way, when the wishes of a chief as to the succession may be expressed during his lifetime. The Ariki Tafua Pukenga, who had been chief before the Ariki I knew in 1929, had been selected mainly as a stop-gap, since the son of the preceding chief, Fokimainiteni, was still young. Before the death of Pukenga there had been some talk of taking his son, Pa Fenutapu, to succeed him, but to this the old man objected. He urged that his son should be 'given a breathing space', that is, that he should be allowed to remain a commoner in order that he might serve as an executive officer (*maru*) to the descendant in the direct line. Later he might be elected if circumstances pointed that way. In fact, the son of Fokimainiteni was elected and Pa Fenutapu and his descendants 'fell to the rear'. By 1929 they were practically out of the chiefly

---

[1] I am not sure if this happened when the Ariki Kafika died in 1955 since Pa Fenuatara appears to have died about the same time. Pa Fenuatara's eldest son, Rakeivave (Pa Farikitonga) succeeded very shortly after.

class and by 1952 they were completely out of the line of succession, though still important people.

It is not possible to decide in all cases what degree of certainty has in fact been present in the apparently free elective choice. The fact that elections did not take place at random is shown by the case of the Ariki Kafika who hid himself, obviously with the idea that he would be called upon. Moreover, the whole history of succession in Tikopia bears with it the presumption that a mature eldest son of a chief is most likely to be chosen. But the issue does not seem to be quite automatic. When the Ariki Taumako whom I knew in 1929 had been elected, the Ariki Tafua was not present. He came later on the scene and it was said became very angry that the issue had been decided. It was held that he had wished that Pae Avakofe, younger brother of the deceased chief, should be taken. It is recorded that he uttered a series of whoops to express his exasperation at having been forestalled. But it was too late. Tikopia custom is definite that once the formal elevation has taken place the succession is irrevocably accomplished. To give effect to any view or to assert any personal interference, it is essential to arrive soon after the death of the former ruler. Yet in the complex workings of Tikopia politics, the action of the Ariki Tafua may not have been a genuine protest. Pae Avakofe was the most respected and influential man in Tikopia. Rather earlier Pa Veterei, the eldest son of Pae Avakofe, had been noted for his physical strength and great influence throughout the land. It was alleged that he had allowed it to be known that he should be taken as the next Ariki Taumako. Actually, so I was told, there was a misconception here. The chiefly family of Kafika, talking together one day privately in their house Mapusanga, had agreed to take the son of the old chief – the man actually chosen later by the Ariki Kafika. But in order to placate Pa Veterei, who it was thought might otherwise have felt aggrieved, it was agreed also by the Kafika people to make some show of gripping him, though not in fact actually to raise him aloft. This was 'to make his face good' (*fakamatamata laui*). In typical Tikopia fashion, news of this decision reached the old Ariki Taumako through one of his daughters in a garbled version – that the Kafika folk were planning to make Pa Veterei chief. The old man was angry. He said, 'Will they allow my son to sit while they take someone from the rear?' – meaning will they neglect the son in favour of the junior branch. Whereupon, it is said, he appealed to his gods and caused Pa Veterei to be poisoned at sea by eating *sumu*, a species of fish, so that he died. This was one *post hoc* explanation of the death of this man; it was given me in 1929 by Pae Sao, a prominent ritual elder. This incident indicates how the Tikopia recognize the possibility of a powerful man of rank aspiring to the chieftainship, although not the most direct heir. Pa Veterei was probably innocent of political ambition. But whether or not he had designs on the chieftainship, popular opinion credited him with some personal interest in the succession. At the time of the death of the Ariki Taumako Pae Avakofe might have been thought to have had some thoughts of the succession. The need for salving wounded feelings is well recognized by the Tikopia. Some concession is often made by a feint. The action of gripping a person as if to elevate him implies that though he just missed selection he is of such great importance that his claims are very seriously considered. Hence, though he may be disappointed, he need not be affronted. Now it is possible that the action of the Ariki Tafua in whooping when he found that he had been forestalled and that Pae Avakofe had not been elected may have been of this feint type. The *fait accompli* might actually have suited him, but his protest was a formal compliment to Pae Avakofe, perhaps still grudging his son's death and still acknowledged to be the most powerful man in Tikopia apart from the chiefs.

Actual competition for the chieftainship is almost unknown. It seems to be possible for a man to indicate privately that he would like to be considered. But a powerful factor operating against any very active move by a candidate is the fear of incurring public reprobation and of prejudicing the chances of his election thereby. I have on record only one instance of such competition – for the chieftainship of Taumako five generations ago. In 1929 the Ariki Tafua told me how Pu Veterei, the chief of the clan a century before, had been lost at sea. His son Pakimoana was still a child, so young that he had not yet donned a waist-cloth – that would be under about ten years of age. Pu Nukuraro, a strong man of Kafika clan, when the news of the death came, took the child and put round his waist the *riri*, the ceremonial bark-cloth which a chief wears on ritual occasions and with which he is invested on his election. He then called out to the assembled people, 'There is your chief.' But Pu Kavasa, a man of the chiefly house of Taumako though not in the direct line, had already put a new waist-cloth on himself as a sign that he had nominated himself as chief. When he heard the announcement he replied propitiatingly, 'I shall sit like this in a dwelling of chiefs, to eat in advance some food for myself; when I die then your offspring shall be lifted into the dwelling place.' In other words, he was rather optimistically offering himself as a stop-gap, pleading in effect for a concession, a kind of notional regency. But he was rudely pushed aside by Pu Nukuraro and the child was accepted as chief.

As competition for the chieftainship is almost unknown, so also is effective refusal of the honour. I have only one case recorded. When Fakatonuara, the Ariki Taumako five generations ago, died, his son Vakasaua did not wish to succeed and advised that the ritual necklet, which is the symbol of chieftainship, be offered to his father's brother. 'Give it to be hung upon him', he said. It was suggested to me that times were then troublous and that he probably felt that he was not strong enough to assume the burdens of office. It is clear then that as far as personal succession goes, a man can refuse election but not secure it.

The descendants of Vakasaua, though senior in kinship to the Taumako chiefly line, from then on counted as inferior in rank. They formed the lineage of Maneve or Resiake. Such a superseded branch did not retain any ritual primacy. They worshipped their own ancestors, but the chief performed the major lineage and clan rituals.

What are the reasons which influence the people who make the selection? Most general seems to be satisfaction in the exercise of power and of making decisions. In the different generations strong men seem to have taken part in more than one election. For example, Pu Nukuraro, who selected the Taumako chief, was also said to have been responsible for the election of Tereiteata, a chief of Tafua. Linked with this is satisfaction in taking the public credit for being responsible for making a chief. The proprietary words of the Arika Kafika quoted earlier illustrate this. But in addition there may be other factors of personal interest. There is no specifically recognized bond of any formal character between the new chief and the people who have elected him. He does not thank them in any way, acknowledge their service by gifts, nor does there seem to be any permanent tie of sentiment between them of the order of bond-friendship. But in particular cases it is possible for some benefits to be secured, taking advantage of the kinship structure. The Ariki Tafua in 1929 made the significant statement to me that people desire to get a maternal nephew made chief. 'They strive that the *tama tapu* (sister's son) may be lifted, they pull him up; because the dwelling place becomes powerful.' He did not specify exactly in what respect, but from the general pattern of the relationship it is clear that possibilities of increased prestige, of influencing the chief's decisions and even of some economic advantage, may be involved. Apart from this, traditionally there was a gain in the religious sphere in that the name of the chief, after his death, could be invoked in the *kava* of his mother's people. This was not to the Tikopia an illusory advantage.

But this choice of a chief on the basis of the personal advantage of the selectors must be subordinated to other factors. In selecting the Ariki Taumako of 1929, for instance, the Ariki Kafika did not choose a maternal nephew of his own but of Tafua, and the Ariki Tafua, in wishing to elect Pae Avakofe, was sponsoring a nephew of Rarovi lineage, of Kafika. On the basis of personal advantage it would have seemed to be more in the interest of the Ariki Kafika to sponsor Pae Avakofe who was married to a woman of his own lineage, since he would thus secure as chief a brother-in-law as well as a man who was a *tama tapu* of the lineage of his clan. Moreover, the Kafika lineage would have been the 'mother's brothers' of the son of Pae Avakofe if he in turn succeeded. The choice of Pa Veterei by the Kafika house would have fulfilled this condition – but as mentioned earlier he was rejected by them.

The other factors of greater weight are the personal qualifications of the candidates and in particular their specific status in terms of seniority in the lineage. As discussed earlier, no member of a commoner lineage, however high be his rank, can become a chief. Again, the Tikopia principle is that if the ancestor from whom a collateral member of the chiefly house traces his descent was never himself a chief, then the eligibility of this collateral member is very greatly decreased. He is 'cast to one side' as the Tikopia say. The principle of legitimacy is clearly that of primogeniture or the nearest substitute.

When the issue of succession is so closely defined by principle, why then is it not assumed as automatic rather than taking the nominal form of selection from a body of candidates? Considering the formal character and high degree of integration of the religious structure of the Tikopia community, it would be plausible to think that on the death of one chief another would automatically succeed him by religious rule. The apparent freedom of the system of selection requires for its interpretation some further consideration of the relations between the chief and the people of the clan whom he represents, and of the Tikopia community as a whole.

The Tikopia system of social control is expressed at one level in terms of the individual fiat of the chief, and there is no co-ordinating central authority to resolve possible conflicts between the chief and his followers – or indeed between chiefs themselves. In practice, however, the actions of a chief are in fact restrained by those of other people of rank both within and without his clan; they express by their behaviour a general body of opinion. This practical control of a chief's idiosyncrasies appears to be reflected in the means whereby his power is conferred upon him. He does not succeed automatically by divine right. If he did, it might be more difficult to check any assertion of his individual attitudes. But he is elected, and not even by his own clan. He receives the mandate of a chieftainship, he cannot claim it. There is then some case for the control of the chief by people even outside his clan. I do not mean to say that the situation is viewed by the Tikopia very consciously and in a sophisticated way from this sociological angle. But blunt statements that 'a chief is made by the body of the land' – as the Ariki Tafua said to me in 1929 – express the essence of this view. Pa·Maneve in 1952 said to me, 'An expression of opinion from of old, from the gods, is that the chief was taken by the body of the land to watch over the body of the land. If a man is hungry, the chief feeds him. If a man is evil, the chief will speak to him. Whatever may be wrong with the land, the chief will speak of it that the land may be good.'

In the Tikopia system, election of the chief is by proclamation and public acclaim, not by any process of choice by voting. The system allows room for a certain amount of power politics, for the operation of factional interests. These assert themselves not so much perhaps in the struggle to raise competing candidates to the chieftainship as in some competitive urgency to reach the scene first and have the credit of elevating the obvious candidate. The occasional incidence of debatable cases when the succession is not

clear serves to reinforce the general principle that election as
chief is dependent upon the will of the people and not upon an
automatic right.

I conclude by a few observations on the effects of the election
upon the man mainly involved. The election of a man as chief
means an abrupt change in his social condition. He has been a
'common man' until now. At one stroke as an *ariki* he is invested
with a new set of privileges and becomes responsible for a complex series of ritual duties. It is not possible for me to describe in
detail how such a man behaves upon this lightning assumption of
power, since I saw no election, but one may assume that the
embarrassment which he must feel is mitigated to some extent by
a useful mechanism. This is the conventional practice of the other
chiefs of taking him aside and giving him instruction in ritual
matters and sometimes also private advice. This coaching in new
duties is not automatic and is never extensive. But on his election
other reigning chiefs regard it as part of their responsibility to see
that the newcomer to their ranks is versed in the ceremonial of
his clan. According to tradition, they gather together and question
him about his *kava* – not as an examination to put him to the
proof, but in order to assist him if his knowledge is faulty. This is
known as *te fuatanga o paito ariki* (the dirge of chiefly lineages), I
was told by the Ariki Kafika in 1929. The separation of the new
chief from his former associates is helped by certain other mechanisms. The change in his status is symbolized linguistically. He at
once assumes a new title, that of the leader of his clan; he drops
his former house name and takes that of the clan as a whole. Thus,
he who was once Pa Teve became Pa Kafika. He who was Pa
Rangifuri became Pa Tafua. He who was Pa Raniniu became Pa
Taumako. Such a new name may well help in the creation of a
new social personality. In it, too, is implicit the idea that the chief
is the head or father of his clan since he bears the collective name
as part of his title. In kinship, too, some change occurs. The chief
tends to be called 'father' more widely than heretofore, and
frequently the kinship term is qualified as 'chiefly father'. For
instance, in 1929 I heard the eldest son of the Ariki Taumako,
speaking of the Ariki Kafika, say 'Chiefly father is right' (*e tonu
e pa ariki*). Such an expression conforms to the ordinary usages of
kinship and still preserves something of the special dignity of the
chief. The series of personal taboos involving a bodily segregation

of the chief from commoners and respectful behaviour by them towards him must tend also to assist the chief in adapting himself to his changed position.

Moreover, the transition cannot be always unexpected. Granted that no man has absolute certainty of succession, but a chief's eldest son if mature may be reasonably sure of it. When such a man is obviously in the line of succession, then his father and other men usually instruct him in the details of chiefly behaviour and especially in the lore of the gods – ritual, formulae and mythology. Moreover, he will have been trained in the exercise of responsibility and in the recognition that a chief has obligations as well as privileges.

Now that after 1956 all the chiefs of Tikopia have become Christians, they are no longer able or necessary to carry on the performance of the traditional religion and take responsibility ritually for the welfare of the land. But the Tikopia chief appears still to be a cultural symbol in general to his people and to have a primary responsibility for social order. The principles of succession to this office will presumably, therefore, remain of significance for a long time to come.

A problem of some delicacy may arise if the chiefs are made instruments of administration by the British Solomon Islands Protectorate Government. In such case the administrative requirements of efficiency might seem to point to the advisability of succession of a man as chief who would not necessarily be chosen by the traditional process of election. It is difficult to predict the outcome of such a situation. But a discreet and private sounding out of local opinion, especially among the other chiefs, would seem prudent at an early stage if the government interest in the succession were strong. In general the respect which the chiefs show to public opinion might well inhibit them from acting as very effective innovators of policy on behalf of the government, if any procedure of 'indirect rule' were adopted. On the other hand, deference of the people to chiefly authority might give a council of chiefs an even greater power than at present.[1]

[1] Cf. Firth, 1959, p. 297.

PART II
MEANINGS AND VALUES

Introductory Notes

Philosophically the idea of meaning is a difficult one. Argument about how far the principle of verification must be used as a criterion of meaning, and not only as a criterion of truth, may now have lost its force. But there is still plenty of room for difference of opinion. Outside the philosophical sphere the word meaning, as Ayer has pointed out, is commonly used in a variety of senses, some of which may allow a statement to be meaningful even although it is neither analytic nor empirically verifiable.[1] Modern linguists and linguistic philosophers have dealt from various points of view with the meaning of discourse – sentences, propositions or other statements of a verbal order. For social anthropologists semantic problems are presented in two orders of analysis – verbal and non-verbal contextualization – which have been as yet but loosely linked. Sociologically, the ascertainment of meaning has been indicated by Ayer[2] as an empirical inquiry concerning the *psychological effect* (my italics) which the occurrence of certain symbols has on a certain group of people. At this 'commonsense' level the meaning of a social action must then be concerned primarily with identification of the observed behaviour leading to or arising from the act in question. Social anthropologists are concerned not so much with the psychological or mental effects – though their existence must be presumed – as with those effects which can be studied by reference to overt behaviour in words and in non-verbal acts. Moreover, such overt behaviour is interpreted as being that of individuals in social relationship.

In social usage it may be difficult to distinguish the notion of meaning from that of value. Dictionaries tend to equate 'meaning' with 'significance', and although some philosophers may separate these two for their own purposes (e.g. as Bertrand Russell calls 'significance' what Carnap has called 'meaning'),[3] it seems convenient for us to retain such a general equation. This implies that

---

[1] Ayer, 1946, pp. 15, 69; cf. Russell, 1940, pp. 306 *et seq.*
[2] *Op. cit.*, p. 69.   [3] Russell, *op. cit.*, p. 306.

in considering meaning we are concerned with a system of signs or clues to behaviour. These may be 'signs proper' – any direct or intrinsic relation between elements in an action situation – or they may be any arbitrary or indirect relation of a symbolic order.[1]

Individuals in society solve many of their problems in a straightforward, material, economic sense, balancing comparative advantage in realistic terms. Many of their acts, therefore, have meaning for them and for others in these terms, and radical changes in the economic and political forms of a society may result therefrom. Some of their problems, however, either defy solution in this way or present to them sacrifices which they feel unable to bear. Some problems remain unsolved, but others they cope with in a figurative, symbolic form. Here meaning, as Lévy-Bruhl has emphasized, lies in an emotional rather than an intellectual apperception of relationships by the people concerned. It is ascribed socially and individually to objects and actions of which the significance is not identifiable by the observer through reference either to generalized human experience or to the environmental situation. The meaning is much more specific to the social situation. Social anthropologists are concerned with 'making sense' of what are often alien modes of behaviour. They try to understand such symbolic meanings comparatively in their human, social context, and to explain them. By 'explanation' here one does not imply necessarily a specific cause in individual terms; one implies rather a demonstration of the relation between phenomena in the particular social system. As I have stated in Chapter, IX there may be no way of ascribing meaning beyond the closed system, but within this its behaviour can be 'explained' in so far as it can be given a social context.

In the use both of signs and of symbols, value elements are involved. The notion of value involves that of comparison, an estimate of worth relative to something else. (What are termed 'ultimate values' are considered to be of greater, even immeasurably greater, worth than any others.) The notion of value then is connected with the notion of standard, whereas the notion of meaning need not so be connected.

I do not wish unduly to split apart these two conceptions for anthropological usage. But I think there is convenience in using

[1] Cf. Parsons, 1949, pp. 636–7; Firth, 1951, p. 176.

the term *meaning* for the identification of social actions by their context in the broadest sense, and in using the term *value* for the referential norms by which meaning is judged – implicitly if not explicitly by the people concerned. For example, in Chapter V I have described how the Tikopia, to force an issue of public policy, may seize their chief and raise him from his seat into the air. While he is thus lifted they pay him the greatest signs of respect, pressing their noses to his knee and to the sole of his foot, while they implore him to yield to their request. The meaning of this act is complex. It cannot be understood only by reference to the physical positions of the actors and their statements to one another at the moment. It embodies a sense of respect paid to the chief by the people who abase themselves before him. But it includes also an element of duress; a hint that the chief may have to stay in this awkward though honorific position until he yields to the public request. The act then is not just a token of respect, it is also a mode of constraint. But these meanings are not all separate and individual. They are linked in operative relationship to form a unitary conception – that the people want their chief to yield to their views. The values to which this set of linked meanings may be referred are themselves part of a system: they include the values attached to status of a chief in the Tikopia polity; the values implied in the outward signs of lowering one-self to indicate inferiority in a social relationship; and the values expressed by exile in punishment of offences which outrage public sentiment.

In social anthropology meanings and values are methodologically significant at the individual as well as at the collective level. Our basic aim is the understanding of collective forms of expression, but meanings and values must be individually interpreted, transmitted and acted upon. In a society many values at the collective level seem to be shared in their forms of expression by all members. But the situation is not necessarily uniform; there may be variation and even conflict between sectional values. Even where this is not so, it is still necessary to study the working out of problems in individual terms. The codes which regulate behaviour may be uniformly accepted as proper throughout the community. But situations often arise in which if one code is accepted another must be rejected. This is illustrated, for instance, in Chapter IV, which examines the implication for social behaviour of persons confronted by choice between agnatic code and affinal code. Each is regarded as obligatory in the appropriate circumstances; the problem is for the individual to decide whether his particular changed circumstances are appropriate for the one or the other. It is relevant for social anthropologists to know the reasons why one code rather than the other is selected, and to be able to understand why sets of people behave to one another in a certain way in line with the consequences of a personal decision. I do not think such analyses in social anthropology can be omitted, or simply dismissed as 'psychology'.

The same method of social contextualization can be applied to the study of behaviour which is often classed as irrational. The irrational is not necessarily unintelligible. It is behaviour which cannot be supported by reason at the overt level of statement. But the notion of reason or rationality, however much a subject of argument, is generally held to refer to a perception of the operational relation between ends and means, in particular applying to the kinds of relationship which fit the conception of methods of modern empirical science. In this sense the irrational may refer to behaviour which ignores this type of relationship and tries to draw inferences which are unwarranted by the logical implications of the assumptions. A rather different type of behaviour, which has been termed by contrast non-rational, relates to different kinds of assumptions about the nature of reality. In the last resort these assumptions cannot be checked by empirical science. But action in the selection of such assumptions is not simply random. It may be often shown to conform to some type of problem situation, individual or collective. Although a non-rational assumption may be proclaimed to be a mystery, such assertion in itself can have meaning in a social system of meanings.

I hold that it is part of the function of a social anthropologist to examine the non-rational in terms of the social situations in which its conceptions are operative. To tackle this problem in the field of religion, including mysticism, is in my view an integral part of the study of social organization and of values in the widest sense. I have, therefore, included in this volume some of my most general essays on these themes.

The essay which opens this section falls broadly into the 'value' category. Although it lies in a field well worked by anthropologists, it embodies some propositions and speculations that are of more general relevance. This illustrates one of the variety of tasks which may fall to the lot of an anthropologist. For the meeting of the Sixth Congress of the Universities of the Commonwealth at Oxford in 1948, it was decided to have, 'A critical review, from the points of view of an historian, a philosopher and a sociologist, of the structural and moral changes produced in modern society by scientific and technical advances'. I was invited to participate and appear in lieu of an historian. Despite some misgivings, I accepted because it seemed to me that there were certain things that an anthropologist from his field experience was entitled to say on this theme. My own contribution was preceded by that of a philosopher, who deplored the technological obsession which he saw as having gripped Western culture, but argued that many structural and moral changes of today were due not to science but to the decay of humanist philosophy. We were followed by an economist of broad interests, who discussed the danger to freedom of thought in the tradition of Western civilization through the influence of science and technology and the mechanization of knowledge. The results were published in the Proceedings of the Congress (1951, pp. 101 et seq.).

The references in the essay to a 'colonial situation' may now seem of less significance than they did at that time, when even in British circles the immediate economic claims and ultimate autonomous roles of colonial territories were not generally accepted premisses of public policy. Two years earlier, to a mixed audience of academic and overseas administrative experience, I had felt myself to be rather challenging in stating that the condition of colonial societies should be regarded as an historical phase. 'Whatever the length of the road, the colonial phase is a transient one. The concept of Colonial Societies is therefore not a basic sociological one; that is, it is not grounded in any theory of the ultimate nature of these groups as such. There are other qualities of societies which are more deep-rooted and less capable of change than political status' (Firth, 1946). But much of what is said of 'colonial' societies still applies also to other technologically backward communities which are politically independent.

What I would add to this essay were I now to rewrite it is a reinforcement of the argument about the need for a firmer choice of goals. In the Western world over the last decade or so productivity has been rising, and so have personal incomes and general standards of consumption. So much has happened on the consumer front that the phrase 'standard of comfort' is now tending to replace 'standard of living'. Yet modern machine technology is not only a terrific producer; it is an ever-increasing consumer of resources. Even that great technological giant the United States of America has begun to feel the pinch of attempting to strive equally in all fields of scientific achievement at once. In Western countries which lack a centralized State-directed plan for the utilization of scientific resources, the choice between all-out research in the physical sciences – whether for industrial or military ends – and other forms of research, including social inquiry, is openly becoming more pressing. (It may be equally so in a state-controlled system.) In the societies which are developing from technological backwardness the choices are of a different kind but are none the less significant – whether, for example, for prestige reasons to set up a national airline instead of a new college of technology. But in all cases some choice must be made, even if it is for inaction in the face of a specific problem.

Anthropologists are concerned with the values by which, explicitly or implicitly, the choices are made, and the types of structure that arise in the society making the choices. In such an analysis an anthropologist himself is not necessarily committed to any particular position. It is assumed that he prefers knowledge to ignorance, technical advance to technical backwardness, higher personal incomes to lower incomes, and so on. But what cannot be assumed is that as an anthropologist he has any particular brief for any form of social system as against another, for monogamy over polygamy, for patrilineal inheritance over matrilineal, or even for the forms of democracy over those of an autocratic regime. Every anthropologist has his own personal standpoints in these matters. But his endeavour must be not to let his personal standpoint blind him to the implications of his analysis.

An anthropologist cannot of course avoid value judgements. It is evident too that his value judgements enter into his selection of problems for examination, the specific kind of material he collects and the form in which he presents his generalizations. But in the field in which he is making his observations and drawing his conclusions he is 'value-free' in the sense that he is not committed in advance to any of the value schemes which are assumed by the various other protagonists. Earlier it was often assumed that an anthropologist necessarily shared all the values of the other representatives of the society of which he is ordinarily a member, and that he would therefore concur without question in their views on local custom or development needs. Nowadays the boot may be on the other foot, and the anthropologist is expected by local politicians to conform to their views about the developing structure of the society. His citation of local custom may be stigmatized as an unfair presentation to the outside world, revealing weaknesses where he should indicate strength. It is difficult for a social anthropologist to remain uncommitted, at least overtly, to such assumptions, and to keep free to draw his own conclusions in the light of his own perceptions of what he has observed. Even if he feels himself committed to the aims of the new society, his problems of critical evaluation of develop-ments are not likely to be less.

The study 'Social Changes in the Western Pacific' (Chapter VIII) began as a paper read to the Commonwealth Section of the Royal Society of Arts on 12 March 1953. It was published in the *Journal* of the Society (vol. CI of 2 October 1953). The essay was an attempt to state in a succinct form what seemed to be some of the most significant trends; it was also intended to present the situa-tion of reaction to Western influence in terms of positive achieve-ment, not simply of cultural loss and breakdown. In 1951 and 1952, in my visits to New Guinea and to the Solomon Islands, I had been much impressed by the signs of development, not merely in the technological field but also in new forms of associa-tion, and in more far-reaching political interests. At the same time, in a paper published soon afterwards on the social structure of two New Guinea communities (Firth, 1952), I tried to estimate the degree of retention of traditional social alignment by Koita and Mailu communities in the forty years or so since C. G. Seligman and B. Malinowski respectively studied them. I pointed out that, despite radical innovations in material culture and technology, and much realignment in forms of economic associa-tion, the people in both communities were maintaining symbolic systems which expressed values of their own, additional to what they received and incorporated from European culture. Other more extensive studies in the same areas, e.g., by W. E. H.

Stanner, H. I. Hogbin, C. S. Belshaw and M. C. Groves, have analysed this situation in much more detail. The relation between the traditional forms, modifications of them, and the forms of modern introduction is one of constant interest to a social anthropologist. Amid the general trend towards social and economic development there seems to be also a modified conservation of traditional social resources. In groups, especially minority groups, exposed to and themselves utilizing and contributing to the forces of radical technical, economic and political change, as these changes become intensified a kind of defence mechanism comes into operation. There is a growing tendency to maintain and develop interest in traditional cultural forms, and even to invent new practices based on traditional themes, as a part of a symbolic representation of the people's desire to preserve a social and cultural individuality.

The essay 'The Study of Values by Social Anthropologists' (Chapter IX) was delivered first as the Marett Lecture before the Rector, Fellows and Scholars of Exeter College, Oxford, on 6 June 1953. Since this essay was originally published the study of values by social anthropologists has explored the subject much further, in particular in the project termed 'The Comparative Study of Values in Five Cultures' (informally known as the Values Project), undertaken by the Harvard University Laboratory of Social Relations. Publications by Rapoport (1954), Watson Smith and Roberts (1954) and Florence Kluckhohn and Strodtbeck (1961) have given a rich documentation and analysis from this field, while the theoretical framework by Ethel M. Albert (1956) has given a most useful classificatory scheme. Although value studies by anthropologists are perhaps less fashionable now than when Redfield wrote (1953, p. 141) nearly a decade ago, I think the case for them still stands, provided that they are specifically linked with studies of social structure, and of variant social operations by different sectors of the society. But a good deal of very useful study of values has been done under other heads, as in recent anthropological studies of religion.

The essay 'Problem and Assumption in an Anthropological Study of Religion' (Chapter X) was delivered as a Huxley Memorial Lecture before the Royal Anthropological Institute on 27 November 1959. It was first published in the *Journal of the Royal Anthropological Institute*, vol. 89, pp. 129–48. In this essay I attempted to formulate the general kind of approach which, as I see it, every social anthropologist must make to the study of religion. My own personal approach is also stated therein and will, I think, be especially clear from consideration of the last three chapters together.

Chapter XI, 'Religious Belief and Personal Adjustment', was originally delivered as the second Henry Myers Lecture before the Royal Anthropological Institute on 11 May 1948. Its argument is part of my general view about the nature of religion, and I would draw attention particularly to those passages towards the end where I stress the need for a theory of religion to take account of the possibility of change in belief. (My emphasis upon the disintegrating as well as the integrating force of religion for society ran counter to Radcliffe-Brown's Henry Myers Lecture three years before.)

The essay on mysticism, originally published in the *Rationalist Annual*, 1950, pp. 49–61, is an extension of the general viewpoint put forward in my Henry Myers Lecture. Since the essay deals primarily with religious mysticism as known to the West, and was a very general study, I did not think it necessary to cite the well-known materials, given for example by William James, Evelyn Underhill and the individual mystics themselves. If I were now to rewrite this article I would not alter this basic standpoint, but I would wish to include much additional material to give point to my argument. In particular, I would like to examine sociologically the position of Rulman Merswin and the Friend of God in the Oberland, which raises a very fascinating problem of the relation between idealism and personal integrity, and the externalization of authority, exposed by Denifle and Jundt and re-examined by J. M. Clark. I had not then seen Orr's work on Dadu or Martin Buber's on Hasidism, nor Scholem's great study, which was first published in England in 1955.

My reference to Lévy-Bruhl may look harsh, but in the light of his own *Carnets*, published shortly before, my statement was not inappropriate. Writing specifically on mystical experience among primitive peoples, he himself distinguished his field of study from religious mysticism of a Western type which, he said, was something very different. I did not, therefore, refer to his work. At the same time, as I have indicated, studies of the kinds of experience characteristic of shamans, spirit mediums and others having dreams and visions, indicate how, as with the more conventional mystics of the great religions, personal experience of an ecstatic quality can be a constructive force in a religious field, giving avenues for development and change in the system.

CHAPTER VII

Structural and Moral Changes Produced in Modern Society by Scientific and Technological Advance

(1948)

This address is concerned with a critical evaluation of structural and moral changes. Such a review implies a standard, which can only, I think, be a personal one. For this discussion I am prepared to assume, rather dogmatically, and, I am afraid, very loosely, that this standard must have a social referent. How far do the changes which we are discussing affect the ultimate stability and harmony of society and how far do they contribute to a system of social justice or a system allowing creative freedom to the human individual? Broadly speaking, those are the criteria that I want to apply.

Modern science, as we know, has become a social force. It is not simply a process of dispassionate systematic inquiry and a body of refined knowledge. Its achievements have given it authority, and in popular eyes it has a mystical and almost a magical value. By holding to its technical standards, it has a moral value also in its own sphere. What are the results, then, where the power of science over men is translated into the power of technology?

It is quite clear that a new technology must mean in many ways a new structure of social relations. A factory system, mechanization, obviously means a concentration of human effort, a special organization of workers' lives. Whether they live in slum or in garden city, their linkage with an industrial technology governs not only their employment but also their family life, their recreation, and even their political and their religious ties. It is not merely a local influence. Modern technology draws its raw materials from all over the world. It creates a commercial structure of an international type, with its roots in the daily activities of even the most remote and primitive peoples. I wish to speak of this later, but first I want to say something about the relation of morality to science.

The function of morality is to sanction social relations, so it is easy to assume, I think, that new technical and social structures produce new moral rules. The technological drive for the raw materials of industry gives a direct incentive to the emergence of moral ideas. Development not only gets prizes for efficiency and industry; it also gets moral approval. Reducing nature to the service of man is a sacred task. Peasant peoples who resist having their lands disturbed for the extraction of gold or other minerals are not simply short-sighted economically; they are held to be wrong morally; they are the enemies of progress. The ability to control breeds ideas about the rightness of control. Economic security has been often approved, as Jane Austen illustrated it, by the conversion of property into gentility. The rugged individualism of the earlier stages of industrial capitalism found its justification not only in the economic doctrine of *laissez faire* but also in the moral precepts of wealth and high station as a calling and blessing of God, requiring as a makeweight no more than a measured charity. It is true that personal conduct and class ideals did not by any means always coincide in this respect. As a Scottish clergyman has put it, 'The Almighty is obliged to do many things in his official capacity that he would scorn to do as a private individual.'

How far do science and technology really produce a new morality? Scientists are part of an organization, society, and this conditions the use they make of their instrument. The confused and conflicting aims and values of men, their personal and social background of experience, dictate what shall be done with the products and potentialities of science. Tawney has pointed out that what makes modern industry is not the machine but the brains which use it and the institutional framework in which it is set. Only in a broad way, then, can any set of moral ideas be said to be produced by a scientific or technical system. If we are looking for an antithesis, we might argue that scientific and technological developments themselves originate in and are governed by moral attitudes. Moral approval of intellectual curiosity and of attempts to increase man's command over nature have led science on at every step. Scientific and technical development may be canalized by moral rules associated with a religious system. Historically, the watchful eye kept by religion over science needs no documentation here.

This means that I see difficulty in trying to isolate precisely what moral changes are produced by scientific and technological advance. The relations between morality and science are reciprocal. Morality is as much the guardian of the tree of knowledge as of its fruits. For this reason I have felt that I cannot try to interpret the subject of this discussion too narrowly.

How closely are our technical and our moral systems integrated? The essence of morality is action according to principle. This means the possibility of choice in conformity with what is believed to be right, or selection on the basis of balance of advantage. Nowadays is it principle that we lack or capacity for choice? It may be argued that we have enough moral blue-prints to enable us to use science and technology in conformity with what we regard as our ends, if we can only define them. Two thousand years of philosophy, Eastern and Western, pagan and Christian, have surely given us enough in the way of moral concepts and moral rules for action to confront any development of science. It is not a new moral outlook that is needed; it is decision to abide by the ideals that we already have. Colloquially, it is not goals but guts that are required. Attainment of one end means sacrifice of others. The Western world is in a quandary today not for lack of moral objectives but because it cannot make up its mind what objectives should be in the forefront. Some of us want to secure all the rights of private property at the same time as we acknowledge the validity of the principles of distributive justice. We want to conserve all possible traces of the traditional and the antique at the same time as we sketch out a new aesthetic design for living. We want to be prepared to defend ourselves by force of arms if necessary, and yet nowhere in this country can a troop-training area be found which lovers of nature do not regard as a sacred trust. We try to combine anthropomorphism towards animals with treatment of them as an economic resource and a material for scientific experiment. We make a compound of individual self-interest and social reciprocity and call it business ethics. We want to blend the principles of reason with the dogmas of a mystic transcendental value system. In short, we are attempting in the Western world to compromise between diverse ideals with differing moral components. In this country indeed we have made this compromise itself into an ideal, the English virtue of compromise.

Ultimately, however, we cannot expect compromise from science. Its search for truth is cumulative. Its values are international. We cannot escape the implications of scientific discovery, and we cannot reverse the processes of technological development. They may be halted for the moment, they may even be dissipated by war, and their achievements may be congealed by some form of institutional action, but the process never really turns back on itself. Hence compromise is futile if it is conceived as a permanent measure. It is valid only if it is conceived as a transition.

One general trend of organization in modern society may be assumed to be in the direction of greater control over the individual handling of property rights. But is it, as Marx argued, the true democratization of authority in control over the means of production? Is it a political entropy which is the inevitable outcome? Will the economic machine necessarily be firmly founded on the broadest possible basis, the working masses? Are we, as Lenin said, 'marching to the very end of the division of society into classes'? We in England know that we are witnessing one phase of the struggle to establish the broadest basis without all the sacrifices that are called for by a revolutionary theory. What we do not know is whether we are in process of trading efficiency for freedom. We see in Russia, as in her satellite countries, the working masses represented by a narrow party leadership. Progress in technology has helped to give them their opportunity, by providing one initial condition for revolt, an obvious inconsistency between ownership and use of the means of production. It has given them a human material which by advances in the techniques of propaganda can be led to see its strength. Above all, it has given them the means of maintaining power once it has been seized. Whatever be their idealism, rights to the direct services of others for what is conceived as the common benefit become the set of goods for the possession of which they struggle. To the property of the bourgeoisie in personal goods succeeds the property of the executive in personal power. Their rule is not a technocratic one or a managerial one. It is a bureaucratic rule, with, it may be, monocracy as the concealed spring. Is this an example which cannot be avoided on the organizational plane? Does it demand a moral counter-offensive?

As a proto-sociologist, I want to illustrate some of these general reflections from a comparative field. Until almost yesterday, these problems were thought to belong essentially to the Western world. Yet they apply now with almost more force to the Oriental peasantry, on the one hand, and to the less-developed peoples, such as those of Africa, on the other hand. All these peoples have been subjected to an intensive dosage of Western applied science, so rapidly in some cases that, in terms of consumer technology, they have leaped from the hoe to the tractor plough and from the canoe to the aeroplane in a generation. Poor, often ridden by debt, educationally backward, socially and politically under-privileged in a number of ways, they are now beginning to articulate common aims and to realize that change can be not merely wished for but enforced. Some of them have been touched by Christianity, but many of them retain their own religious forms. To most of them it is the economics and not the religion of the West that appeals.

The modern colonial system, held together by world markets, rests essentially on the scientific knowledge and the technical achievements of the Western industrial revolution. While these achievements are not necessarily denied to the colonial people themselves, they are primarily at the command of representatives of the controlling power. They are not thoroughly integrated into the local economy and social system, so they tend to promote class structures marked by sharp differentiation, with little mobility. Racial characteristics often symbolize social inequality. The two groups in contact have different moral standards, whether about polygamy, the position of women, the claims of kinsfolk, or the general status of work as a social need. As contact develops, the new technology gets a firmer grip on the peasant. The South African peasant leaves his farm for the mines, the Malay takes to growing rubber, the Ashanti or Ga in Ghana grows cocoa, and they step into the orbit of the Western industrial system. The new skills and the cash nexus of wage labour or commercial crop production create forms of organization unknown to those societies before. New chances arise for individual initiative and industry, and new systems of contract and ownership are forged to meet the demands of the new economic relationships. Perhaps most significant of all, impersonal relations on an economic basis tend to replace the personal relations on a social basis, which characterize the traditional society. As in the break-up of the feudal system in Europe, only some of those who held superior status in the traditional system can hope to get it or hold it in the new. Some structural displacement inevitably takes place. If it were only the reduction of those who held power in the old régime it might be fully approved. But the emphasis on individual rights and individual initiative throws much weight against some of the basic relations of small groups in the traditional society. Family life in particular is threatened. The labourer going into industry or commerce has had either to separate from his wife and children or to house them in unsuitable surroundings. In the novels of Mulk Raj Anand we can read about the appalling surroundings of the Indian industrial worker. They may be neither typical nor contemporary, but similar conditions are reflected in the story of the growth of industry in China. Here human beings, including women and children, were treated as economic and not social material because capital was dear and labour was cheap. The solidarity and moral values of the traditional Chinese family system have acted to some extent as a buffer in this situation, but even these have been eaten into in the process. A similar situation is found in Africa. The temporary urbanization of African mining employees has thrown strains on the native family system which it becomes increasingly unable to bear without legal provisions and other social assistance. The old ties are breaking down and a new system is taking their place, a system in which the individual rather than the group is regarded as being the factor of prime importance.

The new technology does not of itself create the psychological foundation of a new morality. But its structural results favour the expression of some elements in human personality until now restrained, which take on the shape of newer demands and obligations, backed by sanctions of right and wrong.

There is also another side to the introduction of science and the new technology into these societies. The people who accept them for economic purposes may be those outside the community. The impact of them may be resisted by the elders and the over-privileged and also by the society as a whole. Backwardness may be not simply technological; it may also be a continued orientation to traditional values. Such backwardness is brought into relief in a society such as that in Malaya. There the old traditional Malay attitudes are faced by those of the Chinese, who seize with enterprise and avidity all the opportunities presented to them by the new technology. Here is a situation in which the recognition of the value of conservatism can easily be mistaken for or pass into a morality of backwardness. I would argue that it is very easy even in these days to support in effect a morality of backwardness from what are regarded as the best interests of the people concerned.

The humanitarianism of the nineteenth century, which was in itself a reaction from the asperities of the industrial revolution, was responsible for a vast improvement in the social conditions of the backward peoples. But more than social betterment is necessary if we are going to implement the moral values which we have. Action in the colonial fields must follow on a clear realization of our objectives. The colonial territories, at least in British eyes, are destined to self-government, yet, especially by reason of the contraction of our resources, they have become increasingly more important to the metropolitan country. We can perhaps detect the crystallizing of a view that the new programmes of colonial development, with regard to food production, for instance, should be primarily in our own interest in this country. It is true that such ideas are always phrased in terms of the mutual benefit to be derived. But we are in danger, I think, of trying to harness together diverse interests which are bound to pull apart in the end. As a short-term programme, we can justify our action, but, if we are really aiming at self-government, we must recognize that British social and economic privilege cannot long survive the opening of the political door.

There must be a moral basis for action, but it cannot be of a dual kind. We cannot love our neighbour and ourselves with the same intensity. If there are any fundamental principles of right and wrong, basic to our conduct in society, they must apply to everyday affairs and they must operate through an institutional expression. The principles of morality cannot remain indifferent to social change. They must be geared to the new social and economic situations. I have said that in application to the colonial field, but I think it also has a wider application.

Religion is often appealed to as the only source of a morality which can measure up to the magnitude of modern technological advance. But in the Western world religion has by its compromises allowed some of the most important symbols of distributive justice to pass to its opponents. Christianity, since its inception as an institutionalized form of religion, has always been faced by two dilemmas: what to do about wealth and what to do about political power. Its founder was uncompromising. He wanted none of either, but the Church has been walking on a tightrope ever since. For those who advocate Christian faith as a basis for the cure of modern ills, the first requisite is a positive economic industrial morality, which will emphasize the importance of sacrifice of traditional privilege. For those who believe that the foundations of morality are social and humanistic and need no religious backing, the challenge is still of the same order. Science has as its one supreme value intellectual freedom and, as its aim, understanding. It proceeds by reason, and therein lies its strength. In the world today, including the colonial world of which I have spoken, what may be called the system of permissive democracy is in peril. To retain it and enlarge it, and not to have it replaced by a democracy of obligatory form, we must recognize that the implications of modern science and technology require the translation of a political democracy into a social and economic democracy.

CHAPTER VIII

Social Changes in the Western Pacific
(1953)

The Second World War brought major changes into the lives of the native peoples of the Western Pacific. Even apart from this, the influences of commerce, Christian missions and the government have had an immense cumulative effect over the last century. An analysis of the main changes, and of the social processes at work, is important, for two practical reasons. One is that much of the Western Pacific is administered by members of the Commonwealth, and we have an interest in those local problems. The second reason is that the native peoples there have shown some originality in their reactions to civilization, and a more exact knowledge of those reactions bears on the wider question of the chances of achieving our democratic and humanitarian aims in the less-developed parts of the world today. There is also another reason, less practical, but of even more concern to me as a social anthropologist: the varieties of combination of rational and irrational elements in the activities of these people are very illuminating for our understanding of human behaviour.

For the most part, my discussion refers to New Guinea and the Solomon Islands, where most of my personal experience has been.[1] But I think that as far as major trends go, some of the conclusions will be found to apply more generally.

Let us consider briefly some of the modern goals of the people of the Western Pacific, and their implications.

The first point to be made is that these people are now, without exception, committed to the *material* civilization which is the hallmark of the West. There was a time when white men, not least

[1] The 1951–2 field work on which this paper is based was done as part of my association with the Research School of Pacific Studies of the Australian National University, to which I am indebted for this opportunity. I am also indebted to the authorities in Papua and New Guinea, and in the British Solomon Islands Protectorate, for much help in my travels and inquiries. I am grateful, too, to my colleagues Professors J. W. Davidson and O. H. K. Spate, and Mr. J. Spillius for helpful comments.

anthropologists, could talk of leaving the more isolated groups of the Western Pacific alone, so that the natives would not be disturbed and destroyed by our interference. That time has long passed. Every Pacific community has declared its avid interest in the goods of the white man. In the most remote areas it is little more than the traditional trade goods that are in demand – axes, knives, calico, beads, tobacco. But so far has this gone that even in the remote interior of New Guinea there are few stone tools in use today; they have been replaced by steel. On the isolated islands of the Solomons, such as Tikopia (where I lived for a year a generation ago, and recently again, for some months), mosquito nets and electric torches used to be looked on as white man's goods alone, whereas now they are regarded as legitimate native requirements. Native people near the towns such as Port Moresby or Rabaul have a keen interest in a wide range of clothing, foods, toys, musical instruments, bicycles, and tools. Though dwellings are still for the most part of a simple thatch type, a few of more elaborate structure are symptomatic of standards towards which native consumers are beginning to rise. One such I saw near Rabaul, of asbestos board and corrugated iron roof, neatly finished and tastefully painted. It was built for a chief by his three sons, all trained in mechanical crafts, and the cost, which was mainly in materials, was £300. Another house, the property also of a chief in the same general area, was two-storied, of timber and plywood, with concrete foundations and good solid floors and stairs; this had a kerosene refrigerator, which worked, and the total cost was about £1,000.

A second point is that native political aims are changing. Until recent years most government of natives in the Western Pacific was by direct control, with nominated headmen or other agents as intermediaries. Even when there was some measure of responsibility for local affairs, it was only in minor matters. In many spheres natives and non-natives were subject to different laws. In taxation, regulations about firearms and liquor, rules for marriage and divorce, treatment of adultery and many other offences, provision was made for natives quite distinct from that for other members of the society. Natives had no part, either as representatives of their own people or as citizens of the wider community, in decisions on territorial policy. Nor did they show any particular interest in these matters. Since the war, in particular, native

political attitudes have taken on a wider scope and a clearer definition. There is much keener interest in securing local executive and
even judicial functions. Some natives are concerned with major
policy issues, especially in education and economic development.
The war, especially by the entry of United States forces into the
Western Pacific, brought home the notion of differences in
national sovereignty and national attitudes between white men.
In some native minds it gave rise to at least the theoretical possibility of change in political allegiance. There has been some positive response to this by Governments. A strong development of
Native Councils has been fostered in some areas. Natives have
been appointed to the New Guinea Legislative Council, and to
the Advisory Council of the British Solomon Islands Protectorate.
Yet these measures, mild as they are, have not gone without
challenge by some Europeans as giving the native responsibility at
too fast a pace. On the other hand, from the native side it still
appears that the real direction of affairs, at both the local and the
central levels, remains in European hands.

Underlying much of this new atmosphere is the alteration in
the native income structure. Since the beginning of the war there
has been a great increase of overall native income in monetary
terms, and to a considerable extent, also, in real terms. This is
largely a direct reflex of the world increase in raw material prices.
A quarter of a century ago the local price of copra in the islands
was generally less than £20 per ton, and in the depths of the
depression years it went at times to even below £5 per ton. But
recently copra has been fetching more than £60 per ton on a
guaranteed price basis, and very much more at times on the free
market. Native copra producers in New Guinea, New Britain
and the other western islands, have taken full advantage of this
situation and, with relatively low overheads, have increased their
net incomes accordingly. Similar income changes, though on a
much smaller scale, have taken place with trochus shell and green-
snail. And a few natives have begun to get a substantial income
from a new crop in the Western Pacific – cocoa. The price reaction has also been felt in the labour market. Before the war it
was common for unskilled labourers in the Solomons and New
Hebrides to receive £1 per month in cash wages and to be 'found'
with rations and a few other supplies. Similar labourers in New
Guinea got substantially less. Now, after the war, these rates have

been doubled or trebled. Moreover, there has been extension of the scale. Semi-skilled labour – cooks, launch-boys, hospital attendants – get considerably more, while in New Guinea at least, skilled men, such as carpenters, plumbers and electricians, can earn £20 a month or so at wage or contract rates. Though they must then provide their own housing and food, it is clear that at these levels the labour élite are beginning to touch the fringe of European conceptions of appreciable income.

But another reason for the increase in native incomes is the provision by natives of goods or services of a new kind, for cash, in a way unknown before. During the war some natives received payments of some size for laundry or other services rendered to troops, while others made a considerable income by the sale of curios. At the present time one way of getting an income is by the supply of fish or vegetables to a cash market, either European or native. A year or so ago the relatively primitive highlanders near Mt. Hagen were growing cabbages, melons, cucumbers, and bringing them in to the government station to exchange for money. Some got as little as threepence apiece, but others, men of rank with families to work for them, took as much as one pound or more. The vegetables were flown down to the coast by air, to help to supply the European population at Lae. The results were not always successful, since at times a glut threatened to kill the market. But it was estimated that with proper outlets a minimum supply of a couple of tons of such vegetables could be maintained each month, at rates which would yield about £200 to the local natives within a radius of five miles or so from the station. Near Rabaul a regular market has been established, served by the local Tolai people with a great mass of fruit, vegetables and other produce. Buyers and sellers number several thousand, and the local European and Chinese population mingle with the throngs of Melanesians. The market is notable in another way: tobacco, cowry shells and cash all serve as media of exchange. In the neighbourhood of Port Moresby an energetic man with a garden can take between fifteen shillings and two pounds per day, depending on the season, if he hawks from door to door his mangoes, tomatoes, bananas, sweetcorn and pumpkins. And a fisherman can get up to ten or fifteen shillings for a good mullet, from native buyers themselves.[1] A type of service which has contributed significantly

[1] Belshaw, 1952, pp. 26–39.

to native income is transport. The hire of a native sailing canoe, or a cutter, along the coast brings in from ten shillings to five or ten pounds, depending on the saleable nature of the cargo, the distance, and the time taken. At times these canoes are hired by Europeans. A peculiarly post-war phenomenon in the transport field is the ownership of large motor-trucks by New Guinea men. These earn considerable incomes by the carriage of passengers and goods, including some European goods. In a village about five miles out from Port Moresby, for example, there are four trucks, native-owned; they are hired out at a pound a trip to the town or at a shilling a head if the party is a large one.

These developments of native enterprise have had an effect on the general labour market. While the demand for plantation, mining and public works labour seems as keen as ever, there has been a definite falling off in supply, especially of unskilled labour. In some areas, especially those in which a 'Cargo cult' or analogous movement developed after the war, there was a disinclination to work for the white man as such. But for the region as a whole the opportunity of alternative occupations, offering a greater return or more attractive work, has probably been more important. Much more investigation, of the kind Belshaw has done in Milne Bay and near Port Moresby, is needed to establish precisely the degree to which such alternative occupations offer valid preferences. But the shortage in supply may well be a function of several related variables: disinclination to accept low-wage employment in the light of modern native standards of consumption; inability of employers to pay higher wages for labour of low efficiency; lack of an adequate training system to fit labour for more skilled work; lack of enough general education to allow them to take proper advantage of training and give them understanding of incentive-output-cost relationships. The situation is complicated by three further elements. One is the fact that in some of the new reservoirs of unskilled labour supply, as in Chimbu in the New Guinea Highlands or Tikopia on the distant south-eastern fringe of the Solomon Islands, to go away and work for the white man is still an adventure, attractive as much for the new experience abroad as for the wages earned. The result is that, unused in any case to European standards of regular hours and diligence, much of this labour is of low quality. The second element is the lack of any clear general policy, among European residents in the islands, of training to raise the general technical standards of the natives. Many Europeans seem quite content that the natives should continue indefinitely to supply unskilled labour, and that no attempt need be made to integrate them more fully into the technological patterns of the economy.[1] The third element is the apparent lack as yet of any clear notion of what should be, or is likely to be, the broad distribution of native manpower through the economy. One hardly ever hears such questions asked as these: What proportion of the people should be engaged in peasant or native plantation agriculture? What in European enterprises of a private character? What in public works? What therefore should be the relative inducements offered to attract the people accordingly?

What has just been said, will have indicated some of the impediments still in the way of the direct advance of the Western Pacific native to economic and social standards comparable to those of Europeans, or even markedly superior, for the mass of the people, to those which they have at present.

Something more may be said here about the educational factors. There is no colour bar in labour in the Western Pacific, and it is not too far-fetched to anticipate the time when all mechanical work, of whatever grade, will be done by New Guinea or Solomon Islands men. But as yet the technical training offered is elementary and for the most part rule-of-thumb. In speaking of the kerosene refrigerator earlier, I thought it advisable to say that it worked. The low level and sparse distribution of mechanical skills among the natives of the Western Pacific often mean that their equipment is poorly serviced. Yet this is not inevitable. Oil engines in boats, for instance, are often carefully looked after. Capacity and interest are there: they need development and on a much wider front.[2] Outside the technical or mechanical sphere, the standard of education is still inordinately low. The gap between what is taught in the schools and the complex requirements of a modern social life is still immense. One retarding factor here is 'pidgin-English'. This has developed sufficient individuality to be considered a language in its own right, and is capable, especially in

---

[1] I was struck in New Guinea by the way in which much work that could be easily performed by trained natives – e.g. serving behind shop counters, driving motor vehicles – is performed by high-cost European labour, often imported especially from Australia.

[2] Recent proposals for vocational training may start such a development. See Derrick, 1953. (In the last decade great advances have been made.)

native use, of a high degree of fluidity in expression. Perhaps its greatest service is the ease with which its rudiments can be learned by any native, and its use as a unifying medium. But great as its developmental contribution has been in the pioneering phases of the Western Pacific, it is definitely inadequate as a long-term investment. Its most obvious and greatest defect is that its user has no key to any but the most restricted literature; the riches of English thought are barred to him, let alone the store of general knowledge contained in even an ordinary newspaper. The native desire for education, especially education in English, is keen, and during the last generation the proportion who have received some kind of higher education has risen appreciably. But it is still far too small a fraction. One reason is of course the great discrepancy between the cost and the capacity of the people to pay. To break the vicious circle of economic and educational inadequacy may require more substantial and better planned financial outlay than at present.

One factor retarding the economic and social advance of Western Pacific peoples is poverty of natural resources. It is coming to be general knowledge that limitations on agriculture in the Western Pacific, as elsewhere in the tropics, are fairly severe. Soil exhaustion and soil erosion are taking their toll. The disturbance of an ecological balance by man is accentuated by the change-over from stone to steel tools, which has led to increase in the rate of clearing off the taller natural vegetation. Communications and transport services are poor almost everywhere. The coming of the aeroplane has facilitated some kinds of contacts. But it is a vehicle for high-price cargoes, and freight costs do not allow of transport of ordinary native exports by air. Ironically, the development of air communication may even have worsened the economic position of many Western Pacific islands by removing part of the incentive to improve road and sea services. As it is, now that the tide of war logistics has receded, many of the ports of New Guinea and the Solomons are in worse condition than before. Developments in new crops, such as cocoa or 'wet rice', in some areas may raise the productivity of native agriculture there substantially. But in other areas the coconut stands are old and need replacing. The natives gain no royalties from mineral developments. The seller's market for primary products may not last for many years. All in all, then, while individuals may advance, a general increase of income to substantially higher figures will be difficult to achieve. Yet the interest in higher incomes has developed.

One of the most relevant indices of participation in a Western economy is the capacity to save money as well as to spend it. This is a social as well as an economic phenomenon. It indicates not merely a new set of preferences, but a conviction that these preferences are justified as against the more conventional older native ways of getting rid of money. Such saving is one of the pronounced features of the native economy of the Western Pacific in the post-war period. In some cases considerable sums have been accumulated. One Mailu village I visited on the south coast of New Guinea had paid £960 into the local savings bank, representing about three months' accumulation. In the Sohano area of Bougainville, according to official information given me, the co-operative societies started with a capital of about £3,000, collected by a European organizer in the form of small subscriptions in a couple of days. Two natives came in with £700 each to invest, not knowing that only limited subscriptions were called for. In New Guinea, the process of capital accumulation has in many cases been given a fillip by War Damage compensation, which was on a generous scale. But in the British Solomon Islands Protectorate, which received no War Damage compensation payments, and where the native people play a lesser role as copra producers, the build-up of savings has been less but not negligible. I heard of one man who gave his employer £500 to invest for him, and while this is exceptional, there must be many Solomon islanders with small capital accumulations. In significant measure, especially in New Guinea and New Britain, some of these capital funds have been invested in productive equipment. A shot-gun for hunting game, a copra-drier, a saw-bench, a transport canoe, a motor-truck, are examples of such investment. One of the most spectacular was the purchase a year or so ago of a schooner of European type, with a cargo, for £8,500. This was the effort of an organization known as the Toaripi Co-operative Societies Association, using funds they had accumulated mainly from copra sales.

The recent introduction of co-operative societies has distinct possibilities of helping the New Guinea native to strengthen his capital position. After experience of the limitations of co-operative organization in Asia, there is now no great tendency to imagine that such a movement can be a cure for all the social and economic ills of the peasant. But the Western Pacific seems to offer a good field for a moderately conceived programme of native co-operation. For producers' organizations the major crop, copra, lends itself to co-operative handling, since it is fairly easily treated, can be stored with little deterioration, and can be received in any amount. Similarly with trochus shell, *bêche-de-mer* and most of the few other native products. On the consumers' side also, the native co-operative store has some advantages. In particular, its overheads are relatively small compared with those of European stores. Where, as in southern New Guinea, the large European firms have few branch establishments in the villages, and there are no Chinese traders, prospects for development of the co-operative store seem good. Where, on the other hand, as in the vicinity of Lae, Rabaul and Honiara, the Chinese are rapidly re-establishing themselves as traders, the success of native consumers' co-operatives may not be easy. In any event, if through a severe fall in the price of copra, or a severe contraction in the native wage-labour force, the amount of native expendable cash were to decrease substantially, the organization of the native co-operatives would suffer and might not be able to stand the strain. Be this as it may, the size of some of these consumers' co-operative societies at present is not negligible. The most successful of them in New Guinea, the Poreporena and Hohodae Co-operative Store, at Hanuabada, had a turnover in 1951 of £16,000, a profit of £1,750 after all costs of administration, etc., had been met (including a monthly wage bill of £35), and it distributed about £250 among its 300 members. The books of this society were kept entirely by its native secretary, as a private job apart from his ordinary work as a government employee. He also acted as auditor for other native societies in the vicinity. From the broader point of view, one of the useful services that the co-operative organization can give is to introduce notions of elementary book-keeping into native trading.

My aim, in giving all these examples, is to emphasize the reality, and the quality, of the native economic advance in recent years. But my primary concern is not with the economic data as such, but with their social implications. The first point to make here is that the native economic development connotes a wider social horizon. The men of New Guinea or the Solomons – at least the more intelligent and more highly educated of them – no longer look at the things and achievements of the white man's world as being utterly beyond their reach. They see themselves as participants, not simply bystanders, in the sharing out of the goods of civilization. Nor are they any longer content to be passive recipients of the allotted tasks; they want some more creative roles: producing things with their own capital, their own equipment, their own management. They have recognized, moreover, that with such new roles comes a new dignity, that the assumption of economic responsibility makes for social status.

In this acquisition of new status a double process is at work. On the one hand, there is much greater opportunity than before for individual differentiation. In the old native economic system the *entrepreneur* was a man who channelled the wealth of a group rather than operating on and building up his own private capital. Modern conditions are allowing the emergence of some men into more individualistic roles – as middlemen in trading, as petty capitalists, as organizers of the labour of others. On another line, but as part of the same general process, is the tendency of some of the more highly educated men to assume administrative functions as clerks to Native Councils, or secretaries to co-operative societies. One outcome of such developments may be the formation of a new native social and economic class, with different conceptions of the use of resources, and different standards of consumption, than the mass of their fellows. The members of this class, at the apex of a native economic pyramid, may find support from, and intermingle with, the group of mixed-bloods. Though small in numbers, these mixed-bloods tend to exercise an important influence on the native society, and some of them are often media of communication between European and native in social as well as economic situations.

But against such an interpretation of economic differentiation as an index of growing social differentiation, can be set one important factor. This is the marked tendency to communal solidarity which still displays itself in Western Pacific communities. Despite the decay of so much of the traditional institutional life, economic advance is still conceived very largely as community or group advance. This is partly an expression of an attitude towards one's village or other group which on its more negative side can be called parochialism, and on its more positive side, civic pride. The former can be seen in the narrow, atomistic view which sometimes leads people of a small area to refuse to combine with their neighbours in a Native Council organization. The latter is seen in the care given to the Native Council meeting houses, and in the enthusiasm shown for even an informal co-operative enterprise which gives some concrete achievement in which the whole community can share. In the recreational field one such type of enterprise which is very popular in some areas is the cricket match. A women's cricket match which I saw in November 1951, at Kilakila, for instance, was a matter of great village interest. The two Port Moresby villages of Hanuabada and Elevala came up to play the local side, arriving in motor-trucks. Each side had two innings, and the visitors won. Then there was a meal, provided by the hostesses, in the house of their 'cricket-master', the captain, and the guests departed amid much display of good feeling, with formal hand-shaking, waving and cheering. This was entirely an affair of the women. Another even more striking display of civic pride with an economic base took place near Port Moresby one Sunday morning. The occasion was a meeting of expatriate members of the Toaripi Association. They wished to make a further contribution towards the cost of the schooner mentioned earlier. About two hundred people, mostly men, assembled in a clear space among the coconut palms, which had had garlands placed on their trunks. Some mats and chairs, a table covered with a clean cloth, and flowers stuck in two bottles had all been arranged by the people for the reception of the government co-operative officer, a European, who was to preside at the gathering. Proceedings began with a hymn and a prayer – the hymn, 'A little ship was on the sea', had been informally but appropriately adopted as the co-operative song of the Toaripi. After speeches giving news of the vessel which was about to be sailed down from Brisbane by a Toaripi crew, with a European administrator as master, contributions were handed in. The men were assembled by villages, came up as their names were called, took their contributions from an organizer who had collected them previously, and presented them formally. All gifts were in bank-notes, some men giving as much as five pounds, and one man even eleven pounds. The total collected was £136 10s. At the end a further sum of over ten pounds was handed in, in silver. This was to provide pocket money for the crew, and it was unanimously agreed that this should be sent to them by telegram.

The public character of this presentation, its formal, almost ritual atmosphere, and the organization involved, all show the serious committal to community purpose which marks so many of the large-scale economic enterprises of the New Guinea people, even when they are operating in a money economy. In fact, one can go a step further in interpretation, and describe a number of these enterprises as having a strong symbolic content. This means that their object is not merely economic gain, but an expression of community prestige.[1] The Toaripi venture seems solidly conceived. But in enterprises of analogous kinds in the Western Pacific the commingling of social with economic goals may lead to inefficient management from the economic point of view.

In all these economic movements the Western Pacific native has preserved his attachment to his social system. This system has suffered many changes, especially on the ritual side. The old institutions of totemism, with their respect for animals and birds with which social groups were believed to be allied, have largely been abandoned. The marriage rules of clan exogamy with their prohibition on union between man and woman of the same unit, have tended to be disregarded or evaded. Rules about theft, adultery, killing, have been radically altered. The relative distribution of compensation and of bodily penalties for offences has been changed. Amounts of property handed over in symbolic exchange for a woman at marriage have been substantially reduced in some cases,[2] while in others the greater earning power has led to an increase. In some cases the traditional social system has been looked on by the people themselves as a stumbling-block in the way of their quick attainment of Western goods and ways, and they have tried to sweep it away or radically alter it by novel means. Villages have been rebuilt in lines on a military model, the

---

[1] This is not novel in the Pacific. A century ago the Maori of New Zealand were building water-mills to grind their wheat into flour, and assembling funds by methods reminiscent of those of the Toaripi. It is significant that one of their aims was often to get a mill which should grind more wheat than that of a rival tribe, and that in consequence of the rivalry and excitement, the work was apt to be poorly done, resulting in some loss of capital. (See Firth, 1929, pp. 458-61.)

[2] Views expressed by Christian missions have often been responsible for such reduction. At Monum, a village in the Markham valley, I was told that £10 was paid as bride-price if the mission did not object, but that owing to their protests, often only £2 or £3 might be paid. '*Before 'e no savvy talk belong God, 'e on top, too much dear. Nau 'e hearim talk belong God, 'e liklik pay.*'

people have been organized into groups, drilled with sticks, given flags, and fitted out with a hierarchy of officers, or even with kings and queens. Dances and other ancient ceremonies have been abandoned. The spectacular rites of the *hevehe* of the Orokolo have been given up by the people, who burned all their masks and regalia. The resettlement of the Purari people in quite new villages, under the influence of their leader Tomu Kabu, has involved the destruction of the large ceremonial houses which were formerly the centre of the cultural life. Such rejection of traditional elements is in part a recognition, however dim, that modern demands cannot be geared effectively to old ways. The modern type of economic activity, with its emphasis on building up capital by individuals, individual saving, regular time schedules of work, fine adjustments of price to market conditions, is not easy to fit closely to patterns of kinship obligation, village loyalty and other demands of the old native social system - hence the notion that by starting with a clean slate the people can get at once on to the basis of the new economic order, the benefits of which they desire. But this rejection of traditional custom is as much symbolic as real. The people are not simply casting out their native heritage. They are abandoning one kind of native life, which they have cherished, in order to try to build another more in tune with their wants, as swiftly as possible, with the notion that formal abandonment in itself is part of means to that end.

It is against such a background that the spectacular movements known as 'Cargo cults' in New Guinea, as 'Marching Rule' in the Solomons, as the 'Naked cult' and the 'John Frum' movement in parts of the New Hebrides have occurred.[1] These movements are part of a process of imperfect social and economic adjustment to conditions arising directly or indirectly from contact with the West. They are not mere passive responses, the blind stirrings of people who feel that they are being pushed around. Absurd as they may seem when considered as rational solutions, they are creative attempts of the people to re-form their own institutions, to meet new demands or withstand new pressures. In the broadest sense their ends are to secure a fuller life. Some of these ends are defined in terms of economic prosperity – the receipt of the 'cargo' which

---

[1] There is a long history of such movements, both in the Pacific and outside it, and a considerable literature, mainly descriptive, has grown up on the subject. (See Ida Leeson, 1952. Cf. also Firth, 1951, pp. 74-5.)

is to equip everyone with all the goods he wants. Some emphasize political autonomy – with freedom from the hampering machinery of white government, and enlistment under the banner of 'Marching Rule' or other leaders. Some emphasize the importance of more satisfactory ritual relationships – the forging of new ties between man and God, or man and the spirit world. Different combinations of these elements occur in different areas. But some component of freer economic choice is usually involved. Usually, too, there is a tendency for some rejection of European influence and guidance – even of the missions. This rejection, psychologically an equivalent of the adolescent's throwing off of the parents' authority, is the basis for the term 'nativistic' often applied to such movements. While in earlier periods this aspect often involved the notion of a reversion to traditional institutions – a revival of the golden age – in later periods it has represented a more forward-looking type of essentially new native society. Symbolic features often appear in highly developed form: language, gestures, material objects associated in some elaborate and arbitrary way with the organization or with its aims. Sometimes as signs of real participation in the movement there appear marked personality disturbances – bodily tremors or trance-like states. Characteristic of these movements is an element of fantasy, of desire outrunning performance, coupled with a conviction of faith in achievement. Linked with this too is a cohering of the people in new group patterns which in themselves are regarded as having virtue.

In these respects there is no absolute hard-and-fast line to be drawn between such movements and the mass economic enterprises discussed earlier. They too have their symbolic elements, which in some cases may block positive material achievement. But to give an economic end a symbolic value may be a good thing. It may provide an extra spur to activity, and may facilitate rather than inhibit realization. The object of those responsible for administrative control then should be to see that as far as possible there is a solid basis of technical training and general education to give reasonable chances of judgement and achievement to the native peoples when, as is inevitable from time to time, they try to redefine their goals in their own terms.

In all this, some basic values of the native social system will continue to be preserved and used. Throughout the Western Pacific there is retention of the essential features of the kinship system, with its complex rights and obligations as a pattern for working groups, and for the multitude of small services of daily life, whether in village or in town or on plantation. Despite the widespread use of money, there is still adherence to the need for symbolic equivalents such as pigs or armshells or strings of shell discs to act as 'native money' and give some kinds of transactions the proper authenticity. Even the very forms of village alignment of houses may be regarded as a proper part of the correct plan for living.[1] The Western Pacific native is not always sure about the adequacy of his social system, and is content to let some parts of it change. But some of its values, especially those connected with relationships between traditional social units, he treats as basic. They provide a range of interests and satisfactions, a pattern for arranging people in groups which gives impetus to many kinds of economic and social action. The importance of continual study of them will be obvious.

[1] Firth, 1952.

CHAPTER IX

The Study of Values by Social Anthropologists
(1953)

In an earlier Marett Lecture, a brilliant essay which, to borrow a transatlantic metaphor, had some of his fellow anthropologists reaching for their guns, Professor Evans-Pritchard discussed some broad problems of the status and method of social anthropology. I am taking a narrower field, though one in which there is also a lively interest. In talking about some of the problems of values as treated by social anthropologists, I shall be expressing a personal view. But I think it timely to give a brief appreciation of issues which many anthropologists think to be important.

Social anthropologists are, in general, concerned with social relations expressed in behaviour – verbal behaviour as well as non-verbal behaviour; words as well as acts. They can give their study various emphases. One emphasis, given by W. H. R. Rivers in outline more than thirty years ago, but vastly developed in recent years, particularly through the lead given by the anthropologists of Oxford University, is that on social structure. As a study of social groups and social relations of a relatively permanent kind, expressed in a very systematic, highly abstract form, this emphasis has been of great service. It has helped us to sift and clarify our material, and to formulate propositions of clear-cut and testable quality. A second emphasis, complementary to the first, is on social organization. This, less clearly formulated, is the study of how social relations actually work out over time. In most fields of social action there are alternative courses open, and there must be selection between them if social life is to be carried on. Such decision-taking has social repercussions – social relations are created or modified and adjusted as a result of the choices made. This continual ordering and reordering of social relations is the process of organization. Even where no choice seems to be involved, but only impulsive action, the consequential adjustments in the activities of others mean social organization. A third emphasis relates to the quality and ends of social relations – the material for choice and decision. The preferences in social relations, their worthwhileness, the standards of judgement applied, give a content and meaning to social action. This is the field for the study of values.

Take an example from the Polynesian society of Tikopia, which I have recently restudied after nearly twenty-five years. I found in 1952 that the chiefs were still, as in 1929, the apex of the ranking system. People still obeyed them, knelt in obeisance before them, and treated them with the greatest respect. Chieftainship had remained an important element in the social structure. But during my long absence several chiefs had died, and had been succeeded by son or grandson. These various acts of succession had involved choices and decisions by their clans, and consequential adjustments in the status and relations of the brothers and other kin of each newly elected chief. All these variations, rearrangements and adjustments were part of the social organization. The social structure, viewed abstractly as the main elements giving the society its characteristic Tikopia form, was the same, but there had been a re-ordering over time of the human components and of the social relations in respect of them. Social organization is dynamic, part of the social process. During the years I had been away changes had taken place in the religious sphere too. Christianity, which had some hold when I was there earlier, had first suffered a setback, then swept on again. In particular one chief, when newly elected, had reverted to paganism, and gone over to play once again the traditional role of his office in the rites of worship of the ancient gods. Later, he was re-evangelized, repented of his backsliding and joined the Church once again. These were significant changes in his personal conduct, due to the shifting interplay of a complex set of personal and social values, which left the chieftainship unimpaired, but involved change of functions and readjustment among his followers. In the chief's decisions many value elements were mingled, including his belief in the powers of his ancient gods, his respect for representatives of foreign spiritual authority, his economic interest in the gifts they brought, his attachment to traditional ceremonial among his peers, his feeling of the importance of his own status. And these elements were operative in varying degree also among other members of the community and affected the issue. To understand what happened in the society it is essential to understand the significance and distribution of such values.

THE NOTION OF VALUES

The word 'value' is a hard-worked one, and often used in a vague way. Reduction of the notion to any very precise form to serve anthropologists is difficult. Despite the elaborate analysis of it by philosophers, anthropologists themselves have hardly begun the definition of it – that is, the preliminary demarcation of it – for their purposes. Some wish to avoid the term as far as possible, not deeming it a useful heuristic tool. Some use it in a restricted sense, variously equivalent to ideals, to social imperatives, to the basic assumptions of a society, to the dictates of moral obligation. Some are willing to extend the term to cover all exercise of preference into which an element of worthwhileness enters. Some admit evaluation as a part of social process, a concomitant of social action, while refusing to grant the separation of 'values' as useful isolates for examination.

The importance of such distinctions lies not in their conclusions, but in the refinement of our ideas produced by their discussion. To me the study of values, properly organized, can give a useful systematic frame of reference for the analysis of social behaviour. It gives reality to our structural concepts. Studies of social structures deal by abstraction with the most general, the most common elements in social action. They tell us much about the *form* of action – the nature of society in a relatively stable state, or as imagined in a set of ideal rules. Studies of values help us to understand the *meaning* of action. Moreover, they help us to take account of variation, arising in individual action. By reference to values we help to clarify the theory of stability and change in social action – and in social anthropology we are much concerned with getting an adequate theoretical basis for dynamic analysis. In fact what have been called studies of social structure have usually incorporated a great deal of study of values (and of social organization) as well.

Of course we must guard against reifying values, much as we should avoid reifying social structures. Our statements about values are inferences from observation of behaviour. Our use of the term 'value' is a way of talking about behaviour.[1] It suggests persistence of a common element over time. We recognize a quality-isolate in antecedent and consequent.

BREADTH OF THE STUDY

In studying values we are not doing anything radically new. For many years, leaders of anthropological thought have been concerned with value data. In Britain, Radcliffe-Brown long ago examined what he called the social values of the Andamanese, the social effects of their use of fire, and food and marriage. Malinowski included traditionally established values at the core of his notion of the charter of institutions. Evans-Pritchard pointed out how important are the political values, including feelings of unity, in the life of the Nuer. He and Fortes have set common ritual or mystical values as the ideological superstructure of an African political organization. In the United States Linton put the acquisition of common values as basic to the development of individuals and to the perpetuation of society. Kroeber stressed the importance of a study of values as part of a natural science of society. Redfield has consistently emphasized a humanistic aspect of anthropology which gives full weight to personal preferences and community values. Kluckhohn has explicitly defined the concept of values and formulated an elaborate field scheme for their study.

Why does the anthropologist study values at all? Primarily because he thinks his analysis of society is otherwise incomplete. But obviously he alone cannot be responsible for value study. He cannot match the analytical rigour of philosopher or economist, or the minute examination and experiment of the psychologist. He has not the range of knowledge of his own society in its geographical and historical perspective which the ordinary sociologist has. What then can he give? His contribution lies mainly in two directions. In the first place he can give material to others. He covers a wider field of comparative data than do any of his colleagues. The exotic character – to Western views – of many of the value judgements he records is a challenge to produce a rational theory of social relations and of the foundations of social action. Sociologists and philosophers from Durkheim and Hobhouse to

[1] Any conception of 'ultimate values' which are inaccessible to scientific study by their very nature does not fall within this field. But by definition such values (if they exist) are not anthropological material and do not concern us here.

Parsons, Ginsberg and Macbeath have drawn upon these findings. In the second place, most of this material is empirical in origin. One pivotal feature in the anthropologist's method is to apply field observation consistently to check his theories. His notions of what values are and how they are used are verified by systematic appeal to his experience. This experience is partly obtained by listening to what people say about what they believe and do. But it is largely given by watching what they do. So while conceptually the anthropologist's notions of values may change in accordance with a changing climate of opinion, empirically a constantly growing body of field data is accumulated as a test of his ideas. The anthropological definition of values in its widest meaning is an operational one.

But if the anthropologist is a producer of raw materials, he also processes them. He provides interpretation. In this he works with a framework of theory about societies. He is not content with an *a priori* position derived from a Western or other particular cultural upbringing. If necessary he is prepared to take the analysis back to first principles. He asks what are the fundamental elements in a social system, its simplest components. Hardly any principles of human action are admitted without question to be 'natural' or given by some principles of order outside those provided by human association itself. So, as compared with that of his colleagues in the social sciences, the anthropologist's treatment of values tends to be broader in cultural scope, more realistic in illustration, and still fitted to a general social theory. Partly because of this, it is sometimes more naïve. Philosophically such anthropological views may have their shortcomings. As guides to action they may be ineffective. But they are sincere attempts to meet on more than an empirical level the problem of diversity of judgements and conflicts of codes in circumstances when they are claimed to be right by the people concerned.

UNEVENNESS OF TREATMENT

But the anthropological treatment of values has been very uneven. When judgements on conduct are described, or theoretical analyses of social action given, it is only recently that value terms have come to be much used. Durkheim's great body of work, with its emphatic and elaborate analysis of moral obligation and the moral character of consensus, has probably influenced anthropological thinking on values at least as much as that of any other writer in this field. But though there are a few scattered references to the term *valeur* in most of his writings, it appears as a specific subject of discussion only in his essay of 1911.[1] As late as 1942 one of the standard American textbooks gives a whole chapter on economic institutions without mentioning values once; the notion is introduced only when the authors come to the chapter on Money. Such abstentions may be due to a conviction that since values are basic to and inherent in all social action, they are best dealt with indirectly, and discussed in terms of their content, without specific reference. It is perhaps for this reason that contributors to a British series of broadcast talks on the values of primitive society discussed beliefs, behaviour, organization, institutions, modes of thought as much as they did values as such.

But the reason for the lack of discussion in value terms may have also lain in anthropological notions about primitive processes of valuing. When Goldenweiser (1937, pp. 407–26) used the term 'values' sparsely and did not define it, the reason was perhaps the notion that valuation as a cognitive process is foreign to the primitive. Goldenweiser stressed the directness, the pragmatic nature, of primitive pursuits – 'what is aimed at is achievement, not understanding'. Tools and inventions are accepted traditionally and become part of the technical equipment of behaviour, not of thought and understanding. This, he conjectured, explained in part why objective experience in primitive life failed to bring its full intellectual harvest. The primitive is guided by patterns; they are experienced, and the primitive individual identifies himself with his experience, so gratifying his pride and his vanity. There is hardly room for any process of evaluation. This underplaying of primitive conceptualization, with the virtual exclusion of consciousness and deliberate thought, was useful in maintaining the critique of Tylorian intellectualism. But it tended to push values simply into the realm of the irrational and the unconscious. In particular it seemed to give no basis for any change in value judgements. But Goldenweiser did bring out the way in which the patterns of primitive culture in their positive quality prescribe

[1] Durkheim, 1924. Cf. Durkheim, 1932, pp. 5, 7, 8, 12, 17, etc., where he mentions the moral value of the division of labour; the value of dilettantism (negatively); the intrinsic value of civilization, etc. In Durkheim, 1925, p. 637, he alludes to the 'value' attributed to an effect, but cf. also Parsons (1949, pp. 391 *et seq.*) who formulates Durkheim's proposition specifically in terms of 'ultimate values'.

and delineate the *acceptable*. A pattern is not merely a systematic regular chain or modal form of behaviour. It also carries an invitation or command to reproduce the pattern as well as an exclusion and proscription of what is outside it and therefore unacceptable. By implication here is a most important aspect of value, namely its quality of being something wanted and felt to be proper to be wanted.

Most anthropologists so far have treated values mainly in a descriptive way. There is a vast amount of evidence of this kind. We know about the values of cattle in East Africa, of pigs in Melanesia, of a head wrenched in triumph from an enemy in Borneo or the Philippines. Many of these objects of value have symbolic and therefore intricate, even arbitrary aspects. What the anthropologist does is to try to reduce the element of arbitrariness involved. He tries to show how the evaluations correspond to what we ordinarily regard as commonsense requirements of social living. Cattle and pigs have some such recognizable uses. He tries to relate the evaluations to as wide a range as possible of social concomitants – to show that they do not stand alone but have their place in a whole scheme of actions which are characteristic of the society concerned. Ultimately he tries to see them as intelligible in terms of generally recognized human characteristics. So the values of head-taking can be linked with the acquisition of prestige and power, of ritual notions of prosperity and fertility. To go much further into the question of why a *head* has been taken as an object for valuing would demand psychological analysis – for instance, of the importance of eye and mouth, sight and speech, as expressions of personality. But even without all this, and without finding referents in any general human attitudes, values are treated as significant because of the regular systematic social operations which express them. There may be no way of ascribing meaning beyond the closed system, but within it, behaviour can be 'explained' in so far as it can be given a context.

COMPARATIVE APPROACH

When an anthropologist is thus describing the values of a particular society he usually has an implicit comparative approach. F. E. Williams (1930, pp. 316–22) gives a list of what he calls the 'more positive virtues' of the Orokaiva, a northern New Guinea tribe. In this, liberality and good temper come near the top and honesty fairly low down, while sexual continence before marriage has no place at all. In examining Orokaiva ideals, actual conduct and sanctions needed to keep them up to the mark, Williams notes that while their standards are very different from our own, the village life of these people compares by no means unfavourably with ours, in its relative freedom from quarrels and ill-feeling. When C. K. Meek (1937, p. 337) is discussing the legal system of the Ibo of Nigeria he points out too that their sense of values does not coincide with ours. To accuse an unsophisticated Ibo of witchcraft, he says, would be a much more serious matter than to accuse him of having embezzled a large sum of money, whereas an Englishman – a modern one – would think nothing of the one charge and be most deeply concerned at the other. Linked with this is the traditional Ibo notion that to kill a witch is a duty, and that the European legal process which condemns the murderer is unjust and brutal. Both of these studies were by anthropologists for whom such comparisons had a practical administrative relevance. But studies of primitive economic values, made without this interest, have also shown this comparative theme. Malinowski, who first opened up several fruitful aspects of these problems by his field research in the Trobriands, was clearly influenced by his studies at Leipzig under Karl Bücher, who worked on problems of comparative economics, especially the evolution of labour and industry. When Malinowski pointed out that in the Trobriand scheme of things display of food gives social status and therefore abundance is valued as such; that an artifact may be valued the more highly because it is over-ornamented and therefore useless for its original purpose; that an act of exchange may be important for its social implications even more than for the things that change hands, he was doing more than contributing to our understanding of Trobriand values. His propositions were derived from comparative theory, and implied a generality which invited further comparison.

But there are two types of comparison. One is the itemistic type of Westermarck and other older writers. This compares values in their bare judgement or practice – different attitudes to lying, to stealing, to suicide among different societies. The other is more integrative. It compares values in their configuration of social action, in reference to the different structures of the societies in which they operate. The method of Malinowski and most recent anthropologists, while integrative or 'functional' in analysis, has been to offer comparative material rather by implication – by parallelism, one might say. They have co-operated in comparison of values rather than individually engaged in such synthetic work.

A study which does make a frontal attack on the comparative value problems is Ruth Benedict's comparison of Zuñi, Dobu and Kwakiutl societies. This brings out clearly how diversity of custom is not fortuitous, but is explicable in terms of the integration of patterns of behaviour for each type of society. These patterns, fundamental and distinctive, condition the thoughts and emotions of the members of the society. Benedict's conception of a culture as a neatly rounded whole and her attempt to perceive in cultures leading themes which can be characterized as one would describe the character of a person have been rightly much criticized. So also has her inability to make adequate allowance for the conflicts of values within a society, for individual selection and variation. But the appeal of her study in circles outside anthropology was undoubtedly not only its over-simplification but also its emphatic suggestion of passing judgement on our own civilization. People at large are interested not in the Zuñi or the Dobu but in their own discontents. The growing reputation of the anthropologist rests in part on a conviction – sometimes ill-founded – that if he cannot find the cure at least he can help in the diagnosis of our social ills. What in essence Ruth Benedict seemed to offer was an explanation of dominant traits of civilization in terms of cultural choice, and the possibility of a more self-conscious direction of social process on a new value basis. But at the same time she was stressing the importance of cultural relativity, of recognizing as equally valid the pattern of life which each type of society has created. In doing this she was giving her Western readers the chance for self-criticism and for an apologia. She was also implicated in a value standpoint which has become of considerable interest to anthropologists themselves.

MARETT AND CULTURAL RELATIVISM

These issues recall to us the contribution of R. R. Marett. A great deal of Marett's work was concerned, implicitly at least, with questions of values, infused as always by a warm humanistic approach. One of his earliest writings, he tells us, was an essay on the ethics of savage races, which gained him the Green Moral

Philosophy Prize in 1891 not long after his election to a Fellowship of Exeter College. Forty years after this early account (which was never published) he went so far as to define social anthropology itself in value terms – as 'the study of moral institutions and ideas' (1931, pp. 395–430). This was an outline of social anthropology for general readers and he was concerned with what he termed the historical development of morality. Like Durkheim he saw moral values as regulating mechanisms of culture, though he disagreed with the stringency of Durkheim's view of the coercive nature of social facts. In his usual trenchant style he said that the deterministic interpretation of the pressure they undoubtedly exercise is a sheer piece of exaggeration more suited for a rhetorical than for a scientific context. Marett was latitudinarian in his view of exotic moral codes. He warned the student of civilization against treating culture of a Western type as an ultimate ˙fact and so mistaking relative values for absolute ones. But he, unlike Benedict and some other later writers, was not a thoroughgoing ethical relativist. He held that a Science of Man was bound indirectly to a firm comment upon human progress. There are, he thought, significant human goals, defined by notions of the ideal and perfect derived from an infusion of hope into our observation of actuality. These are to be realized in a degree of social equilibrium controlling impulses in a healthy and, he said, therefore 'happy' system. Marett's contribution in this field lay then as much in what has been called 'meta-anthropology' as in value study proper. It is true that in an essay on 'Fact and Value' in 1934 he was concerned to stress that sociology (in which he clearly meant to include anthropology) studies values as facts. Such a treatment he held is neutral and can be satisfied with relativity not professing to be absolute. Facts so treated, he thought, can be used for the criticism of values. They show the existence of a field of choices, leaving the choice itself to others, the framers of ideals. In his vivid metaphor he said, 'The sociologist presides over a bazaar of social experiments, open to all customers to buy or not to buy as they please; his business being simply to see to it that the goods displayed are so labelled that bankrupt stock can be distinguished from the products of some leading house' (1935, pp. 43–61).

Yet the use of the term bankrupt suggests that his own treatment is not perhaps so neutral after all. Indeed in this essay he does give to what (following Bouglé) he terms 'polytelism', the multiple value system of modern liberal democracy, a kindly pat on the head.

In these and more recent anthropological analyses arise the problems of the general status of values and the relation of the observer to them. The most forthright statement, picking up the torch of Westermarck and Benedict, is that of Herskovits, in terms of 'cultural relativism'. All evaluations, he argues, are relative to the cultural background out of which they arise. The primary mechanism that makes for the evaluation of culture is ethnocentrism, the point of view that one's own way of life is to be preferred to all others. In a culture like that of the West, where the existence of absolute values has been stressed for so long, it is difficult to understand the relativism of a world that encompasses many ways of living. Here, it is argued, is where the anthropologist steps in. He studies customs and values in their context, and can so get away from the ethnocentrism of the ordinary man. The principle of cultural relativism springs from a vast array of factual evidence, obtained, Herskovits says, by field techniques that have allowed us 'to penetrate the underlying value systems of societies having diverse customs'. 'It is not chance', he says, 'that a philosophy of cultural relativism . . . has had to await the development of adequate ethnographic knowledge' (1948, pp. 63, 68, 78; 1952, p. 688). Moreover, Herskovits sees the essence of cultural relativism in a respect for the values of other societies, leading directly to the practical implication that an attempt should be made to harmonize these variant goals, not destroy them.

The aspect of the theme of relativism to be paraphrased as 'there's nothing either good or bad but culture makes it so' has a distinguished ancestry, in which perhaps Nietzsche and certainly Westermarck deserve to be remembered. But there are some differences from the way in which modern anthropological thought has developed which should be noted. Much of the traditional discussion in these terms, especially in literature, has been in rebuttal, not in acceptance, of the role of culture. In *The Maid's Tragedy*, where so much of the action hinges, as it usually does in such plays, on conventional values, Beaumont and Fletcher make Amintor say:

> The thing that we call honour bears us all
> Headlong into sin, and yet itself is nothing.

In Henry de Montherlant's drama of Pasiphaë, the Chorus tells the hesitating unhappy woman that she is hitting at bars that do not exist. There is no absoluteness, the Chorus says, in the moral value that human and animal worlds shall not be confused. It is not her passion which is unhealthy, but her belief in the judgement upon it – 'shameful vapours from the human brain'. This differs from the 'cultural relativism' view of morals. The latter is not concerned to defend the right of the actor to disregard public opinion and create and follow his own values. If not asserting that the act *is* wrong because of the social judgement upon it, cultural relativism assumes that the actor would be well advised to behave *as if* it were wrong, otherwise unpleasant consequences will follow, to himself and to the society.[1]

Now turn to the question of systematic comparison. In asserting like Nietzsche that moral judgements have no objective validity, but are of emotional origin, Westermarck did not overlook their social basis. But if his arguments lack that tight positivist framework which A. J. Ayer and others who shared his ideas in this respect have used, they are also without that close context which the modern anthropologist provides. There is little demonstration of the intimate connexion between value judgement, form of the society and actions of its members. On the other hand, it is clear that while recent ethnographical data could have reinforced Westermarck's argument for ethical relativity, it does not depend upon them. The variety of custom he cites from classical antiquity alone could have served him for illustration. In other words, in so far as Herskovits's principle of 'cultural relativism' is not simply a plea for the proper contextual study of values – an up-to-date statement of Malinowski's functionalism – it requires philosophical, not merely anthropological proof. Propositions relating the diversity of value judgements to the specific cultural contexts in which they are formulated help us to greater understanding. They also may make us realize that our own ethical codes may be capable of improvement. But they do not lead inevitably to the proposition that there are no ultimate values, that there is no absolute criterion. To borrow an analogy (from the Italian novelist Marotta), it is as if the fact that so many clocks

---

[1] Cf. Herskovits, 1948, p. 77. 'Cultural relativism must be sharply distinguished from concepts of individual behaviour, which would negate all social controls over conduct. . . . Conformity to a code of the group is a requirement for any regularity in life.'

were out of order had made one lose faith in the existence of Time. Moreover, as Redfield (1953, p. 147, etc.) and also Bidney (1953, p. 690) have shown, the affirmation that we should have respect and tolerance for the values of other cultures is itself a value which is not derivable from the proposition that all values are relative. An anthropologist may wish to hold such a position. But if he does so, it must be on other grounds.

DETACHMENT IN VALUE STUDIES

Anthropologists have often talked about the degree of detachment they can really bring to their value studies. That there must be some personal involvement on the spot is clear. But how far is this emotional interest transferred from field situation to lecture room or book? It is fairly simple to note the occasional overt judgement that slips through. Audrey Richards liked the courtesy and etiquette of the Bemba, and thought European manners apt to be crude and boorish by comparison. Evans-Pritchard has said he thought the Nuer interest in cattle hypertrophied. Clyde Kluckhohn saw Navaho culture becoming an ugly patchwork of meaningless and unrelated pieces instead of a patterned mosaic. At the broad comparative level, even those who argue strongly for cultural relativism can hardly avoid giving marks at times to the values and institutions they examine, as Ruth Benedict did, in terms of a scale of social costs or social waste. Such anthropological judgements seem to be of aesthetic rather than moral order. But what is far more difficult to estimate is how far the anthropologist's description of the form or the functioning of the society is in part a response to some of his own hidden evaluations. To take a hypothetical example, how far is an expression of kinship relations in terms of tension a reflection of some of the anthropologist's own early family experience?

Most of us at one time or other have attempted a statement on the conventional problems of the relation of the scientist to the man. One of my own, years ago (1936, p. 599), is probably representative of one viewpoint. It pointed out how the anthropologist has his own bias, due to his own conditioning and personal interests; and while this must influence his findings, that bias should be consciously faced, the possibility of other initial assumptions be realized and allowance be made for the implications of each in the course of analysis.

Brave words, as I read them now! How can a man face a bias which, even with a psychoanalyst at his elbow, he may not be able to identify? The work of correction may have to be done by others. But it is not uncommon in the university world to have to distinguish between personal and academic interests. And if one does not set objectivity as a goal and strive towards it, however stumbling by the way, one may fall into an obscurantist attitude which seeks and protrudes the irrational, instead of trying to reduce it.

One need not try to defend all values by reason. My own preferences for the music of J. S. Bach and for Romanesque architecture and sculpture – or indeed for the study of anthropology rather than of economics – I find to be without any particular rational grounds. Imaginative and emotional elements are fundamental components of every personality. But this does not mean that they must have a mystical foundation, that they can have no place in a theory of personality. I think there is little doubt that for some people outside anthropology the study of values is attractive because it is thought to be anti-intellectualistic. It is conceived as a kind of restoration of *laissez faire* to social theory, the establishment of a personal retreat from the implications of an imagined social determinism, a quasi-mystical reply to the rationalist temper of much anthropological thought. And who then at some point does not echo Nietzsche and say he is sick to death of all this subjectivity and its confounded *ipsissimosity*! It is the role of the sociologist to extend, not circumscribe the field of reason in scientific study. And so I think there are sounder attitudes towards value study.

But to come back for a moment to the problems of the values in the role of the anthropologist himself. Robert Redfield, in a recent illuminating discussion of this whole problem, holds the scales fairly evenly. He points out the rules of objectivity: the marshalling of evidence that may be confirmed by others, the persistent doubting and testing of all important descriptive formulations, the humility before the facts and the willingness to confess oneself wrong and begin again. 'I hope I may always strive to obey these rules', he says. 'But I think now that what I see men do, and understand as something that human beings do, is seen often with a valuing of it. I like or dislike as I go. This is how I reach understanding of it' (1953, p. 165). This humility seems to me of the spirit of science. Acceptance of oneself as a valuing instrument with an initial bias doesn't need to make one claim that the bias is either essential or correct.

There has always been some tendency for anthropologists to express their personal values, often of a humanistic kind, and identify them with some extra-cultural norms or universals. The international history of the last two decades stimulated this. The boldest and most interesting essay of this type is the attempt by Bronislaw Malinowski (1947) to give an objective basis for the definition of freedom. Writing during the war, with the rise of Hitler strongly in mind, Malinowski tried to show from a study of the minimal conditions of human organization how freedom is essential to civilization. Not to be equated with mere absence of restraint, it is achieved, he argued, by co-operation in conditions of greatest efficiency. Yet while many of his fellow anthropologists may share the main value judgements of Malinowski's essay, few find his arguments self-contained. The concepts of efficiency and of legitimacy of control which he finds essential to his definition cannot be derived effectively from the ethnographical data.

ANTHROPOLOGICAL DEFINITION OF VALUES

From all this you may get the impression that as Marett once said, 'we [sociologists and anthropologists] are notoriously vague, not to say confused in respect to our architectonic' (1935, p. 43). This might be confirmed by a quick look at the way in which we have defined the notion of values. Values are sentiments (Malinowski and Evans-Pritchard); conceptions (Kluckhohn and Murray); generalized meanings (Florence Kluckhohn); unconscious assumptions (Homans); relations of interest (Radcliffe-Brown); ethos (Bateson and Kroeber). Sometimes values are identified with things, sometimes with motives, sometimes with ends. It would be harsh to argue that there is a temptation in the social sciences to make up in language what is lacking in clarity of ideas. But the lack of agreed definition makes for overlapping in the use of what Thomas Hobbes called 'metaphors, tropes and other rhetorical figures, instead of words proper'. It is true too that at times the treatment of values by anthropologists assumes almost the character of a dimension of the whole of social life.

The notion of values is clearly complex. But much anthropological treatment seems to agree in essence though the wording may differ. To speak of values implies recognition of preference qualities of relationships between means and ends in social contexts. Values involve a grading of things and actions in terms of their relative desirability. The emphasis is positive. (A glance at the dictionary gives the Latin *valere*, 'to be strong', and the Old French *valoir*, 'to be worth', as related terms – cf. J. L. and J. P. Gillin, 1948, p. 157; S. F. Nadel, 1951, p. 264.) It also implies systematic behaviour, not simply random choice. Values have a cognitive aspect, they may be conceptualized, have a shape in ideas. They have also an emotional charge. This may be at a minimum with values of a technological or economic kind. But even here this element exists. In the notion of the economic value of a book or the worth, technically speaking, of its binding, there are elements of feeling tone, a small emotional charge expressed in attitudes such as that the price of the book is fair or unfair, or that the binding has been well or shoddily done. It is this emotional element in values in particular which makes them promote and guide conduct. A. J. Ayer (1946, p. 108) has said that ethical judgements are calculated to arouse feeling and so to stimulate action. So Malinowski (1947, pp. 127–31) pointed out how values are important for the exercise of choice among alternatives to action, and provide the force and integration for action. Or as Clyde Kluckhohn has said, 'values are ideas formulating action commitments' (1951b, p. 396). Hence they tend to have an obligatory character – an element of 'ought' as well as of 'want'.

As stimuli to action, values operate from the early years of childhood, once there is some systematic organization of experience into forms which perpetuate motivation. Values are learned, and some very useful work has been done by anthropologists on the way in which different processes of child-training in different societies provide diverse sets of values. But the genetics of value systems, both for individuals and societies, is a subject on which much anthropological work has still to be done.

AN EMPIRICAL CLASSIFICATION

As yet, too, anthropologists have made little attempt to classify values in any very systematic way. I find this a difficult problem, if only because values vary in quality and in intensity. But I find it convenient to distinguish at an empirical level between technological, economic, aesthetic, normative and ritual elements in any value configuration.[1] In doing so I make three points. The first is that these value elements are of different orders. As such, while conceptually separable, in practice they may all be present in an evaluation. A problem for the anthropologist is the identification of them and estimation of their relative weight. The second point is that in some cases it is possible to abstract and capitalize a value element which is especially marked in a range of situations, and refer to these situations as showing 'values' of a particular type. Thus while a normative quality may be ascribed to all evaluating, it is a specific characteristic of evaluations of an ethical or moral kind, where the notion of a standard is in the forefront. These are the 'normative values' *par excellence*. The third point is that I think it is expedient for the present at least to recognize the use of the term values in a wide connotation. There is a case for wishing to confine the term to those basic conceptions or assumptions which are 'obligatory'; which are regarded as predominant in regulating the life of the society. There is no doubt that a most important task in anthropology lies in clarifying these 'grand values', as they have been called. But to stop there is difficult. On this basis economic values would be excluded, since they often relate to trivially motivated demands. Yet Durkheim himself has argued that they must be included, that all types of values are species of the same genus. There is then a case for using the term value, like structure, as an inclusive label without too precise definition.

Some of these elements have socially and for individuals a more relative or optional character than others. The definition of economic value in terms of supply and demand relations shows a specific assignment which is less perceptible in values of other types. In technological values, concerned with standards of efficiency, despite immense variation in range of objects involved in different cultures, there is more common measure of agreement than in other fields. Yet while demand for more efficient tools may be a spur to cultural change, differences of view may arise over the question: efficient for what? The argument whether technological achievement is to be preferred to another value in given circumstances is typical of many such conflicts.

[1] I have previously (Firth, 1951, p. 43) included the category of 'associational' in such a list. But if one is speaking of 'value elements' rather than 'values' this should be omitted since it refers rather to a field of operations than to a special quality of preference.

It is taken for granted that values are not randomly distributed, either for an individual or a society. They are interconnected in some systematic way. But the degree of integration of the system may vary. If with an individual the integration is very low, then his actions are incoherent. If with a society, there is conflict. In studies of primitive societies anthropologists have shown the high degree of integration of the kinship system. Values in behaviour between cross-cousins, for instance, are linked with values attributed to father's sister and mother's brother; and these in turn are linked with values attaching to property and social status. Field research done by anthropologists in London and elsewhere in this country indicates that kinship outside the elementary family has likewise significant values in our Western type of European society.

But one may adopt the assumption that in all social life there is necessarily and inescapably a clash between interests or values of individual and society. Even if one does not, it is clear that there are many spheres of discrepancy. In an economically under-developed territory nowadays, values described as rights to self-government, political freedom and responsibility may be in conflict with values attached to the requirements of technical efficiency. Both in turn may conflict with traditional values of the local people about their class or caste structure, their religion, or their use of leisure. Anthropologists have already contributed towards both theoretical and practical knowledge of the cross-cutting planes in such value systems. Redfield's studies of Chan Kom illustrate how significant kin group and generation cleavages may be here. Results from the elaborate 'Rimrock Project', in studying Navaho war veterans (Vogt, 1951), suggest how important are early individual experiences in shaping reaction to major social changes, and that it is the implicit values not normally put into words which are most resistant to change. They also reinforce the generalization made by others that change is often easier in the religious orientation than in social organization.

In a clash between values in a social system those in what may be called the associational field often seem to assert their primacy. In South Africa the *apartheid* policy in some respects flies directly in the face of those economic values which call for the preservation of an African labour force as an intimate part of both rural and urban white enterprises. This policy also maintains and is supported by a special sectarian interpretation of Biblical values. Similarly in the southern United States the segregation policy draws an almost surrealist distinction between brown men and pink men – meaning by the latter term a physical and not a political complexion. As Myrdal has pointed out, with anthropological support, many Southern white men find themselves in a grave dilemma in trying to justify with all kinds of rationalization the basic inconsistency between the American Creed and the Christian religion on the one hand, and the various forms of discrimination and segregation on the other. The values, both positive and negative, arising from and attached to close association with other human beings have immense weight.

This example bears upon what are often called 'ultimate values'. These, it is presumed, are the most important, the fundamental mainsprings of human action. They are frequently identified with, or thought to reside in, religion. This view is to some extent a matter of definitions. For the anthropologist as a scientist, his ultimate values include knowledge and truth, for which he may or may not feel the need of religious validation. Apart from this, in his material, empirically, he is concerned to extract the basic values in the relations of man to man, man to nature, and man to himself. Here, moral and religious standards, and even economic standards, seem often *de facto* to yield and be redefined in favour of standards of what is agreeable or disagreeable to have in close human association. Preference qualities of such association, what may be called the 'companionship value' or 'sharing value', seem to be basic in social judgement. In trying to establish some universals in human values – a search which I think not in vain – the anthropologist can turn his attention to defining even more closely than hitherto the conditions in which such sharing operates as a positive preference.

CHAPTER X

Problem and Assumption in an Anthropological Study of Religion

(1959)

Since this annual lecture commemorates the name of Thomas Henry Huxley I have asked myself in what sense can a social anthropologist commemorate his work.[1] Huxley's major work was in zoology. Such observations and sketches as he made of Australian and New Guinea peoples during the voyage of H.M.S. *Rattlesnake* were enthusiastic but unsystematic and even naïve (J. Huxley, 1936, pp. 120, 124–8). His 'Essay on the Methods and Results of Ethnology' did not deal adequately with issues of the importance suggested by the title. Yet we are in Huxley's debt for three reasons. The first is that his classic work, *Man's Place in Nature* (1863), helped to free anthropologists to study human beings by the same methods which had already been used to study other animals, and helped to lead the way for Darwin's *Descent of Man*. Secondly, his uncompromising passion, not only for truth as he saw it – 'veracity is the heart of morality' – but also for testing opinion on what is true by as wide a range of fact as possible, helped to raise and perpetuate a standard of scientific integrity which is basic to all our work. To Huxley's continued pronouncements on scientific method and demonstrations of the discipline it demands, we probably owe far more than we now realize. His scientific caution, his rectitude and his essential humility are given eloquent utterance. 'To promote the increase of natural knowledge and forward the application of scientific methods of investigation to all the problems of life'; 'to teach my aspirations to confirm [*sic*] themselves to fact, not to try to make facts harmonize with my aspirations'; 'to be indifferent as to whether

---

[1] In the biological sciences of course the situation is clear, as evidenced by the Huxley Memorial Lectures begun in 1925 at the Imperial College of Science and Technology, where (as the Royal College of Science) Huxley had worked from 1854 to 1895, and of which he became the first Dean in 1881.

work is recognized as mine or not, so long as it is done'[1] – we should like these goals, seen in his practice as well as in his public utterances, to be also ours today.

The third way in which Huxley made a contribution to anthropology was in his treatment of religion. He regarded the study of the spirit entities broadly falling under the head of theology as legitimately coming within the province of anthropology. He himself discussed beliefs in ghosts and worship of ancestors on the basis of comparative evidence. He noted that 'the characteristics of the gods in Tongan theology are exactly those of men whose shape they are pleased to possess, only they have more intelligence and greater power'. He also pointed out how religious beliefs offered a sanction for conduct, as when 'the majority of mankind may find the practice of morality made easier by the use of theological symbols'. But his observations on religion in terms of any ethnographic or institutional content were slight. His rational temper and scientific zeal led him to much more direct considerations. They came to expression in the view that where such symbols are dealt with as real incidents, and are converted into dogmatic ideals, men of science have a duty to show that they have no greater values than the fabrications of men's hands, the sticks and stones which they have replaced (T. H. Huxley, 1892, pp. 161–83, 208). Noted for his religious controversies, Huxley, as we may remember, was the inventor of the term agnostic, which he thought up as a label for himself in a newly formed Metaphysical Society which included labelled religious thinkers of all brands. By this term, he declared his belief in the unverifiable character of all metaphysical solutions of the problems of the nature and origin of the universe, and he adopted it rather lightheartedly as an antithesis to what he termed Christian gnosticism which, he said, professed to know so much. In this he was far more concerned with the lack of evidence for the affirmations of knowledge than he was with denial of the possibility of knowing.

But it is rarely remembered that the agnostic Huxley, by legend Darwin's 'public relations man', provocative, polemical, and antagonistic to revealed religion, regarded by the orthodox as the champion of the scientific imperialism of his day, did not regard

---

[1] For evidence of Huxley's views see Poulton, 1925, pp. 666, 704 (with quotation from chapter entitled 'Autobiography', written by Huxley, 1893, and published in *Methods and Results*, pp. 16–17); Petersen, 1932, pp. 128, 194. See also Irvine, 1955.

himself as a materialist. Believing in the universal validity of what he called the law of causation, he held that this universality cannot be proved by any amount of experience, let alone that which comes to us through the senses. He argued that it is one thing to say that the logical methods of physical science are of universal applicability, but quite another to affirm that all subjects of thought lie within the province of physical science. He rejected materialism because he understood it to maintain that there is nothing in the universe but matter and force, and he accepted the fact of consciousness as a datum of reality, not derivable from matter and force. He said that if he had to choose between materialism and idealism he would accept the latter, but he did not feel that he was under any compulsion to choose either. He held aloof from spiritualism, partly because of its frequent use of trickery and imposture, which revolted his scientific canons of procedure, and partly because it seemed to him to be little better than materialism turned upside down – the concept of spirit, like that of force, having no meaning apart from its qualities, which in this case were the phenomena of consciousness. He was prepared to judge the case of miracles on the evidence. He argued that we do not say miracles are impossible; we say they are so improbable that unusually clear and strong evidence must be presented for them, and in his opinion, such evidence is never forthcoming (T. H. Huxley, 1894, pp. 117–46; Petersen, 1932, pp. 167, 182, 211).

Huxley's particular views are of historical, not theoretic interest. But what comes out from so much of his correspondence and his essays is the moving sincerity and lack of dogmatism in his whole attitude, his conviction of the validity of scientific thought, his sense of obligation upon the scientist to defend the freedom of his thought and to expose the social consequences of failure to utilize it adequately. Whether we share all these opinions or not, and however critical we may be of the limitations in Huxley's own expression of them, as anthropologists we must recognize that they are a significant part of the tradition of that neutralist endeavour to understand human action and human belief by empirical study, to which we are all committed.

In the study of religion the climate of opinion has changed much since Huxley's day. Most marked, perhaps, have been the shift of interest from literal to symbolic and functional interpretations of religious phenomena, and the open acceptance of non-rational and irrational alongside rational components in the data of human personality. Anthropological studies of religion have both contributed to and been influenced by these trends. One important concomitant of this has been the development among anthropologists of a more sympathetic attitude towards religious material in the societies they study. The most exotic religious practices and statements are not now regarded as paralogistic, a product of false reasoning with a gap between premises and conclusions. Even Lévy-Bruhl, in his notebooks towards the end of his life, abandoned the thesis that primitive religious concepts were prelogical, not making the same logical demands as our civilized ideas, in favour of the view that primitive and civilized share the same ways of thinking, including a mystical component, though this is more marked and more easily observable among the 'primitives'.[1] The significance of this mystical component was recognized by others, including Marett and Lowie, in various phrasing. But it needed to be linked with social material and interpreted by structural concepts to yield more manageable propositions, as in the modern analysis of symbolic behaviour. The primitive religious material now tends to be regarded as presenting not so much alien as common themes in symbolic statement – forms alternative to, even if simpler than those in the more widely known 'great' religions. But one implication from this realignment, too little perceived as yet by anthropologists, is that we can no longer afford to neglect the more professional theoretical analyses of religion – not only by sociologists, with whom we have kept in comparative general touch, but also by psychologists, historians, philosophers, theologians, and other students of comparative religion, some of whom have displayed a growing sociological awareness. Another implication from the altered climate of opinion is a growing recognition of the need to re-examine our basic approach. Here is my problem – what is it legitimate to assume in an anthropological study of religion? I consider this question in two main aspects, at different levels. First I discuss the anthropologist's own attitude to the nature of religious pheno-

[1] Lévy-Bruhl died in 1939. His series of works on primitive mentality, with their apparatus of prelogical thinking, mystic participation, etc., are well known. Much less well known are his notebooks of 1938–9, rescued after the war by one of his sons, and published in 1949. In these revealing documents Lévy-Bruhl sets out his growing doubts on the validity of some of the central concepts of his theory, and gives his reasons for his ultimate rejection of the term prelogical, and of the notion of participation as a law – a remarkably frank, objective analysis, which does him credit as a scientist.

mena; and then I look at the kind of framework which has tended to govern the study of the relation of religion to society.

The search for a single defining characteristic of religion has historically proved unsatisfactory. The criteria of Tylor, a belief in spirit entities; of Durkheim, the existence of a special quality, the sacred; of Otto, a special kind of experience, of the holy; or of Tillich, a general function, man's 'ultimate concern', do not fit all situations. There are political symbols treated as sacred objects and yielding comparable experiences of exaltation, yet lacking in that attribution of extra-human quality so that what seems to some people the contradictory term of 'secular religion' has been applied to them. These should probably fall outside the religious category; if they are admitted, the defining characteristic of a 'non-secular' religion has still to be supplied. There are many aspects of belief in spirits and the after-life where a single criterion – the holy, the sacred, the 'ultimate concern' – does not seem to fit, yet on other counts in most people's judgement the phenomena would seem to be entitled to fall inside the religious category. To me, resting the definition of religion on a single criterion is like balancing a pyramid on its point – in theory it can be done, but it is an unstable position and not a very helpful exercise. I prefer a demarcation of the field in more empirical terms, in configurational or multi-factorial fashion. This must allow for the possibility that in any one case not every element in the configuration will be present, and that every element present will not necessarily be there to the same degree.

In this sense, religion may be defined as a concern of man in society with basic human ends and standards of value, seen in relation to non-human entities or powers. This concern is manifested in terms of problems of health and welfare in the mental as well as the physical sphere; and it includes the problems of providing meaning to human existence. The means, conceived ultimately as extra-human in nature, embody concepts of non-empirical existence and sanctions; experiences held to be true, of supernatural entities and forces; and modes of action, including symbolic statement, designed to relate these concepts and experiences to human desires, in ways which will 'make sense' of them. The actions, the concepts, the symbolic statements and objects are endowed with a special quality of sacredness which tends to set them apart from those of ordinary non-religious life, and to involve a commitment, an obligation, in respect of them. They are also shared socially with others in some group or 'church' relationship. Yet religion operates in fields of choice and dilemma; and it creates as well as solves problems. Even the sharing may help to raise the problem of the role of religion itself as personal guide – the question of religion as risk, in Martin Buber's phrase, ready to give itself up for the enrichment of personal experience.

This eclectic definition is substantial rather than formal. It is intended to underline the significance of the questions raised by implication in the propositions, not to attempt any very precise delineation. Any social anthropologist, whether he is doing a comparative study or describing and analysing the religion of a single community, must consider many basic questions, such as the following: What, empirically ascertained, are the matters of grave concern to a people? Are they of concern to all in the society, or only to selected persons or categories of persons? How far are they dealt with in terms of secular or of non-secular procedures? How far do the non-secular procedures involve systematic, compatible relationships? How far is there recognition of incompatibles? How clearly formulated are the notions of a non-empirical sphere; how personalized is it; how unified its structure and the source of its sanctions? What is the character of the experiences stated to have occurred with the supernatural; how is the evidence for them regarded by the members of the society, in terms of faith and scepticism? How adequate are such concepts as 'otherworldly', 'super-natural', 'extra-human'; and what meaning have they as categories within the religious system studied? What is the range of a concept such as the 'sacred' in the definition of religious phenomena; are there types of religious action to which this applies exclusively, or as Leach has argued, is it an aspect of situations, found together with the aspect of the profane, in varying proportions according to context? How far does an aggregate of ritual actions, religious concepts, symbolic objects constitute a system, with a structure of articulate relationships between the elements? If it is a system, how is it related in whole or in part to the social system as specifically defined in terms of social groups, status structure and other standardized social relationships? Does the religious system require a special organization of its own for its maintenance, or does it draw substantially upon the social system, as by a fusion of roles – say, lineage head and local priest?

In attempting to answer such questions on the basis of empirical materials from any religious system, various assumptions have to be made. These are of different orders. Of one order are the assumptions about the representativeness of the data we use, and the degree to which they can be taken to indicate the uniformity or variance of concept and action of people operating the system studied. Assumptions of this order can be tested by sampling, at a particular time level. Another order of assumption consists in the relation conceived to exist between the religious system, or elements of it, and the social system. Proper testing of this type of assumption is helped by studies of the systematic relationship over a time period. Another order of assumption concerns the relation of human action in the religious system to human actions outside that system, and to the possibility of extra-human action and existence. Assumptions of this order cannot be tested, but they can usefully be stated and examined for their plausibility and explanatory power, and for their implications.

This whole question can be looked at in terms of finding meanings for the phenomena observed or inferred and classified as religious. 'Meaning' is a gross label, but as C. H. Morris has observed, a useful one in everyday analysis. I shall take the problems of the meaning of religious phenomena also as being of different orders, as arising at different levels. This conception of orders or levels of meaning is an arbitrary one. It is but an attempt to provide fairly simple categories for a range of contexts and relationships. Let us approach it first from the point of view of a field anthropologist. Of primary order are the problems of immediate translation – though they are not necessarily the simplest. The anthropologist observing the phenomena of an alien religion is faced by the problem of understanding the meaning not only of words and phrases but also of a whole range of items of non-verbal behaviour. The assignment of even limited meanings to these, so that they can be understood in their immediate context, is a continuing and arduous process, and I doubt if we would claim more than rough and ready meanings for much of our work. Another order of meaning is the more general understanding of the major aspects and qualities of the religious system under consideration. Success in comprehension of the overall systematic form of the religion may come slowly and piecemeal. The meaning of a rite may be clear as being, say, an offering made to a specified spirit. But the connexion between this offering and the scheme of religious offerings as a whole, and that spirit and the corpus of spirit beliefs as a whole, may for long remain obscure. Meaning here is an understanding of the articulation between elements, not just of the immediate context of each element. A further order of meaning is that in which the religious system, in its parts and as a whole, is related to other features of the social system. A series of actions, with accompanying words, may mean an offering; this offering may have significance as one of a series linking a set of men, such as the members of a kin group, with a set of spirits, such as those of their ancestors. But the offering may have meaning in other ways. Much depends upon who furnishes it, and who is entitled to withdraw it and use the materials after the religious use has been observed. In fact the offering may be a link in a chain of economic contributions which help to bind the members of a group more closely to their leader and which express status considerations, loyalty, and the importance of certain basic social ties. Finally, there is an order of meaning which considers the relation of the most general characteristics of the religious system to major issues of the social life and individual participation in it. It is in this sense that it can be said that religion is man's ultimate answer to the problem of meaning. Yet issues of human frailty and human destiny, of the nature of man and the nature of life, of good and evil and their consequences are as much raised as answered by religion. Religions deal differently with these issues, and it is important to discover what are the issues on which a particular religion appears to 'make sense' and those which it appears to leave open or – like the problem of theodicy among the Tikopia or the Nupe – it appears to ignore.

From this point of view the search for meaning by the social anthropologist is a twofold process. He is concerned to discover the set of meanings within the religious system itself, and also the correlates of the religious system with other aspects of the social system, and with the most general problems of society. Granting differences in phraseology, so much would I think be conceded by any social anthropologist.

But there is another type of meaning which may be held to constitute a separate order, but which is intimately connected with the others. This is what is often referred to as the individual level of meaning. It has been argued that anthropologists are not, or should not be, concerned with individual meanings. I cannot share this opinion. For me, it is not a question as to whether anthropologists should admit such material relating to individuals, but in what conditions and for what purposes we should consider it. We should not be concerned with idiosyncratic meanings alone. But in at least three ways individual meanings have social relevance. Firstly, many individual actions, based on personal religious meanings, tend to have structural effect. As part of the decision-making process, the interpretations that individuals put on situations and the kind of action they promote, may be very relevant for an understanding of the religious system as a whole. Secondly, individual meanings are important in religious systems where seeking meaning is built in as part of the system. Here the seeking by some individuals – for example, mystics – may affect in many respects the conduct of other individuals, who draw for their own interpretations and actions on the accounts given of their experiences by the seekers. Thirdly, and more generally, individual meanings are important for the establishment of the degree of uniformity and variation in a religious system. The raw material which the anthropologist obtains in helping him to understand the meanings of things said and done in the religious as in other fields, is derived primarily from the statements of individuals. They may be couched in personal terms, or they may purport to express the situation from a more general point of view, but they still remain statements by individuals. The anthropologist's opinion of the general meaning of a rite for a society is then an aggregate or composite of the opinions of individual members of the society – fused with his own conceptions of the significance of the behaviour. No amount of talk about the necessity for abstraction can get away from the fact that the degree of congruence and the nature of variation in these individual opinions is highly relevant for the anthropologist's understanding of typology. Where there is variance, some of the reasons may lie outside the sphere to which it is convenient and efficient for the anthropologist to restrict himself. Such correlates as depend on differences in individual perceptions, or in personality dispositions, seem to me to fall into this category. But variations in meaning which can be linked with differences in an individual's social position seem to me to be very significant for anthropological study. For example, an offering to an ancestor may symbolize attachment to a social group. But if it can be shown that the meaning of the offering when explained by the chief of the group is much more highly charged with statements about moral obligation to make gifts to the spirit than when explained by a junior member of the group, this has to be incorporated into any statement about the 'general' meaning of the rite and related to the final use of the material of the offering. The difference may also be very relevant for possible modification in the religious system if new conditions allow the junior more alternative ways of using his resources. A whole set of possible reactions can easily be envisaged. It is true that we are not concerned with the individual meaning as a final product; its function is to provide type or category – meaning to chiefs, meaning to juniors, etc. But within our field of study there may be only one member in a category – as, for example, formulator of a doctrine, or innovator of a change. Hence the examination of individual meanings is a constant dimension of our problem of religious study, not an order or level alien to it. A principal reason why it has to be faced is that without such properly sampled data we cannot give satisfactory answers to the problems of religious transformation. Variations in religious meaning, in the interpretation of religious symbols, may be treated eclectically, as the Nupe seem to treat wide personal divergences in the notions of spirit. Or they may be treated, as in some religious sects, within a fairly narrow frame of orthodoxy and heresy. But ultimately, religious transformations in systems as a whole must be expressed as differences in personal religion. As an hypothesis, one might say that such religious transformations never occur in isolation, but are always associated with social, especially economic and political, changes. But it would be wrong to say that these economic and political changes alone are the cause of the religious transformations. The latter must be triggered off, given meaning by religious interpretation, and this in the last resort must be meaning for individuals. Such meaning is not purely emotional; it is also intellectual. And one important function of the religious transformation is probably in giving meaning to economic and social conditions – not simply to justify them, in saying that they are right, but in 'making sense' of them in terms of causes and results.

Another dimension of importance is the set of meanings which anthropologists themselves bring to the study of religious phenomena. In organizing the results of observation and in articulation of the itemistic data, the influence of these personal meanings of the anthropologist, and their individual variance, would seem minimal. At the level of consideration of the meaning of the religious experience as such and the significance of the religious system in 'making sense' of the major issues of social existence, however, these personal emphases may come more to the fore.

It is not easy to disentangle these personal assumptions from the presentation of most anthropological material. For the primitive religions with which we have been mainly concerned, I know no modern anthropological assertion that the experiences purported to have occurred therein must be taken as the literal truth. I have heard a missionary bishop affirm his belief that the spirits of a pagan religion were veritable Powers of Darkness; and some of us may have met local residents who held that there was 'something in' killing by bone-pointing or similar sorcery procedures. But no anthropologist I know allows the surface reality of totemic claims to kinship with animals, of witchcraft claims to injure by projective intent, of dream claims to meet a soul wandering apart from its body. No anthropologist dismisses these claims as absurd. But he does not take the specific beliefs at face value. He sees them as symbolic modes of statement which are ways of expressing, within particular social and cultural milieus, significant human relationships of people to one another, singly and in groups, and of people to natural phenomena. So much is common ground.[1]

A wholehearted acceptance of the significance of symbolic statement in primitive religion, of the validity of the non-empirical, the non-rational, even the mysterious as qualities in religious experience, pose certain problems of interpretation. If, for instance, a belief in witchcraft is merely erroneous, an attribution to willed personal causation of what in fact is the result of chance operation of physical causes, then interpretation consists primarily in charting the limits of the phenomenon, its functional equivalents elsewhere, and its social effects, including those of the measures thought

[1] From the considerable literature on this theme I mention only as examples: Gluckman (1950); Monica Hunter Wilson (1951); P. Mayer (1954); Nadel (1952); Firth (1958); Anne Parsons (1956). For an 'open-ended' treatment of the truth or falsity of witchcraft see Christian Council of the Gold Coast (1932).

necessary to counteract it. If it be regarded as a set of symbolic statements, then the further question arises – symbolic of what? The current anthropological answer is, symbolic of tensions, incompatibilities, conflicts in the structure of the society. Statements are made, and actions performed, in terms of the existence of invisible power, usually malevolent, activated by the hostility, envy, etc., of persons in specific social categories relative to others. Witchcraft accusations and behaviour related thereto represent one way of saying things about other members of the society which cannot be said more overtly because of lack of sophistication in analysis, or of inhibition in other forms of manifesting aggression. To say 'She is a witch' is equivalent to saying, 'As my neighbour or daughter-in-law . . . [according to the structure of the society] she presents an incompatibility in our respective social positions and categories of interest, and I am expressing it by this form of imagery.' By the standards of Western science, somewhere along the line there has been failure of observation, faulty diagnosis of cause, incorrect attribution of meaning to a person's behaviour. With ignorance and emotional involvement added there may well have resulted a demonstrable gap between premises and conclusions so that the whole witchcraft complex may be properly termed irrational. But our interpretation in terms of symbolic statement can mean that the area of this irrationality is greatly reduced. If to the question, 'What do you mean by saying your daughter-in-law is a witch?' the answer is given, 'What I really mean is that she and I must necessarily clash over domestic relationships!' then the problem of interpretation is rendered into a study of the ramifications of a special kind of idiom or metaphor on the one hand, and of the reasons, social and personal, for incompatibility of affinal kin on the other. But this is for the conventional social anthropologist. Should it not also imply study of unconscious mental processes also?

It is not suggested by anthropologists that the witchcraft allegations they study are to be taken simply metaphorically. But I think there is some lack of clarity in the use of the term symbolic, which has almost become a catchword. Should it, as Nadel has argued, be restricted to those cases where the relation between object and image can be identified as a conscious one? Where no consciousness of the link can be found, should one speak of a statement *expressing* rather than *symbolizing* a social relationship?

And unless the anthropologist is prepared to commit himself as to the mental process – for example, if he insists in declaring that this is a matter for the psychologist – is he entitled to do more than say there is a *correspondence*, a *correlation* between a set of observed statements about witchcraft and a set of observed social relationships of specified kind?

But granted that one can speak rather loosely of symbolization here, is the anthropologist certain that he has correctly identified the significatum, the referend, of the symbolic statement? For us, in handling the symbolism of witchcraft, the problem is fairly simple. Whatever be the specific answer, the referend must lie in the field of human and physical relations, and there alone. We do not believe in the validity of witchcraft, in the sense of the autonomous existence of invisible, personally controlled evil powers of the order described by our informants. If we did, our problem of interpretation would be different. We should still have to decide what types of social relationships lend themselves most easily to the witchcraft idiom. But also we should be concerned with other questions. How far are the observed witchcraft phenomena merely an imperfect reproduction of some more powerful original mystic forces of evil, perhaps personified, in the traditional manner of Western thought, in the Devil? How far can the social relationship be regarded as having been distorted by the existence or entry of this autonomous power? How far are the evidences displayed to be interpreted as true or false indices of superhuman power? Our disbelief in the validity of witchcraft propositions relieves us from the necessity of having to consider these matters which, allowing for the assumptions, could still be treated in a genuine inquiring 'scientific' manner. In particular, it thrusts into the background the problem of truth or falsity, which is limited to the consideration of the marginal area of conscious deception, which is usually small. My point here is that it is not important for an anthropological study whether witches exist or not – though it may be vitally serious in personal terms for members of the society concerned. But the assumption that we are dealing here only with human relations has freed us in our analysis to focus on a new set of problems, to have a different perspective, and more understanding. I think this can be applied further.

I have deliberately chosen an example on which there is unlikely to be much disagreement. But in the general field of religion, anthropological views on basic realities are less uniform and do raise a problem. While I do not think this issue need be in the forefront of our interests, it is an important factor in interpretation. It merits mention if only to separate from it and demarcate what is common to all our analysis. Some anthropologists refer religion directly to the complex nature of man and the demands of his social existence. Others go further, and in various ways, depending on the particular personal value they find in Western or Oriental religious tenets, adopt a kind of monism in regard to the primitive material. They would see in this and other expressions of belief, symbolic statements referring to universal truths which go beyond the human, physical, and mental sphere altogether. These are truths, it is implied, which however vaguely set forth in the primitive concepts, figure or reflect the existence of an Ultimate Reality, whether or not this takes the form of a personal Mind or Being responsible for the universe and its moral order.

Such alternative assumptions about ultimate meanings can affect the interpretation of our empirical data, by posing further questions about the referend of symbolic statement – as, for example, in offering and sacrifice to spirits and deities. In the case of witchcraft behaviour this does not arise, since we do not believe in its validity – though the logical grounds for the rejection of such belief are not always obvious. But what is of most importance in this whole problem is to have a clear indication of the basis of analysis, of the fundamental assumptions which the anthropologist has adopted in approaching the subject of religion. Such a demand may be thought indelicate. But while as private citizens we have the right to discretion, to keep our own counsel in these matters, as anthropologists whose job is to link conclusions to premises by processes of logical reasoning, we can claim no immunity for our premises. My own assumption is of course, as I have stated elsewhere (Firth, 1951), that religious experience is not a completely separate order of experience, but is essentially a product of human problems, dispositions and relationships. It belongs in my view to the same order of creative imaginative reality as the arts, sharing the same general kind of non-empirical assumptions. In its own rather different way it is to some extent an alternative to art, symbolizing and attributing value to human existence and human endeavour. But the provisions of religion

offer meanings and solutions which are ordinarily more pragmatic and more inclusive than those of art, involving usually a
deeper commitment. At the level of human dilemma, creative
activity and symbolic imagery, indeed, religious concepts and
values can be taken as real; they are true in their context. With
the claim that their basic postulates have an autonomous, absolute
validity I do not agree. But to us anthropologists the important
thing is their *affirmation* of their autonomy, their validity, their
truth – not the metaphysical question whether they are correct in
saying so. Basically, in an anthropological study of religion, as
in studies of art, we are concerned with the relevance of such
affirmations rather than with their ultimate validity. This means
also that as far as an anthropologist's own approach is involved,
we are more interested in the assumptions he actually makes for
the purposes of his analysis than with his own personal viewpoint.

There is a methodological rider to this proposition. Linked
with the monistic attitude that there is a validity to all religious
experience, of any kind, in terms of some common transcendental
reality is an implication that the personal conviction of such experience in one religion may be a necessary element in a proper
appreciation of the phenomena in any other. I have not met with
this view. But if it were put forward I think the kind of appreciation to which it would refer would fall outside the anthropological field. Of course there is significance and satisfaction in a sense
of being moved by apparently comparable religious ideas and
objects. And as in so many other human situations, sympathy
may be an aid to understanding. But in a strict sense of the terms,
sympathy need not mean empathy, identification, a sharing of
roles. Only the mystic is capable of fully understanding, in the
sense of being able to reproduce, the transports of what he calls
the unitive state. Yet the subjective description of this state provides only data, not the analytical frame, for the understanding of
its human aetiology. Intuitional, non-rational assumptions and appreciations have their place in scientific analysis, but they operate
throughout the whole field of a discipline; they do not belong by
prescription to only one empirical sector of it. In other words, I
am very far indeed from decrying the basic value of intuition,
emotion and non-rational perception in human affairs. The most
glorious liberation and intensification of the qualities of the

human spirit may come by exercise of these faculties, in active human relationships as well as in the more withdrawn appreciations of music, painting, or poetry. I am not arguing either that such exercise is not possible in an anthropologist studying primitive institutions. But I am emphasizing strongly that this cannot be made a requirement any more in a study of religion than in a study of kinship, politics, or law. The non-rational is already built into the structure of our thinking; it should not be sought as a scientific tool.

Differences in basic assumption about the nature and interpretation of religious experiences are apt to be disguised among anthropologists by what I would call the As-If attitude, an appearance of accepting at face value the phenomena of the religion they study.[1] This has taken several forms. In the field-research context it is practised extensively in the collection of data. The field anthropologist is not sitting down to speculate on religion, he is actively engaged in learning about it by listening to people talk, seeing what they do, and even taking part himself in their ritual activities. Scepticism or challenge is at times a very useful stimulant in discussion, and irritation of an informant can lead to valuable explanation. But this can be only a temporary expedient. Basically, confidence on the one side and sympathy on the other are very important. Contradiction, or any other contra-action, by

[1] This position is reminiscent of views of Forberg 160 years ago, of Kant, whom he re-interpreted, and of Jeremy Bentham in his theory of fictions. It has analogy with some elements also in the viewpoint of Charles S. Peirce and other pragmatists. Forberg, as cited by Vaihinger, from whom of course I have borrowed the 'As-If' terminology, held that duty lay not in belief but in action. It is not a duty to believe that there exists a moral world-government or a God as a moral world-ruler, he argued; our duty is simply to act *as if* we believed it. In thinking the matter over, or in discussing it, we can take what position we will according as we think we can justify ourselves in the form of speculative reason. Only in real life, where we must act, is it our duty. Forberg's view was expressed in an essay (in German) on 'The Development of the Concept of Religion' in the *Philosophische Journal* in 1798, and Kant's views especially in his posthumous papers published in the *Altpreussische Monatschrift*, vols. 19–21, 1881–4. I have not been able to consult the originals, but both are quoted and analysed by Vaihinger (1935, esp. pp. 318–27). Bentham's work, C. K. Ogden pointed out, anticipated in some respects that of Vaihinger (which Ogden translated) especially in his recognition that assumptions which might be false as hypotheses might nevertheless constitute 'important and useful fictions'. Here of course I am not concerned with the philosophical status of affirmations about the openness of speculation and the necessity for action, but with the anthropological consequences. To the field anthropologist, the duty laid upon him is inferential only, and temporary – to adopt such techniques as will enable him best to gain systematic insight into the character of the religious beliefs and practices of the people in his chosen field. So in Bentham's terms what he does is to manipulate a set of fictitious entities – objects the existence of which is feigned by the imagination, feigned for the purpose of discourse, and which, when so formed, are spoken of as real.

the anthropologist would impair rapport with his informants or co-participants. He behaves then, in word and in deed, *as if* he believes in the religious system he is observing, *as if* it were true.[1] And I think other anthropologists will probably agree that such role-playing in a social drama comes with unexpected ease. It is usually aided by the temper of the primitive religious system, in which the beliefs of people are not often questioned; they are simply inferred from people's actions. The test of religious conformity is practice. Provided that a man makes the offerings, performs the sacrifices, it is assumed that he believes in the gods or ancestors to whom these things are putatively addressed. The odds are heavily in favour of the assumption that he does. But even the anthropologist, who is known not to share views in some other fields, is not often asked specifically what he believes. My own experience among the Tikopia was that I was often asked if the spirits – the gods and ancestors worshipped – were true or not, but not whether I myself believed in them. The inquiry was to get my opinion, not to test my allegiance. In this sense primitive religions have no dogma.

But the 'as if' position, though of a very different order, may occur among adherents to a religious system too. It would seem to be uncommon in a primitive religious system though it may sometimes be inferred. Participants in a rite may be judged as conforming for political rather than for religious reasons, especially when a choice of religious but not of political affiliation is open. Shaman or diviner may be interpreted as trying to simulate results which for the moment he cannot obtain because the demands of his clientele are for 'normal' type of reactions. Some 'as if' behaviour seems logically to be a significant feature of all religious systems which lay emphasis on tests of belief. At some points the demands of the religious ideology are in opposition to those of the secular system and the private interests – including intellectual interests – of the person concerned. Most primitive religions stress primarily performance and not faith. If not, then there must be some easing of the strain, some mechanisms whereby conformity can be secured without too much sacrifice, too much violence to personal life. Maintenance of social relations then is held by implication to be of more significance than avowed nonconformity. Such inner incompatibility between profession and

[1] For examples of this in my own work see Firth, 1940, pp. i, 70; 1959, p. 24.

practice is up to a point an inevitable reaction to any religion which demands a surrender of the personality as its final price.

Anthropologically, in our 'as if' position we do not only behave in the field as if we believe in gods and spirits, shades of the dead and supernatural events, we also present much of our material in the same way. Up to a point this is a necessary economy. It is less cumbersome and more vivid to talk of a spirit entering a man, changing shape, flying, telling about other spirits, than to say that a man in a state of dissociation spoke as if he were a spirit, purported in this state to do acts beyond human compass, saying that they were those of a spirit, though he gave no visible sign of such behaviour, etc. Such 'as if' description is not only a language of temporary convenience; it also helps to bring out the emotional tone of the situation, and to demonstrate the logic in the situation by supplying the 'built-in' elements directly. But this is only at the descriptive level. At the analytical level we have to leave this kind of presentation, or some types of relationships in the material will remain obscure. Ambiguities may remain in the referend of symbolic behaviour. And in particular, significant problems about operations and relations in the situation described do not get formulated.

A brief example will illustrate this. R. H. Lowie, in line with his definition of shamanism as receipt of a communication from the supernatural, described a feud between two Crow shamans, Big-Ox and White-Thigh. Big-Ox seduced the wife of a kinsman of White-Thigh. This man undertook to avenge the grievance, and prayed against Big-Ox the next time he went on the war-path. The war-party failed. For a while each of the two medicine-men thwarted the other's undertakings. Finally, Big-Ox cursed his rival and made him poor and blind, but White-Thigh retaliated by making Big-Ox lose all his next of kin, so that he was obliged to wander from camp to camp in his old age. 'In these contests it is of course at bottom not the human competitors but their supernatural monitors that are pitted against each other' (Lowie, 1922, pp. 344–5; 1936, pp. 17–18). Now I do not think Lowie believed in the reality of these 'supernatural monitors', but by leaving the story at that quasi-vernacular level he ignored some of the most important theoretical questions in the interpretation. He did quote informants who said they saw Big-Ox perform certain rituals to destroy his enemy, and he did say that the feud was repeatedly referred to by various informants. But he apparently did not consider questions of how far the attribution of supernatural invocation was *post hoc*, what was the relative leadership position of the shamans *de facto*, whether their feud was pursued outside the religious field, what amount of public support each had, whether they were spurred on in emulation, and were thus really expressing standard group cleavages . . . and so on. A modern study would probably not overlook such questions. Yet as I shall show later, the meaning of shaman behaviour and spirit mediumship is still inadequately exposed by the continued phraseology of what may be termed incomplete symbolization.

I return now to the problem of individual and general meanings in the religious material. By the anthropologist, ritual can be directly observed, whereas meaning can only be inferred. If the ritual is a collective one, its meaning for all the participants may be uniform or discrepant. If the individual meanings are uniform, then collective action is presumably simple. But if the individual meanings are discrepant, then how is collective action, including the collective use of symbolic objects, managed? Several possibilities are open. There may be an intellectual resolution of the diversity – some overriding consideration which is logically defensible, which allows the participants to 'make sense' of their differences. Diversity of meaning may be equated with diversity of ritual function or with length of religious experience, or it may be recognized as complementary, making ultimately for a unitary entity. There may be a blank refusal to admit incompatibility, a compartmenting of judgements which continues to affirm the unity denied by the reports of the observer. There may be a compromise, an intellectual resolution of another order, involving some concessions – as in making a contrast between 'ideal' and 'real' conditions, with special allowance for the latter.[1]

Let us assume then that if meanings are common there is no problem in regard to action, but that if meanings are diverse then problems arise, either at the level of action or at the level of intellectual concern. Then we may ask how far do anthropologists

[1] An example of such compromise is Heiler's view of fixed prayer. For him the essence of prayer is the spontaneous expression of the individual personality and he stigmatizes the formal prayer, the liturgical prayer, for its lack of spirituality and inwardness. Yet he concedes that only a few favoured souls can reach the ideal. 'The great mass of average people need fixed religious forms to which in their spiritual dependence they can cling; they need some stern compulsion to drive them away from the concerns of daily life and lift them up to a higher world' (Heiler, 1932, pp. 350-2).

tackle these problems? Do we assume uniformity too easily? What criteria do we use to measure diversity of meaning? How far does meaning in the religious sphere involve secular as well as sacred elements?

We have many accounts of religious systems in populations of upwards of hundreds of thousands where generalizations must have been made on the basis of an assumption of homogeneity in belief matching that of a homogeneity in observed action. Take one of the most brilliant analyses of a religious system by an anthropologist that I know – that of the Nupe by the late S. F. Nadel. We find such a statement as this, 'There is no doubt in the minds of the Nupe that God, as he created the world, so he can also control it and intervene in its course' (Nadel, 1954, p. 13). What is the evidence for this, its empirical referent? The generalization would appear to be the anthropologist's inference rather than direct Nupe statement. What the anthropologist actually cites as evidence or supporting data are examples in translation of everyday speech expressing wishes that God may help in specific things. The same linguistic forms are used as of ordinary human action, at a mundane level. Moreover, while the Nupe God may be conceived to have the power to intervene there is stated to be little certainty that he will in fact do so – he is far, aloof, outside the world – 'which tenet overrules all other notions'. It is a bold thing to assert that in the minds of 300,000 people there is 'no doubt' about the power of their God in regard to the 'course of the world'. Even so, for general descriptive and classificatory purposes, I am quite prepared to accept Nadel's categorization. But if one is concerned with the problem of religious experience, one would have to go deeper and demand more specific evidence of the translation from concrete into abstract, from personal into general, from formal into meaningful expression. In fact, the frequent Nupe use of the term for God in many everyday contexts, including swearing, could imply that they gave little or no thought to God's possible control and intervention in the course of the world, but used his name as a conventional verbal counter, and for their own personal troubles alone. To show the difficulties which confront us, I have taken this example from the Nupe analysis because Nadel has shown great sophistication in approaching the general problems. From my own experience, I am impressed by the ease with which it is possible to add one's own personal dimension to the interpretation of an alien religious ideology, to raise the generalizations to a higher power than the empirical context of the material warrants. A certain 'flatfooted-ness' in the attribution of meaning is especially advisable when, as in the case of the Dogon, the complex relationships and identifica-tions in the data obviously lend themselves to quasi-philosophical speculation.

What can be inferred from the preceding example so far is I think this: that in discussing meanings we must differentiate be-tween levels of *religious contact* and levels of *religious experience*. The Nupe use of the name of God in swearing may be of the order of religious contact only – the acquaintance with the reli-gious ideology is superficial. In using a symbol-carrier, say an oath, people do not necessarily use the symbol. Yet how often in speaking of a primitive religion do we not make inferential state-ments about symbolic behaviour because we see some people carrying or handling objects which others have stated are sym-bolic!

In discussing the meaning of religious action one is entitled to assume uniformity much more readily than with religious ideo-logy, because of the greater accessibility to observation. Assump-tions of uniformity or typicality of representativeness in religious ideas may justifiably vary according to the purpose of the analysis. If it be to elucidate major characteristics of a religious idea found among some of the people concerned, though not necessarily all, in order to establish the highest level of religious experience in that society, for implied comparison, then one is entitled to talk of the Nupe, etc., idea of God. But if the purpose is, say, to relate the religious meanings held by the members of the society to the structure of the society, then further empirical measures are neces-sary. For a proper handling of these problems I see no way but more systematic inquiry into religious meanings than anthropo-logists have normally conducted, using the techniques, for ex-ample, of stratified random sampling. It is true that in societies of small scale we often have produced a rough approximation to such a sample by attempting to draw information from a range of persons of different status and interests: e.g. religious leaders, political leaders without religious functions, women, young people, etc. But questions of bias in selection and limits of the universe to be examined are often not squarely faced.

I want now to examine this problem of religious meaning from another angle – the relation of religious forms to the structure of the society. In any society religious phenomena are implicated with social conditions to some degree. It seems clear that in many circumstances religion is a positive element in a total social system. In general terms, it unites members of the society in common rituals; its beliefs, dogmatic and non-dogmatic, supply organizing principles for the social structure, and sanctions for the recognition of a natural and a moral order. Through religious acts, formulae and objects, aid is given to the expression of important aspects of social existence in symbolic patterns. In short, religion helps to maintain, to support the system of social values upon which the continuance of the society depends. From another angle, religion reflects the structure of the society. To use an expression which is becoming popular, the social structure is seen as a parameter, an independent variable used as a constant, by reference to which the religious system may be at least in part defined.

Yet are we satisfied with these fine words? Religion does not always perform these stated social functions. Religious systems may change in accordance with changes in the social structure; but they may also change for demographic or ecological reasons, because of personal decisions by leaders, or from the logic of the internal character of the system. Such changes occur even in what are apparently static societies. The pre-Christian Tikopia saw the development of cults, both in replication of existing rites and in elaboration of them. The pagan Tikopia after the coming of Christianity saw fairly substantial modification of their religion: a reduction both in volume and type of ritual owing to the conversion of some of their number; some alteration through environmental causes; and some variation in detail through status-motivated personal decision on the part of newly elected leaders. Only in part were these changes correlated with structural features of the society.

Dispute over religious features and privileges may precipitate or even initiate a structural cleavage. The Hopi of Oraibi have been known as a very conservative group of people, who have maintained their elaborate ritual against the pressure of Christianity for several hundreds of years. They have used these religious procedures, mainly in secret, as a kind of exclusive cultural weapon to keep the major values of their community, and its structure, intact.[1] It comes as no surprise, then, to read Titiev's statement (1944, p. 3) that it is plain that the religious beliefs and practices of the Hopi had been devised as a supernatural buttress to support the weakest points of their social organization. Yet as the missionary Voth, a careful observer who was in Oraibi from 1893 to 1903, has shown (1903, p. 291; 1912, p. 45), the Hopi have long ago made variation in their religious rites for personal reasons. And as Titiev's excellent analysis shows, in more recent times very serious ritual cleavage and reformation were associated with deep status cleavage which needed personal choice and decision to come to full expression. In so doing the Hopi both copied (faked) traditional sacra and created new ceremonial officers. Religion here did not reflect the structure of the society; it led to a social realignment. When at the critical period an uneven allocation of leadership and control of economic resources had weakened the social structure, the religious rites and beliefs, so far from keeping it from splitting, were the very instrument of the split. The community divided along kinship and power-faction lines, not along ritual association lines, but control of religious affairs was the overt reason for forcing the issue.

This instance shows the value of data over a time period to test the validity of an assumption about basic relations between religious forms and social forms.

I want now to carry this analysis further. I am concerned here with the processes which relate individual action to religious pattern, and which *inter alia* provide conditions or mechanisms of religious change. Taking necessarily a limited field, I illustrate from some aspects of Tikopia spirit mediumship, which I observed in 1928-9 and 1952. (I am aware that this example lacks some methodological strictness—see note to Table.)

First, some preliminary definitions. I think we can usefully distinguish spirit possession, spirit mediumship, and shamanism. *Spirit possession* is a form of trance in which behaviour actions of a person are interpreted as evidence of a control of his behaviour by a spirit normally external to him. *Spirit mediumship* is normally a form of possession in which the person is conceived as serving as

[1] For any understanding I may have of the Hopi I am indebted primarily to Fred and Dorothy Eggan, from whose publications and personal explanations I have drawn so much. A brief trip under their auspices in April 1959 enabled me to appreciate at least the elements of the Hopi situation. They are of course not responsible for this interpretation.

an intermediary between spirits and men.[1] The accent here is on communication; the actions and words of the medium must be translatable, which differentiates them from mere spirit possession or madness. *Shamanism* is a term I prefer to use in the limited North Asiatic sense, of a master of spirits. Normally himself a spirit medium, the shaman is thought to control spirits by ritual techniques, and in some societies, as in Kelantan (Malaya), he may not himself be in a trance state when he does this, but be controlling the spirits in another medium. But we are talking about human actions, whatever be our As-If language, so I shall speak of a *spirit presentation* to indicate the entity believed to be represented at any given moment by the spirit medium. In Tikopia as elsewhere, spirit mediums operate in situations of problem, dilemma, uncertainty, either private or public, and their utterances assist in the decision-making process, in the resolution of choice. Here the character of the mechanism used, the spirit presentation, is of distinct social importance.

This is an extremely complex matter, with social and personal elements intricately involved, elaborate imagery, and expression of fantasy. I can take here only one aspect, the structural identification of these spirit presentations. Despite the erudite and massive analyses of the personality, powers, and role of shaman or spirit medium, we still have very little data on exactly who these spirit presentations purport to be in terms of the social order. We have usually to be content with statements such as those by Marcelle Bouteiller that the North American Indian shaman, a most profoundly social being, incarnates the ancestors, or the spirits of the tribe (1950, p. 25, etc.), or by Eliade, that the female protecting spirit of a shaman, conceived as a celestial spouse, indubitably reflects matriarchal conceptions (1951, p. 88). We can go further than this. Putting the matter in another way, we want to know to what degree the spirit presentations of the medium are of a personal idiosyncratic order, or are part of a system of general religious entities common to the whole society, or symbolize specific elements of the social order.

In spirit mediumship we have essentially a conjunction of public and private meanings. The anthropologist conducting a study of a primitive religion often makes the translation of private into

[1] There are also clairvoyant mediums, though this phenomenon seems to be mainly restricted to Western and Oriental society.

public meanings himself. He takes down what an informant has to say – on the nature of God or spirit, on the referend of a symbol, on the interpretation of a rite – and treats this as an expression of a general meaning. The utterances of a spirit medium are normally made in a public or semi-public context, and they are received as having meaning for others than the medium himself. This meaning is sometimes diversified; members of the audience may not be able to agree on the significance of what the medium is saying. But usually, in Tikopia, a consensus of opinion is fairly soon reached. This consensus indicates that the community is agreed in regarding the medium's utterances as transcending his own personality. His words are regarded as valid in the sense of being held to be utterances by another entity of different type, a spirit. They are valid also in the sense that what the purported spirit says is normally held to be true, relevant, and obligatory. The utterances then are legitimate. But what the community has done in effect is to have bound itself up to a point to recognize as legitimate expressions of its own views those views expressed by one of its own members – or in rare cases, a non-member – who may not necessarily be a person ordinarily entrusted with the making of community decisions. It would not be quite correct to describe the medium as a catalytic agent, aiding the reactions of the community but himself remaining unchanged, because it is in fact through his change of state that the community view is promoted. But he does serve as an agent of crystallization of opinion, enabling action of others to go forward with sanction, altering events, while himself returning to the original state. This is one of the various forms of what I would call 'solution-techniques' for resolving personal or community dilemmas – the solution is still made by human agency, but given an added force and cogency by being expressed through a superhuman frame. But realistically, what is happening here? The community in effect is manifesting a faith in experiment. It assumes virtually that a member of the community from whom the usual controls of mundane challenge and status alignment have been removed will operate with more imaginative or more definitive views on an issue, and will yet retain enough sense of community responsibility to render those views significant and utilizable. Yet as the actual expressions of the medium, the physical man, they embody elements of his own personality. If they are not just nonsense

syllables, which is rare from the intrinsic nature of spirit mediumship as a means of communication, they must correspond with
some set of personal meanings for the medium. They may not
represent any very conscious set of associations in ordinary life,
but symbols which only a state of dissociation could allow to come
to expression. But while socially conditioned, there must be
something to which they correspond in the medium's make-up,
and some elements in this correspondence can often be elucidated
indirectly by discussion with the medium outside the dissociated
state. This can be seen in inquiry about the spirits by whom the
medium is allegedly possessed.

In examining from the structural point of view the classification
of the spirits who allegedly possess the Tikopia mediums, it is
useful for contrast to give first the situation in Kelantan where I
have observed analogous phenomena. The Kelantan village Malays,
among whom spirit mediumship and shamanship are common,
have no corporate descent groups. It is interesting then to note
that the spirits possessing their mediums are not those of their
ancestors, but of an elaborate range of Indonesian, Hindu, and
Muslim god and spirit characters not linked by kinship to the
medium at all, but arranged in a loose hierarchy with much
endowment of social and political titles. The Kelantan medium's
spirit troop then reflects his social structure in its absence of kinship bonds and its free use of status labels. The Tikopia situation
is almost the reverse. The society has corporate descent groups of
patrilineage type, and strong links of persons with their matrilateral kin. While the system of chieftainship is given very great
respect, there is a strong proliferation of titles in a status system.
Correspondingly, there is a strong kin tie and specific lineal
element in the Tikopia mediumship.

Some data are given in the Table.[1] Two-thirds of the 'spirit
presentations' of the mediums I knew best in 1928–9 were of kin
and gods of the medium's patrilineage; in 1952 the proportion
was less than one half, but two-thirds of the male mediums had

[1] The Table has imperfections. By my count in 1928–9 there were in Tikopia twenty-
seven spirit mediums, and in 1952 there were twenty-six. The Table gives data for only
slightly more than half of these. Moreover, while in 1952 the proportion of men to women
and pagan to Christian in the sample is roughly proportionate to those in the total, in the
earlier period the proportion of pagans, and of women, is too low. And while I think I
managed to list all the main spirit presentations of the mediums, I did not list all the minor
presentations. Hence while I think the results are plausible as a general statement, they are
diagnostic rather than definitive, and illustrate some of the weaknesses mentioned.

at least one male patrilineal ancestor or kinsman as a spirit, and the rest each had a patrilineal god, who possessed them.

The spirits which possessed mediums also included a proportion of chiefs, normally appearing through their descendants. Further, the social divisions of ordinary life were preserved to some extent in the spirit presentations: the spirits of great gods and of chiefs did not normally present themselves through commoners, and the spirits of women (who had few religious offices in the pagan system) did not normally present themselves through men. The Tikopia spirit mediumship, then, reflects the patrilineal social structure, and this conclusion is reinforced by the control case of Kelantan. But it is highly selective in the major principles it reflects; it makes no use of the very important matrilateral principle—unlike the invocation of ancestors in the *kava*.

Classification of 'Spirit' Presentations by Tikopia 'Mediums'

Sex and Religion of Mediums	No.	Category of 'Spirit'								Total
		Father	Patl. Anc.	Patl. God	Kin/ God of Spouse	Other Kin	Person of Note	Foetal Spirit	Spirit Child	
1929										
Male										
Pagan	7	I	2	7	.	.	4	.	.	14
Christian	2	I	2	6	.	.	3	3	I	16
Female										
Pagan	3	.	.	5	.	.	.	.	.	5
Christian	0	.	.	.	.	.	.	.	.	.
	12	2	4	18	0	0	7	3	I	35
1952										
Male										
Pagan	4	I	2	2	.	I	.	.	4	10
Christian	7	2	4	5	.	3	4	3	I	22
Female										
Pagan	3	.	.	I	6	.	.	I	I	9
Christian	2	2	.	.	I	I	.	I	.	5
	16	5	6	8	7	5	4	5	6	46

But let us look at the Table again. By 1952, with the great advance of Christianity in Tikopia there was much less need for the services of a spirit medium on formal ritual occasions, and this is reflected to some degree in the decline in the number of pagan gods appearing as spirit presentations. Alternative structural principles were operative. This was especially noticeable with women mediums, who now utilized the spirit presentations of their husband's lineage instead of those of their own patrilineage. Four of the female mediums had seven spirits representative of their husband's group (two being spirits of their late husband, one a husband's brother, two a husband's patrilineal ancestor, and two more being gods of the husband's lineage). These instances, it would seem, reflect the importance of the principle of marital tie, and of the way in which a woman may take on significant links with her husband's lineage. Yet this poses an interesting problem. Symbolic expression of the marital tie comes as an alternative to expression of the lineage tie. A Tikopia woman as a medium has a range of spirit presentations from her own patrilineage ancestors and gods open to her. The information I obtained in 1928–9 showed that women utilized these. Yet their successors seem to have switched to the affinal side. Why? In one case, I was told that a wife acted as medium for her husband's ancestors and gods because the more appropriate medium, the husband's brother, had died. Granting this substitution, why still should women find themselves taking on roles of male spirits when men rarely take on roles of female spirits? Here the most plausible explanation would seem to be that women, denied office in the regular system of religious officiants, compensated themselves by assuming it in the field of spirit mediumship, where their claims to power could not be very effectively refused.

But we see from this that the relation between a religious element and the social structure can be complex. The religious element may reflect the social structure directly, that is, it may symbolize in a simple, positive, and easily comprehended way an important social principle – say, the lineage principle. But the religious element may take an alternate form, and the decision as to which of two structural principles is selected for emphasis – in this case, lineage tie and affinal tie – may be determined not structurally but organizationally (see *supra*, Chapters II and III) in terms of domestic or analogous considerations. Again, the symbolization in the religious element may express not a positive but a negative feature of the social structure. If women, whose sex has no office, become male spirits when dissociated, while men, whose sex has office, do not become female spirits, the religious feature expresses a social asymmetry in reverse. In all these ways, religion may be said to reflect the social structure – but it does so in very different forms.

But the structural determinism of the 'spirit' presentations is very imperfect. In Tikopia society, where respect for the father is so deeply engrained by learning from the earliest years, and the father may be regarded as the principle of authority incarnate, it is interesting to see how few of the mediums showed a 'spirit' presentation of their fathers. Few also used the father's father. More remote ancestors and gods seemed more favoured as personality expressions, that is, figures whom the medium had never known in the flesh. These might be interpreted as more truly symbols of the social structure than the recent patrilineal kin, as being more stripped of personal and more representative of social attributes. (Alternatively, selection of them to detriment of father and father's father might mean rejection of the paternal authority principle when occasion arose, in the dissociated personality.) But even granting this, there is no regularity discernible in the order of such ancestors and gods. Sometimes a founding ancestor, sometimes a father's brother, sometimes a major and sometimes a minor god appears as a regular presentation. In other words, it seems as if in effect the society offers the dissociating person a list of social representations or symbols, and he or she pricks off those particular figures which through their special characteristics have a special appeal for the medium.

But there is a further significant feature. The Tikopia medium does not simply choose from the list of spirits furnished him by his society; he creates some of his own. Very important figures in the spirit presentations of many mediums are foetal spirits, the product of miscarriages, abortions, stillbirths, or occasionally, of infanticide – imperfect social beings whose death was not celebrated and whose burying received no funeral rites. So far from such creatures being discarded because they never formed part of the social structure, they are conceived as being among the most powerful spirits. Never having been men, they are not clogged by having had a developing and ageing body; they are light, swift, and powerful. They are more important because of their lack of social form – and they can be created *ad hoc* by the medium since society has never had a check on the personality he claims to represent. They are endowed with all kinds of qualities and attributes. Here is a field of personal creative activity of which mediums have taken differential advantage.

Putting this last point more trenchantly, so far from the religion of the Tikopia merely reflecting or maintaining the social structure, in some of its aspects it offers avenues of *escape from* society, into personal fantasy, which is then allowed social recognition and credited with social functions. The picture then is much more complex than the conventional one of a direct set of relations between structural principles and religious symbolization. Moreover, it is useless to try to dodge the issue by pleading that such materials 'relate to individuals' or 'are psychological'. There are problems for the psychologist in examining the processes involved – quality of the trance phenomena, family and social history of the subject, aspects of the personality expressed, etc. But the anthropologist cannot ignore the different categories of spirit presentation assumed, because to the degree that they serve as indicators of social principles they show how far the society sets the norms in advance for control of social affairs or leaves the initiative in the hands of personal judgement and imagination.

The need to question conventional assumptions about the support religion gives the social structure is shown by a comparison of the position of Tikopia spirit mediums with that of chiefs, in 1928–9 and again in 1952. It seemed to me in 1928–9 that Tikopia pagan religion was what may be termed a *permeating system*, deeply implicated with the Tikopia social structure, including the political structure. Spirit mediums, who had no particular status in the society apart from the immediate context of their mediumship, operated their religious craft partly in support of their lineage and clan structure and their chief, and partly independently, using their own creative imagery as a technique of contributing to their solution of social and personal problems. But the chiefs were involved at almost every point with religious affairs. Their persons were taboo, they had powers of *mana* and sorcery attributed to them, they were the priests of the community *par excellence*, the repositories of the most sacred knowledge, which they were believed to be able to use for the prosperity and welfare of their own group and of the whole land. Religion, it seemed, gave much powerful support to the political structure. Even the one Christian chief seemed to be supported by such sanctions, since he still recognized and at times even worshipped his pagan gods. I had thought that with the growth of Christianity, the transfer of the priestly role to others, and the secularization of the chieftainship as the old chiefs died and were replaced, the office would lose much of its status and power, if the institution did not actually collapse. I also expected to find spirit mediumship much diminished owing to less formal public occasions for its demonstration, though still perpetuated to cater for personal problems. I found after a generation that despite a great diminution in the pagan cultic body, and a reduction in pagan rites, spirit mediumship was flourishing on much the same scale as before. Moreover the new major Christian chief, who had been baptized in infancy, held a status and power equal to that of his pagan peers. Some social changes had occurred with the advance of Christianity, particularly in the status of lineage heads. But in fact it appeared that the Tikopia had been fully capable of detaching the religious symbolism and sanction from their chief, while still maintaining him in his political, economic, and social roles. The Tikopia seemed to have pinned their faith on chieftainship as a cardinal, even absolute political value, independent of the religious system. When in 1955–6, for a variety of reasons, the remaining pagans abandoned their ancient religion and the whole community became Christian, their chiefs, no longer cult-supported, remained solidly at their head, and continued to symbolize Tikopia society. Religion then provided avenues of expression for the political relationships and values, and helped to buttress them but was not indispensable to them.

This may be put another way. That part of the traditional Tikopia religion which was most closely linked with the social structure was the rites associated with the *kava* performance, which invoked a lineage ideology, used lineage-based recruitment to provide its priests, and was chief-orientated in its system of offerings and obligations. This was the part of the traditional religion which gave way first slowly, then completely. That part of the traditional religion which supported the social structure much more weakly was spirit mediumship, which used a much broader kin and non-kin ideology, was not primarily lineage-based in its ideology, and was not orientated in its performances towards the chiefs. It was this sector of the religion which catered for non-structural interests, for personal dilemmas, which survived, and flourished in spite of Mission opposition. In Tikopia the society in its major form carried on, with its kinship system, its chieftainship system unimpaired. The traditional religion, so closely linked with it, faced by the attack of an alternative system backed up by economic induce-ments and intellectual and moral arguments, succumbed to the pressure in all its main structural features leaving the minor rela-tively unstructured aspect of spirit mediumship to continue. In other words, religion as a configuration, or certain sectors of religion, can operate as semi-independent variables. The hypo-thesis might be advanced that the more public the cult, the more closely it is related to cardinal features of the social structure, the more liable it is to change when affected by external forces. Methodologically, it is significant to note that study of a situation over time may be necessary in order to allow the relative move-ment and weighting of factors to be perceived clearly.

I have not tried to give here any very detailed blue-print of method for the anthropological study of religion. But I have tried to face frankly some of the major difficulties we encounter in tackling our problems, especially in regard to assumptions which we must necessarily incorporate into our approach. I think there is need for such exposition. I have shown how in studies of reli-gious meaning we cannot remain content with general affirma-tions but have to consider different orders of meaning. I have shown how individual meaning, systematically treated, has socio-logical significance both for continuity and for change in religious systems. In all this, I hold that studies of process have an equal place with studies of pattern and structure. Finally, it seems to me that as anthropologists, while we are no longer content with the older positivist approach, we have no need to be afraid of sub-scribing to an intellectual, rationalist view, but on the contrary should assert its validity in scientific analysis of religion, and its capacity to perceive the relevance of the non-empirical, both as content and as instrument of religious study.

CHAPTER XI

Religious Belief and Personal Adjustment
(1948)

An anthropologist addressing an audience on the subject of religion realizes that he is probably facing great divergences of view. While some may regard all religious professions as illusory, others, like More's Utopians, may hold that it falls below the dignity of human nature to believe that the soul perishes with the body or that the world is governed by chance and not by divine providence. The anthropologist trusts that his scientific inquiry will reveal something of the nature of religious phenomena, but he knows that he does not stand as the sole interpreter. Apart from the theologian who claims a proprietary right, historian and sociologist, philosopher and psychologist, and even an occasional natural scientist, all proffer their interpretations of what William James summarized as the feelings, acts and experiences of men apprehending themselves to stand in solemn relation to what they consider to be the divine. Through the scope of his comparative method the anthropologist has contributed a universalism which the study lacked before. His primary observation of primitive cults has added much to its depth. Yet where so much is clouded over by emotion and feeling in the study of those heights of the human spirit which we call religious, the anthropologist's first justification is his sincerity in his attempt to gain as clear an intellectual comprehension of it as possible. His approach has been for the most part humanistic, seeking to understand on the plane of man's activities. It has also been socially positivist, in attributing to religious phenomena important social functions irrespective of the nature of their reality.

Anyone who has the honour of being invited to deliver a Henry Myers lecture before the Royal Anthropological Institute must therefore be conscious of his responsibility. Moreover, religion, the general theme of these lectures, has been the matter of examination by so many eminent men in the history of this Institute and of British anthropology. Tylor, Robertson Smith, Frazer, Marett, Westermarck, Rivers, Seligman, Malinowski – all are classic names, and to them must be added that of our most distinguished contemporary Radcliffe-Brown, who opened this series. Where their contributions stand like polished granite, my own must appear rough-hewn. But I hope it will serve as an introduction to argument.

My subject is religious belief. My basic hypothesis is that religious beliefs are related, in content, form and expression, to the attempts of individuals to secure coherence in their universe of relations, both physical and social. Recent anthropological studies of religion have concentrated more on the analysis of ritual than on that of belief. Religious beliefs appear less stable than ritual, more open to personal variation and modification. Their vagueness and lack of definition are seen in two respects. Different individuals in the same religious communion vary in their beliefs on a given topic, which makes it difficult to assign to any synoptic expression a truly representative value. Again, a single individual is often unable to formulate clearly his belief on even such fundamental concepts as God, Heaven or the soul. Variation in ritual is significant in the interpretation of the role which ritual has in the life of different individuals. Variation and lack of precision in belief, too, have analogous significance. Though they may complicate the analyses of the sociologist, they are not fortuitous; they are characteristic and indeed essential to the functions which religious belief fulfils.

Consider first the notion of belief itself. It has been called the subjective side of judgement. It is a set of ideas more or less integrated by reason but held with a conviction that they are true, that they are meaningful in relation to reality. Elements of knowledge, of emotion or feeling tone, and of volitional activity can be distinguished therein, each capable of being present to varying degree. But however adequate it may be to isolate belief as a psychological concept for examination, for sociological analysis it is necessary to consider it in terms of classes. For our immediate purposes any exact classification is not important. A convenient grouping comprises: empirical, mathematical, philosophical, aesthetical, ethical and religious. What is noteworthy is how religious belief differs from the others essentially in its content of the supernatural and in its quality of the sacred. In religious belief above all, the element of emotion in whatever be the kind of experience that gives the basis to the belief provides it with a strong flavour of reality. At one level, the nature of this experience is a specific question for psychology – as William James, Leuba and many others have amply shown. At another level, as a general question for philosophy, it has occupied the minds of men for over two thousand years. No one wishes deliberately to pass off metaphysics as science. But it has always seemed to me rather naïve to imagine that a personal metaphysical position can be entirely irrelevant to the analysis of religious phenomena. So a little later I shall say something about what I think is the object of religious belief.

For my present analysis it is primarily the content of belief as expressed in verbal behaviour with which I am concerned. One can study belief in its non-verbal expression as well. But one interest of the word, either spoken or written, as an index of belief, is that it can be studied at different levels – overt, or indicative of much that the author does not suspect is revealed. What I want to emphasize here is that religious beliefs, in their immediate expression, are a mode of action. They are not merely passive fixed items of mental furniture; their emotional component alone would suggest this cannot be so. They are active weapons in the process of adjustment by the person who holds them. What I mean by personal adjustment is the continual process of striving for order by the individual in his relations on the one hand with his physical and social universe, and on the other with his own logical system of categories of thought and his own set of impulses, desires and emotions. I think it will be admitted that there is a continual and real need for such adjustment or adaptation on the part of every individual. In this respect the vagueness and lack of precise definition of religious belief is, up to a point, an asset. It allows of a plastic treatment. Modification takes place in detail, often almost imperceptibly to the external observer, and it may be unconsciously by the individual himself.

If this be agreed, then certain implications can be considered. As greater precision in the definition of belief occurs, the greater is the necessity to cope with the change in external circumstances by reinforcing the belief. We shall be concerned with some examination of the processes of reinforcing or buttressing religious belief later. An alternative process is to make a radical alteration in belief by what is known as conversion. In any process of adjustment the content of belief, which varies according to the cultural situation, may be of considerable importance. For example, a belief in an ancestor cult is not of such a type as to allow easily the affiliation of other persons from a different society, who can have the original ancestors ascribed to them only by a series of elaborate fictions. Moreover, the range of religious belief can be expected to vary according to the range of possible social situations. In a simple society the personal adjustments which an individual may have to make are as great in magnitude as in a highly differentiated society such as our own, but are less in diversity.

Each individual has a configuration of religious beliefs corresponding to or representing a configuration of his personal adjustments. These adjustments can have degrees of completeness or adequacy according as the situation to which adjustment is required is more or less adequately conceived. To the degree that there is ignorance or error so there is imperfect adjustment, either recognized or not recognized as such. This conception of the individual's relation to the situations he has to meet is very different from that of a system of equilibrium. It is possible, in fact probable, that each individual has a configuration of more or less imperfect adjustments to reality – always lagging behind or varying from the current situation that he has to face. To conclude this series of propositions for the moment – it is through the continuous operation of personal adjustment in terms of belief that change in religious forms becomes possible.

The attempt to secure personal adjustment rests upon a perception that some degree of adaptation between self and environment is necessary to effective action in view of the ends the individual is pursuing. It rests also upon the emotional drive for sympathy and inter-communion. In the process of adjustment various motivations are at work. These include the search for order, for certitude, for self-expression and for feeling for others, for the exercise of intellectual curiosity. It is conceivable that individuals in any society might be content to place reliance on themselves or on their fellows alone for these elements of adjustment; some do so, especially in the more highly differentiated social systems. And a young child presumably relies on its parents for these matters. But the obvious human insufficiency to cover all the range of circumstances is only too plain. Peoples' limitations, their fallibility, their exercise of their own individualistic impulses, are soon discerned, even where sentiment of a strong kind may lead to trust. The requirements demanded are secured in the highest degree by the postulates of religious belief.

Such belief is always culturally defined, whether explicitly recognized as such or not. It has a nucleus or core, which is firmly held and in essentials usually simple to state; a set of ancillaries or personal variations of a fluctuating kind; and a periphery which is vague, involving either difficulties of formulation or lack of certainty or conviction. The nucleus of the belief may be comprised in part by the dogma of the religion concerned, that is, by the set of doctrines regarded as proper to be believed in by all who profess that religion. It may be assisted in utterance by creeds, expressions of the essential dogma in formal terms. But this is not inevitably the case. Most primitive religions have no creeds, and their dogmas are to be inferred from activity rather than from any specific formulation.

For evidence of this let me briefly refer to material from my own studies. In Tikopia there is a nuclear belief held, as far as could be verified, by all persons, in what may be termed a separable soul-essence of man. Different people have varying ancillaries attributing or denying soul-essence to birds and animals, to stones and trees, and to material goods. There are varying ancillaries also relating to the fate of souls after death. One man, a chief, linked their fate with their interest in life in the basic religious rite, the *kava*. Those who ignored the *kava* in life were themselves ignored after death; their souls, he maintained, were not borne to the spirit world, but left to stand in the path and annoy people. Another man, also a chief and with a similar interest in maintaining the prestige of the *kava*, believed that the souls of the dead came in due course to a stone crossing a void barring the way to the future world. If the soul was that of a man who had sought the *kava*, all was well; the stone stayed firm and the soul crossed it to its future abode. If the man had spurned the *kava*, the stone began to rock and finally precipitated the soul down into the gulf, to be lost. A question as to where the soul goes then showed belief on the periphery – on one occasion the chief said he didn't know, the soul simply vanished; on another occasion he said the soul wandered blindly about. A third man, son of a chief, was not so concerned to interpret the stone in terms of moral or ritual duties. He regarded it as a matter of paying dues, as to a Cerberus. The soul arrives with bark-cloth, areca-nut, oil and valuables. If he wishes to pass, he offers them to the female demon dwelling in the stone. Should he not do this, and try to cross, she makes the stone slippery, the soul loses its footing and tumbles down below. As a further ancillary belief, a description was given of certain flying souls. They have 'speed', that is, power, and evade toll by taking wing, rising up above and darting onwards through the air like fish in the sea. The personal interests of the chiefs are clear in these beliefs. They compensate for inability to punish ritual laggards directly, by adjustment of belief to imagine them suffering future punishment. To the extent that such views get popular credence, the ritual obligations are reinforced.

Similar differences of belief occur in regard to those souls that arrive in the afterworld. The general scheme is that of a number of different heavens, stratified. Each set of strata is associated with a major social group and is situated at a different point of the compass. This is nuclear belief. But there are many individual ancillaries, as regards the names and number of the heavens, and the behaviour of the spirits of the dead there. In particular, this type of belief serves in citation of names in tales and songs, thus acting as material of revelation for spirit mediums. A new name is an effort of the creative imagination, which appeals to other people as a piece of new knowledge, in effect, property. Hence there is a tendency for spirit mediums in their recitals to elaborate the furniture of the other world, in nomenclature and activities; in so doing they help to bolster up their own authenticity by the production of such novel information, in which they appear to believe firmly.

Examination of Malay religious beliefs in a fishing community gave analogous data. Every person held nuclear beliefs in spirits, the ubiquitous *hantu*, and in the powers of selected human individuals to control them. But very different beliefs were held about the powers of a specific *hantu*, or specific human controls. Two dramatic events brought this out to me – the advent of a conjurer claiming to produce sugar, biscuits, and even live birds by materialization; and the practices of a religious man who without experience of the sea and its lore, claimed modestly to be able to increase the catch of fish by well-timed rites with a candle and an egg. The resulting controversies illustrated a variety of ancillary beliefs and their dependence on problems of personal adjustment.

In examining belief in the simpler religious systems, the anthropologist relates the concepts under scrutiny to human needs, desires, emotions. He sees how the various kinds of spirit powers believed in, for example, can be interpreted as essentially socialized projections of the believer's own psychological requirements and faculties. Applied on a comparative basis, such findings may lead him to stress the subjective character of all religious experience and belief. His hypothesis may be that even those concepts which are normally regarded as basic in a religious system are not independent of the individual human believer, but are part of his total adjustment, in common with that of his fellows, to their general field of problems.

Let us pursue this theme in terms of the way in which certain basic beliefs have been formulated. Anthropologists ordinarily study particularist religions, i.e. those in which the system of beliefs and practices is regarded by the adherents as applying to their particular society alone, and not by implication to mankind as a whole. I propose in this lecture to draw examples also from the universalist religions, to broaden my generalizations. In this part of the analysis I shall examine some of the beliefs concerning the Deity, as being of crucial interest.

It is a commonplace that even in the universalist religions belief in God is often conceived in terms which in providing a definite sanction for behaviour, are appropriate to the particular type of society in which the belief finds expression. For instance, in the Koran, the Faithful are enjoined to fight on God's path. Believers who sit at home free from trouble shall not be treated alike with those who do valiantly in the cause of God with their substance and their persons. God has assigned to the latter a rank and a rich recompense above those who sit at home. If a believer kill a believer by mischance, he is bound to atone by blood-money, setting free a slave who is a believer, or both; or by fasting two months if he has no means otherwise. This is the penance enjoined by God, the Knowing, the Wise. But who shall kill a believer of set purpose shall abide in hell for ever; God shall be wrathful with him, and curse him and prepare for him a great torment.[1] Here the attitudes attributed to God can be regarded as a projection of

[1] The Koran, Sura 4, *Women*, verses 94–97.

the Prophet's desires to safeguard the faith of his creation. The religious sanction is invoked to promote unity and amity among the Faithful and compose differences. The Divine sanction was invoked with a more personal flavour to explain the special dispensation by which the Prophet allowed himself to have as many as nine wives, whereas the maximum number allowed to the Faithful was only four. The Prophet by the Koran was allowed not only the wives whom he had dowered and the daughters of his uncle and of his aunts, but also any believing woman who had given herself up to him, if he desired to wed her – 'a privilege for thee above the rest of the Faithful' as the Prophet's own revelation announced it to him.[1]

Fundamental in the nature of much religious belief is that characteristic which may be called the process of theo-symbolism. The aims of man and the principles which he seeks or thinks he finds in the universe are given shape in the idea of the Deity, who is made their symbolic expression. Social relations or interests empirically observable are explicitly formulated as inherent or transcendental principles. They are represented as arising not from the nature of social action but from the nature of God. To acquire knowledge is to many people a human good and certainly engages a great deal of their energies. Consequently it is held that it must be God's will that men should use to the full what gifts of intellectual curiosity He has endowed them with. Guidance is required in one's contacts with one's fellows. Consequently, it is held that God has a will for the world, and that this will, which is perfect and good, sets a pattern for the life of every man.[2]

This theo-symbolism may also assume an inverted form. Some trust and confidence in one's fellow beings is a prerequisite to effective co-operation and sharing of the products of social endeavour. Hence the concept of faith may be expressed as a two-way process. Not only must man have faith in God; he must also believe that God has faith in him. 'God puts His trust in man; He depends upon him; He commits to him the responsibility for carrying out His purposes for the world. . . . God trusts the indi-

[1] The Koran, Sura 33, *Confederates*, verse 49.
[2] Cf. the view of a Chinese scholar on this point: 'Since men have knowledge, many religions regard God as having knowledge, though there is this difference, that he is omniscient. Since men have power, many religions regard God as having power, though with this difference, that he is omnipotent. Since men have a will, many religions regard God as having a will, though with this difference, that his will is perfectly good.' Fung Yu-Lan, 1947, p. 126.

vidual with the raw materials for the formation of character.'
God's trust is often abused, by human faithlessness, stupidity and
indolence. But God continues to trust; God's trust implies His
patience.[1] Here then is an interesting mechanism whereby a man
first projects his desire for confidence into divine shape, and then
injects this image in turn with a further charge of the desired
element. Human frailty can then be interpreted not merely as
failure to take advantage of facilities offered, but as betrayal of
facilities handed over. The sanction for human action is thus
doubled, and guilt is added to laxity. But there is room for selective adjustment. Assurance is given to the shrinking spirit. Where
one cannot trust one's fellows, where the course of events belies
their fair promise, one can fix one's trust on God, and find that
reciprocity which is so craved by feeling that Divinity returns the
confidence. Again to him who wishes to feel that he is entrusted
with a task, to feel that in a situation of dependence he is the one
who is relied upon for action, a belief that God has committed a
responsibility to him – even if it be the onerous one of formation
of his own character – can be a stimulating and heartening thing.
However mean a creature he may be in his own eyes and those of
his fellows, he is one on whom God depends. If he has faith, he
can set back his shoulders and go forward on his daily business,
feeling that every step he takes in the social world is in discharge
of a personal duty to the Most High.

The same process of attribution helps to provide man with that
sense of order which he desires to see in the flux of events that he
may guide his future actions and have some certainty in what often
seems a sorry tangle. One kind of belief which allows this and
strengthens the doubter is that which assigns the origin of the
world to a Creator who continues to take a controlling interest in
his work. Most religious systems, primitive as well as more developed, have concepts of this type. But once the principle of
order has been admitted, there is also need for the explanation of
contradiction. It is only by the eye of faith that a perfect plan can
be discerned. There are several ways in which this can be achieved.
One, probably the simplest, is to stress human incapacity to
understand. To give a sample citation, 'The divine plan in its totality
is utterly beyond human comprehension, though it must include
the possibility of moral and physical evil, and contain within it

---

[1] From an article 'God's Trust in Man', *The Times*, 13 Nov. 1943.

elements of contingency which are inseparable from human freedom.'[1] Another way is to distinguish between the plan or will of God and the imperfection of the human creature as hampering its execution. It is argued that God's will, which stands sure and unshakable through all the ebb and flow of human history, cannot be finally thwarted. But its fulfilment may be hindered and the progress of His kingdom slowed down by human indifference and perversity, and by man's refusal to co-operate with Him.[2] By this interpretation it would seem that the Deity is content to abide by the implications of the freedom which He Himself has vouchsafed to man. He accepts therefore the limitations of His own plan. But contradiction or inconsistency may be faced another way. Those who hold fast to the belief that there is only one proper vehicle for the propagation of the divine message of Christianity are distressed by the way in which the historic Church has been divided by the secession of numerous reforming dissident bodies. The spectacle of a divided Christendom, it is argued, is intolerable to anyone who realizes what God's will is in regard to His Church. Nevertheless the spectacle of good men and of good works proceeding from nests of false doctrine can hardly be denied. An analogous issue which attained wider currency and even some poignancy arose in the First World War when it was discovered that many of the young soldiers who excelled not only in bravery but also in self-sacrifice and in acts of devotion to their fellows did not profess the Christian faith. To such problems many answers have been given. But among them is the view that God is not bound by His own ordinances.[3] Having laid down what shall be the proper procedure in the implementation of the Divine plan for salvation, He is nevertheless prepared to receive all that serves His purposes, whether it is prepared to come under the formal jurisdiction or not. This view can be of course a most flexible instrument since it can be used to justify almost any act of expediency. But its interest to us in this connexion is the way in which it can serve as a means of adjustment for those who believe in the unique value of one religious faith and have to account for virtue in the adherents of others.

One of the most interesting issues in this general theme is that technically known as theodicy, the problem of the vindication of

---

[1] 'The Will of God – Man's Response', a correspondent in *The Times*, 10 Jan. 1948.
[2] *Ibid.*   [3] See, for example, Randolph, 1923, p. 10.

Divine Providence in view of the existence of pain and evil. This offers an intellectual as well as an emotional challenge to the believer in the conception of the Deity as powerful, wise, good, and concerned with the administration of the universe. For the deeply religious person evil is a problem to be overcome when it manifests itself in concrete behaviour. But it is also a phenomenon demanding some kind of explanation in terms of the consistency of the divine supervision of the affairs of men.

In the religions of the simpler societies behaviour, thought and emotion which are injurious or intended as injurious to man are not usually conceptualized as a single abstraction. Conceptualization takes the form rather of separate type events or institutions, such as death or witchcraft or war. Aetiological myths provide their rationale or a defence against them. As Malinowski has pointed out, such myths often treat cosmic events as the product of the simplest human or even animal lapse or omission. Take the myth of death, which is normally regarded as the supreme evil. The ancient Maori people believed that death came from the Goddess Hine-nui-te-po, the Great Lady of Darkness. The culture-hero Maui thought that he could win life for man if he penetrated the body of the Goddess and touched her heart. In due course he made his attempt, entering her while she lay sleeping by the way from which all men are born. But accident intervened. A little bird, the fantail, seeing Maui's legs kicking in the air as he began the perilous passage, was overcome with laughter at the ridiculous sight and the sound of his mirth woke the sleeping Goddess. She closed her body upon Maui and killed him; so death continued its hold over man. One Tikopia myth of death also places man's fate in animal hands. A rat and a crab disputed as to what should happen to man when he grew old. Said the crab, 'Let him cast his skin as I do, emerge freshly and continue to live on.' The rat objected to this, saying, 'No, let him die and be buried in the ground, that his body may rot away.' Here the myths supply explanation and allocate responsibility on a scale and in a way which allows simple comprehension of the great inescapable yet mysterious element in human destiny.

Most primitive societies, in conformity with their lack of effective international relations and emphasis on small group organization, have not proceeded to ideas of a unitary god and a unitary principle of evil. Some of the more advanced religions subsume the phenomena of the universe under integrative principles but do not view these as having any personified character. For the Chinese Confucianist philosopher Hsün Ch'ing, for instance, Heaven, roughly equivalent to Nature, was the unchanging process of action responsible for the final accomplishment of events. 'The true sage does not try to know Heaven' though he sees the results. Man's body and spirit are the work of Heaven. Concerning the fundamental nature of man he and other philosophers were often in disagreement. Mencius maintained the innate goodness of man's nature, with evil as due to bad upbringing. Hsün Ch'ing maintained its basic evil to be corrected by the character acquired through the purposive thinking and practice of the sages and expressed in ritual and rightness.[1] Buddhism proclaims the unitary principle of the universe, but will hardly call it God even as a symbolic expression. The problem of theodicy hardly arises directly then. The issue is handled by admitting the validity of evil as a real phenomenon, but stressing that it is all part of human involvement in desire.[2] The Taoist view, as expressed in the opening of the Tractate on Actions (Kan Ying P'ien), is that 'Woe and weal have no gates, men call them on themselves', that is, they are not predestined, but the result of the heart rising to goodness or rising to evil.[3]

In the monotheistic religions various other solutions to the problem, each allowing a considerable degree of personal inter-

---

[1] Hughes, 1942, pp. 100, 321–5; Fung Yu-Lan, 1947; Soothill, 1929, p. 205.

[2] The Lotus Sutra, the great canonical book of Mahayana Buddhism, expresses the teaching thus:

> 'The cause of all suffering
> Is rooted in desire.
> If desire be extinguished,
> Suffering has no foothold.'

In this form of the religion, salvation, freedom from suffering, pain and evil is attained by faith in the Buddha and Boddhisattvas, and in the Sutra which proclaims the Way of the Law (Soothill, 1930, pp. 97–8 et passim). The inclusive pantheistic doctrines of the Tendai sect lay stress on the absolute nature of the Buddha, in which animate and inanimate are of the same essence; in the last resort, therefore, evil is also comprised therein. 'Since we are all of the same nature, some good can be found in the lowest of us, and reciprocally there is also some evil, in Buddha.' The idea is also held that the world is compounded of three thousand dharmas, or fundamental elements. 'The spiritual, and that which appears to us as material, good and evil, all our sentient universe and our illusions, are the different aspects under which the play of these three thousand dharmas reveal themselves to our senses and to our mind. . . . This universe is so constructed that although it is constituted in its infinity by these three thousand dharmas, a single thought, mean as it may be, contains them all. . . . The dharmas form the world and are all in our thought' (Steinilber-Oberlin, 1938, pp. 77–8).

[3] Soothill, pp. 222–4.

pretation, allocate responsibility differently. The Zoroastrian sees the problem in terms of two active conflicting principles, Good and Evil, each of equal validity. They struggle for mastery in a contest almost indefinitely to be prolonged, though it is hoped that Good will prevail in the end. The Muslim, following the Koran, has a fairly clear-cut set of propositions on which to rely, and which place responsibility for the ills of the world on man's own shoulders. God has breathed into the soul its wickedness and its piety, but these are only potentials. Man himself creates his own ills. The believer is told, 'Whatever good betideth thee is from God and whatever betideth thee of evil is from thyself.'[1] In Christianity the existence of evil rests presumably on the ultimate acquiescence of God. But in terms of human affairs its application is understood by reference to the doctrine of the Fall on the one hand, and the principle of human freedom and responsibility on the other. The myth of the original sin of our first parents being due to a simple act of yielding to curiosity is reminiscent of the myths of the more primitive religions. To make death and the source of all our woe really spring from one single yielding to caprice by an unsophisticated woman almost at the beginning of the world is poising this scheme of things on a very slender foundation. Evil and the fruits of evil must therefore have entered into the Great Design before the Creation; the Fall was the symbol, not the source.

Theological argument about the problem of evil has brought various explanations, including doctrines of self-limitation on the part of God. It is difficult to keep this separate from the idea that He is a finite being and therefore not omnipotent. But it does help to alleviate the burden of the mystery of evil. Another explanation relies largely on the recognition of the instrumental worth of evil – the value of physical pain and suffering in moulding character, and that of moral evil as part of the general discipline of education in combating it. Moral evil has been described as the 'discord without which there would be no harmony, shade without which there would be no light'.[2] Such an essentially monistic view of the problem preserves the omnipotence of God at the cost of the absoluteness of evil. It is reminiscent of the Hindu view that good and evil alike are phenomenal expressions of the one

[1] The Koran, Sura xci, *The Sun*, verses 7–10; Sura iv, *Women*, verse 81.
[2] Hasting's *Encyclopædia*, article s.v. 'Theodicy'.

divine substance or energy; as they operate, often in cyclical opposition, in the world, they are but manifestations of Māyā, the mirage-like illusory character of all existence.[1]

Here then we have a set of beliefs regarding the nature of evil and its place in the scheme of human life, with several emphases. One is an empiricist attitude, accepting the existence of evil as a given element in the nature of things, whether present as an active principle in the world, or as innate in man's constitution, or the product of his desires. Another associates evil more directly with the permissive control of a Deity, as part of his cosmic plan, either as embedded in the great design or called into operation by some fatal action of man. The more enlarged the conception of the Deity, the more difficult becomes the problem of justification of the Divine providence. In all cases an element of human activity is involved, both in setting the processes of evil in motion and in putting an end to them and their consequences. Freedom from evil and its results can be attained according to some religious beliefs by the acts of self-restraint of a more or less positive kind, forming a virtuous life. According to other beliefs, it is reached by the acts of faith, accompanied by some degree of regret or repentance for what has been done, and leading of themselves to salvation. Emotionally the acts of faith are more attractive and easier as a solution than the acts of self-discipline without reference to Divine grace. Intellectually, it may be more difficult to say honestly 'I believe . . .' than to see the reasonableness of altering one's way of life. With every profession of faith is mingled a modicum of reason. But for the man who endeavours to guide himself by thought and not simply by emotion, the sedative of faith is not enough; it must be balanced by the stimulant of argument. For belief to be effective as an instrument of personal adjustment, therefore, one expects to find elaborate intellectual analysis mingled with the statement of what are conceived as the results of experience.

So far we have been examining what may be called public expressions of belief; now let us consider some more individual formulations. These are to be found in particular as far as Christianity goes in the sphere of speculative theism – in arguments for the existence of God, and about the attributes of God. I would

[1] Cf. Zimmer, 1946, p. 136. 'Hindu wisdom, Hindu religion, accepts the doom and forms of death as the dark-tones of a cosmic symphony. . . .'

emphasize that I am concerned not with the logical validity of the arguments, but with their form and content as sociological expressions, reflecting interests and providing means of action. The ontological argument of Anselm, and its reformulation by Descartes, the aetiological and other arguments of Leibnitz, the Thomist arguments from motion and so on, are all attempts to buttress by the power of logic those convictions which rest on the basis of faith. The reasoned sequences of propositions regarding the dependence of conception upon existence; the necessity of an Existent which is not contingent but carries within it its own cause or reason; the relation of order and intelligibility in the world to an intelligent, planning Creator are religious as well as metaphysical exercises. The urgency of the argument that in each case the inference *must* be so reveals how the imperative that drives the disputant emerges from his own need for intellectual reassurance, rather than from the rigour of the implications of the premisses.[1] Nowadays, all this brave show brings only feeble applause.

It is true that a generation ago one daring spirit reformulated the ontological argument, with certain additions relating to emotional content, to give the concept of a personal God what he termed value as well as logical validity. But he surpassed himself by proving by the same line of reasoning that if God marks the upper limit of our conceptions there must be a corresponding lower limit. Rather disconcerted, he concludes that this can only be the Devil. With some relief he affirms that this Devil is not personal, though the impersonal devil, or evil, must be reckoned as eternal. At this point his courage cracks a little and he almost begs to be proved wrong. 'I confess', he says, 'to being uncomfortable over my deduction from Anselm's argument, but perhaps

---

[1] Muslim theology has its parallels in this field. For example, take the arguments of Ibn Maskawaih, a medieval historian who died in the early years of the eleventh century, nearly 150 years before St. Thomas. In his 'Proof of the Maker', the first chapter of his book entitled *The Smaller Work on Salvation*, he puts forward a case very similar to that of Aquinas, and probably derived from the same Aristotelian sources, for the existence of God in terms of a need for a Prime Mover, who is the cause of all effects but not himself the effect of any cause. The proposition that God exists, he holds, is as obvious as, if not more so than, the proposition that the Sun exists. The difference is that the latter is clear to the senses whereas the former is clear to the reason. To free reason from its veils and reach the knowledge of God and the real, i.e. spiritual world, requires discipline. And who lacks reason is debarred from apprehension of God's existence, as a bat from the lack of the appropriate sensory faculties is debarred from an apprehension of the Sun's existence. (See Hamid, 1946.) Here we meet the thesis familiar in other contexts, that failure of an opponent to agree on the nature of the phenomena under discussion must be attributed to a gap in his perception, and not to error in the original identification.

my critics will show that the reality of the devil is after all only a pseudo-reality'—a regulative notion, in distinction from the reality of God.[1]

But ever since Kant's powerful attack, the case for thinking that God's existence can be inevitably demonstrated by reasoning from basic propositions about mind or matter has been greatly weakened. C. C. J. Webb has pointed out that 'the proofs of the existence of God which were so important a factor in the eighteenth century defence of religion are now very largely discredited'. In carefully weighed terms he continues, 'it is vain to suppose that, apart from some specifically religious experience in our hearer we can, so to say, force religion upon a reluctant mind by means of such reasonings'.[2] And J. L. Stocks indicates the singular character of the assertion of the existence of God on *a priori* grounds. 'The proofs themselves rest on the uniqueness of their problem.'[3]

The logical arguments put forward for the existence of God have always in religious history been supported also by the appeal to empirical experience. Events in the external world have been regarded as countersigning, so to speak, the evidence provided on other grounds. Such events are of two types – normal and miraculous. In all religions which base part of their claim to recognition upon the purity of their ethical principles, witness to their truth is sought in the conduct of those who follow their doctrines. Each of the major religions has its saints, whose lives have been marked by an extreme of piety, self-abnegation, and moral refinement. But each has been able to count also multitudes of ordinary adherents who have shown such control of themselves and such care for their fellow men that it is concluded they could only be animated by belief of a true kind. One of the arguments put forward not merely for the superiority but also for the correctness of Christian belief, for instance, is the general character of the achievements of Western civilization in liberating men from physical and mental bonds. However, it is difficult for even those who maintain such views to regard them as conclusive or

[1] Cock, 1918, p. 20.

[2] Webb, 1929, pp. 36–40. He proceeds indeed to draw a comparison between the recalcitrance of such a hearer and resistance to poetry or music in a soul incapable of aesthetic emotions. But this is an imperfect analogy since only in a figurative way is it ever suggested that aesthetic expression carries within it any qualities of a personal suprahuman kind akin to those claimed for religion.

[3] Stocks, 1934, pp. 19–20.

final evidences for the truth of the religion concerned. The achievements of Christian like those of other religious organizations have often been base as well as noble. And men of pure life with ethical systems of a lofty selfless kind are not the prerogative of any one religious faith. In fact many modern theologians are coming to acknowledge that the social influence of Christianity is not the prime argument for its validity, that it is only a by-product. Its aim of promoting social justice on this view, if not illusory, is certainly secondary. The world is impermanent; it is the future, the eternal, that should be sought, by the road to salvation through faith and grace.

The argument of evidence from miracle seems to be at present in a transitional state – at least as far as Christian circles go. Whereas a century ago sceptics were few, there are probably now large numbers of professing Christians who believe that most if not all of the miracles described in the Scriptures are at best allegorical. Miracle, by definition, is an event which stands outside the ordinary processes of nature, is remarkable for its discontinuity, and is not explainable by physical principles. As has often been pointed out – if we could explain it, it would not be a miracle. Nevertheless there is an attempt to reconcile modern scientific views with Scriptural account as far as possible. This takes three forms. The first is to waive any idea of physical anomalies or variations from natural laws and to treat a miracle as a symbol – an account in terms of physical behaviour of what was in fact mental behaviour. On this view the miracle of feeding the hungry multitude from a small quantity of loaves and fishes is a beautiful story illustrating the importance of compassion, the virtues of sharing, and the way in which the effects of a gift are multiplied manifold. Another view is that the Scriptural account describes an actual event, but in terms somewhat different from what in fact must have happened. Ritchie's explanation, for example, is that the crowd had come to hear the Master already furnished with provender concealed about their garments. But in the character of suspicious Oriental peasantry they were unwilling to take out what they had and share with their neighbours. The Master, knowing this, called up to him a small boy; then, breaking up and dividing the food, by his personal magnetic example He induced the crowd to follow suit. The miracle lay not in multiplication of the food itself, but in dissipating suspicion and securing co-operation from the hard-bitten, slow-moving peasant assembly.[1] Still another view is that which tries to save the miracle by an appeal to modern science. The miracles of healing are thus interpreted as an early use of psychotherapy. The miracle of the feeding of the five thousand is explained by concepts analogous to those of atomic fission, of which the Master is believed to have had the secret. The following is one view: 'That Our Lord in creating the solid matter of which the food was formed had at His intuitive disposal and control the vast energy which we now know to have been necessary, gives to the Christian believer a new realisation of His power, and to the unbeliever a further difficulty.'[2] Within the whole range of miracles there are, however, grades in what is treated as matter for belief. Many who give credence to Biblical miracles deny this to the miracles recorded since Apostolic times, regarding them as not supported by evidence of the same weight. The newer the miracle, the less it is believed. Even within the New Testament range a distinction is drawn between such ancillary events as the feeding of the multitude and the cardinal events of the Virgin Birth and the Resurrection. That which is central to the whole religious system cannot be so easily abandoned, however incredible it may seem. The surest course to adopt is that which has been hallowed by long usage – to believe even though it is incredible. 'Strange to all our experience and inscrutable to all our science', as one writer has put it, such stupendous miracles are part of the attraction of faith. Belief in them is part of the test of faith itself. *Credo quia incredibile* becomes a matter of pride.

In the last resort, it is not intellectual or moral proofs for belief in the existence of God, or in other religious concepts that have prime validity; it is the emotional proofs. This was demonstrated more than a century ago by the German theologian Schleiermacher. Seeing the inadequacy of basing evidences for the truth of Christianity upon human reason alone, he developed the theme of the importance of man's feeling of dependence on God. This to him was the true basis of dogma. An essentially similar view, it will be remembered, was put forward as the basis of religion on scientific grounds by Radcliffe-Brown in his lecture in this series three years ago.[3]

[1] Ritchie, 1945, pp. 73-4.　　　　　　　　[2] Thornton, 1930, p. 27.
[3] William James (1929, p. 27) has argued that this is only one of many sentiments which can be put as the basis of religion.

But basing belief on emotion, on non-rational attachment of the will, does not mean suspension or abnegation of all reasoning processes. This can be so even in the acceptance of miracles. The view that the events described as miracles actually happened because the Gospel record is based on eyewitness or near eyewitness accounts is interesting. Every anthropologist is familiar with the miracles of magic, faith-healing, spirit-mediumship, and ancestral intervention – apparently much better authenticated from contemporary sources. What impresses is not the value of the evidence adduced. But the mental attitude on the part of the believer indicates the strength of the need that is felt for support to what is believed. It is felt that there should be some demonstration of relation between antecedent and consequent. In the case of the Resurrection, verification is at times held to lie in experiences of the disciples, transmitted to other followers who wrote their words down. The believer in the miracle thus transfers his reasoning – he abandons any attempt to place the event in a physical order, since it is characterized by discontinuity in natural process. But he sets it in the framework of a rational human order by relying on a case for the credibility of witnesses and faithfulness of the written record. Suggestion has even been made that the evidence would bear scrutiny comparable with that given in a modern court of law.

My point is here that belief is emotionally based but intellectually supported. Its use as part of the processes of personal adjustment requires that the emotion be organized in an intellectual or para-intellectual system.

The furthest removes from this are the emotional extremes of frenzy (such as that following on, say, bereavement) or of transcendental mysticism. It is symptomatic of the general attitudes of believers that though the same propositions of belief may be shared, there is often an attempt to restrain the exhibition of transports of emotion by others. And among writers on religion who are primarily concerned with intellectual analysis, there is a tendency to deprecate any ranking of transcendental mysticism too high on the scale of religious experience.[1] On the other hand there is the simple attitude of the intuitional claim – 'I believe because I know.' In this, as for example in the identification of the object of knowing with a transcendent Being, there is a refusal to carry the intellectual analysis beyond an affirmation.

[1] Webb, *op. cit.*, p. 8; Temple, 1924.

But let us continue with the arguments which buttress faith.

In line with modern ideas of development is the view that God is being made known to man more exactly and completely by progressive revelation. Few Christians will go so far, perhaps, as to admit that the nature of God himself may have changed from that of a jealous tribal god to one of love for all humanity, even though it is one implication from the Biblical record.[1] But only the most ardent Fundamentalist nowadays will maintain that the days of the Creation were spaces of twelve hours or so between dawn and dusk, that man was formed of the dust of the ground, and woman from one of the ribs of man, and that the Lord God walked in the cool of one evening in a garden, eastward in Eden, which had a tree giving the fruits of the knowledge of good and evil.[2] The argument for progressive revelation is used in two ways. One way is in buttressing the general validity of religion, while meeting the difficulty of the existence of a diversity of faiths or creeds, each claiming to have the sole key to the truth. If all are wrong but the one championed by the particular believer, then intellectually doubt may creep in as to the possibility of error in that one. But if all are admitted to have in some measure a partial revelation of the Divine, then, to some types of minds at least, it becomes easier to think that one's own faith must be right, and being so is the closest to the truth. The argument can be applied even to the religious conceptions of the people of the simpler societies, often formerly dismissed as absurd by Christian missionaries. Thus a few years ago the Moderator of the Presbyterian Assembly in New Zealand, in opening the annual conference spoke of the ancient Maori conception of Io – represented by European scholars as the supreme god – as remarkable. In his view it 'could only be accounted for by the statement that, while they felt after Him in the darkness, God's spirit revealed to them as much of the Divine nature as could be conveyed to men in their stage of development'.[3] Such an opinion reflects the speaker's conviction of his church's own attainment. But the reverse attitude can also be emphasized.

[1] This idea is dramatically and movingly expressed in Marc Connelly's play *Green Pastures*, which symbolizes God learning from experience – specifically, the experience of suffering. See also the preface to the play by Vincent Long.

[2] The metaphorical nature of beliefs formerly held as literal, for example the spatial notions of heaven and hell expressed in the Apostles' Creed, is examined by Ritchie, *op. cit.*, pp. 75–6.

[3] Rev. J. G. Laughton, as reported in the *Auckland Weekly News*, 18 Nov. 1942.

The second way of using the argument for progressive revelation is in emphasizing the relativity of our own present knowledge, and so warding off criticism. This may be of two kinds. Internal criticism alleges that a change or development in interpretation of doctrine is not an improvement but a perversion, a heresy. External criticism alleges that changes in doctrine are still further evidence that the religion as a whole is a human fabrication – that what are claimed as refinements in understanding the spiritual world are nothing but inevitable adjustments to the flux of events in the material world. The notion of progressive revelation meets both these attacks.

One of the most brilliant achievements in the use of this concept to face internal criticism is given by the Lotus Sutra, the Mahayana Buddhist text. It would appear that this work had in its inception no direct connexion with the Buddha, that though it purports to present the words of the Eternal Saviour, his last testament before his departure, it was composed long, perhaps centuries, after his death. Its essential teaching, salvation by faith, is in flat opposition to the ideas of attainment of Nirvana by self-discipline and good works, which are the essence of the older orthodox 'Hinayana' (Theravada) teaching. The Lotus Sutra, in a series of mystical revelations, discloses through the mouth of the Buddha himself how he had hitherto used the narrow way of doctrine of salvation by works as a preparatory piece of enlightenment, reserving the broad way of salvation by faith for the ultimate gift of knowledge. When asked why he should have first taught and then repudiated the Theravada doctrines, the Buddha answers that he has had to preach the Law as might be expedient. Sinful ignorant men would not have been able to understand the full and wonderful truth at once and therefore he had to use appropriate tactful methods. The Buddha reinforces his argument by the parable of the Burning House. A father sees his children playing about inside, heedless of his warnings, and in danger of burning to death. He lures them outside by promises of rich toys which for the moment he does not have. Overjoyed, they all run outside. Then, when they are in safety, he takes his time and prepares for them the gifts he described. In the Sutra, all his hearers assent that the Buddha's intention and his gift of redemption remove from him all taint of falsehood – that his explanation justifies his message.[1]

[1] Soothill, *op. cit.*, 1930; introduction and chapter ii.

The history of the great religions is full of such arguments of progressive revelation. Christianity uses them to justify itself against Judaism; Islam uses them against Judaism and Christianity both. In the early nineteenth century they were used against Islam in Persia by the reformer Saiyid 'Ali Muhammed of Shiraz. As El Bab, The Door, he put forward what was in effect a new set of religious doctrines about the unity and attributes of God. To the Comte de Gobineau, now rather under a cloud because of his ill-judged essay on the inequality of the races of man, but a sociological observer of acute penetration nevertheless, we owe a valuable record and analysis of the new faith, and its relation to the old. According to Gobineau, the Bab purported to give not a new conception of the Deity, but only a further development of the knowledge of the Divine nature. All the prophets successively, he argued, had stated more on this subject than their predecessors were commissioned to do. It was only in accordance with this regular progress that the Bab had had entrusted to him a task more complete than that of Mohammed, which was more complete than that of Jesus, who in turn had known more than his precursors.[1] 'Ali Muhammed, the Door or Mirror of God, met a fate not unlike that of an earlier prophet who had claimed a new revelation; he was put to death by the authorities as an outrage to the orthodox faith and a threat to civil order.

The idea that the revelation of fundamental truths is progressive is a valuable defence against external challenge. It can always be held that what is being attacked is in fact not the real or complete explanation, but only a partial, perhaps even distorted version. The critic thus spends himself fighting a phantom adversary while the real protagonist, the truth in its blinding entirety, will reveal herself, if ever, only at a later time.[2] When the idea of progressive revelation is linked with that of ultimate incomprehensibility in this life of the final religious truths, then the argument of belief takes on one of its strongest forms. Negatively, it is an aid to rejection of the charge that anthropomorphic concepts of the Divine are an indication that God is man-made. If the ultimate

---

[1] Gobineau, 1933, p. 284. See also Huart s.v., 1941.

[2] The value of the conception of progressive revelation from this point of view has been understood by Ritchie (*op. cit.*, pp. 75–76) who states, 'Unless God is now in process of being revealed to us, whatever revelation there may have been in the past, we must inevitably be atheists. The atheists are those to whom God does not reveal Himself or who reject His revelation.'

reality transcends man's capacity for understanding, then how otherwise can he express his attitudes than by using the terminology and concepts of his own experience? Positively, it strengthens the call for faith. If in this world our knowledge is incomplete and our understanding is difficult, the greater is the importance of a faith which holds before us the complete realization of the mystery in the life to come, be it Nirvana, or union with the Divine.[1]

This brings us to the threshold of the perennial dispute as to the relations between religion and science. We are not concerned here to evaluate carefully the respective views, but primarily to indicate their sociological relevance to an understanding of religious belief. The basic religious attitude is to protect its sphere of faith and ritual from what is regarded as unjustified encroachment by the principles of reason, particularly reason in what is expressed as the materialistic doctrines exemplified by science. The term science ordinarily refers both to a body of knowledge and to a set of methods of investigation. By religion the body of knowledge is nowadays usually accepted, while the competence of the set of methods to pursue knowledge into the religious sphere is denied. But methods of inquiry must start from assumptions about the nature of reality, and here is the fundamental divergence. Three main standpoints may be mentioned – that matter is the ultimate reality; that mind is the ultimate reality; that mind, as ultimate reality, has qualities of an extra-human or supra-human order, such as omniscience, omnipotence or power of incarnation. Different scientists adopt different standpoints on this. Some for example do hold that there is a non-empirical reality or sphere of

---

[1] This point of view is epitomized by St. Paul: 'Now we see through a glass darkly; but then face to face: now I know in part; but then shall I know even as I am known.' The Buddhist *Avatamsakasutra*, a canonical text of the Hosso and Kegon sects, puts it thus:

> 'How exquisite is our physical eye,
> It has not the power to see our condition,
> The affirmation of its power betrays an illusion,
> And it is inapt to understand the incomparable Law. . . .
> The Perfect Law of all the Buddhas is incomprehensible.
> For it surpasses the power of our comprehension. . . .
> Believe in Buddha with the simplicity of thy heart,
> Be unshakable in thy faith, . . .
> Enter in the torrent of Buddhism,
> To reach the beauty and the calm of Wisdom.'

(Steinilber-Oberlin, 1938, pp. 285–6.)

Cf. also the view that in the present period, which is one of degeneracy, 'we are now too corrupt to understand alone the whole light of the Buddha. An act of faith in the sacred text which is suitable for the men of our time is neccessary' (*ibid.*, p. 241).

thought, with which a logical-empirical analysis cannot cope.[1] But recognition of this need not imply the recognition of that supra-human mind or power, which for religion is the essential assumption. And what some scientists take as assumptions, together with a real or imagined body of knowledge and set of methods, is in popular usage lumped together and given a quasi-personal, almost magical value. Science in this sense is the voice of authority or that of the false prophets, according to the point of view.

The arguments of religious belief in respect of science take a variety of forms. One is to stress the essential relativity of scientific discovery and principles. This is in order to show that the findings of science, apparently incontrovertible, will in the end be superseded, and in particular the firm grasp of science on matters fringing the religious sphere will slip away. The essence of this approach is given by a recent Muslim economist. 'My belief', he says, 'is that when Quranic theories come into conflict with the modern scientific theories, I find no reason to trouble my conscience. I firmly believe that the science of today may be the mythology of tomorrow, and that what the Quran has said we may not understand today, but it is likely to become quite clear to us tomorrow.'[2]

Another instance of the way in which stress on the relativity of scientific knowledge is used as a buttress to religious faith is the cordial reception given to Heisenberg's enunciation of the uncertainty principle.[3] This and other discoveries in modern physics which have promoted revision of the classical notions of causal laws and of determinism of a mechanistic kind are thought to prove the case for the inadequacy of science to grasp fundamental reality. The universe is thought to be indeterminate, mysterious, something more than matter.[4] But as Susan Stebbing has shown,

[1] In the social sciences the existence of observer-effect, the participation of the observer as an element in many situations being studied, complicates the problems of determinate measurement. There are phenomena which defy logical and empirical reconstruction – the intuitive processes for instance, as in that ability to perceive hitherto unnoticed relations and integrate them into a general principle which is the mark of the true scientist.

[2] Qureshi, 1945, p. 4. It will be observed that it is not argued that the Koran's ideas of today may become the mythology of tomorrow.

[3] One gathers that by this the more accurate the determination of the position of an electron, the greater is the uncertainty as to its momentum; conversely, the more accurately its momentum is determined, the greater the uncertainty in its position. The degree of uncertainty, which is due to the nature of measurement itself, is laid down by Heisenberg's principle, by which it is assigned a value never less than a specified constant.

[4] The new physics has 'renewed and stimulated a sense of the ontological mystery of the world of matter', Maritain, 1940a, p. 65.

with humour and skill, the physicists' discoveries warrant no such conclusions. Neither idealism nor materialism can benefit.[1] Nor would it seem to follow that the less we know about the seen world the more therefore we know about the unseen world.

Another form of the argument is a denial of the competence of science to pronounce on matters which are regarded as falling within the province of religion. This view is met not only among the professed exponents of religious doctrines, but also among philosophers and among scientists themselves. The real world, it is held, is beyond the shadow-show of space and time. The physical is a manifestation of something other than itself. Religious experience is truly objective, not merely subjective. Contemporary science, including sociology and anthropology, is incapable of passing judgement on any theory concerning the super-sensory or transcendental world, with which religious and philosophical thought deals.[2] A further buttress to religious belief is to claim the reverse – that religion is only another form of science. Made in the most blatant form it is that a religious system is founded on scientific principles primarily because it purports to argue in terms of cause and effect. One such system is Christian Science, alleging that illness, pain and sin can be made to disappear by using the laws of mind properly. Another, an intellectual variety of Saivaism, claims the law of universal causation as its basic postulate. Since this is regarded as being the very foundation of Western science, Saivaism is hailed as embodying the counterpart of the most modern scientific theories of the West. Another view represents science as essentially a part of religion because both are a quest for knowledge and truth in a disinterested way.[3]

An interesting example of the way in which a scientist has worked out his personal adjustment in religious terms comes from an eminent professor of electrical engineering. For him, God is a finite Being, conforming to the laws of mechanics. He has the ether as His abode, and as part of His nature. The visible material universe is God's kenosis, the shedding of part of Himself, part of His output of energy. From these views, rather unorthodox, certain corollaries emerge. If God has surrendered part of Himself in creating matter, is it perhaps true that there is some slight justifica-

---

[1] Stebbing, 1937.
[2] See e.g. Brown, 1946, pp. 35-7, 39, etc.; Wach, 1947, pp. 4-5, 14; Sorokin, 1941, vol. iv, p. 296.
[3] See Fisher, 1933, pp. 62-72, 76 *et passim*; Shivapadasundaram, 1934, p. 14.

tion for the perception of an inner spirit in wood and stone? If the wisdom and foreknowledge of God apply to the laws by which action takes place, and not to the predestination of every fact or event, then must even God try out the laws which He has framed? Can He perhaps not foresee or intend to foresee their consequences in every variant? 'Is He in truth as Creator the Supreme Researcher?' it is argued. 'Is the chemist who makes the compound hitherto unknown or a biologist who succeeds in making new variations of a species, carrying on the work of God as He would have it done?'[1]

Another variant on the same theme is to represent science as only of limited adequacy in its ordinary form and as needing enlargement to take in factors which religion wishes to include in the world view. It is argued, for instance, that a 'bastard' science leaves out all except material factors. 'True' science takes into account the eternal verities, such as character and conscience, religious instinct, parental, conjugal or patriotic love. These cannot be weighed, analysed, dissected, but cannot be excluded from 'true' science.[2]

All these points of view indicate different modes of adjustment whereby, sometimes in most elaborate imaginative constructions, attempts are made to place the facts of emotion within an intellectual system. But whether religion is made to oppose science or to absorb science, the issue needs clarification. Science has as its hallmarks the formulation of hypotheses, testing of them by observation and experiment, and careful relation of conclusions to empirical data. In its use of analytical thought, it must always work with given premises. It is unable to pronounce with certainty on the nature of ultimate reality. From its methods, it is debarred from mere assertion, unsupported by that degree of probability which is ordinarily held to constitute proof. But religion feels no necessity for such limitation. In its certitude lies its strength. It constantly makes assertions about the nature of reality. The proofs produced rest either on argument of which the logic is highly debatable or on further assertion about the intuitive nature of the revelation or other experiences of a special order adduced as evidence. Even where the data are regarded as capable of empirical examination

[1] Thornton, op. cit., pp. 17–8, 23.
[2] e.g. Bishop Walter Carey, in an article entitled 'Can We Ever Think Clearly?' Sunday Dispatch, 1 Sept. 1946.

by an external observer, the initial premisses supplied in the interpretation are usually in excess of those which are the necessary
minimum. No social science may be able to prove or disprove the
reality of such religious categories as God, devil, heaven or angels,
apart from their existence as human concepts. But it can certainly
show the way in which such concepts can be seen to be consistent
with much in human wants and behaviour alone. Revelation and
mystical experience, for instance, whether regarded as proceeding
from an external supra-human source or not, are fundamentally
human states. As such they can be analysed and interpreted with
significance from the scientific point of view. The anthropologist,
like any other scientist, has to base his work upon some assumptions of a metaphysical order. Whatever metaphysical position he
adopts it must be such as to allow him the greatest freedom of
exploration of the whole range of phenomena of man's behaviour.

Freedom is a word which every system nowadays, however
authoritarian, likes to inscribe on its banners. And there are other
old labels too, which are borne on unaccustomed packages. Freedom is held out as a promise by what has been called the new
humanism. It is exemplified in the work of Jacques Maritain, in
whom the neo-Thomists have a philosophical publicist of great elo-
quence. The classical humanism, he argues, had an anthropocentric
idea of man and culture – the idea of human nature as self-enclosed
or self-sufficient. This it put forward instead of what Maritain
would term an open nature and an open reason – which are man's
real nature and his real reason. The classical attitude towards
human existence has been that of the isolation of reason from all
that is supra-rational and irrational in man. Its reaction inevitably
has been the counter-humanism of Kierkegaard and Karl Barth
with its emphasis on personal anguish.[1]

The new humanism as conceived by Maritain is of a Christian
order; he has termed it 'the humanism of the Incarnation', integral
and progressive. It is claimed as springing from the concrete logic
of the events of history. It involves the conception of the wholeness
of man in his natural and supernatural being and of the descent of
the divine into man. Faith supplies the key to fundamental questions of being; the supra-rational is regarded as equally essential as

---

[1] 'The terrible voices which rise up in man crying out Enough of lying optimism and
illusory moralities . . . of liberty . . . of idealism; take us back to the great spiritual fruit-
fulness of the abyss, of the absurd, and of the ethics of despair' (Maritain, 1940b, p. 5).

the rational in the interpretation and government of human affairs. This new humanism, it is argued, has its implications not merely for the religious life of the believer. It is conceived as an attitude and doctrine of far-reaching importance – even as affecting our own anthropological science. 'The new humanism', he says, 'must reassume in a purified climate all the work of the classical period; it must re-make anthropology, find the rehabilitation and the "dignification" of the creature not in isolation, not in the creature shut in with itself, but in its openness to the world of the divine and supra-rational.'[1]

This is only one of a group of tendencies which seek to demonstrate the inadequacy of reason not merely for an approach to human contacts and relations with the external world as part of man's everyday behaviour, but also as a mode of analysis of phenomena. One expects to find a championing of the irrational in the sphere of art, where the emphasis upon feeling as a guide and stimulus to aesthetic activity has always been paramount. The abandonment of the medieval artist's subjective attitude to his material in favour of a naturalism derived from the remnants of classical antiquity led inevitably, it is held, to a degeneration of art. By taking nature first as an inspiration for creative form and then as a model the artist was led to become a copyist. As the Church progressively lost her spiritual initiative in Europe the artist progressively became freer from mysticism and religious iconography. In the Renaissance political system this did lead to some of the finest products of art. But the inevitable outcome of this classicism was the translation of the artist into the artisan.[2] But the historian also can exemplify the same attitude. Arnold Toynbee in his monumental study of culture argues that criteria of the growth of civilization are not to be found in increasing command over the human or the physical environment. This, the evidence suggests, is a concomitant of disintegration rather than of growth because of a decline in the spiritual forces which make for purpose and unity. The proper saviour from a disintegrated society is not to be found in the philosophy of detachment like that of Buddhist or Stoic. It is the 'mystery of transfiguration' which alone can work as the effective agent – the God incarnate in a man. This, he argues, represents a truth which we can verify empirically but which is

[1] Maritain, *op. cit.*, 1940b, p. 9.
[2] See e.g. Mazenod, 1943.

also known to us intuitively.[1] One suspects also that recent work by the psychologists on precognition and extra-sensory perception attracts attention for its religious bearing rather than for its scientific interest. This derives ultimately from the hope that negatively these conclusions will place limitations on the claims for the exercise of reason and positively they will encourage belief in the existence of the world of the supra-rational, including forces and powers which religion alone can claim to control.

In the history of religious belief in Europe it would seem such currents can be traced for the last three hundred years. C. C. J. Webb and others have pointed out how in the eighteenth century the idea of God was that of a transcendent Being having a separate existence from the Universe and from man, and standing over sharply against man as the Creator of omnipotent and omniscient power. With the change which the scientists initiated in the idea that cosmic process was to be viewed in terms of evolution rather than of creation, came also the idea of God as immanent, a Being permanently pervading the Universe and in a sense an integral part of the life of the world and man. It was not out of the question that God for the accomplishment of His own purposes was prepared to limit Himself in both power and knowledge, and to participate through His world substance in the evolutionary process. Man, as a semi-autonomous creature, could take part, so to speak, in working out the designs of God. Salvation and human happiness could be sought in the world which represented the evolution of the Great Design. As time has passed, the early glories of the industrial revolution have begun to fade, first one, and then another great war has shaken the fabric of civilization, and all established social order has been challenged to its roots by the Marxist state. Correspondingly the tendency to seek religious values within civilization has begun once again to be regarded as fallacious. The sense of other-worldliness has once more come to be looked upon by many as fundamental in religion. Reinforced by arguments based upon the primacy of feeling, the value of irrationality, and the claims of mystical experience to a validity apart from their subject, this may be described as the new transcendentalism.[2]

---

[1] 'So far as this Civitas Dei enters into the time-dimension at all . . . it is as a spiritual reality interpenetrating the present' (Toynbee, 1946, pp. 527–9).

[2] See for example the illuminating essay by Webb, *loc. cit.*

What is to be the anthropological attitude towards this development? Must we look forward to see our science remade in the light of this approach which, novel in some of its formulations, carries nevertheless the kernel of age-old argument? I suggest that, as before, the anthropologist can only take man as the centre of his study. Emotion, unreason, belief, intuitive knowledge and mystical perception, may all be regarded as modes or bases of action for the individuals to whom they seem appropriate in given circumstances. But they must be regarded as essentially modes of personal adjustment and not as scientific instruments. The rational dispassionate analysis which the anthropologist applies to religious phenomena and in which his own position as the analyst is reduced to a minimum, even though it cannot be eliminated, must still remain our guide.

If this be so it appears to me that the range of phenomena we have been discussing can find an explanation not inconsistent with the point of view which I presented to you at the beginning of this lecture. These phenomena – views on theism, theodicy, and progressive revelation; theo-symbolism and its inversion; belief in the insufficiency of scientific knowledge and in the integral character of the new humanism – are not all aspects of reality beyond the scientist's perception. They are modes of grappling with a reality which is open to observation though by no means adequately measurable by scientific knowledge – at least in the present state of our technique. What is this reality? It is the individual human being himself, in relation to the physical world of which he has cognizance and the society of which he is a member. Man has to face the reality of his own mental make-up, with all its conflicting desires, emotions, intellectual drives and moral sentiments. He prefers to do so in a mirror.

The value of religious belief to him is in meeting his own personal wants. It provides him with a means of reacting in a range of social situations where without it he would be severely hampered. His belief supplies him also with a principle of order – order in his relation to his fellows, including the moral norms he follows, and order in his conception of the universe. This search for an external order in events and things demands that their relationships to one another can be recognized as intelligible and not merely fortuitous association. The principle of order deals with time as well as space; it can comprise even eternity. In the view of such universalistic religion it is this which makes the eternal order authentic. But it is not merely order, it is the assurance that we know where to find guidance upon that order that is desired. Religious belief supplies also a principle of authority or certitude upon which indecision and the need for resolution can seize. The relation of son to father, believer to Church, man to God all exemplify the operation of this principle, in which wisdom is believed to reside in a superior, into whose hands the inferior resigns the decision.

Religious belief also provides objects of attachment for sentiments of dependence and affection. Belief is a comforter in time of trouble. It can also serve as a vehicle for the transports of ecstatic love. This involves not merely self-expression in the sense of ability to give vent to creative interests. It also involves opportunity to exercise those self-regarding sentiments which are part of the personal constitution. There must be outlet, too, for what we may call the 'other-regarding' sentiments, of which there must be at least a minimal exercise for any social existence. All this gives occasion for emphasis upon individuality. The relation of the mystic to the divine with which he seeks union may seem to negate this stress. Yet in all such cases there is emphasis upon the uniqueness of the experience, the particularity of it, as being incapable of being grasped by another person – except perhaps a mystic who has attained the same state. A heightened consciousness of personality in social matters then is correlated with the claim to a merging of personality on the supra-rational plane. It is precisely by that capacity of being united with the Divine essence, of grasping reality direct, that the mystic feels he is singled out from his fellows. Over the whole range of religious belief, stress upon the personal relation of God to man is a marked feature. It helps to satisfy that desire for personal recognition and personal assertion which is germinal in every one of us. It can serve also those attitudes which, springing from an enlightened self-regarding sentiment, demand the application of principles of equity and justice to the results of conduct. Religious belief usually embodies some concepts whereby behaviour is related to a scheme of consequents, whether or not these are interpreted in terms of moral approbation or disapprobation, and of reward or punishment. Religious belief also offers a prospect for him who is curious for truth. Many things which science and commonsense knowledge cannot provide, religion offers as certainties. If one cannot know the truth by reason one must know it by faith. Certitude, rest from the internal dialectical battle, from the effort of grappling with inconsistencies and half-answers, is undoubtedly one of the great attractions in religious belief. One can always painfully build up one's own ideas, but a framework already put up makes the work much easier. This has always been recognized. Reason and the delights of logical argument, too, find their place in religious belief. There may be disagreement about the extent to which the assumptions from which the analysis starts are data ascertained by experience. But the highest philosophical and dialectical skill can be developed whatever the basis. The intellect can thus be satisfied by the intricacies of formulating and defending religious belief even while it professes to rely on and find truth in other instruments.

This analysis is not an argument in metaphysics nor an essay in the scholarship of comparative religion. It treats some characteristic types of beliefs in a variety of religious systems as modes of adaptation. This is not to deny Durkheim's contribution in relating religious symbols to social forms, nor that of Max Weber in showing how different personal solutions of an integrative kind are to be found in different systems of religious thought.[1] But it is important to show how religious belief can be related to the structure of personality, not merely to social structure. It is an instrument in the maintenance of personal integration, not simply of social integration. And, to get the stamp of conviction, belief must fit somehow into a personal intellectual system, not only into an emotional system. Denying reason with one breath, faith seeks with the next to produce the final compelling reason to justify its own primacy.

In all this, every individual has his own adjustment-points, every belief its own adjustment-values. To a Tyrolese peasant what appeals is God as a simple family Father of a patriarchal, somewhat overbearing type, with the Madonna as a kindly protectress and intercessor, to be represented, as in one homely image, with a cosmic umbrella sheltering herself and the Child, while their suppliants pay their devotions. Not for the peasant the conceptions that meet the intellectual needs of a professor of electrical engineering, with God as the supreme expression of the laws of mechanics,

[1] See the illuminating article of Talcott Parsons, 1944, pp. 176–90.

as the research mind *in excelsis*. The more highly elaborate the social organization the greater the diversity of situations open to individuals for resolution, and the greater possible range of adjustment-points. The diversity of religious belief tends to increase as science develops. The logico-empirical system of scientific thought can destroy belief – but it can also develop it, stimulate it to erect new variants to buttress itself.

Understanding of these processes is essential in the study of how change in religious belief comes about. New facts are always being presented to individual experience, and new interpretations of experience are always being suggested. There is the impact of the behaviour of fresh personalities, or of known personalities in new situations. New verbalizations of experience are always being demanded. A refusal to make adjustment may lead to heightened emphasis on the customary expressions of belief. But fresh defences are also built up. Wittingly or unwittingly these become substantial alterations to the corpus of belief in the individual religious armoury.

With diversification of the types of situation to be met by an individual, so is there diversification of expression of belief. The anthropologist's concept of a specific belief is a summation of individual views, an abstraction of time-place expressions. The beliefs of even the most primitive religious system are always mobile, sensitive to changes in external circumstances or in social composition. Primitive religion, contrary to a common view,[1] is not devoid of sceptics, heretics, and other unorthodox who have had to meet a personal intellectual or emotional challenge by individual formulations which diverge from the community norm. When a tribal religion is met by Christianity or by Islam, each with a new social and economic system, it is not only fear and respect for the new God, the perception of a higher morality, or the principles of comparative economic advantage that move to conversion. A more complex set of factors is responsible, involving delicate adjustment in more personal terms. Social relations with community members, the sense of communion itself, the appeal of the new beliefs in a universe of greater scope than hitherto imagined, intellectual conviction of the fitness of the new ideas to explain situations difficult to comprehend,

---

[1] Expressed even by Malinowski (1925, pp. 57, 64), who is usually so insistent on the importance of individual variation.

acceptance of the necessity of a new value system – all have weight.[1]

But the demands on the new beliefs may be different from what was at first envisaged. Hence still newer beliefs arise, attempts at more complete adjustment. We are familiar with the variety of new cults that have sprung up in Africa, North America, New Guinea and elsewhere as congeners of or offshoots from Christianity. They have been termed 'nativistic' cults, but they might almost be termed 'adjustment-cults'. The amount of native reversion in them is very variable, while it is their quality of adjustment that is outstanding.[2] They are an attempt to provide an aetiology for new situations of which the implications are but dimly grasped. Something has 'gone wrong' with the process of change – the people have adopted Christianity or other Western culture forms, yet the things of the European have not accrued to them. Traditional forms alone are incompatible with new demands, yet they still meet some wants. The beliefs of the new cult, whatever be their precise content, are attempted adjustment to these anomalies. The greater the anomalies, the more fantastic the beliefs – that all Europeans will vanish, leaving their goods behind; that the spirits of the dead will all return to an earthly Elysium; that if there is fighting for the new cult all the faithful are invulnerable. Faith in many of these cults has smashed on reality, when belief in immediate miracle has failed to redeem its promise. But belief has often been plastic enough to make a fresh adjustment, by buttress rather than by complete modification.

I do not deny the value of Malinowski's theory of religion as satisfying basic human needs, especially that for personal continuity – 'building out heaven beyond the grave', in William James's expression. But this theory needs reformulation. It does not explain why change of belief takes place, how conversion, heresy and apostasy can occur. The views of Radcliffe-Brown need qualification in the same way. The function of ritual, he argues, is in the perpetuation of sentiments – especially the prime one of dependence – on which the maintenance of society depends. But if an ancestral cult, for instance, expresses this, why does it not continue, no matter what be the change in external events? The

---

[1] Allier (1925, I, p. 525) argues that conversion does not consist in intellectual conviction – but that such conviction must necessarily follow if the conversion is not to be sooner or later only a memory of violent though fleeting emotions.

[2] See e.g. Stanner, 1947, pp. 31–4.

ancestors do not change; in time of stress, then, why not appeal even more to them, and cling to them? Emile Nolly has given in his novel *La Barque Annamite* a skilful analysis of the desperate attachment of an old man to his ancestral cult in the face of the new forces of civilization. But this fails to satisfy the hopes, thwarted passions and new interests of his dearest kin. The basic human needs in such a case are still there; the response is inadequate, fails to satisfy intellectually as well as emotionally the demands of the individual in the changed environment. The Tikopia, among whom I worked when Christianity and some Western cultural items had already gained a foothold, are a case in point. Christian and heathen all still had a sense of dependence on their ancestors, and all participated in some minimal ancestral rites. But differential reaction to the new wants and opportunities emerged not only in conversions, but also in modification of the beliefs of different heathen. Some defended their ancient faith stoutly, others placed God in the native deity system. Some assigned supernatural powers to the Bishop and other Europeans, and some produced versions of myths which accounted for the distribution of iron between Tikopia and European.

Such new developments of belief show adjustment in terms of rational logical thought as well as of emotional reaction. So trenchant was the attack of Durkheim, Marett and others on the early anthropologists for over-intellectualization of religion, that emphasis has tended to be placed almost entirely on the elements of feeling and emotion in belief. Reason, it is claimed, cannot destroy faith. I would argue that it can. Faith buttresses itself. But what may be termed the covert atheism of large numbers of putative Christians is evidence of some rational inference as to the incompatibility between traditional religion and contemporary social and economic circumstances.

I think that the implications of what I have said necessitate some change in the emphases of current anthropological views on religion. Clearly, religion is much more than a sentiment-carrier for society. The hypothesis that religion is an integrating force is more closely applicable to the simpler than to the more highly complex societies. With social and economic differentiation religion often becomes a banner for sectionalism. Society is split, not welded together by religious development. Individual interpretations of accepted religious truths find backing from others whose personal adjustment-points they meet, and emerge in modifications of dogma and rite. Temperamental differences are reflected there too. The history of schism, sectarianism, heresy, of conservative and modernist movements, of ascetic groups and those to whom austerity has no appeal all give evidence of such tendencies. The establishment of a religious organization may rend the society by the creation of monopoly or strong vested interests in social and economic affairs. Religious enterprise may drive the social order into specific channels – as the role of monastic institutions in commerce affected the development of capitalism in Western Europe.

Religion may also perform an important social role in providing an outlet for individual sentiments, where other institutions in the society may be inadequate. Individual desires for prestige and advancement, incapable of finding temporal channels, turn to religion as a vent. I am not thinking here only of the worldly clerics, like those cardinals displayed in the plays of Webster and James Shirley, with their 'purple pride that wants to govern all', the reflection of a long line of priest-politicians. I have in mind rather those who through dogmatic assertion and conviction of righteousness find their imagined level of superiority over their fellows. Social relations may be embittered rather than improved thereby. If social integration be promoted by such behaviour, it is integration by catharsis.

A cathartic function of a more creative kind is given by the way in which religion provides a powerful vehicle for aesthetic expression. A conventional way of regarding the relation of religion to art is to point to the manner in which religious emotion provides the stimulus to artistic creation. To my mind the reverse is more often the case – religion provides the medium. This is a point of view admirably examined in detail by Yrjö Hirn[1] who has demonstrated how much of Catholic doctrine results from speculation directed by aesthetic aspirations. In general, in a society where religious institutions occupy an important part of the total field, religion may be a recognized means of canalization for aesthetic impulses. The trappings of the religion are embellished, the imagery elaborately worked out. Religious belief is externalized as part of the process of a personal adjustment in art. I suspect that Michelangelo's Sistine Chapel designs, Bach's cantatas and passion music are good art not because they were inspired by religion;

[1] Hirn, 1912.

they are religious in theme because when they were created religion was one of the most effective channels and media for the production of good art. The poverty of good religious art at the present time is probably the result less of a decline in religious sentiments of inspiration than of the existence of many other avenues for the expression of the artist's creative urge. Similarly religion attempts to provide a framework and supervised outlet for metaphysical and allied speculations. For nearly a thousand years Christendom controlled in Western Europe the intellectual forces which would otherwise have rebounded on society. It thus acted as a shock-absorber for thought. It would seem indeed that as societies develop, technologically and economically, institutions other than religion must arise to allow of the exercise of the creative imagination. Otherwise this might burst religion itself apart.

This study of religious belief has stressed its importance in the action systems of individuals. It has shown also how essential is this consideration for an understanding of religious change. But what of the ultimate content of belief? This question, though not the subject of inquiry by science, stands behind many of the inquiries made. If there be an external reality, transcendent, providing its own cause, author of the moral order, and illuminant of the life of man, this would be a significant assumption behind our theories. There is a common belief that God is real since the effects attributed to Him are real. Whether man exists only in the mind of God, or God exists only in the mind of man, seems to me unproven, and as far as I can judge, unprovable. The evidence produced for a supra-human mind and will is I think of the same order – though on a high plane – as other anthropological data concerning belief. A preferable and more economical assumption, offering what to me is a greater degree of probability, is that this is all part of man's attempt to make the supreme, final and unique but really unattainable adjustment – the search after the complete formula for the synthesis of human conduct.

CHAPTER XII

An Anthropological View of Mysticism
(1950)

Mysticism is to the ordinary person a vague term. It has a flair of the unseen, a notion of something spiritual about it, and it is used in contrast to normal behaviour. Mystical belief and behaviour are religious where one expects a matter-of-fact approach, and have a veiled, hidden element where one expects plain circumstances. They therefore give the idea of something mysterious, secret, even occult. More precisely, this hidden element can be defined in terms of a special attitude towards reality. The mystic lays claim to a particular awareness, a special kind of experience of a non-rational order, giving insight into the essential nature of things. But mysticism is used in a more limited sense still to indicate those forms of religion in which the insight into reality involves the conception of an intimate relation with the Divine. So close is this said to be that it may mean a direct and intuitive awareness of God, and even union with the Divine personality. Visionary raptures, ecstatic transports, a curious kinship with the sensuous experiences of physical love, often mark this state. The language used to describe these experiences, powerful and sincere, rich in symbolism and glowing with the notion of a warm inner light, may reach true poetic values.

This is intriguing material for philosophy, psychology, and aesthetics, as well as for the student of comparative religion. For the anthropologist, too, it offers data for his attempts to understand the nature of social process through the actions of individuals. The mystic is not simply a person who concentrates on spiritual values or is subject to supernatural exaltations. He is a member of a society and usually of a religious body in that society. As such, he is a paratrooper of religion. He goes on the more dangerous adventures of the soul, often secretly and alone or in the company of a select few. His experiences challenge the unbeliever more radically and violently than do those of his more orthodox fellows. He compels their admiration for the way in which he plants the banner of faith on heights of assertion that they can never reach, far behind the enemy's rational lines. Yet this self-reliance can raise its head against the authority of friends as well as against enemies. To assert that one is in union, not just communion, with the Divine is a boldness which can shock the more timid of the faithful. The drill and discipline of the religious order may be rejected as fit only for the mundane rank and file of ordinary believers. The mystic may be so convinced of his inner knowledge and rightness that he arrogates to himself decisions on the moral law. Through the ages, then, the mystic has been a problem to religion as well as to science.

It is this situation which the anthropologist is interested to explore. The anthropologist sees the mystic not merely as a question-mark to man's approach to reality, or as a sample of an abnormal type of personality. He is an item in the structure and organization of religious experience in a social milieu. Some anthropologists, doubtless, are content to abandon reason as their guide after a certain point, and to concede the validity of the mystic's claims. I think this is unnecessary. A simpler hypothesis is that the claims of the mystic are part of his adjustment to a refractory social and physical environment. They need involve no wholesale revision of our everyday attitudes towards reality, reinforced by science; on the contrary, they themselves form part of the material for scientific analysis of the nature and functions of religion.

Analysis of mysticism has hitherto played a small part in anthropological studies of religion. There has been a revulsion from the muddled approach of Lévy-Bruhl, who characterized the mode of thinking of primitive peoples as 'mystic participation'. In seeking to prove such pre-logical mentality he cast his net so wide and confused so thoroughly the empirical and non-empirical fields of savage thought, the rational and the emotional, that he failed to study carefully the precise nature of the mystical attitudes that do exist. Primitive peoples – that is, those with simple forms of technology – have types of what may be called mystical experience in totemism, spirit-medium cults, and guardian-spirit cults. In the first, some form of spirit entity representing a social group blends almost indistinguishably into some natural object or species, such as a plant or animal or stone. In the second type, a spirit enters a human being and uses his voice and limbs as a means of communication with other people. In the third type, a spirit gets into rapport with a human being, but does not necessarily enter his body. But mystical concepts of an elaborate analytical intellectual order are not found there. The primitive phenomena lack, as a rule, either the quality of ineffability, of non-impartable experience which is the hall-mark of the developed mystical visitation, or the completeness of union, the fusion of personality which is held to be the culmination of mystical striving. In totemism the relation believed to exist is diffused, not highly personalized, and is projected into a natural object. In spirit-medium phenomena the medium may be united with his God, but only as a vessel is united with the sacred liquid it contains. In the guardian-spirit cult the worshipper has a dream or vision of his spirit protector, but does not normally have a personal union with him.

Yet study of the more primitive forms of mysticism does two things. By making us see the cultural range of the mystical attitude it emphasizes its comparative interest – that to understand it we should focus attention less on the particular content of the mysticism in any one religious system than on the common features which can be seen in a range of systems. By showing mysticism as operating essentially in an institutional setting it makes us realize how much the attitudes of the mystic are socially orientated, despite all his claims to a purely personal type of experience. In fact, one might argue that the stress on the very personal intimate character of the developed mysticism of civilized society is to some degree a reflection of the greater scale of the intellectual and emotional demands which this type of society makes upon the individual.

Here I shall be discussing mystical phenomena of the more developed type, primarily that of the West. Despite the analyses of William James, Leuba, Delacroix, Maréchal, Howley, and many others, there is still room for examination of the material from a more sociological point of view.

The goal of mystical perception is the unitive state, in which the soul unites with the Divine or whatever is conceived as the absolute principle of reality. Normally, the motive force of greatest power in assisting to this union is love. For this love to operate effectively there must be detachment of the self from earthly affairs, and purification; self-love must be forgotten. Each school of mysticism has its own techniques for attaining the desired end, usually demanding some ascetic and moral discipline. Often a series of stages must be passed through before the mystic reaches what a Sufi – a Muslim mystic – has described as the state 'Where "I" and "Thou" have ceased to exist, and the Quest and the Way and the Seeker are One.'

Basic to the concept of the mystical state is the belief that the process of grasping the Truth is not by reason, but by a unique mode of perception, which is sometimes described as a spiritual sense, sometimes as intuition. The results are not supposed to be accessible to experimental verification and other scientific tests. The mystical state, it is said, is not merely one of feeling; it is one of knowledge. In defending such claims, the mystic does not disdain reasoned argument, though he uses it rather as an outer screen to his fortress; he withdraws to his assumption of inner knowledge when pressed, as to a citadel. He reinforces his argument by the assertion that such non-verifiable knowledge is not merely possible, but essential to our proper comprehension of reality. He may go further and hold that such inner knowledge gives the only reality.

Such warnings cannot deter the scientist. He can agree to the existence of non-empirical spheres of judgement, to evaluations not based on reason. But he cannot agree that where perception and evaluation are not so controllable by rational process of inquiry and verification, every type of assertion is equally probable. In particular, he cannot be prevented from relating assertions to their personal and social context. To the sociologist or anthropologist the significance of mystical experience is to be sought as much in how and why the mystic expresses it as in its manifest content of subject-matter. That the mystic feels it so necessary to insist on the impregnability of his experience to ordinary observation and analysis is one of the significant elements in it.

The simplest material for us to take in this brief examination of mysticism is what the mystics themselves have said. One thing that they stress is that the experience is incommunicable. Words are inadequate, and even the mental imagery the mystic uses to himself is only a translation, an inaccurate representation of what occurs. A Buddhist philosopher has stated that the intuitionalist position needs pointers rather than ideas to express itself, and that these pointers are enigmatic and non-rational. Says St. John of the Cross: 'This mystical theology . . . is so simple, so spiritual and generalized, that the intelligence receives it without being enveloped in any kind of image or of representation capable of being received by the senses.' St. Teresa de Jésus, reviewing the statement of another mystic that the inward eye of the soul sees God without corporeal form more clearly than one man can see another, though words and imagination cannot express how, comments 'one doesn't see anything, even with the eyes of the imagination, to which one can properly speaking give the name of *view*'. Nevertheless, the impression produced is of a strong emotional focusing on an object of interest, accompanied by some degree of visualization of it. If ideas are thought to be inadequate to describe the experience, words must be still less effective. As the author of the Persian poem *The Mystic Rose Garden* put it:

> Let reason go and abide in the Truth.
> The eye of a bat endures not the bright sun. . . .
> Prosody and rhyme weigh not mysteries,
> The pearl of mystery cannot be compressed in letters;
> The Red Sea is not contained in a jug.[1]

That words are inadequate to express strong emotional experiences is a fact known to others than mystics. Moreover, mystics, like other people, do use words to express the incommunicable. They cannot stay silent. As William James has pointed out, one of the characteristics of the transcendental mystical state at its height is its brevity, its transience; it can rarely be sustained for longer than an hour or two, and then it fades. Some memory of it remains, and a feeling that it is profoundly important, and it continues to affect the inner life of the mystic between whiles. Nevertheless, memory needs stimulation, even for the mystic himself. Some means has to be at hand to recall the state, to exchange recollection of it with others of similar experience, to present at least the outline of it to others who are incapable of having it. In this task of expression some mystics are much better than others at handling the tools. The clarity of their thought, the precision of their reasoning within the bounds allotted, the vividness of their imagery, show aptitudes which measure closely alongside those of non-mystical writers. Whether it be the intense character of their

[1] Quoted from E. H. Whinfield's translation of *Gulshan I Raz: The Mystic Rose Garden of Sa'd Ud Din Mahmud Shabistari*, 1880. Other Muslim material is cited mainly from R. A. Nicholson, 1914, and Margaret Smith, 1931.

mystical experience or not, some have shown that aesthetic exaltation which has produced great literature. St. John of the Cross, says Allison Peers, was 'primarily a poet, and as such among the first in Spanish literature'. And it is to Sufism that Islam would appear to owe so much of her major verse, including that by the much-quoted Omar Khayyám. Despite the fact that the mystic, on his own showing, is always struggling against the world of rational, empirical knowledge, he is always leaning on it, symbolically and socially. He seeks to pass beyond the symbol to a direct non-symbolic expression of reality. Yet all the time he must express himself in words, and use these words as an instrument to proclaim his faith, analyse and define his experience, and even to enlarge the aesthetic horizon of himself and others.

Not every mystic is articulate. But for an ineffable, incommunicable type of experience it is significant what a volume of words have been expended to give it expression and communication! One can conclude, then, that this association is not haphazard; that the verbal expression of mystical experience plays an important role, and in fact is to be regarded normally as an integral part of the total phenomenon. Belief must emerge in action, and a valuable part of the action is in attempting to put into words the quality of the experience. It is important, I think, to look on the mystic's experience as a part of the activity of his personality. William James has noted the passive element in the experience – the mystic feels that his will is in abeyance, as if he is grasped and held by a superior power. But it would be wrong to look on the experience as something that simply happens to the mystic. Proven theory in psycho-pathology shows how obscure motivations in the personality lie behind the occurrence of even the most unlikely events of an apparently accidental character. So is it also with the mystical state – the subject is not dissociated from it, a mere passive recipient of novel experience, but is actively associated with it and uses its outcome as an instrument in forwarding his personal ends, however much these may be disguised or refracted through a screen of social purpose.

How, then, does mysticism further any such ends?

We can conveniently open this question by a reference to Max Weber's view that the mystic, unlike the ascetic, is against the world – or rather against his action in the world. He rejects the world, argues Weber, refuses to participate in it, engages in contemplative flight from it. This cannot be taken too literally. In ordinary life the mystic does not necessarily stay unique and aloof; he (or she) may take a very active role in society. One of the most famous of the Spanish mystics of the sixteenth century, St. Teresa de Jésus, took a primary part in creating an order of Carmelite nuns in Ávila, and led a most busy practical life as an organizer and administrator. The mystical element in behaviour is not against action *in* the world, but against action *by* the world. It is primarily a defence of the personality against the world's interference, not a refusal to interfere in the world. This point is reinforced by considering the role of many mystics as social as well as religious leaders. By what are conceded to be their extraordinary qualities as recipients of personal revelation, such mystics often exercise important functions as sources of authority. Most important, also, they act as providers of evidence as to the truth of the supernatural for the body of believers who are not endowed with mystical capacity. In Sumatra, for instance, it has been noted that teachers of mysticism have more influence over the people than do teachers in the Muslim universities. As a consequence, all Muslim religious teachers try to incorporate mystical exposition in their teaching, and even professors become members of mystical orders so that their reputations may be improved.

The sociological relevance of mysticism comes out also in dominant types of imagery used to describe the experience. One such is the imagery of light; another is the imagery of love. The association of light with the mystical state is very general, among both Christians and Muslims. Sometimes it is introduced simply as a metaphor; sometimes it is held to be a concrete condition; sometimes, again, it is a diffused perception by both the eye and the soul. A prayer said to have been taught by the Archangel Gabriel to the Prophet Mohammed, but probably of Sufi origin, runs: 'O light of the heavens and of the earth. . . . Give me light in my heart and light in my tomb, and light in my hearing and light in my sight . . . to possess such light means to be contemplated eternally by the Light of light.' St. John of the Cross makes powerful play of the antithesis of darkness and light in his famous work, the 'Night of the Soul', in which the spirit is laid bare and beaten upon by the light of Divine wisdom. With many other mystics, the first experience begins with the perception of a great light. Psycho-physically and symbolically, this theme of the great illumination has much significance. From the sociological angle it can be interpreted as a diffuse individual affirmation of the positive role of the mystic towards his environment, and of his assumption of control of it. Opposed to the negation, ignorance, and frustration of darkness is the symbolic assertion of the clarity of his knowledge, the competence of his insight, his ability to understand his difficulties and master them. Though phrased in passive expressions of his being flooded with light, the imagery is really an active statement by the mystic that he has reached the point from which he can survey his world with equanimity, because he is armed against it.

The sociological interpretation of the imagery of love, with its wealth of symbolism and its analogies drawn so boldly, if so delicately, from the physical acts of erotic dalliance and consummation, carries us still further. The development of the love theme, as Allport has shown, provides organization and extension for a variety of dispositions of importance to the personality. For a mystic, it provides a focus for many social sentiments, including his social goals, aesthetic interests, sexual orientations, moral standards. It also reflects, unwittingly, much cultural material from the society in which the mystic lives. But while serving as an integrative agency for the mystic's personality, the love imagery can also threaten the harmony of the religious community within which he moves. The early Muslim mystics were wont to use the imagery of the wine of love and the cup poured out for the lover to drink. 'Drink the wine of His love for thee, that He may intoxicate thee with thy love for Him', said Dhu al-Nun. And Jalaluddin Rumi said,

> God is the Cupbearer and the Wine;
> He knows what manner of love is mine.

Others again, like mystical poets everywhere, celebrated the beauty of the Lover in language of glowing adoration, or stressed the completeness of the mystic unity as that of body as well as of soul. Hence the statement made by one authority that it is easy to mistake a Sufi mystical hymn for a drinking song or a serenade. To this the controversies over the sacred or profane intent of Solomon's Song give point. Little wonder, then, that Ibn al'Arabi had to write a commentary on some of his poems to avoid the charge of scandal that they were to celebrate the charms of his mistress, or that Luis de León, a teaching brother, was imprisoned for four years, allegedly in part because of his translation of the Song of Songs into the vernacular.

But in the history of mysticism the line between being unjustly suspected of scandalous statement and really being prepared to override the orthodox moral law is sometimes a fine one. The mystic may refuse to be bound by moral codes, since the unitive state, he alleges, has given him freedom through his true knowledge of good and evil.

> The man of God is made wise by the Truth. . . .
> The man of God is beyond infidelity and faith.
> To the man of God right and wrong are alike.

Evil, according to many mystics, has no real existence; it is only not-being. This concept may, as with so many Buddhists, be associated simply with a contemplative refusal to engage in such useless activity. But as with the Bektashis and other 'lawless' orders of dervishes it may involve a refusal to abide by the ordinary constraints of morality, and an active pursuance of mystical exaltation by erotic or other forbidden means. This clearly sets a problem to any religious organization which has such mystics within its fold. The reality and value of their experiences are believed in, but the authorities are unwilling to concede their freedom from rules of discipline.

A much more serious threat to organized religion comes from the doctrinal consequences of mystical illumination. The claim to direct knowledge of the reality of God involves the possible rejection of the general external authority and dogma of the Church. Any religion such as Christianity, involving the doctrinal concept of a Mediator, clearly cannot look unmoved on assertions from within its fold of unmediated union with God. The conduct of mystics is very variable in the degree to which they push their individual interpretations of doctrine and actual behaviour *vis-à-vis* the dogma and ritual of the orthodox Church. But the acid remark of Salomon Reinach, that if the Church has beatified or canonized many mystics, she has silenced many more, is not without point here.

The high emotional temperature of the unitive state has at times called forth the claim, not merely that the individual passes away as self and is incorporated with God, but that the process of identification also operates in reverse. Meister Eckhart quotes a saying of St. Augustine that man *is* what he loves, adding, 'If he loves a stone he is a stone; if he loves a man he is a man; if he loves God – I dare say no more, for if I said that he would then be God, ye might stone me.' But the Sufi, as Nicholson has indicated in comment on this, is sometimes freer and bolder:

> O my soul, I searched from end to end: I saw in thee naught
>   save the Beloved;
> Call me not infidel, O my soul, if I say that thou thyself art He.

Such affirmations of identity of man with godhead are interesting, if only because they are usually made with such hesitation. Here the mystic is careful to avoid the triumphant proclamation of the sureness of his knowledge. He may know he is God, but he is very cautious about saying so. This is not merely his recognition of the logical relations between part and whole. His hesitation has definite social foundations. Like Meister Eckhart, he may be unwilling to incur social disapprobation by blasphemy. Again, he cannot escape the effects of the basic religious ideology in which he was brought up and which has always presented to him the difference between a holy God and profane Man. For this there is good cause. The mystic's claim to the superlative, to complete suffusion with the highest in Truth, Beauty, Goodness and Love, to utter completeness and unity with God, can be interpreted as the culmination of the search made by every human being for a fixed point in a shifting universe, an ultimate meaning, a certainty in physical and social existence. Men want assurance, a final explanation of their problems, a final solution to their difficulties, which will solve their emotional as well as their intellectual wants. The claim of the mystic is that he has found the final answer, that it is reality itself, that it is the summation of the aesthetic and moral order, and that it is inaccessible to attack by any means, including those of reasoning. The mystical life, then, presents satisfactions of an intense kind, and its nature, including the reality of its manifestations, must be sought in this. When the mystic says that knowledge, the knower, and the known are One, it is because they are all manifestations of a human psyche which has found its utmost extensions and most complete affirmations in this development of its own capacities. Yet the mystic cannot go too far. United with God, he can master the universe, he thinks, at least in so far as his own contacts with it are significant for him. But as God he would not merely be in control of his own destiny, but also be responsible for the destiny of others. This responsibility he cannot, dare not, face except in a very few cases. Mohammed was content to remain the Prophet of God, and 'Ali Muhammed of Shiraz called himself El Bab, the Door. Jesus of Nazareth; Mirza Ghulam Ahmad Khan, founder of Ahmadiyya; and Shembe, the Black Christ of Ohlange, are among the few who have borne the claims of divinity with some success.

My analysis may now be summarized and reorientated.

All religious systems are concerned with the relation of persons to extra-human, spiritual beings or powers. This relation is in some sense a reflection of the relation between the individual and his social and physical environment. As such, the individual's religious experience is of prime importance to him as one means of coping with his problems. Mystical experience is part of such a way. Only a limited number of people have the particular psycho-physical disposition which allows them to experience the voices, the illumination, the emotional and physical transports of the mystical state. But to such people its value is in allowing them emotional expression beyond the bounds ordinarily allotted by the religious system to which they adhere. The unity theme which it expresses to such a high degree allows of an abnormal development of the identification feeling with all that can be selected as of interest in the environment. By the emphasis on love as a crucial factor in the experience the personality can be enlarged by the incorporation of external elements and standards. Opportunity is given for the free exercise of symbolic creation and for other aesthetic effort. Of extreme importance to the personality also is the provision of a covered road to reality – the assertion of untouchable knowledge, which gives, if not certainty, at least a high degree of conviction as to the individual's interpretation of his situation, and his capacity, control, and rightness of action in the face of his problems. More specifically, the wish to share experiences originates in some cases fellowships of mystics, select communions of a more restricted kind than those of the mass of worshippers in the general religious system.

There are broader social concomitants. Mystical formulations, however much fantasy they embody, are socialized in their expression and are significant for society. To some extent they ingest

and reformulate material of social import, such as doctrinal concepts, religious and moral conventions and sanctions. They re-
assert its validity with emotional force, and crown it with the
affirmation that its truth is unassailable. Hence to the religious
body of which the mystic is a member, and to his society in
general, he has value, though his contemporaries may not be able
to share or fully understand his experiences. Though they may
even suspect or reject the letter of his message, they accept its
spirit. Moreover, the socialized fantasy of the mystic offers a
safety-valve to the uninitiated. The mystic often expresses what
they themselves would like to indulge in, could they and would
they dare. He is part of the emotional and intellectual catharsis
necessary to the maintenance of any integrated religious system.
This is seen most clearly in Islam, where, as has been pointed out
more than once, the Sufi has usually been accepted despite most
of his wildest challenges to doctrinal orthodoxy. The formal
transcendentalism of the orthodox idea of God, and the limited
expression for emotional release in the Muslim ritual, have left
him a valid role.

   This synthetic function helps to explain why mystics of one
religious faith are so often held in regard by the orthodox of
another. The mystical values and experiences of one religious
system help to reinforce the ideology of others by assertion of
values common to all. By reaching out, as many mystical developments of a metaphysical kind do, beyond the confines of the
dogma of a single religion, mysticism helps to promote the interests of religion as such. Thus the Principal of Mansfield College,
Dr. Micklem, argues that while the perils of delusion and self-
deception are apparent in mysticism, those who have in their own
experience felt the 'Spirit of the Highest' to any degree will be
unwilling to set limits to the extent of union with God possible to
mortal man. Such acquiescence is relevant to our main argument.
For the claims of the mystic, one would think, should be accepted
in toto, if the mystical standpoint is adopted at all. If there be a
sphere where private feeling has the value of universal knowledge,
then who is to pick and choose between what the mystic offers?
To concede general truth while denying specific claims is inconsistent and places the defender of mysticism in a serious dilemma.
What standards of evaluation is he to apply?

   This dilemma disappears if the matter be looked at anthropologically, in terms of the mystic's relation to a religious system. Mysticism is a two-edged instrument for a religious body to recognize or employ. On the one hand, it helps to maintain religious integration by setting standards – of intense concentration on religious matters, of the supreme value of human orientation towards a concept of divinity, and of association of that concept with social values of truth and goodness, and aesthetic values of beauty. By making religious interests appear identical with these important social interests it gives both a strong reinforcement. Its assertions of the reality of specific religious experience are a shield against the darts of the infidel. As we have seen, both leadership and catharsis may be provided by mysticism. On the other hand, by its insistence on the ultimately personal nature of religious experience it offers a challenge to organized religious institutions. The way of escape can be used too easily. Authority can find that the shield is held by a free-lance, not by any soldier of the regiment. Hence the mystic is looked on jealously by the controllers of any organized religious body, lest his utterances fall outside the normal bounds of the ideology. And if pressed too hard he may abandon his Church and look to found a new unit in which his own brand of interpretation of reality will be more acceptable. How many religious cults of today are not the products of the splinter groups of mysticism? The real importance of the mystic, then, is his social relevance, not his views on the nature of reality.

References

AIYAPPAN, A., 1945. *Iravas and Culture Change.* Bull. Madras Govt. Mus., n.s., vol. v, no. 1. Madras.

ALBERT, ETHEL M., 1956. 'The Classification of Values: A Method and Illustration'. *Amer. Anthrop.,* vol. 58, pp. 221–48.

ALLIER, R., 1925. *La Psychologie de la Conversion chez les Peuples Non-Civilisés.* 2 vols. Paris.

AYER, A. J., 1946. *Language, Truth and Logic.* 2nd ed. London.

BAILEY, F. G., 1960. *Tribe, Caste and Nation.* Manchester.

BALANDIER, G., 1952. 'Contribution à une sociologie de la dépendance'. *Cahiers Int. Sociol.,* vol. xii, pp. 47–69.

BARBEAU, M., 1950. *Totem Poles.* 2 vols. Bull. Nat. Mus. Canada, 119, Anthrop. ser. no. 30.

BARNES, H. E., 1960. In Dole, G. E. and Carneiro, R. L., pp. xi–xlvi. New York.

BARNES, J. A., 1949. 'Measures of Divorce Frequency in Simple Societies'. *J. Roy. Anthrop. Inst.,* vol. 79, pp. 37–62.

—— 1954. 'Class and Committees in a Norwegian Island Parish'. *Human Relations,* vol. 7, pp. 39–58.

BATESON, G., 1936. *Naven.* Cambridge.

—— 1949. 'Bali: The Value System of a Steady State' in *Social Structure: Studies Presented to A. R. Radcliffe-Brown* (M. Fortes, ed.), pp. 35–53. Oxford.

BAUMOL, W. J., 1948. 'Notes on Some Economic Models'. *Econ. J.,* vol. 58, pp. 506–21.

—— 1959. *Economic Dynamics.* 2nd ed. New York.

BEAGLEHOLE, E., 1957. *Social Change in the South Pacific.* New York.

BELSHAW, C. S., 1952. 'Port Moresby Canoe Traders'. *Oceania,* vol. xxiii, pp. 26–39. Sydney.

—— 1954. *Changing Melanesia.* Melbourne.

—— 1957. *The Great Village.* London.

BERNDT, R. M., 1952. 'A Cargo Movement in the Eastern Central Highlands of New Guinea'. *Oceania,* vol. XXIII, pp. 40–65, 137–58, 202–34. Sydney.

BIDNEY, D., 1953. 'The Concept of Value in Modern Anthropology' in *Anthropology Today* (A. L. Kroeber, ed.), pp. 682–99. Chicago.

BIRNBAUM, N., 1953. 'Conflicting Interpretations of the Rise of Capitalism: Marx and Weber'. *Brit. J. Sociol.,* vol. iv, pp. 125–41.

BOUTEILLER, MARCELLE, 1950. *Chamanisme et Guérison Magique.* Paris.

BRANDON, S. G. F., 1955. 'Divine Kings and Dying Gods'. *Hibbert J.*, vol. 53, pp. 327–33.

BRINKLEY, F., 1915. *A History of the Japanese People*. New York and London.

BROTZ, H., 1961. 'Function and Dynamic Analysis'. *European Journal of Sociology*, pp. 170–9.

BROWN, G. G. and BARNETT, J. H., 1942. 'Social Organization and Social Structure'. *Amer. Anthrop.*, vol. 44, pp. 31–6.

BROWN, W., 1946. *Personality and Religion*. London.

BUBER, M., 1948. *Hasidism*. New York.

BURROWS, E. G. and SPIRO, M. E., 1953. *An Atoll Culture: Ethnography of Ifaluk in the Central Carolines*. HRAF. New Haven.

CARR-SAUNDERS, A. M. and CARADOG JONES, D., 1927. *A Survey of the Social Structure of England and Wales as Illustrated by Statistics*. Oxford.

CASSIRER, E., 1953. *The Philosophy of Symbolic Forms*. I. *Language* (trans. by R. Mannheim, with preface and introd. by C. W. Hendl). New Haven.

CHILVER, E. M., 1960. 'Feudalism in the Interlacustrine Kingdoms' in Richards, Audrey I., *East African Chiefs*, pp. 378–93. London

CHRISTIAN COUNCIL OF THE GOLD COAST, THE, 1932. *Report on Common Beliefs with Regard to Witchcraft*. Accra.

CLARK, J. M., 1949. *The Great German Mystics*. Oxford.

COCK, A. A., 1918. 'The Ontological Argument for the Existence of God'. *Proc. Aristotelian Soc.*, 10 June.

COLSON, ELIZABETH and GLUCKMAN, M. (eds.). 1951. *Seven Tribes of British Central Africa*. London.

CONNELLY, M., 1941. *Green Pastures*. Penguin Books, London.

COOLEY, C. H., 1909. *Social Organization: A Study of the Larger Mind*. New York.

COSER, L., 1956. *The Functions of Social Conflict*. London.

CROOK, D. and ISABEL, 1959. *Revolution in a Chinese Village: Ten Mile Inn*. London.

DAHRENDORF, R., 1959. *Class and Class Conflict in an Industrial Society*. London.

DERRICK, R. A., 1953. *Vocational Training in the South Pacific*. Oxford.

DOLE, GERTRUDE E. and CARNEIRO, R. L. (eds.), 1960. *Essays in the Science of Culture in Honor of Leslie A. White*. New York.

DOSSER, D., 1961. 'Tax Incidence and Growth'. *Economic Journal*, vol. LXXI, pp. 572–91.

DURKHEIM, E., 1924. 'Jugements de Valeur et Jugements de Réalité'. *Sociologie et Philosophie*. Paris.

—— 1925. *Formes Elémentaires de la Vie Religieuse*. 2nd ed. Paris.

—— 1932. *De la Division du Travail Social*. 6th ed. Paris.

EGGAN, F., 1949. 'The Hopi and the Lineage Principle' in *Social Structure: Studies Presented to A. R. Radcliffe-Brown* (M. Fortes, ed.), pp. 121–44. Oxford.

—— 1950. *Social Organization of the Western Pueblos.* Chicago.

ELIADE, M., 1951. *Le Chamanisme et Les Techniques Archaiques de l'Extase.* Paris.

EPSTEIN, A. L., 1953. *The Administration of Justice and the Urban African: A Study of Urban Native Courts in Northern Rhodesia.* Col. Res. Ser. no. 7. London.

—— 1954. *Juridical Technique and the Judicial Process.* Manchester.

EVANS-PRITCHARD, E. E., 1940. *The Nuer.* Oxford.

—— 1948. *The Divine Kingship of the Shilluk of the Nilotic Sudan.* Cambridge.

—— 1950a. 'Kinship and the Local Community among the Nuer' in *African Systems of Kinship and Marriage* (A. R. Radcliffe-Brown and D. Forde, eds.), pp. 360–91. Oxford.

——1950b. 'Social Anthropology: Past and Present'. *Man,* vol. L, no. 198.

—— 1951. *Kinship and Marriage among the Nuer.* Oxford.

—— (ed.), 1954. *The Institutions of Primitive Society.* Oxford.

FAUCONNET, P., 1928. *La Responsabilité: Etude de Sociologie.* 2nd ed. Paris.

FEI, H. T., 1946. 'Peasantry and Gentry: An Interpretation of Chinese Social Structure and its Changes'. *Amer. J. Sociol.,* vol. 52, pp. 1–17.

FIRTH, R., 1929. *Primitive Economics of the New Zealand Maori.* (2nd ed., 1959 – *Economics of the New Zealand Maori.* Wellington, N.Z.) London.

—— 1936. *We the Tikopia: A Sociological Study of Kinship in Primitive Polynesia* (2nd ed., 1957). London.

—— 1939. *Primitive Polynesian Economy.* London.

—— 1940. *The Work of the Gods in Tikopia.* London School of Economics Monographs on Social Anthropology, nos. 1 and 2. London.

—— 1947. Introduction to Lin Yueh-Hwa, *The Golden Wing.* London.

—— 1951. *Elements of Social Organization* (3rd ed. 1961). London.

—— 1952. 'Notes on the Social Structure of some South-Eastern New Guinea Communities'. *Man,* vol. LII, nos. 99, 123.

—— 1954. 'The Sociology of "Magic" in Tikopia'. *Sociologus,* n.s., vol. 4, pp. 97–116.

—— 1956. *Human Types: An Introduction to Social Anthropology.* Rev. ed. Edinburgh.

—— 1957. 'A Note on Descent Groups in Polynesia'. *Man,* vol. LVII, no. 2.

—— 1958. *Social Anthropology as Science and as Art.* Dunedin, N.Z.

—— 1959. *Social Change in Tikopia: Re-Study of a Polynesian Community after a Generation.* London.

—— 1961a. 'Suicide and Risk-Taking in Tikopia Society'. *Psychiatry,* vol. 24, pp. 1–17.

—— 1961b. *History and Traditions of Tikopia.* Wellington, New Zealand.

FIRTH, R. et al., 1957. 'Factions in Indian and Overseas Indian Societies'. *British Journal of Sociology,* vol. VIII, pp. 291–342.

FISHER, H. A. L., 1933. *Our New Religion.* (Thinker's Library, no. 31.) London.

FORDE, C. D., 1950. 'Double Descent among the Yakö' in *African Systems of Kinship and Marriage* (A. R. Radcliffe-Brown and C. D. Forde, eds.), pp. 285–332. Oxford.

FORTES, M., 1945. *Dynamics of Clanship among the Tallensi.* Oxford.

—— 1949a. *The Web of Kinship among the Tallensi.* Oxford.

—— 1949b. 'Time and Social Structure: An Ashanti Case Study' in *Social Structure: Studies Presented to A. R. Radcliffe-Brown* (M. Fortes, ed.), pp. 54–84. Oxford.

—— 1953. 'The Structure of Unilineal Descent Groups'. *Amer. Anthrop.*, vol. 55, n.s., pp. 17–41.

—— 1955. 'Radcliffe-Brown's Contributions to the Study of Social Organization'. *Brit. J. Sociol.*, vol. VI, pp. 16–30

—— and EVANS-PRITCHARD, E. E. (eds.)., 1940. *African Political Systems.* Oxford.

FORTUNE, R. F., 1932. *Sorcerers of Dobu.* London.

FOX, J. R., 1961. 'Veterans and Factions in Pueblo Society'. *Man*, vol. LXI, no. 201.

FREEDMAN, M., 1950. 'Colonial Law and Chinese Society'. *J. Roy. Anthrop. Inst.*, vol. 80, pp. 97–126.

FUNG, YU-LAN, 1947. *Spirit of Chinese Philosophy* (trans. E. R. Hughes). London.

GEERTZ, C., 1957. 'Ritual and Social Change: A Javanese Example'. *American Anthropologist*, vol. 59, pp. 32–54.

—— 1960. *The Religion of Java.* Glencoe, Illinois.

GILLIN, J. L. and GILLIN, J. P., 1948. *Cultural Sociology.* New York.

GILLIN, J. P., 1960. 'Some Signposts for Policy' in Adams, R. N. *et al.*, *Social Change in Latin America Today*, pp. 14–62, New York.

GLUCKMAN, M., 1940. 'Analysis of a Social Situation in Zululand'. *Bantu Stud.*, vol. 14, pp. 1–30, 147–74.

—— 1950. 'Social Beliefs and Individual Thinking in Primitive Society'. *Mem. & Proc. Manchester Lit. & Phil. Soc.*, vol. 91, pp. 1–26.

—— 1954. *Rituals of Rebellion in South-East Africa.* Manchester.

—— 1955a. *The Judicial Process among the Barotse of Northern Rhodesia.* Manchester.

—— 1955b. *Custom and Conflict in Africa.* Oxford.

GOBINEAU, J. A. de (Comte), 1933. *Religions et Philosophies dans L'Asie Centrale.* 6th ed. Paris.

GOLDENWEISER, A. A., 1937. *Anthropology.* London.

GOUGH, E. KATHLEEN, 1952. 'Changing Kinship Usages in the Setting of Political and Economic Change among the Nayars of Malabar'. *J. Roy. Anthrop. Inst.*, vol. 82, pp. 71–87.

GREER, S. A., 1955. *Social Organization.* New York.

GROVES, M. C., 1960. 'Motu Pottery'. *J. Polynesian Society*, vol. 69, pp. 3–22.

HADER, J. J. and LINDEMAN, E. C., 1933. *Dynamic Social Research*. London.

HAMID, K. A., 1946. *Ibn Maskawaih: A Study of his Al-Fauz Al - Asghar*. London.

HASTINGS, J. (ed.), 1908. 'Theodicy'. *Encyclopaedia of Religion and Ethics*. London.

HEILER, F. J., 1932. *Prayer: A Study in the History and Psychology of Religion* (ed. S. McComb). Oxford.

HERSKOVITS, M. J., 1948. *Man and his Works*. New York.

—— 1952. 'Cultural Anthropology in Area Studies'. *Internat. Soc. Sci. Bull.*, vol. IV, no. 4. Paris.

HIELD, W., 1954. 'The Study of Change in Social Science'. *Brit. J. Sociol.*, vol. V, pp. 1–12.

HIRN, Y., 1912. *The Sacred Shrine*. London.

HOGBIN, H. I., 1939. *Experiments in Civilization: The Effects of European Culture on a Native Community of the Solomon Islands*. London.

—— 1947. 'Native Christianity in a New Guinea Village'. *Oceania*, vol. XVIII, pp. 1–35.

—— 1951. *Transformation Scene: The Changing Culture of a New Guinea Village* London.

HOMANS, G. C., 1950. *The Human Group*. New York.

HUART, C., 1941. 'Bab'. *Handwörterbuch des Islam*. Leiden.

HUGHES, E. R. (ed.), 1942. *Chinese Philosophy in Classical Times*. London.

HUNTER, MONICA (afterwards WILSON), 1936. *Reaction to Conquest: Effects of Contact with Europeans on the Pondo of South Africa*. Oxford.

HUXLEY, J. (ed.), 1936. *T. H. Huxley's Diary of the Voyage of H.M.S. 'Rattle-snake'*. New York.

HUXLEY, L. (ed.), 1900. *Life and Letters of T. H. Huxley*. London.

HUXLEY, T. H., 1892. *Essays upon Some Controverted Questions*. London.

—— 1894. *Evolution and Ethics and Other Essays*. London.

IRVINE, W., 1955. *Apes, Angels and Victorians: A Joint Biography of Darwin and Huxley*. London.

JAMES, W., 1929. *Varieties of Religious Experience*. London.

JARVIE, I. C., 1961. 'Nadel on the Aims and Methods of Social Anthropology'. *British J. for the Philosophy of Science*, vol. XIII, pp. 1–24.

KABERRY, PHYLLIS M., 1945. Introduction to Malinowski, B. *The Dynamics of Culture Change*. New Haven.

KAGAROV, E., 1933. 'The Ethnography of Foreign Countries in Soviet Science'. VOKS, fourth year, vol. IV. *Ethnography, Folklore and Archaeology in the U.S.S.R.*, pp. 88–99. Moscow.

KEESING, F. M., 1928. *The Changing Maori*. Mem. Maori Bd. Ethnol. Research, vol. 14. New Plymouth, N.Z.

KLUCKHOHN, C., 1941. 'Patterning as Exemplified in Navaho Culture' in *Language, Culture and Personality* (L. Spier, ed.), pp. 109–30. Wisconsin.

KLUCKHOHN, C., 1951a. 'A Comparative Study of Values of Five Cultures' in E. Z. Vogt, *Navaho Veterans: a Study of Changing Values*. Papers Peabody Mus., Harvard, vol. XLI, pt. i, pp. vii–ix.

—— 1951b. 'Values and Value-Orientations in the Theory of Action: An Exploration in Definition and Classification' in T. Parsons and E. A. Shils, *Towards a General Theory of Social Action*, pp. 388–433. Cambridge, Mass.

—— and LEIGHTON, DOROTHEA, 1946. *The Navaho*. Cambridge, Mass.

KLUCKHOHN, FLORENCE R. and STRODTBECK, F. L., 1961. *Variations in Value Orientations*. Evanston.

KORAN, THE (see RODWELL, J. M.).

KORSCH, K., 1938. *Karl Marx*. London.

KRIGE, E. J. and KRIGE, J. D., 1943. *The Realm of a Rain Queen: A Study of the Pattern of Lovedu Society*. Oxford.

KROEBER, A. L., 1944. *Configurations of Culture Growth*. Berkeley and Los Angeles.

—— 1948. *Anthropology*. New ed. New York, London.

KROUPIANSKAIA, V., POTAPOV, L., TERENTIEVA, L., 1960. 'Problèmes Essentiels de l'Etude Ethnographique des Peuples de l'URSS'. *Communications de la délégation Soviétique au VI Congrès International des Sciences Anthropologiques et Ethnologiques*. Moscow.

KUPER, HILDA, 1947. *An African Aristocracy: Rank among the Swazi*. Oxford.

LASKI, H. J., 1948. *Communist Manifesto: Socialist Landmark*. London.

LAWRENCE, P., 1954. 'Cargo Cult and Religious Beliefs among the Garia'. *Int. Archiv. Ethnogr.*, vol. 47, pp. 1–20.

LEACH, E. R., 1945 (1949). 'Jinghpaw Kinship Terminology. An Experiment in Ethnographic Algebra'. *J. Roy. Anthrop. Inst.*, vol. 75, pp. 59–72.

—— 1954. *Political Systems of Highland Burma*. London.

LEESON, IDA, 1952. *Bibliography of Cargo Cults and other Nativistic Movements in the South Pacific*. South Pacific Commissions, Technical Paper no. 30. Sydney.

LE VINE, R. A., 1961. 'Anthropology and the Study of Conflict: An Introduction'. *Journal of Conflict Resolution*, vol. V, pp. 3–15.

LÉVI-STRAUSS, C., 1949. *Les structures élémentaires de la Parenté*. Paris.

—— 1953. 'Social Structure' in *Anthropology Today* (A. L. Kroeber, ed.), pp. 524–53. Chicago.

LÉVY-BRUHL, L., 1938. *L'Experience Mystique et les Symboles Chez Les Primitifs*. Paris.

—— 1949. *Les Carnets de Lucien Lévy-Bruhl*. Paris.

LEWIS, O., 1951. *Life in a Mexican Village: Tepoztlán Restudied*. Urbana.

—— 1954. *Group Dynamics in a North-Indian Village: A Study of Factions*. Delhi.

LEWIS, W. A., 1955. *The Theory of Economic Growth*. London.

LI AN-CHE, 1937. 'Zuni: Some Observations and Queries'. *Amer. Anthrop.*, vol. 39, pp. 62–76.

LOWIE, R. H., 1922. 'The Religion of the Crow Indians'. *Anthrop. Papers Amer. Mus. Nat. Hist.*, vol. xxv, pp. 309–444.

—— 1936. *Primitive Religion*. London.

—— 1948. *Social Organization*. New York.

MACRAE, D. G., 1961. *Ideology and Society*. London.

MAINE, H. S., 1875. *Lectures on the Early History of Institutions*. London.

MAIR, L. P. (ed.), 1938. *Methods of Study of Culture Contact in Africa*. Reprinted from *Africa*, 7, 8 and 9, with an Introductory Essay by B. Malinowski. Memor. Int. Inst. Afr. Lang., no. 15. Oxford.

—— 1957. *Studies in Applied Anthropology*. London School of Economics Monographs on Social Anthropology, no. 16. London.

MALINOWSKI, B., 1925. 'Magic, Science and Religion' in J. A. Needham (ed.), *Science, Religion and Reality*, pp. 19–84. London.

—— 1927a. *The Father in Primitive Psychology* (reprinted in *The Sexual Life of Savages*, ch. 7, 1929). London.

—— 1927b. *Sex and Repression in Savage Society*. London.

—— 1932. *The Sexual Life of Savages in North-Western Melanesia*. 3rd ed. London.

—— 1935. *Coral Gardens and their Magic*. 2 vols. London.

—— 1938. 'Modern Anthropology and European Rule in Africa'. *Reale Accademia D'Italia*, viii. Convegno 'Volta'. Rome (also 1940).

—— 1944. *A Scientific Theory of Culture and Other Essays*. Chapel Hill.

—— 1945. *The Dynamics of Culture Change*. New Haven.

—— 1947. *Freedom and Civilisation*. London.

MARETT, R. R., 1931. 'The Beginnings of Morals and Culture: An Introduction to Social Anthropology' in W. Rose (ed.), *An Outline of Modern Knowledge*, pp. 395–430. London.

—— 1935. *Head, Heart and Hands in Human Evolution*. London.

MARITAIN, J., 1940a. *Science and Wisdom* (trans.). London.

—— 1940b. *Scholasticism and Politics* (trans.). London.

MARSHALL, A., 1922. *Principles of Economics: An Introductory Volume*. 8th ed. London.

MARX, K., 1930. *Capital* (*A Critique of Political Economy*), trans. 4th German ed., by Eden and Cedar Paul. 2 vols. London.

MATORIN, N., 1933. 'Soviet Ethnography'. VOKS, fourth year, vol. IV. *Ethnography, Folklore and Archaeology in the U.S.S.R.*, pp. 3–18. Moscow.

MAYER, A. C., 1952. *Land and Society in Malabar*. Bombay.

MAYER, P., 1954. *Witches* (Inaugural Lecture delivered at Rhodes University). Grahamstown.

MAZENOD, L., 1943. Avant-propos to *L'Art Roman en Suisse*. Geneva.

MEEK, C. K., 1937. *Law and Authority in a Nigerian Tribe*. London.

MILLS, C. WRIGHT, 1959. *The Sociological Imagination*. New York.

MITCHELL, J. C., 1951. *The Yao of Southern Nyasaland* in Colson and Gluckman (eds.), pp. 292–253. London.

MOSS, F. J., 1894. 'The Maori Polity in the Island of Rarotonga'. *Journal Polynesian Society*, vol. III, pp. 20–6. New Plymouth, N.Z.

MURPHY, R. F., 1957. 'Intergroup Hostility and Social Cohesion'. *American Anthrop.*, vol. 59, pp. 1018–36.

NADEL, S. F., 1947. *The Nuba: An Anthropological Study of the Hill Tribes in Kordofan*. Oxford.

—— 1951. *The Foundations of Social Anthropology*. London.

—— 1952. 'Witchcraft in Four African Societies: An Essay in Comparison'. *American Anthropologist*, vol. 54, pp. 18–29.

—— 1953. 'Social Control and Self-Regulation'. *J. Soc. Forces*, vol. 31, pp. 265–73.

—— 1954. *Nupe Religion*. London.

—— 1957. *The Theory of Social Structure*. London.

NGATA, SIR A. T., 1931. 'Native Land Development'. Statement by the Hon. Sir Apirana T. Ngata, Native Minister. App. to *J. House Rep. N.Z.*, ii (G.10). Wellington.

—— 1940. 'Tribal Organization', ch. 5 of *The Maori People Today, a General Survey* (I. L. G. Sutherland, ed.), pp. 155–81. Christchurch.

NICHOLSON, R. A., 1914. *The Mystics of Islam*. London.

OBERG, K., 1940. 'The Kingdom of Ankole in Uganda' in M. Fortes and E. E. Evans-Pritchard (eds.), *African Political Systems*, pp. 121–62. Oxford.

OGDEN, C. K. (ed.), 1931. *The Theory of Legislation* by Jeremy Bentham. Trans. from the French of (Pierre) Etienne (Louis) Dumont, of *Traités de legislation* (3 vols., Paris, 1802) by Richard (properly Robert) Hildreth. London.

—— 1932. *Bentham's Theory of Fictions*. London.

OPLER, MORRIS E., 1962. 'Two Converging Lines of Interest in Cultural Evolutionary Theory'. *American Anthropologist*, vol. 64, pp. 524–47.

ORR, W. G., 1947. *A Sixteenth Century Indian Mystic*. London.

PARSONS, ANNE, 1956. 'Expressive Symbolism in Witchcraft and Delusion: A Comparative Study'. *Rev. Inter. d'Ethnopsychologie Normale et Pathologique*, vol. 1, pp. 199–19.

PARSONS, T., 1944. 'The Theoretical Development of the Sociology of Religion'. *J. Hist. of Ideas*, vol. 5, New York (reprinted in *Essays in Sociological Theory*, revised ed., 1954, Glencoe, Illinois, pp. 197–211).

—— 1949. *The Structure of Social Action*. 2nd ed. Glencoe, Illinois.

—— and SMELSER, N. J., 1956. *Economy and Society*. London.

PETERSEN, H., 1932. *Huxley Prophet of Science*. London.

PHILLIPS, A. (ed.), 1953. *Survey of African Marriage and Family Life*. London.

PHILLIPS, A. W., 1950. 'Mechanical Models in Economic Dynamics'. *Economica*, n.s., vol. 17, pp. 283–305.

PITT-RIVERS, G. H. L. F., 1927. *The Clash of Cultures and Contact of Races*. London.

PITT-RIVERS, J. A., 1954. *The People of the Sierras*. London.

PLEKHANOV, G. V., 1929. *Fundamental Problems of Marxism* (trans. Eden and Cedar Paul). London.

POTEKHIN, I. I., 1956. 'Clan Relations in the System of Social Relations of the Present-Day African Village'. (Papers presented by Soviet Delegation at Vth Int. Congress Anthrop. and Ethnological Sciences.) pp. 11–18. Moscow.

POULTON, E. B., 1925. 'Thomas Henry Huxley'. *Nature*, supplement 9 May; reprinted in *Huxley Memorial Lectures*, 1925–32, Imperial College of Science, 1932. London.

POWELL, H. A., 1960. 'Competitive Leadership in Trobriand Political Organization'. *Journal Royal Anthrop. Inst.*, vol. 90, pp. 118–45.

QURESHI, A. I., 1945. *Islam and the Theory of Interest*. Lahore.

RADCLIFFE-BROWN, A. R., 1924. 'The Mother's Brother in South Africa'. *S. Afr. J. Sci.*, vol. 21, pp. 542–55. (Reprinted (1952) in *Structure and Function in Primitive Society: Essays and Addresses by A. R. Radcliffe-Brown*, pp. 15–31. London.)

—— 1930. *The Social Organization of Australian Tribes*. Oceania Monogr., no. 1. Melbourne.

—— 1940. 'On Social Structure'. *J. Roy. Anthrop. Inst.*, vol. 70, pp. 1–12. (Reprinted (1952) in *Structure and Function in Primitive Society: Essays and Addresses by A. R. Radcliffe-Brown*, pp. 188–204. London.)

—— 1945. 'Religion and Society'. *J. Roy. Anthrop. Inst.*, vol. lxxv, pp. 33–43. (Reprinted (1952) in *Structure and Function in Primitive Society: Essays and Addresses by A. R. Radcliffe-Brown*, pp. 153–77. London.)

—— 1950. Introduction to *African Systems of Kinship and Marriage* (A. R. Radcliffe-Brown and D. Forde, eds.), pp. 1–85. Oxford.

—— 1952. *Structure and Function in Primitive Society*. London.

RANDOLPH, B. W., 1923. *Marriage Orders and Unction*. (Congress Books, no. 32.) London.

RAPOPORT, R. N., 1954. *Changing Navaho Religious Values*. Papers Peabody Mus., Harvard, vol. xli, No. 2. Cambridge, Mass.

RATTRAY, R. S., 1923. *Ashanti*. 348 pp. Oxford.

READ, MARGARET, 1942. 'Migrant Labour in Africa and its Effects on Tribal Life'. *Int. Labour Rev.*, vol. 45, pp. 605–31.

REDFIELD, R., 1930. *Tepoztlan: A Mexican Village. A Study of Folk Life*. Chicago.

—— 1941. *The Folk Culture of Yucatan*. Chicago.

—— 1950. *A Village that Chose Progress: Chan Kom Revisited*. Chicago.

—— 1953. *The Primitive World and Its Transformations*. Ithaca.

—— and VILLA ROJAS, A., 1934. *Chan Kom, a Maya Village*. Publ. Carnegie Instn., no. 448. Washington.

RICHARDS, AUDREY I., 1940a. *Bemba Marriage and Present Economic Conditions*. Rhodes-Livingstone Pap., no. 4. Livingstone.

—— 1940b. 'The Political System of the Bemba Tribe – North-Eastern Rhodesia' in M. Fortes and E. E. Evans-Pritchard (eds.), *African Political Systems*, pp. 83–120. Oxford.

—— 1941. 'A Problem of Anthropological Approach'. *Bantu Studies*, pp. 45–52.

—— 1954. *Economic Development and Tribal Change: A Study of Immigrant Labour in Buganda*. Cambridge.

—— (ed.), 1960. *East African Chiefs*. London.

RITCHIE, A. D., 1945. *Civilization, Science and Religion*. Penguin Books, London.

RIVERS, W. H. R., 1914a. *Kinship and Social Organization*. London.

—— 1914b. *The History of Melanesian Society*. 2 vols. Cambridge.

—— 1924. *Social Organization* (W. J. Perry, ed.). London.

ROBINSON, JOAN, 1952. 'The Model of an Expanding Economy'. *Econ. J.*, vol. 62, pp. 42–53.

RODWELL, J. M., 1876. *The Koran* (trans.). London.

ROSTOW, W. W., 1961. *The Stages of Economic Growth*. Cambridge.

ROYAL ANTHROPOLOGICAL INSTITUTE, 1951. *Notes and Queries on Anthropology*. 6th ed. London.

RUSSELL, B., 1940. *An Inquiry into Meaning and Truth*. London.

SADLER, A. L., 1946. *A Short History of Japan*. Sydney.

SAHLINS, M. D., 1958. *Social Stratification in Polynesia*. Seattle.

—— 1960. 'Political Power and the Economy in Primitive Society' in Dole, G. E. and Carneiro, R. L., pp. 390–415. New York.

SCHAPERA, I., 1928. 'Economic Changes in South African Native Life'. *Africa*, vol. I, pp. 170–88.

—— 1933. 'Pre-Marital Pregnancy and Public Opinion'. *Africa*, vol. 6, pp. 59–89.

—— 1938. *Handbook of Tswana Law and Custom*. London.

—— 1940. *Married Life in an African Tribe*. London.

—— 1947. *Migrant Labour and Tribal Life: A Study of Conditions in the Bechuanaland Protectorate*. London.

—— 1950. 'Kinship and Marriage among the Tswana' in *African Systems of Kinship and Marriage* (A. R. Radcliffe-Brown and D. Forde, eds.), pp. 140–65. London.

SCHOLEM, G. G., 1955. *Major Trends in Jewish Mysticism*. 3rd ed. London.

SELZNICK, P., 1948. 'Foundations of the Theory of Organization'. *Amer. Sociol. Rev.*, vol. 13, pp. 25–35.

SHIVAPADASUNDARAM, S., 1934. *The Saiva School of Hinduism*. London.

SIEGEL, B. J. and BEALS, A. R., 1960. 'Conflict and Factionalist Dispute'. *Journal Royal Anthrop. Inst.*, vol. 90, pp. 107–17.

SMITH, MARGARET, 1931. *Studies in Early Mysticism in the Near and Middle East*. London.

SMITH, WATSON and ROBERTS, J. M., 1954. *Zuni Law: A Field of Values*. Papers Peabody Mus. Harvard, vol. xliii, no. 1. Cambridge, Mass..

SOOTHILL, W. E., 1929. *The Three Religions of China*. Oxford.

—— 1930. *The Lotus of the Wonderful Law*. Oxford.

SOROKIN, P., 1941. *Social and Cultural Dynamics*, vol. IV. New York.

SPENCER, H., 1862. *First Principles*. London. (Thinker's Library, 1937.)

—— 1885. *The Principles of Sociology*. 3 vols. (1876–96), I. (*A System of Synthetic Philosophy*, VI.) 3rd ed. rev. and enl. (1885). London and Edinburgh.

SPOEHR, A., 1949. 'Majuro. A Village in the Marshall Islands'. Fieldiana: Anthrop., vol. 39. Chicago.

STANNER, W. E. H., 1947. *Reconstruction in the South Pacific Islands: A Preliminary Report*. New York: Institute of Pacific Relations (mim).

—— 1953. *The South Seas in Transition*. Sydney.

STEBBING, L. S., 1937. *Philosophy and the Physicists*. London.

STEINILBER-OBERLIN, N., 1938. *The Buddhist Sects of Japan* (trans. from French by M. Loge). London.

STILLMAN, C. W., 1955. 'Academic Imperialism and its Resolution: The Case of Economics and Anthropology'. *Amer. Scientist*, vol. 43, pp. 77–88.

STOCKS, J. L., 1934. *On the Nature and Grounds of Religious Belief*. (Riddell Memorial Lecture.) Oxford.

STONE, R., 1948. 'The Theory of Games'. *Econ. J.*, vol. 58, pp. 185–201.

—— and JACKSON, E. F., 1946. 'Economic Models with Special Reference to Mr. Kaldor's System'. *Econ. J.*, vol. 56, pp. 554–67.

SUNDKLER, G. M., 1948. *Bantu Prophets in South Africa*. London.

TAX, S., 1937. 'Some Problems of Social Organization' in *Social Anthropology of North American Indian Tribes: Essays in Social Organization, Law and Religion presented to Professor A. R. Radcliffe-Brown*, etc. (Fred Eggan, ed.), pp. 3–32. Chicago.

TEMPLE, W., 1924. 'Some Implications of Theism' in *Contemporary British Philosophy* (J. H. Muirhead, ed.), pp. 414–28. London.

THORNTON, W. M., 1930. *The Scientific Background of the Christian Creeds*. (Riddell Memorial Lecture.) Newcastle-on-Tyne: University of Durham.

TITIEV, M., 1944. *Old Oraibi*. Papers Peabody Mus. Harvard, vol. XXIII, no. 1. Cambridge, Mass.

TOYNBEE, A., 1946. *A Study of History*, abridgement by C. D. Somervell. London.

TURNER, V. W., 1957. *Schism and Continuity in an African Society*. Manchester.

TURVEY, R., 1948. 'The Multiplier'. *Economica*, n.s., vol. 15, pp. 259–69.

VAIHINGER, H., 1935. *The Philosophy of 'As If'* (trans. C. K. Ogden). 2nd ed. London.

VOGT, E. Z., 1951. *Navaho Veterans: A Study of Changing Values.* Papers Peabody Mus. Harvard, vol. xli, no. 1. Cambridge, Mass.

VON NEUMANN, J. and MORGENSTERN, O., 1947. *Theory of Games and Economic Behavior.* 2nd ed. Princeton.

VOTH, H. R., 1903. *The Oraibi Summer Snake Ceremony.* Field Columbian Mus. Pub., no. 83, Anthrop. ser., vol. 3, no. 4. Chicago.

—— 1912. *The Oraibi Marau Ceremony.* Field Mus. Nat. Hist., publ. 156, Anthrop. ser., vol. II, no. 1. Chicago.

WACH, J., 1947. *Sociology of Religion.* London.

WEBB, C. C. J., 1929. *Religion and the Thought of Today* (Riddell Memorial Lecture). Oxford.

WEBER, MAX, 1947. *The Theory of Social and Economic Organization.* Trans. of Part I of *Wirtschaft und Gesellschaft* (2nd ed. 2 vols. Tubingen, 1925) by A. R. Henderson and Talcott Parsons. Edinburgh.

WHINFIELD, E. H., 1880. *Gulshan I Raz: The Mystic Rose Garden of Sa'd Ud Din Mahmud Shabistari.* London.

WILLIAMS, F. E., 1928. 'The Taro Cult: A Study of a Primitive Religious Movement' in *Orokaiva Magic,* pp. 3-101. Oxford.

—— 1930. *Orokaiva Society.* London.

WILSON, B. R., 1962. 'The Teacher's Role – A Sociological Analysis'. *British J. Sociology,* vol. XIII, pp. 15-32.

WILSON, G., 1941-2. *An Essay on the Economics of Detribalization in Northern Rhodesia.* 2 pts. Rhodes-Livingstone Pap., nos. 5 and 6.

—— 1951. 'The Nyakyusa of South-Western Tanganyika' in E. Colson and M. Gluckman (eds.), *Seven Tribes of British Central Africa,* pp. 252-91. London.

—— and MONICA, H. 1945. *The Analysis of Social Change; Based on Observations in Central Africa.* Cambridge.

WILSON, MONICA H., 1950. 'Nyakyusa Kinship' in *African Systems of Kinship and Marriage* (A. R. Radcliffe-Brown and D. Forde, eds.), pp. 111-39. Oxford.

—— 1951. 'Witch Beliefs and Social Structure'. *Amer. J. Sociol.,* vol. 56, pp. 307-13.

WORSLEY, P. M., 1957. *The Trumpet Shall Sound: A Study of 'Cargo' Cults in Melanesia.* London.

—— 1961. 'The Analysis of Rebellion and Revolution in Modern British Social Anthropology'. *Science and Society,* vol. XXI, pp. 26-37.

ZIMMER, H., 1946. *Myths and Symbols in Indian Art and Civilisation.* London.

Index

LONDON SCHOOL OF ECONOMICS
MONOGRAPHS ON SOCIAL ANTHROPOLOGY

Titles marked with an asterisk are now out of print. Those marked with a dagger
have been reprinted in paperback editions and are only available in this form.
A double dagger indicates availability in both hardcover and paperback editions.

1, 2. RAYMOND FIRTH
 The Works of the Gods in Tikopia, 2 vols., 1940. (2nd edition in 1 vol., 1967.)
  3. E. R. LEACH
 Social and Economic Organization of the Rowanduz Kurds, 1940. (Available
 from University Microfilms Ltd.)
 *4. E. E. EVANS-PRITCHARD
 The Political System of the Anuak of the Anglo-Egyptian Sudan, 1940. (New
 edition in preparation.)
  5. DARYLL FORDE
 Marriage and the Family among the Yakö in South-Eastern Nigeria, 1941.
 (Available from University Microfilms Ltd.)
 *6. M. M. GREEN
 Land Tenure of an Ibo Village in South-Eastern Nigeria, 1941.
  7. ROSEMARY FIRTH
 Housekeeping among Malay Peasants, 1943. Second edition, 1966.
 *8. A. M. AMMAR
 A Demographic Study of an Egyptian Province (Sharquiya) 1943.
 *9. I. SCHAPERA
 Tribal Legislation among the Tswana of the Bechuanaland Protectorate, 1943.
 (Replaced by new volume, No. 43)
 *10. W. H. BECKETT
 Akokoaso: A Survey of a Gold Coast Village, 1944.
 *11. I. SCHAPERA
 The Ethnic Composition of Tswana Tribes, 1952.
 *12. JU-K'ANG T'IEN
 The Chinese of Sarawak: A study of Social Structure, 1953. (New edition
 revised and with an Introduction by Barbara Ward in preparation.)
 *13. GUTORM GJESSING
 Changing Lapps, 1954.
 *14. ALAN J. A. ELLIOTT
 Chinese Spirit-Medium Cults in Singapore, 1955.
 *15. RAYMOND FIRTH
 Two Studies of Kinship in London, 1956.
 *16. LUCY MAIR
 Studies in Applied Anthropology, 1957.
 †17. J. M. GULLICK
 Indigenous Political Systems of Western Malaya, 1958.
 †18. MAURICE FREEDMAN
 Lineage Organization in South-Eastern China, 1958.
 †19. FREDRIK BARTH
 Political Leadership among Swat Pathans, 1959.

†20. L. H. PALMIER
Social Status and Power in Java, 1960.
†21. JUDITH DJAMOUR
Malay Kinship and Marriage in Singapore, 1959.
†22. E. R. LEACH
Rethinking Anthropology, 1961.
★23. S. M. SALIM
Marsh Dwellers of the Euphrates Delta, 1962.
†24. S. VAN DER SPRENKEL
Legal Institutions in Manchu, China, 1962.
25. CHANDRA JAYAWARDENA
Conflict and Solidarity in a Guianese Plantation, 1963.
26. H. IAN HOGBIN
Kinship and Marriage in a New Guinea Village, 1963.
27. JOAN METGE
A New Maori Migration: Rural and Urban Relations in Northern New Zealand, 1964.
‡28. RAYMOND FIRTH
Essays on Social Organization and Values, 1964.
29. M. G. SWIFT
Malay Peasant Society in Jelebu, 1965.
†30. JEREMY BOISSEVAIN
Saints and Fireworks: Religion and Politics in Rural Malta, 1965.
31. JUDITH DJAMOUR
The Muslim Matrimonial Court in Singapore, 1966.
32. CHIE NAKANE
Kinship and Economic Organization in Rural Japan, 1967.
33. MAURICE FREEDMAN
Chinese Lineage and Society: Fukien and Kwantung, 1966.
34. W. H. R. RIVERS
Kinship and Social Organization, reprinted with commentaries by David Schneider and Raymond Firth, 1968.
35. ROBIN FOX
The Keresan Bridge: A Problem in Pueblo Ethnology, 1967.
36. MARSHALL MURPHREE
Christianity and the Shona, 1969.
37. G. K. NUKUNYA
Kinship and Marriage among the Anlo Ewe, 1969.
38. LUCY MAIR
Anthropology and Social Change, 1969.
39. SANDRA WALLMAN
Take Out Hunger: Two Case Studies of Rural Development in Basutoland, 1969.
40. MEYER FORTES
Time and Social Structure and Other Essays, in press.
41. J. D. FREEMAN
Report on the Iban, in press.
42. W. E. WILLMOTT
The Political Structure of the Chinese Community in Cambodia, in press.
43. I. SCHAPERA
Tribal Innovators: Tswana Chiefs and Social Change 1795-1940, in press.